NEW AFFINITIES

ANCA ROSU • WENDOLYN TETLOW

Pearson
Custom
Publishing

Cover art: *The Tilled Field,* by Joan Miro,
Oil on canvas (1923–1924), 66 x 92.7 cms (26 x 36 ½ inches),
Solomon R. Guggenheim Museum, New York.
Photograph by David Heald © The Solomon R. Guggenheim
Foundation, New York.

Please visit our web site at www.pearsoncustom.com

ISBN 0–536–62977–3

BA 993054

PEARSON CUSTOM PUBLISHING
75 Arlington Street, Suite 300, Boston, MA 02116
A Pearson Education Company

For our students and colleagues

Contents

Affinities

    Ullman argues that recent technologies promote isolation and
    cripple our abilities to interact with other people.
    This poem is about questioning received values and being oneself.
    In an essay full of personal anecdotes, Williams argues that interracial
    relations have achieved a level of complexity that borders on the
    perverse.
    This is a nice theoretical debate about the nature of reality in relation
    to the development of computer technology.

Instead of Introduction: Write On!

What do they teach in a writing class? What do we learn in a writing class? In a writing class we just write, right? But that means we know how to write, why do we have to take a class anyway? We are not here to become writers, are we? One can ask such questions and invoke their obvious answers, only if one has never seriously thought of writing and its reason to be. Pause to think about it, and writing unfolds as a complicated business. There are as many varieties of writing as there are purposes and audiences for it. However, all these kinds of writing share two important characteristics: they result from deeply personal, natural thought processes, and they take on widely public, conventional forms.

Although we think of it as remote from everything technical, writing is actually a technology. It was invented for the purpose of simplifying record keeping in commercial transactions. Thus, one of the first achievements of writing was to make it possible for some people to leave a record for the future. It also made it possible for others to look back on the records of the past.

This victory against time may be the reason why, in his note "Write and Wrong," the poet and artist Breyten Breytenbach brings up writing as he explores the relation between past and future: "The past is the ink with which we write the present—and in the process and the flow of writing the words, the concepts and ideas, the images, the flights become…just *ink*. Whereas what we'd probably like to write would be an open hand wherein time, which is the future of the present movement, could find its fit and its fist" (22-23). While struggling with metaphors for our sense of history, Breytenbach also creates a metaphor of writing. The passage from the past to the present, or the continuity of past, present, and future is seen as writing. Writing is a way of representing ourselves in time, and if we think of it functionally, keeping records, or aiding memory is perhaps the first thing that comes to mind. When we write, we are, in a sense, historians.

Although the record keeping function seems the most obvious, when we say "writing," we most often have in mind works of literature. Writers fall into the same category with poets. In this case, writing is an artistic activity, one that produces, like painting or carving, images of the world for our understanding and delight. Art requires talent and dedication, and this is perhaps why those of us who do not write professionally tend to think of writing as some mystical gift. "I cannot write. I am no good at it." I have heard these sentences from my students more often than I care to remember. They share the belief that writing is an art, made possible by some divine gift. But as Ved Mehta points out in his essay "Lightning and the Lightning Bug," "for every natural writer there are ten or more writers that have to labor over their craft" (176). Mehta talks about craft, not art, suggesting that we can all learn to write.

What his essay describes is a learning experience, which embraces both writing and other kinds of knowledge. In trying to perfect his writing style, Mehta reads and learns to appreciate the best-known authors of English literature, for instance. Most interestingly, he talks about how the writing and learning processes are hard to distinguish from each other: "I found I had first to decide what, exactly, I wanted to say, even if in the course of writing I should find myself saying something totally different. (All ideas grow and develop as one writes, I learned, since one's memory expands through the process of association)" (175). Mehta's experience reveals to us yet another dimension of writing, where beyond record keeping and artistry, a learning process emerges. Associations that expand memory develop as one writes. It is perhaps this aspect of writing that should interest us most when we are students: writing as learning and discovery of new ideas.

Mehta's experience, however, is marked by labor and constraint. In spite of the passion he develops for writing, one cannot ignore his struggle. What is most striking in this struggle is perhaps the feeling of inferiority. He continuously evaluates himself as he writes: "I remember that I was struck by the elegance and luster of many of the essays written by my English contemporaries. Compared to theirs, my best efforts came across as dull and lame" (175). Mehta's feeling may have to do with the fact that he was not born English, although he learned the language early enough in his life to call it his own. But beyond his origin, the inferiority complex is fostered, if not even created, by his teacher: "My tutor's questioning of one infelicitous word effectively unraveled my confidence in my writing even as it began to sensitize me to the nuances of words. For some time thereafter, whenever I wrote a sentence, I would read it as my tutor might, and conclude that almost everything was wrong with it" (175). Even when the tutor is absent, his presence is felt by the student writer. In his imagination, the tutor's intervention is magnified and becomes an obstacle in the way of his desire to write. The student's inner self seems to be invaded by the voice of the tutor.

Mehta's teacher appears more as a censor than as a mentor. The way Mehta internalized the opinion of his tutor looks quite similar to the way writers internalize the point of view of the censors described by J.M. Coetzee in his essay "Emerging from Censorship." Coetzee shows how censorship is fueled by paranoia, an irrational fear of whatever may question the power of the authorities. Censors are watchdogs set against opinions contrary or irreverent to political authority. But the restrictions they impose on writers become part of the writer's consciousness: "By forcing the writer to see what he has written through the censor's eyes, the censor forces him to internalize a contaminating reading" (51). The contamination consists, according to Coetzee, in the writer becoming as paranoid as the censor. And indeed Mehta's state of mind as he writes could well be called paranoia.

This paranoia involves a hostile relationship with the reader, a relationship perverted, according to Coetzee, precisely because we always write for someone else, but someone we conceive of as a beloved. Writing is, according to Coetzee, "a transaction with some such figure of the beloved, that tries to please her (but that also tries continually though surreptitiously to revise and recreate her as the-one-who-will-be-pleased)" (52). Coetzee's image of writing here is personalized, a transaction that takes place between two people, although obviously the writer is writing alone. The second figure, the reader, is created and recreated as someone who will not censor but will appreciate the writing.

Perhaps the censorship exercised by Mehta's teacher is partly due to Mehta's own inner effort to create his reader. Because he is a student in a foreign university of great prestige, he imagines his reader as intimidating and censorious. Instead of recreating the reader into "the-one-who-will-be-pleased," Mehta recreates himself into the inferior, submissive student, who must study the masters in order to form his own style. Although he becomes a good writer, Mehta seems to be adversely affected by the process. Mehta is not the only one to make this mistake. Many students write only to please their teacher, and the effort leaves them depleted of the ability to deal with other writing situations. Too often, the relationship between the mentor and the pupil becomes too personal, and both lose sight of what is at stake in writing. In a sense, the teacher must be pleased, but only in so far as he or she represents the reading public. But even in an ideal situation the writing self may still be hurt in the process.

The most difficult task of the writer is thus to balance the two aspects of writing: the personal and the public. On the one hand, writing is personal, intimate, private. It is, as Coetzee's metaphor suggests, an act of love. To an extent, it is useful to think about writing that way. Love not only endows the beloved with the best qualities, but it also brings up the best in us. When we fall in love, we are excited and elated, we want to show and give what we have best. Unlike the student, as portrayed by Mehta, the lover is confident, daring, and creative. Many of my students feel that way: "I can write when I am interested in the topic." "I can write well about what I like." In such statements, writing seems to be no more than a fine romance, where the writer finds self-fulfillment. But notice that the satisfaction does not quite take the other, the beloved reader, into account. It is the topic, or the theme that my students are infatuated with, not the audience for whom they write. The readers, because they are not present, are banished from the student writers' minds.

It is, however, dangerous to forget the audience. Writing becomes then a closed self-reflection. Here is how Breytenbach, with his unchecked metaphors, intuits the impulse to make writing an affair with oneself: "You must polish the word—not to have it shiny or smooth but to make it as clear as a mirror or a pebble in which you can see your face, and may see that your face is death" (23). Why is death the ultimate reflection? Though the writer polishing the words seems to be a solitary creature, he or she looks in the mirror he has created and sees something or someone else—death. What we may learn from Breytenbach's turn of words is that whenever we write, no matter how joyfully alone we feel doing it, we establish a relation with another. The other is imagined here as death, probably because as long as the reader has not been created by the writer, there is nothing there but death. An uncalled reader, or worse, one that does not feel welcome to the text, can be as harsh and censorious as Mehta's Oxford tutor. But is any reader, an actual, not an imagined reader, any better than Mehta's teacher, any better than a reflection of death? Where are we to find the benevolent beloved who will indeed help us accomplish the writing romance?

To Coetzee, the reader is someone the writer creates and recreates in his mind while he writes. In real life situations, however, a writer encounters people, who are not always willing to let themselves be recreated by his or her will. Romance itself does not take place in a vacuum, and its relation to social norms is not always easy. In her essay "Adultery," Laura Kipnis says, "Romance is, quite obviously, a socially sanctioned zone for wishing and desiring as well as a repository of excess. Mobilized by unconscious fantasy, it's potentially a profoundly antisocial form as well" (154). Romance shares with writing the impossibility of separating its public from its private aspect. Though we think of it as intimate and personal, it is, in so far as it includes another, a social form. If the intimate and personal aspect flourishes in romance, it is because it is socially sanctioned. But when fantasy takes over, romance becomes antisocial.

It is hard, if one thinks of writing as the form of self-reflection, as a romance with oneself, to suffer anyone else to read it. One can see this reluctance in the jealousy with which teenagers guard their personal journals. One should perhaps keep separate the writing done for oneself, the writing with maximum personal involvement, and the other writing, the writing for others, for the public. Some people do just that. I have read as many impersonal, cold, and indifferent papers, as I have read confessions, so personal as to make me feel embarrassed. Where does this split come from? What are we sometimes too afraid and sometimes too willing to expose?

Past rhetoricians thought of writing as exclusively public, and the desire to assert oneself (and sometimes expose oneself) in writing may have to do with the delicate balance between the private and the public spheres in our times. As Jonathan Franzen points out in "Imperial Bedroom," today everyone feels that privacy is threatened. But in Franzen's opinion, "What is threatened isn't the private sphere. It's the public sphere" (128). Franzen attracts our attention to the counterpart of privacy, the seldom-mentioned public domain in which we live. Without the public sphere, the private sphere does not make sense, and ultimately it does not exist. The reason why the threat is differently understood by the public and by Franzen may have to do with the fact that it comes from a cancellation of differences. What is threatened, I would say, is the difference between what is private and what is public.

Much of the erasure of differences is due to new technologies like the computer, the personal phone, the TV, VCR, etc., which enable us to do our job from home, or enjoy entertainment that once was available only in public, in the comfort of our bedroom. Ellen Ullman sees the progress of such technologies, especially of the Internet, as a threat to shared experience:

> The Net ideal represents a retreat not only from political life but also from culture—from that tumultuous conversation in which we try to talk to one another about our shared experience. As members of a culture, we see the same movie, read the same book, hear the same string quartet. Although it is difficult for us to agree on what we might have seen, read or heard, it is out of that difficult conversation that real culture arises. Whether or not we come to an agreement or understand-

ing, even if some decide that understanding and meaning are impossible, we are still sitting around the same campfire. (292)

Ullman sees in the new technology of the Internet the same threat that our ancestors must have seen when writing came about. Before writing was invented, people talked to each other, they shared news, traditions, emotions, and experiences. One can say that inventing writing was the first step toward becoming the solitary creatures we are today. But we do not feel so solitary when we pick up a book. The very nature of language has made it possible to preserve the relation with another even in writing. Our ability to speak is inextricably related to our social nature. No one speaks, or writes, exclusively for oneself.

As Ullman notes, though, the social relation, the cultural conversation is not easy. Sharing is hard. Making others understand us is harder. It is as hard as understanding others. Breytenbach's metaphors let us see this difficulty in its tragic dimension: "The recognition and the acceptance of the Other's humanity (or humanness) is a maiming of the self. You have to wound the self, cut it in strips, in order to *know* that you are similar and of the same substance as shadows" (23). It seems paradoxical and sacrificial, but Breytenbach's insight applies to our everyday transactions with each other. Whenever we listen to others, we have to keep our selves silent. Does this mean that the self is sacrificed on the altar of knowledge and of community? Does this mean that in order to know and speak to others, we have to annihilate the self? Notice that Breytenbach says only maim, cut into strips. From those strips we can weave another self, one that has the knowledge of oneself and of the other.

Breytenbach is not the only one to describe the contact between self and other as hurtful. Certainly Mehta's self as a student seems maimed in spite of the fact that the maiming leads to his achievement as a writer. Robert Scholes also describes the relation with the other in a negative metaphor. In "On Reading a Videotext," he speaks of reading as surrender. Although he refers to videotexts, which are, in his opinion, more powerful seducers than written texts, his image of reading as surrender to another's voice, another's view, another's thought is quite appropriate for any kind of text. For sheer understanding of what someone else says, we have to listen passively. Scholes warns us, however, that from surrender we must recover, and that "Recovery, in fact, may depend upon critical analysis" (263). Scholes speaks at once about the personal side of processing texts and the relationship implied in this process. When we read, as when we write, something happens to us, but it happens in relation to another. Whether it is a maiming or a surrender of the self, we need to recover as ourselves again. However, when we do, what do we do with our new critical knowledge if not share it, yet again, with another?

With Scholes, the reading and writing appear as parts of a never-ending cycle, in which knowledge is circulating both *within* and *between* persons. It is easy to see the importance of being part of such a cycle: the very act of being human, no matter how much technology is involved, is a shared and sharing experience. The self does not make sense without its opening to another, without its maiming, surrender, and recovery, any more than the private can make sense without the public. No matter how self-sufficient and independent we are, we do not make sense without others. We make sense from others and for others.

Scholes's lesson about reading videotexts is also explaining to us the process by virtue of which we become willing to surrender. We are in possession of a culture, of a shared experience, even as, if we are to trust Ullman, we are in danger of losing it. We draw our opinions and beliefs from that culture. Ultimately thus, our selves have always been made up of others. Coetzee sees it that way: "The self, as we understand the self today, is not the unity it was assumed to be by classical rationalism. On the contrary, it is multiple and multiply divided against itself. It is, to speak in figures, a zoo in which a multitude of beasts have residence, over which the anxious, overworked zookeeper of rationality exercises a rather limited control" (52). Perhaps what we ordinarily call self is the zookeeper that tries to exercise control. But when we write and address others, it is important to achieve not only control but unity as well. There should be some consensus among the animals of the zoo in order for the keeper to be able to report to someone outside.

Let us imagine ourselves ready to write, to address an audience that for the moment will remain imaginary, an audience that shares our culture and can therefore understand us. What do we have to tell this audience? Where do we start? To be part of the great conversation, of the culture Ullman talked about, we have to pick up where others left off. Before we write for others, we have to read others. Many times, we tend to see the reading as an imposition, as something we would rather not do. But that is unfair. If we write, and implicitly, we want someone else to read our writing, then we have to reciprocate, and read what others have written. Sometimes, what we read goes directly to our heart. The writer seems to be of one mind with ourselves, and we are ready to surrender. Scholes thinks the cause of this readiness to surrender is cultural reinforcement. And he explains: "By cultural reinforcement, I mean the process through which video texts confirm viewers in their ideological positions and reassure them as to their membership in a collective cultural body" (261). Scholes refers to videotexts, of course, but the same is true about written texts. We are all satisfied and reassured when someone agrees with us. As Ullman argues, we need such reassurance in order to share experience.

The question is, however, what would happen if our opinions were constantly reinforced and we would continue to reinforce them for others? We would probably be happy, but nothing new would ever emerge. The critical analysis, I have to agree with Scholes, is indeed the necessary means not only to recover from the surrender to the text but also to be able to create something new. Analysis means separating things into their component elements to see what they are made of, or what their nature is. It comes from a Greek word that means to undo, to loosen throughout. And although we usually think of "critical" as judging, we must not forget that it comes from crisis, which means a crucial point, or a turning point. We thus have to undo first what the others have done in order to turn it around and recreate it in our own way.

This description of our job as writers seems focused only on its public side, on the relationship with other authors we read and with our prospective readers. It would appear that nothing is in it for the self, that when recreating, we cannot create. But that is a one-sided view. In critically processing others' ideas, we enrich ourselves, bring more animals to our inner zoo, if we are to stick with Coetzee's metaphor. Once we know these animals well, we are free to steer and control our zoo the way we want to. And it is not only in the interest of our beloved reader that we have to harness the force of our inner zoo, but also in our own interest. Inner order makes us more secure even as it makes us more capable and ready to meet the others.

You may have noticed that in the course of this essay I have referred to many sources. I have deliberately chosen sources from this book, because I want you, my audience, to be able to consult them easily. Much of the essay's shape has been determined by you and by the sources. In spite of my reliance on these sources throughout, I can claim this essay for my own, and it is indeed the result of my experience in writing. By opening myself to the texts and to you, I have been able to shape an argument that gives a richer meaning to my experience as a writer. I can understand now why criticism has always hurt, and why it has been so hard to satisfy my audiences. I have also learned that reading others critically, carefully, considerately can make me richer intellectually. I know now how to respect my readers, to share my experience in reading with care and clarity. The notes I write for myself are animals from my inner zoo. What I write for the public though is measured and under control.

Control is difficult to achieve these days, when we are bombarded with information. If you have ever worked on a research project, you know that the problem with information is not that it is scarce but that there is too much of it. Some people become complacent because information is so readily available, especially on the Internet. But information does not help unless it is organized into some meaningful whole. In "Intelligent Electronics," Andrei Codrescu also feels the threat of a loss of meaning due to virtuality: "Once virtuality has been built out of all the information we have, it becomes meaningless" (47). In order to have meaning, we have to manage information, to include, but also to exclude, and above all, to make connections between the pieces of information we have and to bring them together.

To achieve this meaningful whole is to write. To write is thus to abandon oneself to reading and readers and to recover oneself from reading for one's readers. It is to undo and remake the readings and oneself; therefore, it is the most intensely private and the most riskily public experience and the most exhilarating. Whether we are writing a poem, a novel, an essay, a report, or a memo, the process is the same. We gather information from without, make it meaningful within, and write it out again for our readers.

My colleagues, my co-author, and I have gathered here a number of texts for your reading. Some will please you, some will challenge you, but we hope you will read them all with curiosity and an open mind. We hope you will surrender to them temporarily and then recover your stance through critical analysis. We also hope you are ready to cut the self into strips and reweave it into a newer, and richer you. And we hope that writing will be the process by which you enrich yourselves and enrich the world. Write on!

Anca Rosu

Acknowledgments

This book has its roots in the experience and practice of the teachers at DeVry College in North Brunswick. Wendolyn Tetlow and Martin Gloege were the initial editors, and we owe the existence of the book to them. We also owe debts of gratitude to all the colleagues who participated in the debates of Club Affinities, which we hope to resurrect soon. Among the most frequent participants were Barbara Burke, Barbara Lindquist, Al Armstrong, Susan (Charlie) Groth, and Jeanne Roach-Baptiste. Special thanks to Barbara Lindquist, Susan (Charlie) Groth, Samantha Napier, Alyson Mosquera, and Mark Hinrichs for reading and commenting on the new selections. And very special thanks to Matt Reed who served as proof-reader and generally supported the project with enthusiasm and competence. Last, but not least, we thank our editor from Pearson Custom, Will Vogel, who gave us his encouragement and the benefit of his expertise.

My Pin-Up

Hilton Als

Hilton Als is staff writer for The New Yorker *magazine and advisory editor at* Grand Street Magazine. *He has written on photography and is recognized as a member of the field. His first book,* The Women *(1997)—part memoir, part psychological study, part sociopolitical manifesto—was published by Farrar, Strauss and Giroux. Als writes from the point of view of marginalized categories to which, in some way or another, he belongs: blacks, immigrants, women, gays, the poor. His statements and ideas are at times controversial but his compelling writing talent gains him admirers everywhere. The following essay was included in* The Women.

By now, the word "Negress" has become to mean many things. The Negress is perceived less as a mind than as an emotional being. In the popular imagination, she lives one or several cliché-ridden narratives. One narrative: she is colored, female, and a single mother, reduced by circumstances to tireless depression and public "aid" and working off the books in one low-paying job after another in an attempt to support her children—children whom, according to tax-paying, law-abiding public consensus, she should not have had. Like my mother.

Another narrative: she can be defined as a romantic wedded to despair, since she has little time or inclination to analyze how she is regarded by America's social welfare system, which sees her as a statistic, part of the world's rapacious silent majority. Like my mother.

Another narrative: she gives birth to children who grow up to be lawless; she becomes involved with men who leave her for other women; she is subject to illness and depression. Her depression is so numbing that she rarely lets news of the outside world (television, radio, newspapers) enter her sphere of consciousness, and much

1

of her time is spent shielding herself and her children against the news of emotional disaster she sees day after day in the adult faces that surround the faces of her children, who, in turn, look to her to make sense of it all. Like my mother.

What the Negress has always been: a symbol of America's now forgotten strain of Puritanical selflessness. The Negress is a perennial source of "news" and "copy" in the newspapers and magazines she does not read, because she is a formidable character in the internal drama with which most Americans surround the issue of self-abnegation. If the Negress is represented in the media, it is as a good neighbor who is staunch in her defense of the idea that being a good neighbor makes a difference in this common world. And this: she is a good neighbor uncritical of her faith, even as her intellect searches through the Byzantine language of the Bible for a truth other than her own. Her ability to meld language with belief without becoming sarcastic (sarcasm defines our sense of contemporary speech) is one reason the Negress is both abhorred and adored. Take, for instance, this story, reported in the *New York Post:*

> The Trinidad woman who lost her legs in a subway purse-snatching is not looking for revenge—but she hopes her mugger will become "a better person" in prison. . . . Samella Thompson, 56, fell onto the tracks in the Van Wyck Boulevard Station in Jamaica, Queens. . . . She was trying to jump onto the platform from an F train as she chased a homeless man who had grabbed her sister's purse. . . . The feisty mother of five's attitude is "you have to take life as it comes." Thompson wished [her attacker] would know God.

The Negress serves as a reminder to our sentimental nation that its countrymen are shaped by a nonverbal confusion about and, ultimately, abhorrence of the good-neighbor principle, which they absorb through the language-based tenets of Judaism and Christianity. And since most Americans are suspicious of language and spend a great deal of time and energy on Entertainment and Relaxation in an attempt to avoid its net result (Reflection), this absorption leads to a deep emotional confusion about the "good."

To women who are not Negresses—some are white—the Negress, whether she calls herself that or not, is a specter of dignity—selfless to a fault. But eventually, she troubles her noncolored female admirer, since the latter feels compelled to compare herself and finds herself both privileged and lacking. This inversion or competitiveness among women vis-à-vis their "oppressed" stance says something about why friendships between women are rare, and especially so between noncolored women and Negresses.

The Negress's will to survive is enhanced by her need to survive for her children. But being the source of such strength is sometimes too much for the Negress. Sometimes she contrives to marry something other than herself or her children in order to escape it, that something being a black male. When maleness manages to brush up against the Negress, it is usually violent, so its presence is felt. But it eventually absents itself from the Negress because her intellectual and physical focus on surviving leaves no room for maleness's self-centeredness.

Man Seized in Rape of 3-Year-Old in Public

A Manhattan man raped his 3-year-old niece about 25 feet from the Franklin D. Roosevelt Drive at the start of the rush hour Friday evening. . . . The suspect, Leroy Saunders, 29, was caught a few blocks away after assaulting the girl under a tree on a grassy knoll. . . . Mr. Saunders, with his pants down to his ankles, assaulted the girl, who was naked below the waist. . . . The girl's mother, who is Mr. Saunder's sister, said, "You just don't expect that from kin." But she declined to talk further about the case. "I just want to go to my apartment to rest," she said. . . . Neighbors said the mother, whose surname differs from her brother's, had six children.

The New York Times, July 17, 1991.

The fact that Leroy Saunders's sister, mother of six, three of whom were in foster homes, had to "rest" after her daughter's attack on a grassy knoll and perhaps consider the facts later was not unusual given what I assumed when I read her story: that she was a Negress. What was, or perhaps was not, unusual, given that there was no photograph accompanying *Man Seized in Rape of 3-Year-Old,* was that immediately upon reading it, I attached black faces to this narrative of "kin" gone awry, a grassy knoll, pants down around the ankles, and a mother's need for rest after an atrocity committed against her child.

That Leroy Saunders's sister has a surname different from her brother's is not among the pertinent facts that make up the Negress in her. The fact that she did not expect such behavior from "kin" is. This word—"kin"—is a regional colloquialism peculiar to the South; it evokes a narrative. One can imagine Leroy Saunders's sister as an inbred Negress, saddled with bad men and children swollen with need and the welfare system. No husband or father is reported as being attached to her "different" name or to her children. But the use of the word "kin" implicates her in Saunders's crime: in a common world, her actions are crimes too. Her use of the word "kin" not only indicates her commonness to her readers, but also her forbearance, her unwillingness to give her brother up, regardless of the facts.

The story of the Negress is not difficult to understand if you listen. My sisters spoke the same language of kin, one saying of another: "She is so nasty. Having one baby after another, and none of them by the same father. Like a dog." I assumed that Leroy Saunders's sister was another Negress living in strict avoidance of the facts, just as I assumed his niece was another Negress left in a world where her future actions would probably illustrate Leroy Saunders's turn of mind against her. What the *Times* made clear was how Leroy Saunders's sister and niece would not be a story were it not for him. Generally the Negress wears the rouge of a peculiar emotional verbosity that is not, in fact, verbal.

I grew up with the youngest of my four older sisters, who was eleven years my senior, during the '70s, a period characterized by a breakdown in the traditional social order, at least as we had known it. The '70s were a synthetic version of the more galvanizing active radicalism of the '60s. As a leftover time, the '70s suited us, perfectly, since we considered ourselves leftover people, Negresses like our mother. Being younger and, in some respects, less intelligent than our mother, we were conscious of wanting to develop our own social stance, even as we affected her stance of disinterest, because we admired her. I think we misread our mother's exhausted concern as lack of concern; she never didn't care.

Unlike our mother, we affected an interest in people who, because they had the same skin color as our own, presumed we were interested in the race and its struggle. We were not interested in the race and its struggle. We were not interested in strident abstractions, being so emotionally abstract ourselves. We were West Indians living in New York; we were smug in our sense of displacement; we took freely from both cultures in order to be interesting. The furor and energy that our black American contemporaries focused on dreams and hopes we found ridiculous. Their ideology was totalitarianism made simple: economic independence from "the man" and an entirely black-run government. We were especially distanced by the movement's xenophobia: members of the Black Power movement referred to West Indians, and their ambitious progeny, as black Jews.

My sister discovered Black Power around the same time she discovered her need for a father; as a concept, the movement lent itself to the idea of "serious" black men who were "committed." She was drawn to Black Power because of its distinctly American male cast of mind. As a girl of West Indian descent, she considered American black men exotic, charming in their narcissism, and in their generally ahistorical stance.

It would not be excessive for me to say that my sister and I probably also considered American blacks disgusting on some level, even though we didn't admit this to ourselves, given our melodramatic silence. We weren't attracted to much that we didn't find repugnant. We couldn't be in love with something we could not control. Disdain is controllable, no matter how feigned; love is not. And we believed we would feel less overwhelmed and more distanced from our difference vis-à-vis American blacks if we were disdainful of them—a romantic view. Our romantic view of American blacks included feeling "bad" for them because they weren't us. We wanted to save them from themselves. We were very big on rescuing people, having had a mother like ours.

Although we did not know it then, my sister and I used our cursory involvement in the Black Power movement—sit-ins in Harlem, many, many poetry readings in the Bronx, and demonstrations everywhere—to catapult ourselves past our mother's non-verbal emotional verbosity, her increasing disinterest in the world at large. The outings I looked forward to most were not those that involved picketing, or canvassing votes for now forgotten community "leaders," but listening to the women who sometimes took the stand at rallies and spoke, the women who wrote and published books and recited their words in public, unlike my sister who hid or burned her diary and buried her language in the creases of her careless lovers' necks.

The women we heard read—Sonia Sanchez or Nikki Giovanni—were addressed as "Sister." They wore brightly colored dashikis, head wraps, and robes. Their poetic skills were limited. Their work was strident, empty, and invigorating. It valorized the black male. The black male those poetesses and my sister imagined did not exist—which is one reason they had to imagine him. Those women embraced the ideology spouted during the revolution that was always about to happen because they wanted to maintain the fantasy that the revolution was the assertion of a black masculinity that was about to be. That masculinity would serve my sister's purpose: it would be forceful enough to dismantle Negressity and its aura of depression.

That many of the male members of the black revolutionary movement were irresponsible and childlike was beside the point. That they were in search of the same authority figure whom most of them had never known in their matriarchal households—Dad—as their female comrades was also beside the point. What made the women different from the men in the movement was the will they applied to *creating* Dad for themselves.

The poetesses my sister and I listened to commanded the respect of their male "comrades" because they reinvented them as officers of war. As those women poets spoke, in their conspiratorial, self-congratulatory, syncopated voices, another tone broke in, a tone which expressed their need for Daddy to shut them up. It became clear to me that their language was not the product of reflection or the desire to reflect; if they thought before they spoke, they'd be forced to realize that what they were screaming about was their need to be silenced. Instead, they identified their need to be oppressed by their idea of a black male as an "emergent black tradition," its foundation being the abstractions of Black Motherhood and Black Pride.

The movement's most popular poet, Nikki Giovanni, wrote in a poem titled "Seduction," which was published in 1970:

> one day
> you gonna walk in this house
> and I'm gonna have a long African
> gown
> you'll sit down and say "The Black . . ."
> and i'm gonna take one arm out
> then you—not noticing me at all—will say "What
> about this brother . . ."
> and i'm going to be slipping it over my head
> and you'll rapp on about "The revolution . . ."
> while i rest your hand against my stomach
> you'll go on—as you always do—saying
> "I just can't dig . . ."
> while i'm moving your hand up and down

and i'll be taking your dashiki off . . .
then you'll notice
your state of undress
and knowing you you'll just say
"Nikki,
isn't this counterrevolutionary . . . ?"

And Sonia Sanchez wrote in "Black Magic" in 1978:

magic
   my man
is you
   turning
my body into
a thousand
smiles.
   black
magic is your
touch
   making
me breathe.

The images these poetesses offered in verse—a simple, uncomplicated, thuggish sexuality projected onto their construction of the black male—were perfectly legitimate but dumb, easily co-opted by the pornographic imagination that continues to produce such magazines as *Black Tail, Sugah,* and *Ebony Heat.* During the revolution, the Negress replaced her starched cap of servitude with a brightly colored turban made of knit cloth, but she did not reinvent her internal structure.

When the Negress is seen in books, such as Toni Morrison's *Beloved* or Terry McMillan's *Waiting to Exhale,* that are marketed according to their "anger" quotient, or in films, such as Charles Burnett's *To Sleep With Anger,* that are remarkable for their willful construction of the "benign" Negress, or in theater pieces, such as *Having Our Say*, that avoid reference to class issues among Negresses, she is shown as less than herself, but is still more than our current cultural climate can handle. Angry or silent, she carries a tray loaded with forgiveness, bitterness, rancor, defensiveness, and slatternliness. She had rejected language. In most of the books about her, the authors do not question what the Negress is, because they cannot face her. The Negress in their books is shut off from ideas or speech of her own, like a mad, woolly relative. Like the Negress in Toni Cade Bambara's *Gorilla, My Love:*

It does no good to write autobiographical fiction cause the minute the book hits the stand here comes your mama screaming how could you and sighin death where is thy sting and she snatches you up out your bed to

6

grill you about what was going down back there in Brooklyn when she was working three jobs and trying to improve the quality of your life and come to find . . . that you were messin around with that nasty boy up the block and breaks into sobs . . .

Or the Negress in Toni Morrison's *Sula:*

Hannah rubbed no edges, made no demands, made the man feel as though he were complete and wonderful just as he was—he didn't need fixing. . . .

What would the Negress be if she were stripped of her role? Would she be just another banal woman undone by domestic despair, fortified by her class aspirations and fantasies about being fulfilled through marriage? It is difficult to imagine the Negress being anything other than what she has come to symbolize in contemporary literature: authorial conceit and ambition. The writers who present the Negress are intent on building an empirical universe in which the only voices heard are their own, and since the Negress does not speak, but *moves* through their fiction as either an adventurer or a victim, her existence depends entirely upon the fictional system they build for her. They create the Negress in order to kill her, because she represents the matriarchal society they are at pains to forget, even as they cling to her because of her ability to milk sympathy from the audience—or provide it.

The Negress in literature is a construct who does not exist independently of her creator's need to fulfill his or her audience's expectations of "black" writing. She signifies "oppression" and, by extension, blackness. They make the Negress bigger than she is in order to mythologize her. As a myth, she does not have to be complex or subtle. She is larger than life, like Pilate in Toni Morrison's *Song of Solomon.* She is uglier than life, like Celie in Alice Walker's *The Color Purple.* And she appears to superb theatrical effect from time to time, especially when her presence represents someone else's failure of expression, as in the late British playwright John Osborne's *The Entertainer:*

Archie: Did I ever tell you the most moving thing that I ever heard? It was when I was in Canada—I managed to slip over the border sometimes to some people I knew, and one night I heard some negress singing in a bar. Now you're going to smile at this, you're going to smile your educated English head off, because I suppose you've never sat lonely and half slewed in some bar among strangers a thousand miles from anything you think you understand. But if ever I saw any hope or strength in the human race, it was in the face of that old fat negress getting up to sing about Jesus or something like that. She was poor and lonely and oppressed like nobody you've ever known. Or me, for that matter. I never even liked that kind of music, but to see that old black whore singing her heart out to the whole world, you knew somehow in your heart that it didn't matter how much you kick people, the real people, how much you despise them, if they can stand up and make a pure, just natural noise like that, there's nothing wrong with them, only with everybody else. . . . There's nobody who can feel like that. I wish to God I could, I wish to God I could feel like that old black bitch with her fat cheeks, and sing.

When describing the Negress, writers describe themselves away from her, as they rush headlong into the void of patriarchy. In their books, the Negress is replete with tears. She smiles. Her chest heaves. Her body is that of a servant not begging for respite. She burns brightly in the imagination, like a dull witch.

In order to understand her, I have written my life in the margins of hers. Is this love? How did I love my mother? After a certain point, I rarely expressed it physically for fear her touch would be so hideous and lonely. How do I love her still? In my imagination.

Xerox and Infinity

Jean Baudrillard

Jean Baudrillard is a well-known sociologist and a theorist of contemporary culture. Born in Reims in 1929, he moved to Paris where he taught at the University of Paris X (Nanterre). Among his works translated in English are In the Shadow of the Silent Majorities, Simulations and Simulacra, Fatal Strategies, Seduction, America, *and* Cool Memories. *His most recent works in French include* The Gulf War Never Took Place *and* The Illusion of the End. *The following essay is a chapter in* The Transparency of Evil *published in English in 1993.*

If men create intelligent machines, or fantasize about them, it is either because they secretly despair of their own intelligence or because they are in danger of succumbing to the weight of a monstrous and useless intelligence which they seek to exorcise by transferring it to machines, where they can play with it and make fun of it. By entrusting this burdensome intelligence to machines we are released from any responsibility to knowledge, much as entrusting power to politicians allows us to disdain any aspiration of our own to power.

If men dream of machines that are unique, that are endowed with genius, it is because they despair of their own uniqueness, or because they prefer to do without it—to enjoy it by proxy, so to speak, thanks to machines. What such machines offer is the spectacle of thought, and in manipulating them people devote themselves more to the spectacle of thought than to thought itself.

It is not for nothing that they are described as 'virtual', for they put thought on hold indefinitely, tying its emergence to the achievement of a complete knowledge. The act of thinking itself is thus put off for ever. Indeed, the question of thought can no more be raised than the question of the freedom of future generations, who will pass through life as we travel through the air, strapped into their seats. These Men of

"Xerox and Infinity," by Jean Baudrillard, reprinted from *The Transparency of Evil*, 1993, Verso.

Artificial Intelligence will traverse their own mental space bound hand and foot to their computers. Immobile in front of his computer, Virtual Man makes love via the screen and gives lessons by means of the teleconference. He is a physical—and no doubt also a mental—cripple. That is the price he pays for being operational. Just as eyeglasses and contact lenses will arguably one day evolve into implanted prostheses for a species that has lost its sight, it is similarly to be feared that artificial intelligence and the hardware that supports it will become a mental prosthesis for a species without the capacity for thought.

Artificial intelligence is devoid of intelligence because it is devoid of artifice. True artifice is the artifice of the body in the throes of passion, the artifice of the sign in seduction, the artifice of ambivalence in gesture, the artifice of ellipsis in language, the artifice of the mask before the face, the artifice of the pithy remark that completely alters meaning. So-called intelligent machines deploy artifice only in the feeblest sense of the word, breaking linguistic, sexual or cognitive acts down into their simplest elements and digitizing them so that they can be resynthesized according to models. They can generate all the possibilities of a program or of a potential object. But artifice is in no way concerned with what *generates,* merely with what *alters,* reality. Artifice is the power of illusion. These machines have the artlessness of pure calculation, and the games they offer are based solely on commutations and combinations. In this sense they may be said to be virtuous, as well as virtual: they can never succumb to their own object; they are immune even to the seduction of their own knowledge. Their virtue resides in their transparency, their functionality, their absence of passion and artifice. Artificial Intelligence is a celibate machine.

What must always distinguish the way humans function from the way machines function, even the most intelligent of machines, is the intoxication, the sheer pleasure, that humans get from functioning. The invention of a machine that can feel pleasure is something—happily—that is still beyond human capacity. All kinds of spare parts are available to humans to help them achieve gratification, but none has yet been devised that could take pleasure in their stead. There are prostheses that can work better than humans, 'think' or move around better than humans (or in place of humans), but there is no such thing, from the point of view of technology or in terms of the media, as a replacement for human pleasure, or for the pleasure of being human. For that to exist, machines would have to have an idea of man, have to be able to invent man—but inasmuch as man has already invented *them,* it is too late for that. That is why man can always be more than he is, whereas machines can never be more than they are. Even the most intelligent among machines are just what they are—except, perhaps, when accidents or failures occur, events which might conceivably be attributed to some obscure desire on the part of the machine. Nor do machines manifest that ironical surplus or excess functioning which contributes the pleasure, or suffering, thanks to which human beings transcend their determinations—and thus come closer to their *raison d'être.* Alas for the machine, it can never transcend its own operation—which, perhaps, explains the profound melancholy of the computer. All machines are celibate.

(All the same, the recent epidemic of computer viruses does embody a striking anomaly: it is almost as though machines were able to obtain a sly pleasure by producing perverse effects. This is an ironic and fascinating turn of events. Could it be that artificial intelligence, by manifesting this viral pathology, is engaging in self-parody—and thus acceding to some sort of genuine intelligence?)

The celibacy of the machine entails the celibacy of Telecomputer Man. Thanks to his computer or word processor, Telecomputer Man offers himself the spectacle of his own brain, his own intelligence, at work. Similarly, through his chat line or his Minitel, he can offer himself the spectacle of his own phantasies, of a strictly virtual pleasure. He exorcises both intelligence and pleasure at the interface with the machine. The Other, the interlocutor, is never really involved: the screen works much like a mirror, for the screen itself as locus of the interface is the prime concern. An interactive screen transforms the process of relating into a process of commutation between One and the Same. The secret of the interface is that the Other here is virtually the Same: otherness is surreptitiously conjured away by the machine. The most probable scenario of communication here is that Minitel users gravitate from the screen to telephone conversations, thence to face-to-face meetings, and . . . then what? Well, it's 'let's phone each other', and, finally, back to the Minitel—which is, after all, more erotic because it is at once both esoteric and transparent. This is communication in its purest form, for there is no intimacy here except with the screen, and with an electronic text that is no more than a design filigreed onto life. A new Plato's retreat whence to observe shadow-forms of bodily pleasure filing past. Why speak to one another, when it is so simple to communicate?

We lived once in a world where the realm of the imaginary was governed by the mirror, by dividing one into two, by theatre, by otherness and alienation. Today that realm is the realm of the screen, of interfaces and duplication, of contiguity and networks. All our machines are screens, and the interactivity of humans has been replaced by the interactivity of screens. Nothing inscribed on these screens is ever intended to be deciphered in any depth: rather, it is supposed to be explored instantaneously, in an abreaction immediate to meaning, a short-circuiting of the poles of representation.

Reading a screenful of information is quite a different thing from *looking*. It is a digital form of exploration in which the eye moves along an endless broken line. The relationship to the interlocutor in communication, like the relationship to knowledge in data-handling, is similar: tactile and exploratory. A computer-generated voice, even a voice over the telephone, is a tactile voice, neutral and functional. It is no longer in fact exactly a voice, any more than looking at a screen is exactly looking. The whole paradigm of the sensory has changed. The tactility here is not the organic sense of touch: it implies merely an epidermal contiguity of eye and image, the collapse of the aesthetic distance involved in looking. We draw ever closer to the surface of the screen; our gaze is, as it were, strewn across the image. We no longer have the spectator's distance from the stage—all theatrical conventions are gone. That we fall so easily into the screen's coma of the imagination is due to the fact that the screen presents a perpetual void that we are invited to fill. Proxemics of images: promiscuity of images: tactile pornography of images. Yet the image is always light years away. It is invariably a tele-image—an image located at a very special kind of distance which can only be described as *unbridgeable by the body.* The body can cross the distance that separates it from language, from the stage, or from the mirror—this is what keeps it human and allows it to partake in exchange. But the screen is merely virtual—and hence unbridgeable. This is why it partakes only of that abstract—definitively abstract—form known as communication.

Within the space of communication, words, gestures, looks are in a continual state of contiguity, yet they never touch. The fact is that distance and proximity here are simply not relationships obtaining between the body and its surroundings. The screen of our images, the interactive screen, the telecomputing screen, are at once too close and too far away: too close to be true (to have the dramatic intensity of a stage)—and too far away to be false (to embody the collusive distance of artifice). They thus create a dimension that is no longer quite human, an eccentric dimension corresponding to the depolarization of space and the indistinctness of bodily forms of expression.

There is no better model of the way in which the computer screen and the mental screen of our own brain are interwoven than Moebius's topology, with its peculiar contiguity of near and far, inside and outside, object and subject within the same spiral. It is in accordance with this same model that information and communication are constantly turning round upon themselves in an incestuous circumvolution, a superficial conflation of subject and object, within and without, question and answer, event and image, and so on. The form is inevitably that of a twisted ring reminiscent of the mathematical symbol for infinity.

The same may be said of our relationship with our 'virtual' machines. Telecomputer Man is assigned to an apparatus, just as the apparatus is assigned to him, by virtue of an involution of each into the other, a refraction of each by the other. The machine does what the human wants it to do, but by the same token the human puts into execution only what the machine has been programmed to do. The operator is working with virtuality: only apparently is the aim to obtain information or to communicate; the real purpose is to explore all the possibilities of a program, rather as a gambler seeks to exhaust the permutations in a game of chance. Consider the way the camera is used now. Its possibilities are no longer those of a subject who 'reflects' the world according to his personal vision; rather, they are the possibilities of the lens, as exploited by the object. The camera is thus a machine that vitiates all will, erases all intentionality and leaves nothing but the pure reflex needed to take pictures. Looking itself disappears without trace, replaced by a lens now in collusion with the object—and hence with an inversion of vision. The magic lies precisely in the subject's retroversion to a camera obscura—the reduction of his vision to the impersonal vision of a mechanical device. In a mirror, it is the subject who gives free rein to the realm of the imaginary. In the camera lens, and on-screen in general, it is the object, potentially, that unburdens itself—to the benefit of all media and telecommunications techniques.

This is why images of *anything* are now a possibility. This is why everything is translatable into computer terms, commutable into digital form, just as each individual is commutable into his own particular genetic code. (The whole object, in fact, is to exhaust all the virtualities of such analogues of the genetic code: this is one of artificial intelligence's most fundamental aspects.) What this means on a more concrete level is that there is no longer any such thing as an act or event which is not refracted into a technical image or onto a screen, any such thing as an action which does not in some sense *want* to be photographed, filmed or tape-recorded, does not desire to be stored in memory so as to become reproducible for all eternity. No such thing as an action which does not aspire to self-transcendence into a virtual eternity—not, now, the durable eternity that follows death, but rather the ephemeral eternity of ever-ramifying artificial memory.

The compulsion of the virtual is the compulsion to exist *in potentia* on all screens, to be embedded in all programs, and it acquires a magical force: the Siren call of the black box.

Where is the freedom in all this? Nowhere! There is no choice here, no final decision. All decisions concerning networks, screens, information or communication are serial in character, partial, fragmentary, fractal. A mere succession of partial decisions, a microscopic series of partial sequences and objectives, constitute as much the photographer's way of proceeding as that of Telecomputer Man in general, or even that called for by our own most trivial television viewing. All such behaviour is structured in quantum fashion, composed of haphazard sequences of discrete decisions. The fascination derives from the pull of the black box, the appeal of an uncertainty which puts paid to our freedom.

Am I a man or a machine? This anthropological question no longer has an answer. We are thus in some sense witness to the end of anthropology, now being conjured away by the most recent machines and technologies. The uncertainty here is born of the perfecting of machine networks, just as sexual uncertainty (Am I a man or a woman? What has the difference between the sexes become?) is born of increasingly sophisticated manipulation of the unconscious and of the body, and just as science's uncertainty about the status of its object is born of the sophistication of analysis in the microsciences.

Am I a man or a machine? There is no ambiguity in the traditional relationship between man and machine: the worker is always, in a way, a stranger to the machine he operates, and alienated by it. But at least he retains the precious status of alienated man. The new technologies, with their new machines, new images and interactive screens, do *not* alienate me. Rather, they form an integrated circuit with me. Video screens, televisions, computers and Minitels resemble nothing so much as contact lenses in that they are so many transparent prostheses, integrated into the body to the

13

point of being almost part of its genetic make-up: they are like pacemakers—or like Philip K. Dick's 'papula', a tiny implant, grafted onto the body at birth as a 'free gift', which serves the organism as an alarm signal. All our relationships with networks and screens, whether willed or not, are of this order. Their structure is one of subordination, not of alienation—the structure of the integrated circuit. Man or machine? Impossible to tell.

Surely the extraordinary success of artificial intelligence is attributable to the fact that it frees us from real intelligence, that by hypertrophying thought as an operational process it frees us from thought's ambiguity and from the insoluble puzzle of its relationship to the world. Surely the success of all these technologies is a result of the way in which they make it impossible even to raise the timeless question of liberty. What a relief! Thanks to the machinery of the virtual, all your problems are over! You are no longer either subject or object, no longer either free or alienated—and no longer either one or the other: you are *the same,* and enraptured by the commutations of that sameness. We have left the hell of other people for the ecstasy of the same, the purgatory of otherness for the artificial paradises of identity. Some might call this an even worse servitude, but Telecomputer Man, having no will of his own, knows nothing of serfdom. Alienation of man by man is a thing of the past: now man is plunged into homeostasis by machines.

If the River Was Whiskey

T. Coraghessan Boyle

Born in the Hudson Valley of New York State, T. Coraghessan Boyle is the author of numerous short stories and novels. His novels include East Is East *and* The Road to Wellville *(1993), and his novel* World's End *won the 1988 PEN/Faulkner Award for Fiction. Boyle's short fiction has been published in* The New Yorker, Harper's, The Atlantic, *and* Playboy, *and collected in* Without A Hero *and* If the River Was Whiskey. *He lives near Santa Barbara, California.*

The water was a heartbeat, a pulse, it stole the heat from his body and pumped it to his brain. Beneath the surface, magnified through the shimmering lens of his face mask, were silver shoals of fish, forests of weed, a silence broken only by the distant throbbing hum of an outboard. Above, there was the sun, the white flash of a faraway sailboat, the weatherbeaten dock with its weatherbeaten rowboat, his mother in her deck chair, and the vast depthless green of the world beyond.

He surfaced like a dolphin, spewing water from the vent of his snorkel, and sliced back to the dock. The lake came with him, two bony arms and the wedge of a foot, the great heaving splash of himself flat out on the dock like something thrown up in a storm. And then, without pausing even to snatch up a towel, he had the spinning rod in hand and the silver lure was sizzling out over the water, breaking the surface just above the shadowy arena he'd fixed in his mind. His mother looked up at the splash. "Tiller," she called, "come get a towel."

His shoulders quaked. He huddled and stamped his feet, but he never took his eyes off the tip of the rod. Twitching it suggestively, he reeled with the jerky, hesitant motion that would drive lunker fish to a frenzy. Or so he'd read, anyway.

"Tilden, do you hear me?"

"I saw a Northern," he said. "A big one. Two feet maybe." The lure was in. A flick of his wrist sent it back. Still reeling, he ducked his head to wipe his nose on his wet

"If the River Was Whiskey," by T. Coraghessan Boyle, reprinted from *Stories*, 1998, Penguin Putnam, Inc.

shoulder. He could feel the sun on his back now and he envisioned the skirted lure in the water, sinuous, sensual, irresistible, and he waited for the line to quicken with the strike.

The porch smelled of pine—old pine, dried up and dead—and it depressed him. In fact, everything depressed him—especially this vacation. Vacation. It was a joke. Vacation from what?

He poured himself a drink—vodka and soda, tall, from the plastic half-gallon jug. It wasn't noon yet, the breakfast dishes were in the sink, and Tiller and Caroline were down at the lake. He couldn't see them through the screen of trees, but he heard the murmur of their voices against the soughing of the branches and the sadness of the birds. He sat heavily in the creaking wicker chair and looked out on nothing. He didn't feel too hot. In fact, he felt as if he'd been cored and dried, as if somebody had taken a pipe cleaner and run it through his veins. His head ached too, but the vodka would take care of that. When he finished it, he'd have another; and then maybe a grilled swiss on rye. Then he'd start to feel good again.

His father was talking to the man and his mother was talking to the woman. They'd met at the bar about twenty drinks ago and his father was into his could-have-been, should-have-been, way-back-when mode, and the man, bald on top and with a ratty beard and long greasy hair like his father's, was trying to steer the conversation back to building supplies. The woman had whole galaxies of freckles on her chest, and she leaned forward in her sundress and told his mother scandalous stories about people she'd never heard of. Tiller had drunk all the Coke and eaten all the beer nuts he could hold. He watched the Pabst Blue Ribbon sign flash on and off above the bar and he watched the woman's freckles move in and out of the gap between her breasts. Outside it was dark and a cool clean scent came in off the lake.

"Uh huh, yeah," his father was saying, "the To the Bone Band. I played rhythm and switched off vocals with Dillie Richards. . . ."

The man had never heard of Dillie Richards.

"Black dude, used to play with Taj Mahal?"

The man had never heard of Taj Mahal.

"Anyway," his father said, "we used to do all this really outrageous stuff by people like Muddy, Howlin' Wolf, Luther Allison—"

"She didn't," his mother said.

The woman threw down her drink and nodded and the front of her dress went crazy. Tiller watched her and felt the skin go tight across his shoulders and the back of his neck, where he'd been burned the first day. He wasn't wearing any underwear, just shorts. He looked away. "Three abortions, two kids," the woman said. "And she never knew who the father of the second one was."

"Drywall isn't worth a damn," the man said. "But what're you going to do?"

"Paneling?" his father offered.

The man cut the air with the flat of his hand. He looked angry. "Don't talk to me about paneling," he said.

16

Mornings, when his parents were asleep and the lake was still, he would take the rowboat to the reedy cove on the far side of the lake where the big pike lurked. He didn't actually know if they lurked there, but if they lurked anywhere, this would be the place. It looked fishy, mysterious, sunken logs looming up dark from the shadows beneath the boat, mist rising like steam, as if the bottom were boiling with ravenous, cold-eyed, killer pike that could slice through monofilament with a snap of their jaws and bolt ducklings in a gulp. Besides, Joe Matochik, the old man who lived in the cabin next door and could charm frogs by stroking their bellies, had told him that this was where he'd find them.

It was cold at dawn and he'd wear a thick homeknit sweater over his T-shirt and shorts, sometimes pulling the stretched-out hem of it down like a skirt to warm his thighs. He'd take an apple with him or a slice of brown bread and peanut butter. And of course the orange lifejacket his mother insisted on.

When he left the dock he was always wearing the lifejacket—for form's sake and for the extra warmth it gave him against the raw morning air. But when he got there, when he stood in the swaying basin of the boat to cast his Hula Popper or Abu Reflex, it got in the way and he took it off. Later, when the sun ran through him and he didn't need the sweater, he balled it up on the seat beside him, and sometimes, if it was good and hot, he shrugged out of his T-shirt and shorts too. No one could see him in the cove, and it made his breath come quick to be naked like that under the morning sun.

"I heard you," he shouted, and he could feel the veins stand out in his neck, the rage come up in him like something killed and dead and brought back to life. "What kind of thing is that to tell a kid, huh? About his own father?"

She wasn't answering. She'd backed up in a corner of the kitchen and she wasn't answering. And what could she say, the bitch? He'd heard her. Dozing on the trundle bed under the stairs, wanting a drink but too weak to get up and make one, he'd heard voices from the kitchen, her voice and Tiller's. "Get used to it," she said, "he's a drunk, your father's a drunk," and then he was up off the bed as if something had exploded inside of him and he had her by the shoulders—always the shoulders and, never the face, that much she'd taught him—and Tiller was gone, out the door and gone. Now, her voice low in her throat, a sick and guilty little smile on her lips, she whispered, "It's true."

"Who are you to talk?—you're shit-faced yourself." She shrank away from him, that sick smile on her lips, her shoulders hunched. He wanted to smash things, kick in the damn stove, make her hurt.

"At least I have a job," she said.

"I'll get another one, don't you worry."

"And what about Tiller? We've been here two weeks and you haven't done one damn thing with him, nothing, zero. You haven't even been down to the lake. Two hundred feet and you haven't even been down there once." She came up out of the corner now, feinting like a boxer, vicious, her sharp little fists balled up to drum on him. She spoke in a snarl. "What kind of father are you?"

He brushed past her, slammed open the cabinet, and grabbed the first bottle he found. It was whiskey, cheap whiskey, Four Roses, the shit she drank. He poured out half a water glass full and drank it down to spite her. "I hate the beach, boats, water, trees. I hate you."

She had her purse and she was halfway out the screen door. She hung there a second, looking as if she'd bitten into something rotten. "The feeling's mutual," she said, and the door banged shut behind her.

There were too many complications, too many things to get between him and the moment, and he tried not to think about them. He tried not to think about his father—or his mother either—in the same way that he tried not to think about the pictures of the bald-headed stick people in Africa or meat in its plastic wrapper and how it got there. But when he did think about his father he thought about the river-was-whiskey day.

It was a Tuesday or Wednesday, middle of the week, and when he came home from school the curtains were drawn and his father's car was in the driveway. At the door, he could hear him, the *chunk-chunk* of the chords and the rasping nasal whine that seemed as if it belonged to someone else. His father was sitting in the dark, hair in his face, bent low over the guitar. There was an open bottle of liquor on the coffee table and a clutter of beer bottles. The room stank of smoke.

It was strange, because his father hardly ever played his guitar anymore—he mainly just talked about it. In the past tense. And it was strange too—and bad—because his father wasn't at work. Tiller dropped his bookbag on the telephone stand. "Hi, Dad," he said.

His father didn't answer. Just bent over the guitar and played the same song, over and over, as if it were the only song he knew. Tiller sat on the sofa and listened. There was a verse—one verse—and his father repeated it three or four times before he broke off and slurred the words into a sort of chant or hum, and then he went back to the words again. After the fourth repetition, Tiller heard it:

> *If the river was whiskey,*
> *And I was a divin' duck,*
> *I'd swim to the bottom,*
> *Drink myself back up.*

For half an hour his father played that song, played it till anything else would have sounded strange. He reached for the bottle when he finally stopped, and that was when he noticed Tiller. He looked surprised. Looked as if he'd just woke up. "Hey, ladykiller Tiller," he said, and took a drink from the mouth of the bottle.

Tiller blushed. There'd been a Sadie Hawkins dance at school and Janet Rumery had picked him for her partner. Ever since, his father had called him ladykiller, and though he wasn't exactly sure what it meant, it made him blush anyway, just from the tone of it. Secretly, it pleased him. "I really liked the song, Dad," he said.

"Yeah?" His father lifted his eyebrows and made a face. "Well, come home to Mama, doggie-o. Here," he said, and he held out an open beer. "You ever have one of these, ladykiller Tiller?" He was grinning. The sleeve of his shirt was torn and his elbow was raw and there was a hard little clot of blood over his shirt pocket. "With your sixth-grade buddies out behind the handball court, maybe? No?"

Tiller shook his head.

"You want one? Go ahead, take a hit."

Tiller took the bottle and sipped tentatively. The taste wasn't much. He looked up at his father. "What does it mean?" he said. "The song, I mean—the one you were singing. About the whiskey and all."

His father gave him a long slow grin and took a drink from the big bottle of clear liquor. "I don't know," he said finally, grinning wider to show his tobacco-stained teeth. "I guess he just liked whiskey, that's all." He picked up a cigarette, made as if to light it, and then put it down again. "Hey," he said, "you want to sing it with me?"

All right, she'd hounded him and she'd threatened him and she was going to leave him, he could see that clear as day. But he was going to show her. And the kid too. He wasn't drinking. Not today. Not a drop.

He stood on the dock with his hands in his pockets while Tiller scrambled around with the fishing poles and oars and the rest of it. Birds were screeching in the trees and there was a smell of diesel fuel on the air. The sun cut into his head like a knife. He was sick already.

"I'm giving you a big pole, Dad, and you can row if you want."

He eased himself into the boat and it fell away beneath him like the mouth of a bottomless pit.

"I made us egg salad, Dad, your favorite. And I brought some birch beer."

He was rowing. The lake was churning underneath him, the wind was up and reeking of things washed up on the shore, and the damn oars kept slipping out of the oarlocks, and he was rowing. At the last minute he'd wanted to go back for a quick drink, but he didn't, and now he was rowing.

"We're going to catch a pike," Tiller said, hunched like a spider in the stern.

There was spray off the water. He was rowing. He felt sick. Sick and depressed.

"We're going to catch a pike, I can feel it. I know we are," Tiller said, "I know it. I just know it."

It was too much for him all at once—the sun, the breeze that was so sweet he could taste it, the novelty of his father rowing, pale arms and a dead cigarette clenched between his teeth, the boat rocking, and the birds whispering—and he closed his eyes a minute, just to keep from going dizzy with the joy of it. They were in deep water already. Tiller was trolling with a plastic worm and spinner, just in case, but he didn't have much faith in catching anything out here. He was taking his father to the cove with the submerged logs and beds of weed—that's where they'd connect, that's where they'd catch pike.

"Jesus," his father said when Tiller spelled him at the oars. Hands shaking, he crouched in the stern and tried to light a cigarette. His face was gray and the hair beat crazily around his face. He went through half a book of matches and then threw the cigarette in the water. "Where are you taking us, anyway," he said, "—the Indian Ocean?"

"The pike place," Tiller told him. "You'll like it, you'll see."

The sun was dropping behind the hills when they got there, and the water went from blue to gray. There was no wind in the cove. Tiller let the boat glide out across the still surface while his father finally got a cigarette lit, and then he dropped anchor. He was excited. Swallows dove at the surface, bullfrogs burped from the reeds. It was the perfect time to fish, the hour when the big lunker pike would cruise among the sunken logs, hunting.

"All right," his father said, "I'm going to catch the biggest damn fish in the lake," and he jerked back his arm and let fly with the heaviest sinker in the tackle box dangling from the end of the rod. The line hissed through the guys and there was a thunderous splash that probably terrified every pike within half a mile. Tiller looked over his shoulder as he reeled in his silver spoon. His father winked at him, but he looked grim.

It was getting dark, his father was out of cigarettes, and Tiller had cast the spoon so many times his arm was sore, when suddenly the big rod began to buck. "Dad! Dad!" Tiller shouted, and his father lurched up as if he'd been stabbed. He'd been dozing, the rod propped against the gunwale, and Tiller had been studying the long suffering-lines in his father's face, the grooves in his forehead, and the puffy discolored flesh beneath his eyes. With his beard and long hair and with the crumpled suffering look on his face, he was the picture of the crucified Christ Tiller had contemplated a hundred times at church. But now the rod was bucking and his father had hold of it and he was playing a fish, a big fish, the tip of the rod dipping all the way down to the surface.

"It's a pike, Dad, it's a pike!"

His father strained at the pole. His only response was a grunt, but Tiller saw something in his eyes he hardly recognized anymore, a connection, a charge, as if the fish were sending a current up the line, through the pole, and into his hands and body and brain. For a full three minutes he played the fish, his slack biceps gone rigid, the cigarette clamped in his mouth, while Tiller hovered over him with the landing net. There was a surge, a splash, and the thing was in the net, and Tiller had it over the side and into the boat. "It's a pike," his father said, "goddamnit, look at the thing, look at the size of it."

It wasn't a pike. Tiller had watched Joe Matochik catch one off the dock one night. Joe's pike had been dangerous, full of teeth, a long, lean, tapering strip of muscle and pounding life. This was no pike. It was a carp. A fat, pouty, stinking, ugly mud carp. Trash fish. They shot them with arrows and threw them up on the shore to rot. Tiller looked at his father and felt like crying.

"It's a pike," his father said, and already the thing in his eyes was gone, already it was over, "it's a pike. Isn't it?"

It was late—past two, anyway—and he was drunk. Or no, he was beyond drunk. He'd been drinking since morning, one tall vodka and soda after another, and he didn't feel a thing. He sat on the porch in the dark and he couldn't see the lake, couldn't hear it, couldn't even smell it. Caroline and Tiller were asleep. The house was dead silent.

Caroline was leaving him, which meant that Tiller was leaving him. He knew it. He could see it in her eyes and he heard it in her voice. She was soft once, his soft-eyed lover, and now she was hard, unyielding, now she was his worst enemy. They'd had the couple from the roadhouse in for drinks and burgers earlier that night and he'd leaned over the table to tell the guy something—Ed, his name was—joking really, nothing serious, just making conversation. "Vodka and soda," he said, "that's my drink. I used to drink vodka and grapefruit juice, but it tore the lining out of my stomach." And then Caroline, who wasn't even listening, stepped in and said, "Yeah, and that"—pointing to the glass—"tore the lining out of your brain." He looked up at her. She wasn't smiling.

All right. That was how it was. What did he care? He hadn't wanted to come up here anyway—it was her father's idea. Take the cabin for a month, the old man had said, pushing, pushing in that way he had, and get yourself turned around. Well, he wasn't turning around, and they could all go to hell.

After a while the chill got to him and he pushed himself up from the chair and went to bed. Caroline said something in her sleep and pulled away from him as he lifted the covers and slid in. He was awake for a minute or two, feeling depressed, so depressed he wished somebody would come in and shoot him, and then he was asleep.

In his dream, he was out in the boat with Tiller. The wind was blowing, his hands were shaking, he couldn't light a cigarette. Tiller was watching him. He pulled at the oars and nothing happened. Then all of a sudden they were going down, the boat sucked out from under them, the water icy and black, beating in on them as if it were alive. Tiller called out to him. He saw his son's face, saw him going down, and there was nothing he could do.

Write and Wrong

Breyten Breytenbach

Breyten Breytenbach is a South African writer, painter, and performing artist. He made his literary debut with a volume of prose, Katastrofes, *and poetry,* Die ysterkoei moet sweet, *in 1964. Due to his marriage to a Vietnamese woman, Breytenbach was persecuted by the Apartheid regime and was not allowed to visit his own country. He returned to South Africa with a false passport in 1975, but was arrested after a few weeks. He was charged with and convicted of terrorism, an experience upon which he based his memoir,* The True Confessions of an Albino Terrorist.

A large number of articles, essays, academic dissertations, doctoral theses and books have been written and published—in Afrikaans, English, French, Dutch, German, Russian, Chinese and Arabic, among others—on Breytenbach's literary and visual work. Several documentaries have been made about his life and work, including the 1998 film, Vision from the Edge: Breyten Breytenbach Painting the Lines.

Breytenbach has published numerous literary works, the most recent being the 1999 prose work, Woordwerk. *He has also won a number of international prizes and awards for literature and art, including the Alan Paton Award for Literature (South Africa), the Libyan Jurists Association Award (Libya) and the Prix d'Ivry pour la Peinture (France).*

I don't know whether I've written this before. One plunders the notebook again and again.

I find: "The past is the ink with which we write the present—and in the process and the flow of writing the words, the concepts and ideas, the images, the

Excerpt from "Note 3 Nov. (Write and Wrong)," by Breyten Breytenbach, reprinted from *The Faces of Ants*, 1999, Harper's Magazine.

flights become . . . just *ink*. Whereas what we'd probably like to write would be an open hand wherein time, which is the future of the present movement, could find its fit and its fist."

A little further I find: "You must polish the word—not to have it shiny or smooth but to make it as clear as a mirror or a pebble in which you can read your face, and may see that your face is death." And then: "The recognition and the acceptance of the Other's humanity (or humanness) is a maiming of self. You have to wound the self, cut it in strips, in order to *know* that you are similar and of the same substance of shadows."

These reflections surface during a visit to Weimar, where I'm to be a member of the jury deciding which philosophical essay best answers the question of how to free the future from the past and the past from the future. It is a curious town, the small provincial capital of Thüringen; egg-yellow facades are washed to keep up a sun-splashed face of classicism and quaint comfort and the late bourgeois charms of GDR democracy—but in the back streets houses are rotting from neglect and decay. The town is flooded with Goethe; he is on every menu; the dogs don't piss against trees and lampposts, they bark snippets of the great man's wisdom. And to a lesser extent there are Schiller and Herder and Liszt, who played his piano in a big room with an ornate ceiling, and Nietzsche, who stroked his madness in his mother's house as if it were a mustache. Their spirits flutter above the rooftops and the steeples the way banners are the remembrance of republics and of battles.

It is dark when we visit the replica of Goethe's *Gartenhaus*. A blonde lady architect guides us through the low-beamed rooms of the exact copy of the small house where the master used to work. Look, she says and points, we photographed the floor tiles of the original dwelling so that we could faithfully reproduce the spots and the scratches; and look, this is the identical copy of his writing desk where we made precisely the same ink stains blot by blot. When she turns her back to escort us to the next room, Andrei Bitov, the Russian author, slips a kopeck into one of the desk's small drawers, "to fuck up the symmetry and destroy the German soul."

But why this? Because we wanted to see if it could be done, the girl guide says. It cost nearly two million deutsche marks to assemble. Now you see it, now you don't. The original, nearby in the dark garden of the night, is for pious ogling; the clone you can run your hands over. But is that not the definition of totalitarianism, "the repetition of the same"? And now, what about aging? Will they touch up the copy to show, in time, the same wear and tear as the original? Or will the original be brought into line with its monstrous shadow?

On Sunday, after adjudicating an essay called "A Dictionary of Winds" the best entry, we go up the hill to visit Buchenwald. It is so close by, a raven could bridge the distance like an open hand writing without thinking a single line of invisible ink! And yet, how distant it is.

There are trees up there, many trees, and clouds racing through a high-domed light-soaked sky, and birds being fluttered by the wind, and probably insects in the soil too. There's a breathtaking view over the gentle surroundings of flowing valleys and peaceful towns where Goethe must have taken his walks. And suddenly

23

it is cold, so desperately cold—as if we'd moved into another world. We shouldn't have come.

A young man takes us through the camp. He is thickset and has dark half-moons under his eyes; he speaks English with a Scottish accent, probably that of a soccer fan, but the German breaks through painfully. He blurts out figures and facts relentlessly. This was a training ground for the SS, he tells us. As early as 1934. They came here young, sometimes only sixteen years old. They were to be the new elite to revolutionize society. The New Man could be unshackled only in a hierarchy of self-abnegation and arbitrary violence and torture. He saw this job as a guide advertised in the newspaper, the young man says, and so he applied. Sometimes he wonders. He has met survivors. He asked them: "What were your first thoughts when you woke up in the mornings here?"

We are shown the barracks. We see the exact replica of the small zoo where officials brought their families on Sunday outings—hardly three meters away from the barbed-wire enclosure keeping in the inmates. We pass through the narrow wrought-iron gate to the inner camp, with its mocking iron letters: *Jedem das Seine* ("To each his own"). Then we see the bare expanse, the broad view from up here overlooking the world with its harvests.

And then we're taken to the execution block, the tiles of the autopsy room, the furrows to sluice away the blood, the instruments shiny and elegant like slivered mirrors or like pebbles. Then the ovens and the urns and in the basement the hooks and the piano wire. . . . We should not have come.

But this I cannot look at. This then is the Other. This is Me. This is what we do. This is what we're like. Vietnam. Rwanda. Kosovo.

We cling to one another. The wind is in our eyes and our throats. A beautiful sunset purples the sky. Grandfather sky and father sky and son sky, and man. Grandmother wind and mother tree and daughter bird and grandchild insect through all the ages, and man once only. Once is enough.

Back in the hotel Andrei Bitov gives me a full glass of vodka, "to take the shiver out of the soul." He clumsily cuts up an apple with a bottle opener. "One must always have an apple with the vodka," he says. "Now go and take a hot bath."

Immediately I fall into a bottomless sleep. I have a first dream.

A bright, sylvan scene. A clearing in the forest. We hear, at the periphery of our eyesight, a thrashing in the undergrowth. As if someone (or something) is observing us from the invisibleness, but clumsily now camouflaging its presence. We then know it is an immortal. How can he be lured forth? Only one thing will work. We peg down a book in the sun-filled glade. This will be the irresistible bait. We know he/she is desperate to know what's written. Does the wind turn over the leaves of the book? Can the wind read? And what is the title?

How rotten with memory this earth is! And how the one thing slides over the other! When does memory become obliterated? Can we write everything? Are we not obliged to approach obliquely, camouflaging our presence, turning away our faces? Can we see Goethe whole?

It should have been burned to the ground and left to the wind. The town, too, should have been given over to the dark ink of time. No memorial, no ceremonies, just the salted earth forever. Because we have no right to remember.

Thereafter the night turns, and it is empty. And when we take leave the next day to return to our respective cities of time and of rhythm, Andrei Bitov and I, as writers from nowhere at the end of this century, exchange the empty bound books that we had been given by the organizers. He writes in the copy that he gives me: *I would like to present you something. But we, in our monastery, have nothing. . . .* Underneath he notes: *For writing nothings.* And in my copy to him I jot: *1. Thou shalt not kill. 2. Thou shalt laugh with thy whole mouth and thy whole belly. 3. Thou shalt study the expressions on the faces of ants.*

The Day the Martels Got the Cable

Pat Cadigan

Pat Cadigan was born in Schenectady, New York in 1954, but grew up in Fitchburg, Massachusetts. She attended the University of Massachusetts on a scholarship, majoring in theater, and eventually transferred to the University of Kansas, where she received her degree. Cadigan was an editor and writer for Hallmark Cards in Kansas City for ten years before embarking on her career as a Science Fiction writer in 1987. Cadigan is the only writer to have won the prestigious Arthur C. Clarke Award twice, in 1992 for Synners *and in 1995 for* Fools. *Her most recent novel is* Tea from an Empty Cup. *She now lives in England with her second husband, Chris Fowler.*

Cadigan's work is part of a special kind of Science Fiction called cyberpunk, which deals with the impact of technology on the future of mankind. The following story is from her first volume entitled Patterns.

Lydia had stayed home from work to take delivery on the washer and dryer. So this time David would have Lydia call him in sick and would wait for the cable TV people to come. Sitting at the kitchen table enjoying the luxury of a second cup of coffee, he skimmed the front page of the newspaper as Lydia hurriedly made herself up in the tiny downstairs bathroom.

"You sure you don't want me to drive you in?" he called over his shoulder.

Lydia poked her head out of the bathroom, holding a mascara brush between two fingers. "Not unless you want the car for some reason. Do you?"

"The Day the Martels Got the Cable," by Pat Cadigan, reprinted from *Patterns*, 1989, TOR Books (St. Martin's Press).

"Nah. I was just thinking though, I always do the driving and you're not really used to the rush-hour traffic. Awake, anyway."

She stuck her tongue out at him. *"That* to you. I was driving in rush hour long before I hooked up with you and I'll be driving in it long after you run off and leave me for a younger woman." She disappeared back into the bathroom.

"That will be the day." He got up and went to the doorway of the bathroom. "When I go, I'm taking the car with me."

"Men," Lydia said, staring down at the hand mirror as she worked her eyelashes. "You're all alike."

"We attend a special school for it when we're young." David looked at her admiringly. She had on what she called her dress-for-success get-up, tailored navy-blue jacket and skirt with a soft white blouse. What the well-dressed board chairperson was wearing this year. David had asked her once if it wasn't a bit overwhelming for an office manager. All in fun, of course. Truth to tell, her career was outstripping his own.

He reached out and stopped her as she was about to apply her lipstick. "Sure you don't want me to call you in sick, too? We could wait for the cable people together and then afterwards not watch the movie channel."

"That would look good, wouldn't it?" She gave him a quick but thorough kiss before she put on her lipstick. "I mean, the both of us working at the same company and we both happen to come down with stomach flu—ho, ho—on the same day. They'd buy that, for sure."

David shrugged. "So? We've got two bathrooms. Two toilets, no waiting. They can send the corporate secret police out to check if they want."

"David."

"I know, I know." He sighed. "It was worth a try."

"Don't think I don't appreciate it." She grinned redly, looking him up and down. "And don't think I'm not tempted. Say, poppa, did anyone ever tell you you do things for a bathrobe and pajamas that no other man can do?"

"Plenty of women, all the time." He stepped in and posed behind her in the mirror over the sink. They made a perfect portrait of the odd married couple, one with her blonde, chin-length hair carefully combed and the other with his tangled hair standing on end and morning stubble shading his cheeks. "Hey, if this were 1956, you'd be the one in the bathrobe, you know."

Lydia looked pained. "Promise me that after we get the cable, you won't tune in Channel 87 in Dry Rot, Egypt, for old *Leave It To Beaver* reruns."

"How about *Ozzie and Harriet?*"

"I *never* liked them." She gave him a push. "Let me out. I gotta go set the world on fire."

David backed up and blocked the doorway. "Last chance, woman. Eight hours of work or sixteen hours of ecstasy—the choice is yours." He made a thrusting motion with his hips.

"Sixteen hours of ecstasy or twenty-six weeks of paid unemployment. Outta my way, hot pajamas." She honked him as she slipped past and he chased her into the living room.

"Anything I should know about this cable thing?" he asked as she rummaged through her shoulder bag for her car keys.

"Like what?"

"I dunno. You're the one who filled out all the forms and made the arrangements. Am I supposed to do anything with the TV before they get here?"

"Not that I know of." Lydia hooked the keyring around her little finger and pushed several papers back into her purse. "Just stand back and don't get in anybody's way."

David put his hands on his hips. "Well, if they come during *Donahue*, they're just going to have to *wait!*" He tossed his head.

"I never liked him either. He's insincere." Lydia offered her cheek a kiss. Instead, he bit her on the neck and gave her an impertinent squeeze.

"Don't you love permanent press?" he whispered in her ear. "You do all sorts of things and your clothes never wrinkle."

She poked his ticklish spot and squirmed away. "Try not to eat too many chocolate-covered cherries while you're watching the soaps this afternoon, dear. And be dressed for when the cable people come, will you?"

"Yes, dear," he said nasally. "Honestly, work, work, work—that's all I ever *do* around this place."

Lydia's smile was only half amused. "And take the chicken out to thaw for supper tonight."

"I will."

"I mean it. Don't forget."

"All right, already. I'll take the chicken out to thaw. I was taking chicken out to thaw long before I hooked up with you and I'll be taking it out to thaw long after you run off and leave me to find yourself."

"Just make sure that you do it *today.*"

"I will. I *promise.* Now go to work before I rip all your clothes off." He did another bump and grind and she escaped out the door, laughing.

He watched from the living room window as she maneuvered the car out of the cramped parking lot in front of the townhouse. Then he went upstairs to take a quick shower, keeping one ear cocked for the sound of the doorbell in case the cable people came early. Why was it cable installers and delivery people could never give you a definite time when they would arrive at your home? They'd just tell you the date and you had to be there. Of course, they didn't come on a Saturday. They worked a straight Monday-to-Friday week, God *forbid* they should arrange their time to accommodate customers with like schedules.

Decadently, he decided not to shave after dressing and went back downstairs to pour himself a fresh cup of coffee and finish the newspaper. At ten o'clock he was fresh out of lazy things to do and just beginning to feel hungry. Well, what the hell—this was a free day. If he wanted to eat lunch early, he could.

The house seemed so quiet, he thought, as he flopped down on the couch with a magazine and a sandwich. As he ate, he turned pages without really looking at them. Playing hooky from work wasn't much fun when there was no one else to share it with.

He laughed at himself. *You sound like an old married man, fella.* An old married man. That wasn't such a bad description, considering whom he was married to. How did that old song go? *Lydia, ho, Lydia . . .* something, something. The Marx Brothers had done it in one of their movies, hadn't they?

Lydia. He'd had some kind of industrial-strength good luck going for him when he'd met her. Everything had just fallen into place—their relationship had progressed to marriage without missing a beat, and their marriage hadn't had anything missing in three and a half years. Companionship, love, sex, and everything in between—it was all there, just the way he might have imagined it. He *had* imagined it a few times, but in an abstract sort of way. There had been no one he would have filled in the woman's part with until Lydia had come into his life.

Not that he was living some kind of fairy tale, though. They had their problems, they argued, and Lydia had the ability to play the bitch just as well as he could be the bastard. But there was nothing seriously wrong, nothing that threatened them. Hell, he didn't even feel funny about her making more money than he did. They were beyond that kind of macho silliness.

David got up and looked out the window at the parking lot. No sign of the cable truck yet. He supposed they would come in a truck with all kinds of equipment, ready to plug him into the wonderful world of pay-TV. He'd had a few misgivings, about it when Lydia first suggested they subscribe to the cable. The image of himself and Lydia sitting in front of the TV, slaves of the tube and its programming hadn't been terribly appetizing. As a rule, they weren't much for TV watching. But there was the movie channel, and the idea of being able to watch uncut films at home appealed to him. It would probably make them lazy about getting out to the theaters, but that wouldn't be so bad. During the week they were both tired, and on the weekends they had to fight the crowds—the terminal acne couples, the families with the restless kids and/or squalling babies, and let's not forget the inveterate chatterboxes who seemed to think they were in their living rooms and didn't refrain from adding their stupid comments at the tops of their lungs. Yeah, cable TV would be worth it if it would spare them that.

At 11 o'clock, when he was already giving thought to having another sandwich, the doorbell rang. "Hallelujah," he muttered and went to answer it.

The small woman smiling up at him on the doorstep had a wildly growing-out permanent and a broad, plain face. There was a length of black cable coiled around one shoulder and she held a bag of tools in her hand. "You Mr. Martel?"

He blinked. "Can I help you?"

"Cable-Rama. I'm here to put in your cable."

David looked past her, saw the truck sitting in their usual parking place. "Oh. Sure. C'mon in."

The woman gave him a big grin, the skin around her eyes crinkling a thousand deep lines. "Every time." She walked in, looked around, and went immediately to the television. David hesitated.

"Just you?" he asked. "I mean, did they send you out all by yourself?"

"Every time," she said again and dropped her tool bag on the carpet.

"Every time what?" David asked, closing the door.

The woman never stopped grinning, even as she rolled the television on its cart out from the wall and knelt behind it. "Every time they open the door and see the cable guy's a woman, their mouth falls open. Or they blink a lot." She showed her teeth cheerily. "Like you. They can't believe I can do it all alone."

David felt his face grow slightly warm. "That's not it at all. I just—well, these days you know, sending a woman by herself to people's houses is a risky kind of thing. I mean, times being what they are." The woman detached the rabbit ears and UHF antenna and set them aside. "Yeah? You mean, like if somebody tries something funny or like that?" She picked up a tool David couldn't imagine a use for, a thing that seemed to be a cross between a wrench and a pair of pliers. "Anybody tries something, I adjust their fine tuning. See?" She wiggled her eyebrows. "They said you guys seemed to be okay."

"Oh, we are, but I thought they'd have to send three, four g— people out to do this."

"Oh, yeah. Back in the early days." She kept working on the back of the television set as she spoke, occasionally reaching for a different tool or gadget from her bag. "Now it's easy. Someday the technology's gonna get so good, you'll be able to install this stuff yourself. Just click it onto the back of your set or something." She grimaced at the tip of a Phillips-head screwdriver and wiped it on her workshirt. "You guys into video games?"

David shook his head.

"Ah. That's good. Video games are shit. Burn your goddam tube out quicker. So do those videotape recorders. But you got a good cable-ready set here, you know that?"

"No."

"Yeah, you do. So you don't have to go unhooking this and hooking it back up again if you get a VCR. Better if you just leave it, unless the set has to go in for servicing."

"I wouldn't know how to remove it anyway."

"S'easy. But best not to fool with it. Play around back here, don't know what you're doing, next thing you know—*zzzzt!* Fried poppa." She raised one eyebrow. "Kids. You got any?"

"Nope."

"Good. I mean, well, you want 'em, you have 'em, I don't care. But if you have any in visiting or anything sometime, don't let them fool with this."

"*Zzzzt,*" said David, smiling.

"You got it." She picked up one end of the cable which she had let slide off her shoulder onto the floor and began connecting it to the back of the television. The other end she screwed into a silvery outlet in the wall. Then she got to her feet. "Gonna play outside for a few minutes now. Don't touch anything. Don't turn the set on, okay? I'll try to get this finished up by the time *Donahue* comes on."

"We don't like him," David said. "We think he's insincere."

"Suit yourself. Half the women in this town get cable just so they can see him better. It's all the same to me." Still grinning, she stepped over the tools and let herself out.

30

All delivery and service people, David decided, had to go to some kind of training camp for vocational-quirkiness lessons. Then again, maybe if he made a living connecting people to *Donahue,* he'd be a character himself. He couldn't wait to tell Lydia about this one. Lydia had thought the two guys who had delivered the washer and dryer had been lunatics.

When the woman hadn't returned for several minutes, he went to the window to check on her. She was standing at the open back of the truck with some kind of meter in her hand. It was attached to a cable that ran out of the truck over the sidewalk and around the side of the house. She seemed to be muttering to herself as she twisted a button or dial on the meter. David raised the window.

"Are you sure you don't need me to turn on the set?" he called.

She looked up at him, startled. "Don't touch it! You *didn't* touch it, did you? Well, don't! Can't take any power right now; you'll blow up all my equipment!"

"Okay." He left the window up and wandered into the kitchen. Was it considered improper to fix yourself something to eat while a service person who was probably dying for lunch herself was still on the premises? Almost certainly. His stomach growled. He snagged a piece of cheese out of the refrigerator and then crammed the whole thing into his mouth as he heard her come back into the house.

"Almost done," she sang. "Few more adjustments, you're ready for the glory of Living Room Cinema. Trademarked."

He went back to the living room, trying to chew inconspicuously. The woman glanced up at him as she connected wires from a small brown box to the back of the set.

"Ah. Lunch. I'm dyin' for lunch. That's what I'm goin' for next, you bet." She pushed her frizz back from her forehead. "Okay. C'mere. I'm gonna show you."

David swallowed the cheese and wiped his hand across his mouth.

"This here on top of the cable selector. S'got two buttons, A and B. One group of stations is on A, the other's on B. A is simple, mostly the local stations. B is complex—satellite stations and movie channel, sports and news networks, that stuff."

"How do I know what channels to turn to?"

"I'll give you a card before I leave, it's got all that stuff on it. And here's a free program guide. Right now, we wanna see how good it comes in, okay? Great. Go for it and turn her on."

David laughed a little and turned on the television. A game show sprang into life on the screen, looking a bit purple.

"Okay. You're on A right now, see? The A button is pushed in. Flip around the dial and let's see everything else."

More game shows, some soap operas and a flurry of commercials lashed on the screen before David returned to the original game show.

"Great picture, huh?" said the woman, tapping his arm lightly with screwdriver. *"Purple* picture."

"You can fix that yourself later. Right now we're just interested in your reception. No snow, no rolling. Great. Isn't that great?"

31

"It's great," David said. Strange how service people always seemed to crave praise for whatever company they represented. "Do *you* have the cable?"

The woman's eyes widened as though he had asked her about her sex life. "Do I look like someone who would need the cable? Try the B channels. No, keep your hand on the dial, in case you've got to fine tune."

David opened his mouth to tell her there was no fine tuning connected with the channel selector and decided to humor her. Then perhaps she'd take her quirky little self out of his living room faster. He was beginning to tire of her and her jackrabbity conversational style.

He reached up with his left hand and touched the box on top of the TV set. It was warm and tingly on his fingertips, and he almost snatched his hand back. The woman shifted her weight impatiently, and he thumbed down the B button.

Something hot and sizzling jumped into his left hand and shot up his arm. To his horror, he couldn't let go of the box. The hot, sizzling feeling hit his chest and streaked down his other arm before it began to burn through his torso. His last thought, as he turned his head toward the woman, was that she was reacting awfully nonchalantly to the electrocution of one of her customers.

The woman stood staring at David with, her arms folded. The fading expression on his face was typical—shock, panic, maybe a little betrayal. Probably thought he was being electrocuted. She'd heard the final connection was something like that, getting fried. *Zzzzt!* She grinned.

When the last bit of emotion had drained from David's face and his eyes had gone opaque, she produced something that might have been a lecturer's metal pointer form her back pocket and stepped around behind the television again. She did something else to the connections she had made, and the TV screen went dark: David's arms dropped abruptly. The woman punched the A button. "Straighten up," she ordered.

David did so, his head still facing where she had been standing previously. She moved back in front of the TV and twisted the channel selector. David took three steps backwards and bumped into the coffee table.

"Easy there, poppa." She patted her pockets and found the small white card she needed. "Okay. Here we go. Channel 4, right. Channel 5." David held his arms out to his sides as if waiting either to catch someone up in a hug or be crucified. She changed the channel again and he bent forward at the waist.

"Lotta talent there." The woman flipped through the channels, watching closely as David bent forward at the waist, bobbed up again, combed his hair with his fingers, pinched his nose and opened his mouth. "Siddown on the couch. Stand up. Stand on your left foot." David obeyed, his movements smooth and almost graceful. "Okay. Now the B channels. Do your stuff, poppa."

David walked around the room, turned on a lamp and shut it off again, mimed opening a drawer and searching through some files and danced a few shuffling steps.

"Great reception," the woman said. "One more and you're set." She consulted the card and turned to Channel 9. David did a bump and grind, slow and then fast. "Relax.

This is only a test." She laughed and switched back to the A button. He stood motionless again, awaiting instructions. "You're doin' great. Siddown."

David collapsed to the floor cross-legged. "Oops. Shoulda told you to sit on the couch. Hell. Just stay there. Gonna take care of momma next. After lunch." She went into the kitchen and found the cheese in the refrigerator. She nibbled at it while she got the peanut butter and a loaf of bread out of the cupboard. As an afterthought, she opened a can of black olives.

Lydia Martel was having a carton of strawberry yogurt for lunch at her desk when the phone rang. She dabbed at her lips with a napkin before picking up the receiver.

"Lydia Martel." She paused, sitting back. "Oh, good. Any problems? How's the reception, any static?" She paused again, listening. "Good. Good. Now, how much did you say the installation fee would be? Uh-huh. And the regular monthly charge is what?" She scribbled the figures on a memo pad. "Yes, it *is* reasonable. That includes everything, right?" Lydia laughed a little indulgently. "I *can't* get away before 4:30.—Yes, there is something. Put him on vacuum before you leave. He knows where it is, even if he's never touched it. *All* the rooms. After that he can clean up the kitchen, I'm sure he left a mess from lunch. Have him take the chicken out to thaw, I'm positive he forgot.

"And, oh, yes—have him shave, will you? Thanks."

San

Lan Samantha Chang

Lan Samantha Chang attended the Iowa Writers' Workshop where she began working on "San." At one point, the story was thirty pages long, at another seven pages. After much revision and a two-year period during which she waited for her perspective on the material to mature, Chang finished the story. Her other fiction has appeared in Prairie Schooner, The Atlantic Monthly, *and* The Best American Short Stories 1994. *She has received support for her fiction writing from the Michener-Copernicus Foundation, the Henfield Foundation, and the estate of Truman Capote. She teaches fiction writing at Stanford University.*

———————————————

My father left my mother and me one rainy summer morning, carrying a new umbrella of mine. From our third-floor window I watched him close the front door and pause to glance at the sky. Then he opened my umbrella. I liked the big red flower pattern—it was *fuqi,* prosperous—but in the hands of a man, even a handsome man like my father, the umbrella looked gaudy and ridiculous. Still, he did not hunch underneath but carried it high up, almost jauntily.

As I watched him walk away, I remembered a Chinese superstition. The Mandarin word for umbrella, *san,* also means "to fall apart." If you acquire an umbrella without paying for it, your life will fall apart. My father had scoffed at such beliefs. The umbrella had been a present from him. Now I stood and watched it go, bright and ill-fated like so many of his promises.

Later that morning the roof of our apartment sprang a leak. Two tiles buckled off the kitchen floor, revealing a surprising layer of mud, as if my mother's mopping over the years had merely pushed the dirt beneath the tiles and all along we'd been living over a floor of soot.

———————————————

"San," by Lan Samantha Chang, reprinted from *Hunger*, 1998, published by W. W. Norton & Company.

My mother knelt with a sponge in one hand. She wouldn't look at me. Her heavy chignon had come undone and a thick lock of hair wavered down her back.

"Can I help?" I asked, standing over her. She did not answer but stroked the tiles with her sponge.

I put the big rice cooker underneath the leak. Then I went to my room. All morning, I studied problems for my summer-school math class. I heard my mother, in the kitchen, start to sob. I felt only fear—a dense stone in my chest—but I put even this aside so I could study. My father had taught me to focus on the equations in front of me, and so I spent the hours after he left thinking about trigonometry, a subject he had loved.

My mathematical talent had sprung from an early backwardness. As a child I could not count past three: my father, my mother, and me.

"Caroline is making progress in her English lessons, but she remains baffled by the natural numbers," read an early report card. "She cannot grasp the *countability* of blocks and other solid objects. For this reason I am recommending that she repeat the first grade."

This comment left my father speechless. He believed I was a brilliant child. And mathematics had been his favorite subject back in China, before the political trouble had forced him to quit school.

"Counting," he said in English, when he was able to talk again. His dark eyebrows swooped over the bridge of his aquiline nose. Despite his drastic ups and downs, bad news always caught him by surprise. But he recovered with typical buoyancy. "Don't worry, Lily," he told my mother. "It's those western teachers. *I'll* teach her how to count."

And so my father, himself an unreliable man, taught me to keep track of things. We counted apples, bean sprouts, grains of rice. I learned to count in pairs, with ivory chopsticks. We stood on the corner of Atlantic Avenue, counting cars to learn big numbers. We spent a lovely afternoon in Prospect Park, counting blades of grass aloud until we both had scratchy throats.

"Keep going," he urged me on as the shadows lengthened. "I want you to be able to count all the money I'm going to make, here in America."

By the time I was seven I had learned the multiplication tables to twenty-times-twenty. In the following year I learned to recite the table of squares and the table of cubes, both so quickly that the words blended together into a single stream, almost meaningless: "Oneeighttwentysevensixtyfouronetwentyfivetwosixteenthree-fortythree . . ."

As I chanted, my father would iron the white shirt and black trousers he wore to his waiter's job, a "temporary" job. Or he stood in the kitchen, Mondays off, with three blue balls and one red ball, juggling expertly beneath the low tin ceiling. Each time the red ball reached his hand I was ordered to stress a syllable. Thus "One, *eight,* twenty-*sev*en, sixty-*four.*"

"Pro*nounce,*" said my father, proud of his clear *r*'s. To succeed in America, he was sure, required good pronunciation as well as math. He often teased my mother for pronouncing my name *Calorin,* "like a diet formula," he said. They had named me Caroline after Caroline Kennedy, who was born shortly before their arrival in the States. After all, my father's name was Jack. And if the name was good enough for a president's daughter, then certainly it was good enough for me.

After I learned to count I began, belatedly, to notice things. Signs of hard luck and good fortune moved through our apartment like sudden storms. A pale stripe on my father's tanned wrist revealed where his watch had been. A new pair of aquamarine slippers shimmered on my mother's feet. A beautiful collection of fourteen cacti, each distinct, bloomed on our fire escape for several summer months and then vanished.

I made careful explorations of our apartment. At the back of the foyer closet, inside the faded red suitcase my mother had brought from China, I discovered a cache of little silk purses wrapped in a cotton shirt. When I heard her footsteps I instinctively closed the suitcase and pretended I was looking for a pair of mittens. Then I went to my room and shut the door, slightly dizzy with anticipation and guilt.

A few days later when my mother was out, I opened one purse. Inside was a swirling gold pin with pearl and coral flowers. I made many secret visits to the closet, a series of small sins. Each time I opened one more treasure. There were bright green, milky white, and blood red jade bracelets. Some of the bracelets were so small I could not fit them over my hand. There was a ring with a pearl as big as a marble. A strand of pearls, each the size of a large pea. A strand of jade beads, each of them green as grass, carved in the shape of small buddhas. A rusty key.

"Do you still have keys to our old house in China?" I asked my father.

"That's the past, Caroline," he said. "*Wanle.* It is gone."

Surrounded by questions, I became intrigued by the answers to things. My report cards showed that I became a good student, a very good student, particularly in math. At twelve, I was the only person from my class to test into a public school for the "gifted" in Manhattan. My father attended the school event where this news was announced. I remember his pleased expression as we approached the small, crowded auditorium. He had piled all of our overcoats and his fedora over one arm, but with the other he opened the door for my mother and me. As I filed past he raised his eyebrows and nodded—proud, but not at all surprised by my achievement.

He believed in the effortless, in splurging and quick riches. While I studied, bent and dogged, and my mother hoarded things, my father strayed from waitering and turned to something bigger. He had a taste for risk, he said to us. A nose for good investments. Some friends were helping him. He began to stay out late and come home with surprises. On good nights, he brought us presents: a sewing kit, a pink silk scarf. Once he climbed out of a taxicab with a hundred silver dollars in my old marble bag.

On bad nights, my father whistled his way home. I sometimes woke to his high music floating from the street. I sat up and spied at him through the venetian blinds. He no longer wore his waiter's clothes; his overcoat was dark. I could just make out the glitter of his shiny shoes. He stepped lightly, always, on bad nights, although he'd whistled clear across the bridge to save on subway fare. He favored Stephen Foster tunes and Broadway musicals. He flung his head back on a long, pure note. When he reached our door he stood still for a moment and squared his shoulders. My mother, too, knew what the whistling meant.

"Stayed up for me?"

"I wasn't tired."

I crept to my door to peek at them. My mother staring at her feet. My father's hopeful face, his exaggerated brightness. My mother said, "Go to sleep, Caroline."

But I had trouble sleeping. I could feel him slipping away from us, drifting far in search of some intoxicating music. Each time he wandered off, it seemed to take more effort to recall us. He began to speak with his head cocked, as if listening for something. He often stood at the living room window, staring at the street.

"Does Baba have a new job?" I asked my mother.

"No." She looked away.

I felt sorry I'd asked. Questions caused my mother pain. But I was afraid to ask my father. In his guarded face he held a flaming knowledge: a certain concentration, a hunger for opportunities that lay beyond my understanding.

All that year I hunted clues, made lists of evidence.

> *Missing on February 3:*
> *carved end table*
> *painting of fruit (from front hallway)*
> *jade buddha*
> *camera (mine)*

I followed him. One evening after I missed my camera, I heard the front door slam. I grabbed my coat and bolted down the stairs. I dodged across the street half a block back, peering around pedestrians and traffic signs, my eyes fixed on his over-coat and fedora. At the subway station I waited by the token booth and dashed into the car behind him, keeping track of his shiny shoes through the swaying windows. I almost missed him when he left the train. Outside it was already dusk. The tall, cold shapes of City Hall and the courthouses loomed over us and I followed at a distance. I felt light as a puff of silk, breathing hard, excited, almost dancing.

Past the pawnshops, the offtrack betting office with its shuffling line of men in old overcoats, toward the dirty, crowded streets of Chinatown, its neon signs wink-ing on for the night. Groups of teenagers, chattering in Cantonese, looked strangely at me and kept walking.

"Incense, candles, incense, *xiaojie?*" A street vendor held a grimy handful toward me.

"No, thanks," I panted. I almost lost him, but then ahead I recognized his elegant stride. He turned into a small, shabby building, nodding to an old man who stood at the door. I hung around outside, stamping my shoes on the icy sidewalk.

After a minute the old man walked over to me. "Your father does not know you followed him," he told me in Chinese. "You must go home. Go home, and I will not tell him you were here."

For a minute I couldn't move. He was exactly my height. His short hair was white but his forehead strangely unlined, and he wore well-fitting western clothes. It was his expensive tweed overcoat that made me turn around. That and the decaying, fetid odor of his teeth, and the fact that he knew my father well enough to recognize my features, knew he would not have wanted me to follow him. I reboarded the train at the Canal Street station. Back in the apartment, I stayed up until well past midnight, but I didn't hear him come home.

I should not have followed him. I should have known that eventually he would show his secret to me, his one pupil. A few months later, on the night before my fourteenth birthday, he motioned me to stay seated after supper. The hanging lamp cast a circle of light over the worn kitchen table.

"I'm going to teach you some math," he said.

I glanced at his face, but his eyes glowed black and expressionless in their sockets, hollow in the lamplight.

Over his shoulder I saw my mother check to see that we were occupied. Then she walked into the foyer and opened the closet door, where the jewelry was. I felt a tingle of fear, even though I had concealed my visits perfectly.

"Concentrate," said my father. "Here is a penny. Each penny has two sides: heads and tails. You understand me, Caroline?"

I nodded. The dull coin looked like a hole in his palm.

"Hao," he said: good. His brown hand danced and the penny flipped onto our kitchen table. Heads. "Now, if I throw this coin many many times, how often would I get heads?"

"One-half of the time."

He nodded.

"Hao," he said. "That is the *huo ran lu*. The *huo ran lu* for heads is one-half. If you know that, you can figure out the *huo ran lu* that I will get two heads if I throw twice in a row." He waited a minute. "Think of it as a limiting of possibilities. The first throw cuts the possibilities in half."

I looked into the dark tunnel of my father's eyes, and following the discipline of his endless drilling, I began to understand where we had been going. Counting, multiplication, the table of squares. "Half of the half," I said. "A quarter."

He set the coins aside and reached into his shirt pocket. Suddenly, with a gesture of his hand, two dice lay in the middle of the yellow circle of light. Two small chunks of ivory, with tiny black pits in them.

"Count the sides," he said.

The little cube felt cold and heavy. "Six."

My father's hand closed over the second die. "What is the *huo ran lu* that I will get a side with only two dots?"

My mind wavered in surprise at his intensity. But I knew the answer. "One-sixth," I said.

He nodded. "You are a smart daughter," he said.

I discovered that I had been holding onto the table leg with my left hand, and I let go. I heard the creak of the hall closet door but my father did not look away from the die in his hand.

"What is the *huo ran lu* that I can roll the side with two dots twice in a row?" he said.

"One thirty-sixth."

"Three times in a row?"

"One two-hundred-and-sixteenth."

"That is very good!" he said. "Now, the *huo ran lu* that I will be able to roll a two is one-sixth. Would it be a reasonable bet that I will not roll a two?"

I nodded.

"We could say, if I roll a two you may have both pennies."

I saw it then, deep in his eyes—a spark of excitement, a piece of joy particularly his. It was there for an instant and disappeared. He frowned and nodded toward the table as if to say: pay attention. Then his hand flourished and the die trickled into the light. I bent eagerly over the table, but my father sat perfectly still, his face impassive again. Two dots.

When I looked up at him in astonishment I noticed my mother standing in the doorway, her two huge eyes burning in her white face.

"Jack."

My father started, but he didn't turn around to look at her. "Yes, Lily," he said.

The die grew wet in my hand.

"What are you doing?"

"Giving the child a lesson."

"And what is she going to learn from this?" My mother's voice trembled but it did not rise, "Where will she go with this?"

"Lily," my father said.

"What will become of us?" my mother almost whispered. She looked around the kitchen. Almost all of the furniture had disappeared. The old kitchen table and the three chairs, plus our rice cooker, were virtually the only things left in the room.

I grabbed the second die and left the table. In my room as I listened to my parents next door in the kitchen I rolled one die two hundred and sixteen times, keeping track by making marks on the back of a school notebook. But I failed to reach a two more than twice in a row.

"The suitcase, Jack. Where is it?"

After a moment my father muttered, "I'll get it back. Don't you believe me?"

"I don't know." She began to cry so loudly that even though I pressed my hands against my ears I could still hear her. My father said nothing. I hunched down over my knees, trying to shut them out.

"You promised me, you promised me you'd never touch them!"

"I was going to bring them back!"

"We have nothing for Caroline's birthday . . ."

Something crashed against the other side of my bedroom wall. I scuttled to the opposite wall and huddled in the corner of my bed.

For a long period after I heard nothing but my mother's sobbing. Then I heard them leave the kitchen. The house was utterly silent. I realized I had wrapped my arms around my knees to keep from trembling. I felt strange and light-headed: oh, but I understood now. My father was a gambler, a *dutu,* an apprentice of chance. Of course.

With the understanding came a desperate need to see both of them. I stood up and walked through the living room to my parents' bedroom. The door was ajar. I peered in.

The moonlight, blue and white, shifted and flickered on the bed, on my mother's long black hair twisting over her arm. Her white fingers moved vaguely. I felt terrified for her. He moved against her body in such a consuming way, as if he might pass through her, as if she were incorporeal, I watched for several minutes before my mother made a sound that frightened me so much I had to leave.

The next morning my eyes felt sandy and strange. We strolled down Atlantic Avenue, holding hands, with me in the middle because it was my birthday. My mother's stride was tentative, but my father walked with the calculated lightness and unconcern of one who has nothing in his pockets. Several gulls flew up before us, and he watched with delight as they wheeled into the cloudy sky. The charm of Brooklyn, this wide shabby street bustling with immigrants like ourselves, was enough to make him feel lucky.

He squeezed my hand, a signal that I should squeeze my mother's for him. We'd played this game many times over the years, but today I hesitated. My mother's hand did not feel like something to hold onto. Despite the warm weather her fingers in mine were cold. I squeezed, however, and she turned. He looked at her over the top of my head, and my mother, seeing his expression, lapsed into a smile that caused the Greek delivery boys from the corner pizza parlor to turn and watch as we passed. She and my father didn't notice.

We walked past a display of furniture on the sidewalk—incomplete sets of dining chairs, hat stands, old sewing table—and I stared for a minute, for I thought I saw something standing behind a battered desk: a rosewood dresser my parents had brought from Taiwan; it used to be in my own bedroom. I once kept my dolls in the bottom left drawer, the one with the little scar where I had nicked it with a roller skate. . . . Perhaps it only had a similar shape. But it could very well be our dresser. I knew better than to point it out. I turned away.

"Oh, Jack, the flowers!" my mother exclaimed in Chinese. She let go of my hand and rushed to DeLorenzio's floral display, sank down to smell the potted gardenias with a grace that brought my father and me to a sudden stop.

My father's black eyebrows came down over his eyes. "*Ni qu gen ni mama tan yi tan,* go talk to your mother," he said, giving me a little push. I frowned.

"Go on."

She was speaking with Mr. DeLorenzio, and I stood instinctively on their far side, trying to act cute despite my age in order to distract them from what my father was doing. He stood before the red geraniums. He picked up a plant, considered it, and set it down with a critical shake of his head.

"And how are you today, sweetheart?" Mr. DeLorenzio bent toward me, offering me a close-up of his gray handlebar mustache. Behind him, my father disappeared from view.

"She's shy," said my mother proudly. After a few minutes I tugged her sleeve, and she said good-bye to the florist. We turned, continued walking down the street.

"Where is your father?"

"I think he's somewhere up there."

I pulled her toward the corner. My father stepped out from behind a pet store, smiling broadly, holding the pot of bright geraniums.

"It's going to rain," he proclaimed, as if he'd planned it himself.

It started to rain. The drops felt light and warm on my face. We ran to the nearest awning, where my mother put on her rain bonnet. Then my father disappeared, leaving us standing on the sidewalk. I didn't notice him leave. All of a sudden he was just gone.

"Where's Baba?" I asked my mother.

"I don't know," she said, calmly tucking her hair into the plastic bonnet. The geraniums stood at her feet. I looked around us. The sidewalks had become slick and dark; people hurried along. The wind blew cool in my face. Then the revolving doors behind us whirled and my father walked out.

"There you are," my mother said.

"Here, Caroline," said my father. He reached into his jacket and pulled out the umbrella. It lay balanced on his palm, its brilliant colors neatly furled, an offering.

I wanted to refuse the umbrella. For a moment I believed that if I did, I could separate myself from both of my parents, and our pains, and everything that bound me to them.

I looked up at my father's face. He was watching me intently. I took the umbrella.

"Thanks," I said. He smiled. The next day, he was gone.

My mother had her hair cut short and dressed in mourning colors; this attitude bestowed on her a haunting, muted beauty. She was hired for the lunch shift at a chic Manhattan Chinese restaurant. Our lives grew stable and very quiet. In the evenings I studied while my mother sat in the kitchen, waiting, cutting carrots and mushroom caps into elaborate shapes for our small stir-frys, or combining birdseed for the feeder on the fire escape in the exact proportions that my father had claimed would bring the most cardinals and the fewest sparrows. I did the homework for advanced placement courses. I planned to enter Columbia with the academic standing of a sophomore. We spoke gently to each other about harmless, tactful things. "Peanut sauce," we said. "Shopping." "Homework." "Apricots."

I studied trigonometry. I grew skillful in that subject without ever liking it. I learned calculus, linear algebra, and liked them less and less, but I kept studying, seeking the comfort that arithmetic had once provided. Things fall apart, it seems, with terrible slowness. I could not see that true mathematics, rather than keeping track of things, moves toward the unexplainable. A swooping line descends from nowhere, turns, escapes to some infinity. Centuries of scholars work to solve a single puzzle. In mathematics, as in love, the riddles matter most.

In the months when I was failing out of Columbia, I spent a lot of my time on the subway. I rode to Coney Island, to the watery edge of Brooklyn, and stayed on the express train as it changed directions and went back deep under the river, into Manhattan. Around City Hall or 14th Street a few Chinese people always got on the train, and I sometimes saw a particular kind of man, no longer young but his face curiously unlined, wearing an expensive but shabby overcoat and shiny shoes. I would watch until he got off at his stop. Then I would sit back and wait as the train pulsed through the dark tunnels under the long island of Manhattan, and sometimes the light would blink out for a minute and I would see blue sparks shooting off the tracks. I was waiting for the moment around 125th Street where the express train rushed into daylight. This sudden openness, this coming out of darkness into a new world, helped me understand how he must have felt. I imagined him bending over a pair of dice that glowed like tiny skulls under the yellow kitchen light. I saw him walking out the door with my flowery umbrella, pausing to look up at the sky and the innumerable, luminous possibilities that lay ahead.

Intelligent Electronics

Andrei Codrescu

Andrei Codrescu, a professor at Louisiana State University in Baton Rouge, is best known as a regular contributor to National Public Radio. Born in Romania, he emigrated to the US in 1966 and started his prodigious writing career. He has published fiction, poetry, essays, and a memoir. He also wrote and starred in the Peabody Award winning movie Road Scholar. *In 1989, he returned to his home country to cover the events leading to the collapse of communism for ABC's* Nightline. *Later he chronicled that experience in the book* The Hole in the Flag, *which became a* New York Times *notable book of the year. His latest book, the historical thriller* The Blood Countess *(1965) was a national bestseller. The following essay is from* The Dog with the Chip in His Neck.

I have gone through the hell of trying to figure out my tenth computer in fifteen years and I am just as baffled and irritated as I'd been that fateful day in 1979 when a KayPro4 landed on my desk in Baltimore and screwed up my life forever.

Most of us—techno-idiots who are swept away by superior sales techniques—find ourselves kind of weary, worn out by the losing battle against ever-newer technology. Each new machine humiliates us with identical problems. In the end, we become a little ashamed of confessing our frustrations because it seems that we should have learned something from the last disaster. The stark truth, however, is that no one ever learns anything: he only pretends that he knows something so he won't look the fool. Fools are encouraged by computer PR to think that they know a lot more than they do through the means of so-called "user-friendly" technologies. There is no such thing: "user-friendly" simply means that our ignorance is now shielded

"Intelligent Electronics," by Andrei Codrescu, St. Martin's Press.

from itself by a screen of faux simplicity that makes it even more difficult to admit our ignorance. Implicitly, both the Macintosh and the Windows programs ask only one question: How can you be so stupid when it's so easy?

Sure. Only I started backwards. From the seeming difficulty of a language called CPM on my KayPro—which looked like a military bunker machine able to take a direct hit from a ten-ton bomb—to the cute faces on my Mac, stretches the vast bridge of fifteen years. For me, these fifteen years represent a certain regression from a poet without any worry or money to the present-day processor of words for articles, radio commentaries, and fiction, and still no money. When I was a young poet in San Francisco in the early seventies, all I needed to practice my profession was a pencil and a bar napkin and the presence in the vicinity of beautiful girls for inspiration. Back then, the streets were full of people who actually lived on them. People used to go to coffeehouses, hang out on their stoops and porches, and gather in large groups to throw Molotov cocktails at the National Guard. I used to write divinely inspired poetry with my pencil on my napkin. I would then read this napkin to a beautiful girl and if she liked it, I would be so inspired I would write another poem on the spot, and if she took me home with her, I would usually write two. Sometimes, I was so poor that I didn't even have a pencil and I used to drink in places where they didn't give you a napkin. On those occasions, my only writing tools might consist of a razor blade and my wrist. With these poetry tools I would then write on the wall—until either a beautiful girl rescued me or the management called an ambulance. That's why I had gotten on to this art in the first place: it was cheap. I didn't need paints and brushes like the painters, or fiddles like the fiddle players, or rich patrons like the sculptors and architects.

Alas. Heaven didn't last long. Enter my first typewriter, a gun blue Smith-Corona 220, ready to fire. Sure enough, I started writing prose: stories, novels, essays. I could only write poetry when I ran out the back door to my bars and cafés. It wasn't easy either: the Smith-Corona was the first of my machines endowed with the ability to hear me leave the house. Often, when I came back late, or left it unattended for a couple of days, the machine would take its revenge on me by smudging or locking or popping a spring.

The KayPro4 marked yet another stage of my enslavement: I have now forgotten just how many months of pain it took finally to produce a printed text through the bowels of it. This "forgetting," by the way, is the computer industry's most precious marketing tool. It is similar to the way women forget the pain of childbirth and go right ahead and have another child. Likewise, we forget the pain of our latest computer: we go right on and get another one. Anyway, the KayPro greatly increased my productivity and severely limited my freedom. Now, this was a paradox because in order to create I needed freedom, but in order to get freedom I had to be away from this machine. It therefore followed that the increased production I obtained from my computer was at the expense of creativity. So I started writing even less poetry.

Don't fear. I will not take you painfully, though it would give me great pleasure, through each and every one of the machines that over the years rapidly turned me into its slave. Suffice it too say that my art became a lot less portable, and even though

I have a Mac Notebook now, I find myself bound by habit to the desktop. Once you turn this thing on it starts to blink like a vampire, demanding its quota of words.

Americans have been conquered by the computer. I say conquered to mean what until recently was being called a revolution, the computer revolution. In my opinion it's no longer a revolution: the "compurevolutionists" have won and there is a New Order in effect. We live in ECC, Era of the Computer Chip, and this technology calls the shots now.

In the previous age, the Early Post-Humanist Age, the issues were about liberation from oppression, freedom from work, spiritual development, the defense of nature, and art. This EPHA (Early Post-Humanist Age) wasn't very long ago, doubtlessly most of us remember it. Some of us may even believe that we are still in it. Dealing with intelligent electronics does not preclude having a social conscience, it could be argued. Maybe not. But let's see.

The first use of computers for the purpose of social betterment was in the ideologically neutral area of *networking*. It would seem that the increased ability to communicate and to link people of like minds would be a great benefit to people working for post-humanist causes. All the people who want to save the whales could get to know each other and they could link up with the defenders of the wolves and so on. But the actual benefits of networking are not in areas of social activism: they are in fund-raising and marketing. People who might have found solace in the disinterested company of fellow altruists find themselves *targeted* instead. The most vulnerable targets are precisely people who don't cover their asses all the time. The best targets for sales and partisan political rhetoric are people whose minds are still open: but instead of opening them to the common good, the savvy networkers open them to the fangs of the commercial vampire. The proof of this is the tremendous rise of shopping channels, soon to come to your beloved Net, and the Republican sales pitches that translated so well in recent elections.

I know the counterargument: there are efforts to keep the big Net commercial-free but that's like saying, "The Visigoths are still five miles from Rome." And, of course, there are more ways to skin a cat than deafening it with a jingle. From what I've seen, most of the stuff out there is either sex or ads or both. And it's all lies in any case. But let's take the case of a friend of mine in New York who started a special talk salon for high IQs in the hope that world problems would get some armchair brainstorms. Guess what? The high IQs, after some high-minded protocol dust, got right down to business: sex and money. If they had been meeting face to face, I doubt that they would have been this crass. Face to face one tries to find one's better nature. If only because one has some vestigial respect, or fear, of the other's soul. In the anonymity of the electronic exchange one finds the crassest thing first. The soul doesn't shine through. Intelligence does, yes, but intelligence without soul is like a fiddle without strings.

Okay, I'm no prude, and I'm not blind to the practical advantages of information in medicine and other industries. It's the creativity angle I'm working. To be creative, a person needs freedom. I've said that before, but let me ask you: is freedom increased or lessened by the use of a computer? I would say lessened if not entirely eliminated. First, you are bound to the keyboard. Second, you must respond to the time-consuming demands of (mostly) useless information. Third, you do not have the luxury of being able to reflect for long periods of time because, most likely, the clock is ticking. Fourth, you are connected willy-nilly to a community of users with whom you have nothing in common but the frustrations of the equipment. Time is a limited commodity, which has become ever more limited since the Industrial Revolution. With the latest computer technology, human time disappears completely: machine time takes over.

Okay, you might say, but this "time," this "freedom" that you say we used to have—it was time for what? Freedom to do what? Here we come to the crux of the problem. The question of information.

ECC (Era of the Computer Chip) is also called, sometimes, the Age of Information. It's not a bad name: it describes succinctly exactly what it is that we produce and consume now. An observer in, let's say, the sixteenth century, would be astonished to see the quantities of sheer information consumed by an average American in an average town on an average day. Our sixteenth-century observer would, at first, faint from the sheer excitement and delight at the volume of knowledge, and then would try to grab as much of it as possible. He or she would, however, be able to grab no more than about five minutes worth from our media before short-circuiting and vanishing in a puff of smoke. Why would a sixteenth-century observer short-circuit? Because a sixteenth-century observer, unlike a twentieth-century consumer, would try to make sense of the information by connecting it. A sixteenth-century human was probably the last being on the planet capable of knowing everything—and not just *knowing,* but having a connected picture of the universe in his or her head.

To be sure, this was a sixteenth-century European, and the *everything* he or she knew was only what had been written and translated in Europe. Still, that was a lot, considering that knowing so much involved making a great many connections in order to make sense of the information. After the Renaissance, the illusion of such knowing vanished: libraries became the repositories of all that humanity knew. It no longer became necessary to know everything: little by little people began to specialize in small areas, trusting that they could find what they needed by looking it up. Instead of a coherent picture of the world that each individual might, by reflection, form for oneself, we entered an age of fragmentation. In this age, no individual had more than a few pieces of the puzzle and they lay disconnected, waiting for this individual to connect them with information from the library. Information increased and libraries grew and grew until there was a problem of storage. Happily, computers showed up.

Now the problem of storage seems to have been solved, leaving—only!—the problem of meaning. This, of course, is not such a great problem: very intelligent computers, very fast ones, could supply information almost as quickly as one's own memory used to when one had a memory. Fast computers are, in effect, a still-clumsy global nervous system that will get less and less clumsy.

So what's the problem? The problem is that the storage space now far exceeds the amount of information we have to store in it. Everything we know can now be stored in a corner of the vast electronic storage bin. The storage space now begins to demand information from us at a faster and faster rate: in order to fill its insatiable and theoretically infinite maw we must now produce faster and faster and more and more. Very soon, like that Renaissance person, we will blow up and go up in smoke, not because we have too much in us to deal with, but because we don't have another thing to give to the machine that's sucked us dry.

When the Renaissance persons put what they knew in books and put these in libraries, they didn't have to hurry. They emptied themselves of the information that held their world together slowly because there was only so much room. We now have to empty ourselves fast of information that literally goes through us. We have no time to reflect on it, we have no time to construct a picture of the world for ourselves. We are simply extensions of the intelligent electronics demanding to be fed.

When I hear "virtual world" or "cyberspace" I think of archeology. I *already* think of this world space as an archeological site, our equivalent of the Roman temple. At this point in time, and maybe for another decade, the temple of virtuality is awake with the swoosh of information it sucks to feed itself. In a decade or so the info will be exhausted. There will be nothing to suck and the whoosh will die down. Already, all the inert info we've busy-stashed like squirrels in books, tapes, and now CD-ROM, has whooshed down the cyber-gullet. The cyber-temple walls are so vast that all our records take only a pinprick's worth of room. So, what happens when the info's been all stored and all the things you can do to move it up and down and sideways have taken their thimble's worth of space? Well, then, what happens is that the temple itself, deprived of its food, will start to eat at its own walls until they collapse on top of everyone in it—and everyone *is* or will be shortly within—and that will be the end of our particular world and culture. Thus, archeology. They'll dig up cyberspace like Apuleium and they'll say: They worshipped their gods in here and when they ran out of sacrifices their gods killed them.

The meaning of virtuality is the information used in constructing it. Virtuality only has meaning as long as it's under construction. Nobody can actually inhabit it: it has no smell. Or, as my friend Larry says: "You can't pass a joint through the Internet!" Once virtuality has been built out of all the information we have, it becomes meaningless. And we are empty, emptied by what we have given virtuality. This is the case of any temple: it has meaning only as long as it has belief. When belief is exhausted it collapses. Information in our age is a dangerous belief: we worship information. We believe in storing it and, in so doing, we are drifted to serve the architecture of the store. The original purpose of information was to mobilize the interior of the mind for deeper understanding. In order to be useful in that way it had to stay within. By giving it up to the computer, we have not only precluded our evolution but have ensured our obsolescence.

Okay, so I'm no Marshall McLuhan, who thought that the global village was just hunky-dory. But I'm no practicing Luddite, either: I'm writing this on my latest tormentor, a Packard-Bell 486, courtesy of my mother, who always had a knack for interrupting whatever I was doing. This particular interruption took a week. Mothers are probably in collusion with intelligent electronics—to keep everybody in where they can keep an eye on them. But mother is too big a subject, let me go back to the questions of freedom and time, "down time" as it is now called.

Yes, freedom, and time, and the question of what does a "coherent picture of the world" mean. Freedom is that referent-free space at the coffeehouse when you scribble on your napkin with the vague perfume of that potential girl in your unfocused nostrils. In that state, time is infinite. Not machine time, not clock time, not set-up time: infinity. (And that's not a car, please!) In this space of infinity-freedom you dream. You float, you dream, you have no boundaries, you are within a potential and generative state of mind. This is the mulch ground of the uncreated, the space prior to inarticulation, a place where articulation is, in fact, suspect. You are . . . in New Orleans.

You look out the frame of the streetcar window and let the live oaks and the big houses with their columns of piquant stories flash by without focusing on any of them. You go to Cafe Brazil and inhale deeply the aroma of espresso and young dancers at work. You go to the Faulkner Bookstore and say hi to his ghost. You hand over some money to the tap dancers on Decatur Street. Get immersed in street music. And this is no interactive program: things smell, resonate, and brace.

Under conditions of freedom and leisure, an individual might construct a picture of the world from the few bits of information still charged by the senses. It won't be the Renaissance cat's erudite, prescientific vision, but it won't be the overnetworked grudge's sense of eternal emergency, either.

Emerging from Censorship

J. M. Coetzee

J. M. Coetzee was born in Cape Town, South Africa in 1940. He studied first at Cape Town, and later earned a Ph.D. degree in literature from the University of Texas at Austin. He returned to South Africa and joined the faculty of the University of Cape Town in 1972.

His first novel, actually two novellas, Dusklands *(1974), examines the parallels between Americans in Vietnam and the early Dutch settlers in South Africa.* Waiting for the Barbarians *(1980), the story of a government magistrate, who questions the government for which he works, won South Africa's highest literary honor, the Central News Agency (CNA) Literary Award, in 1980. He won the premier British award, the Booker Prize, for the first time in 1983, for the* Life and Times of Michael K. *In the same year he was appointed Professor of General Literature at the University of Cape Town, a post he still holds.*

On October 25th 1999, Coetzee became the first author to win the prestigious Booker award twice in its 31-year history, for his current novel, Disgrace. *In addition to novels, he has written several volumes of critical essays. The following essay is part of a chapter in* Giving Offence: Essays on Censorship.

From the early 1960s until about 1980, the Republic of South Africa operated one of the most comprehensive censorship systems in the world. Called in official parlance not censorship but "publications control" (*censorship* was a word it preferred to censor from public discourse about itself),[1] it sought to control the dissemination of signs in whatever form. Not only books, magazines, films, and plays, but T-shirts, key-rings,

---

Excerpt from Chapter 2, "Emerging from Censorship," by J. M. Coetzee, reprinted from *Giving Offence: Essays on Censorship*, 1996, University of Chicago Press.

dolls, toys, and shop-signs—anything, in fact, bearing a message that might be "undesirable"—had to pass the scrutiny of the censorship bureaucracy before it could be made public. In the Soviet Union, there were some 70,000 bureaucrats supervising the activities of some 7,000 writers. The ratio of censors to writers in South Africa was, if anything, higher than ten to one.

Paranoids behave as though the air is filled with coded messages deriding them or plotting their destruction. For decades the South African state lived in a state of paranoia. Paranoia is the pathology of insecure regimes and of dictatorships in particular. One of the features distinguishing modern from earlier dictatorships has been how widely and rapidly paranoia can spread from above to infect the whole of the populace. This diffusion of paranoia is not inadvertent: it is used as a technique of control. Stalin's Soviet Union is the prime example: every citizen was encouraged to suspect every other citizen of being a spy or saboteur; the bonds of human sympathy and trust between people were broken down; and society fragmented into tens of millions of individuals living on individual islets of mutual suspicion.

The Soviet Union was not unique. The Cuban novelist Reinaldo Arenas wrote of an atmosphere of "unceasing official menace" in his country that made a citizen "not only a repressed person, but also a self-repressed one, not only a censored person, but a self-censored one, not only one watched over, but one who watches over himself."[2] "Unceasing official menace" punctuated with spectacles of exemplary punishment inculcates caution, watchfulness. When certain kinds of writing and speech, even certain thoughts, become surreptitious activities, then the paranoia of the state is on its way to being reproduced in the psyche of the subject, and the state can look forward to a future in which the bureaucracies of supervision can be allowed to wither away, their function having been, in effect, privatized.

For it is a revealing feature of censorship that it is not proud of itself, never parades itself. The archaic model for the censor's ban is the ban on blasphemy, and both bans suffer an embarrassing structural paradox, namely, that if a crime is to be satisfactorily attested in court, the testimony will have to repeat the crime. Thus it used to be that in the public sessions of the rabbinical courts witnesses to blasphemy were supplied with codified euphemisms to utter in place of the banned name of the Holy; if the actual blasphemy had to be repeated to make conviction conclusive, the court moved into closed session, and testimony was followed by rituals of purgation on the part of the judges. Embarrassment went even further: the very notion that the name of the Holy as a blasphemous word could curse the Holy was so scandalous that for "curse" the word "bless" had to be substituted.[3] Just as a chain of euphemisms came into being to protect the name of the Holy, so in an age when the state was worshipped the office that protected its name had to be euphemized. That office waits for the day when, its functions having been universally internalized, its name need no longer be spoken.

The tyrant and his watchdog are not the only ones touched by paranoia. There is a pathological edge to the watchfulness of the writer in the paranoid state. For evidence one need only go to the testimony of writers themselves. Time and again they record the feeling of being touched and contaminated by the sickness of the state. In a move typical of "authentic" paranoids, they claim that their minds have been invaded; it is against this invasion that they express their outrage.

The Greek writer George Mangakis, for instance, records the experience of writing in prison under the eyes of his guards. Every few days the guards searched his cell, taking away his writings and returning those which the prison authorities—his censors—considered "permissible." Mangakis recalls suddenly "loathing" his papers as he accepted them from the hands of his guards. "The system is a diabolical device for annihilating your own soul. They want to make you see your thoughts through their eyes and control them yourself, from their point of view."[4] By forcing the writer to see what he has written through the censor's eyes, the censor forces him to internalize a contaminating reading. Mangakis's sudden, revulsive moment is the moment of contamination.

Another passionate account of the operations of introverted censorship is given by Danilo Kis:

> The battle against self-censorship is anonymous, lonely and unwitnessed, and it makes its subject feel humiliated and ashamed of collaborating. [It] means reading your own text with the eyes of another person, a situation where you become your own judge, stricter and more suspicious than anyone else. . . .
>
> The self-appointed censor is the *alter ego* of the writer, an alter ego who leans over his shoulder and sticks his nose into the text. . . . It is impossible to win against this censor, for he is like God—he knows and sees all, he came out of your own mind, your own fears, your own nightmares. . . .
>
> This *alter ego* . . . succeeds in undermining and tainting even the most moral individuals whom outside censorship has not managed to break. By not admitting that it exists, self-censorship aligns itself with lies and spiritual corruption.[5]

The final proof that something has, so to speak, gone wrong with writers like Arenas or Mangakis or Kis is the excessiveness of the language in which they express their experience. Paranoia is not just a figurative way of talking about what has afflicted them. The paranoia is there, on the inside, in their language, in their thinking; the rage one hears in Mangakis' words, the bafflement in Kis's, are rage and bafflement at the most intimate of invasions, an invasion of the very style of the self, by a pathology for which there may be no cure.

Nor am I, as I write here, exempt. In the excessive insistency of its phrasing, its vehemence, its demand for sensitivity to minutiae of style, its overreading and overwriting, I detect in my own language the very pathology I discuss. Having lived through the heyday of South African censorship, seen its consequences not only on the careers of fellow-writers but on the totality of public discourse, and felt within myself some of its more secret and shameful effects, I have every reason to suspect that whatever infected Arenas or Mangakis or Kis, whether real or delusional, has infected me too. That is to say, this very writing may be a specimen of the kind of paranoid discourse it seeks to describe.

For the paranoia I address is not the imprint of censorship on those writers alone who are singled out for official persecution. All writing that in the normal course of events falls under the censor's eye may become tainted in the manner I have described, whether or not the censor passes it. All writers under censorship are at least potentially touched by paranoia, not just those who have their work suppressed.

Why should censorship have such contagious power? I can offer only a speculative answer, an answer based in part on introspection, in part on a scrutiny (perhaps a paranoid scrutiny) of the accounts that other writers (perhaps themselves infected with paranoia) have given of operating under regimes of censorship.

The self, as we understand the self today, is not the unity it was assumed to be by classical rationalism. On the contrary, it is multiple and multiply divided against itself. It is, to speak in figures, a zoo in which a multitude of beasts have residence, over which the anxious, overworked zookeeper of rationality exercises a rather limited control. At night the zookeeper sleeps and the beasts roam about, doing their dreamwork.

In this figural zoo, some of the beasts have names, like figure-of-the-father and figure-of-the-mother; others are memories or fragments of memories in transmuted form, with strong elements of feeling attached to them; a whole subcolony are semitamed but still treacherous earlier versions of the self, each with an inner zoo of its own over which it has less than complete control.

Artists, in Freud's account, are people who can make a tour of the inner menagerie with a degree of confidence and emerge, when they so wish, more or less unscathed. From Freud's account of creative work I take one element: that creativity of a certain kind involves inhabiting and managing and exploiting quite primitive parts of the self. While this is not a particularly dangerous activity it is a delicate one. It may take years of preparation before the artist finally gets the codes and the keys and the balances right, and can move in and out more or less freely. It is also a very private activity, so private that it almost constitutes the definition of privacy: how I am with myself.

Managing the inner selves, making them work for one (making them productive) is a complex matter of pleasing and satisfying and challenging and extorting and wooing and feeding, and sometimes even of putting to death. For writing not only comes out of the zoo but (to be hypermetaphorical) goes back in again. That is to say, insofar as writing is transactional, the figures *for whom* and *to whom* it is done are also figures in the zoo: for instance, the figure-of-the-beloved.

Imagine, then, a project in writing that is, at heart, a transaction with some such figure of the beloved, that tries to please her (but that also tries continually though surreptitiously to revise and recreate her as the-one-who-will-be-pleased); and imagine what will happen if into this transaction is introduced in a massive and undeniable way another figure-of-the-reader, the dark-suited, baldheaded censor, with his pursed lips and his red pen and his irritability and his censoriousness—the censor, in fact, as parodic version of the figure-of-the-father. Then the entire balance of the carefully constructed inner drama will be destroyed, and destroyed in a way that is hard to repair, since the more one tries to ignore (repress) the censor, the larger he swells.

Working under censorship is like being intimate with someone who does not love you, with whom you want no intimacy, but who presses himself in upon you. The censor is an intrusive reader, a reader who forces his way into the intimacy of the writing transaction, forces out the figure of the loved or courted reader, reads your words in a disapproving and *censorious* fashion.

ENDNOTES

[1] Though by no means as extreme, the South African system showed odd parallels with the Soviet system. Andrei Sinyavsky recollects finding no entry for *tzenzura*, "censorship," in a 1977 dictionary of foreign-derived words in Russian: "The word 'censorship' was itself censored." Quoted in Marianna Tax Choldin and Maurice Friedberg, eds., *The Red Pencil* (Boston: Unwin Hyman, 1989), p. 94.

[2] Quoted in Carlos Ripoll, *The Heresy of Words in Cuba* (New York: Freedom House, 1985), p. 36.

[3] Leonard W. Levy, *Treason against God* (New York: Schocken, 1981), pp. 25-26.

[4] George Mangakis, "Letter to Europeans" (1972) in George Theiner, ed., *They Shoot Writers, Don't They?* (London: Faber, 1984), p. 33.

[5] Kis, Danilo. "Censorship/Self-Censorship." *Index on Censorship* 5/1 (January 1986): 45.

The Mathematics of Kindness: Math Proves the Golden Rule

K. C. Cole

K. C. Cole is a science writer for Los Angeles Times, *who lives in Santa Monica, California. In 1995, she won the American Institute of Physics Award for Best Science Writing. She wrote* Sympathetic Vibrations *(1984), a book that explores creativity, art and beauty in relation to physics. In* The Universe and the Teacup: The Mathematics of Truth and Beauty *(1998), from which the following essay was excerpted, she continues to explore the same themes in relation to mathematics.*

Surprisingly, there is a single property which distinguishes the relatively high-scoring entries from the relatively low-scoring entries. This is the property of being NICE. . . .
> —Robert Axelrod, in The Evolution of Cooperation

Life did not take over the globe by combat, but by networking.
> —Lynn Margulis and Dorion Sagan in Microcosmos

"Do unto others as you would have others do unto you." "An eye for an eye." "Get it while the getting's good." "He ain't heavy, he's my brother."

Selfishness and altruism have always been uneasy partners in human affairs. Churches and scout troops exhort us to lend a helping hand to those in need; at the same time, advertisers and politicians encourage us to be as greedy as humanly possible. Indeed, the idea that greed is all to the good has become encoded in a kind of religion of U.S.-style capitalism: The more you're out for yourself, the better off the whole society will be.

This win-at-all costs strategy gains strength because it appears to be founded on Mother Nature's own laws. Charles Darwin's idea of survival of the fittest suggests that only the meanest, most competitive, most selfish individuals will make it to the top of the evolutionary heap. Compromise, cooperation, and kindness are for losers and wimps. In a capitalistic society, failure to be selfish is akin to economic treason.

For a long time, people have accepted this philosophy as undeniably true. But for the past two decades, mathematicians have been studying survival strategies to find out which are truly best. To almost everyone's surprise, they have found that nice guys can and frequently do finish first. In tournaments designed to pick out winners in a variety of conflict situations, the top dog turns out to be not the most ferocious but the most cooperative. Ironically, the strategies that have emerged from the mathematical research sound a lot like old-fashioned homilies: think ahead, cooperate, don't covet your neighbor's success, and be prepared to forgive those who trespass against you.

Much work in game theory has focused on one of the most unsettling paradoxes of all, the so-called prisoner's dilemma. It's usually explained as a familiar cop show scenario. Two partners in crime are kept in isolated cells. Each is told that if he blows the whistle on the other, he might be able to go free. If he remains mute, each prisoner knows, the authorities might not have enough evidence to convict him—unless, of course, the other prisoner rats on him first. Which strategy works best—keep silent or strike a deal?

Variations on this theme, I think, make the inherent paradox even clearer. Assume, for example, that you've outgrown your old car but desperately want a family sailboat for Sunday afternoon excursions. Another person—whom you contact through the newspaper—desperately needs a car like yours and has exactly the sailboat you crave—a boat she no longer uses. You both agree that a swap would be a fair trade.

Now assume for some reason that the trade needs to be kept secret. You both agree to put the car/boat in predesignated places. The problem is: What happens if you leave behind your car, and the boat isn't where it's supposed to be? You've been cheated!

The boat owner faces exactly the same dilemma.

Logically, you might add up the pros and cons this way: If you leave the car, but the other person doesn't leave the boat, you get robbed. If you don't deliver the car, and she doesn't deliver the boat, then you come out even. If you don't leave the car and she does deliver the boat, you get something for nothing.

Logic points you to an inescapable conclusion: No matter what the other person does, you're better off not leaving your car. The other person's logic leads her to the same destination. Outcome? Neither of you gets what you wanted.

A prisoner's dilemma pops up anytime going after your own immediate interests results in disaster if everyone does it. Should you throw your trash out the window, or wait until you find a garbage can? Listen to public radio for free, or pay your way? Abide by disarmament agreements, or cheat and hide your arsenals?

Clearly, if one party cooperates while the other cheats, the cooperator is a sucker. But if both cheat, no one gets anything.

Looking in on the situation from the outside, it may be clear that cooperation is a better tactic for both sides. But from an individual player's point of view, there's always temptation to try to get the better of the other guy; you always have a chance of winning more by *not* cooperating.

Why, then, do people cooperate at all? This is the question that intrigued political scientist Robert Axelrod of the University of Michigan in the 1980s. If dog eat dog is the law of the jungle, why is cooperation so common among humans and other species as well? During trench warfare in World War I, Axelrod points out, soldiers on opposite sides of the front lines formed tacit agreements to live and let live—in direct defiance of orders from commanders. An officer in the British army, writing in his diary in August 1915, recounts how after a Prussian shell exploded in the British camp (during teatime, no less), a German soldier climbed out of his trench and crossed no-man's-land to apologize: "We hope no one was hurt. It is not our fault, it is that damned Prussian artillery."

Closer to home, it's not even clear why people obey traffic signals. Individually, there's not much motivation for stopping at red lights—short of the very off chance of being caught. Yet, most of the time, people do it anyway. They leave tips for waiters they may never see again, pick up after themselves when no one is looking, show kindness to total strangers.

To try to resolve the paradox, in 1980 Axelrod invited experts in game theory to a tournament of repeated games of prisoner's dilemma. Each entrant would submit a strategy, and the various strategies played against each other by means of computers. Points were assigned to outcomes and tabulated.

To almost everyone's surprise, the most successful strategy turned out to be an ingeniously simple program created by Anatol Rapoport at the University of Toronto. Called Tit for Tat, the program's first move is always to cooperate. After that, it simply echoes whatever its opposition does. If the opposition cooperates, Tit for Tat cooperates. If the opposition defects, Tit for Tat retaliates in kind.

In this sense, Tit for Tat embodies both biblical injunctions: an eye for an eye, and the Golden Rule. Or as William Poundstone sums it up in a book about classic game theory problems, the program's message is: "Do unto others as you would have them do unto you—or else!"

By not ever being the first to defect, Tit for Tat was what Axelrod called a "nice" program. As it turns out, most of the winners in computer simulations that Axelrod has run have been nice: most of the losers were not. Tit for Tat could also be forgiving—that is, even after the opposition defected, Tit for Tat would occasionally give cooperation another try. The lesson, says Axelrod, is "be nice and forgiving."

It is also important to be clear. Very complex computer programs fare no better than random ones in such simulated games because no one can figure out what their strategy is and respond in kind.

Axelrod then held a follow-up tournament. This time he got entries not only from game theorists, but also from researchers in biology, physics, and sociology. And this time, everyone knew about the success of Tit for Tat and other "nice" strategies. Nevertheless, Rapoport's simple program won again. The other experts, Axelrod concluded, all "made systematic errors of being too competitive for their own good, not being forgiving enough."

In a final round, Axelrod wanted to see what would happen if he pitted all the programs against each other in a kind of Darwinian evolution, where survival of the fittest meant success for those who produced the most viable offspring in the next generation—the number of offspring being determined by the number of points.

This time, Tit for Tat did well, but so, at first, did some very cut-throat, exploitative strategies. Then a funny thing happened: The exploitative strategies ran out of prey. There was no one left to gobble up. As Axelrod puts it, "in the long run [a strategy that is not nice] can destroy the very environment it needs for its own success."

The tournament also had lessons for the envious. If one strategy envied another's success and tried to do better, it would usually wind up cutting off its nose to spite its face. That is, the only way to get the better of an opponent would be to attack, and that would set off another round of nastiness that would make everyone worse off.

"There is no point in being envious of the success of the other player," says Axelrod, "since [in this kind of game] the other's success is virtually a prerequisite of your doing well yourself."

A final requirement for success was a stable, long-term relationship, where the same opponents would play each other again and again. In such a situation, it paid to be cooperative. This explains the relationship of the World War I soldiers, who faced each other month after month, or people in tight communities, or national leaders who need each other in an ongoing series of negotiations.

More recently, New York University's Steven Brams made great strides in making game theory more realistic.* While he was at it, he got interested in whether it might be possible to use mathematics to model human emotions—and therefore come up with strategies for getting out of frustrating situations.

In his "frustration" games, one player is stuck in a bad position, while another player is satisfied and has no incentive to change his tune. The first player can't get out of the situation without also hurting himself.

An example might be a family with an unruly teenager who refuses to follow any of the parents' rules. The parents don't want to become too Draconian, because that might hurt them, too. (Say the teenager uses the family car to take his little sister to school, and the parents would lose that service if they take away his keys. Or say they impose a no TV rule, but that means they must give up their favorite shows as well.)

If the parents get frustrated enough, however, they might be willing to hurt themselves (at least temporarily) simply to break out of the deadlock.

Another recent and socially relevant twist on game theory illuminates the effects of obvious labels on players—like skin color or nationality or gender. As described by Poundstone, this variation on Tit for Tat changes the rules slightly. Players would always

---

* Details can be found in his book, *Theory of Moves*.

cooperate with other players of the same group, but not with players bearing different labels. Thus, males, or blues, would always cooperate with other males, or blues, but not cooperate in encounter with females, or reds.

Not surprisingly, in this game of Discriminatory Tit for Tat, the majority group always did well, but minorities did very badly. The reason is not difficult to figure out: Where majorities had most of their daily encounters with others of their own kind, and thus were treated "nicely," minorities were forever bumping into their opposites, who would always "defect," or fail to cooperate.

It's possible, Poundstone concludes, that such behavioral dynamics could account for the compelling allure of minority communities—be they religious, racial, or even financial. Even a "ghetto," in this sense, can be "a safe haven where most interactions are likely to be positive."

Curiously, evidence from the world of the living—that is, biology and genetics—seems to confirm some of the "abstract" arguments to come out of game theory. If these notions are right, then the evolution of species has depended a great deal less on "dog eat dog" and a lot more on "dog learns to live cooperatively with other dogs" (not to mention humans) than anyone imagined.

Just because the "fittest" tend to survive, in other words, doesn't necessarily mean the "fittest" are the strongest, or meanest, or even the most reproductively profligate; the fittest may be those who learn best how to use cooperation for their own ends.

Controversial microbiologist Lynn Margulis has vastly extended the idea that symbiosis (living together without the benefit of clergy, one might call it) has been a major force in shaping organisms. From trees to fish to fungus, all kinds of living things take nourishment from each other, build communal housing, use each other, and generally form all sorts of lifelong partnerships and odd arrangements for the mutual benefit of all concerned.

Margulis has suggested that the cell itself arose from such cooperative arrangements among subcellular beings. Cells are packed full of specialized components that metabolize food, produce and store energy, propel the cell, shape its internal structure, and so forth. A good deal of evidence already supports Margulis's idea that cells are more like colonies of cooperating individuals than survivors of some fierce competitive race to "success."

Other biologists have argued—on a variety of different bases—that there is probably a gene for altruism and that humans (not to mention ants and bees and other intensely communal creatures) carry it within them as part of their genetic baggage. Altruism, wrote the late Lewis Thomas, "is essential for continuation of the species, and it exists as an everyday aspect of living."

After all, it's well known that creatures as various as vampire bats and stickleback fish put their own lives at risk to feed their fellows—even when the fellows happen to be unrelated.

In his usual lyric way, Thomas fashioned these facts into a lesson of near-biblical proportion:

I maintain that we are born and grow up with a fondness for each other, and that we have genes for that. We can be talked out of that fondness, for the genetic message is like a distant music, and some of us are hard-of-hearing. Societies are noisy affairs, drowning out the sound of ourselves and our connection. Hard-of-hearing, we go to war. Stone deaf, we make thermonuclear missiles. Nonetheless, the music is there, waiting for more listeners.

He may well be right, but the living genes aren't the only ones hearing the music. Carl Zimmer wrote in *Discover* magazine about a computer whiz named Maja Mataric of Brandeis University. She managed to get fourteen robots to cooperate in such simple tasks as retrieving a puck. Remarkably, cooperation wasn't a talent that she programmed into them. They learned it themselves. Instead of all ganging up on the same prize at the same time, she programmed them to pay attention to what the others were doing. Within fifteen minutes of practice, they acquired a taste for altruism.

What all this says about robots or vampire bats or even mathematicians, I'll leave to further study. Even if cooperation didn't steer human evolution, it probably wasn't completely absent from the picture, either. Perhaps the mathematicians' study of human interaction will someday help point the way out of what seems to be humanity's increasingly common lament—or as Rodney King puts it: "Why can't we all just get along?"

White Angel

Michael Cunningham

Michael Cunningham writes fiction and nonfiction. His stories have appeared in The Atlantic, Redbook, The Paris Review, *and* The New Yorker, *where "White Angel" first appeared. Based very loosely on an incident that happened when he was thirteen near his hometown in Cleveland, Ohio, "White Angel," according to Cunningham, is ninety percent fiction. Ten percent—the boy running through a glass door—provided the kernel for his story.*

Cunningham's first novel, Golden States, *was published in 1984. A Home at the End of the World (1990), a book about the impact of AIDS on four characters' lives, has earned much praise from critics. Born in 1952, Cunningham earned an M.F.A. from the University of Iowa. He is an active member of ACT–UP and has worked for the Carnegie Corporation in New York City since 1986.*

We lived then in Cleveland, in the middle of everything. It was the sixties—our radios sang out love all day long. This of course is history. It was before the city of Cleveland went broke, before its river caught fire. We were four. My mother and father, Carlton and me. Carlton turned sixteen the year I turned nine. Between us were several brothers and sisters, weak flames quenched in our mother's womb. We are not a fruitful or many branched line. Our family name is Morrow.

Our father was a high-school music teacher. Our mother taught children called "exceptional," which meant that they could name the day Christmas would fall in the year 2000 but couldn't remember to take down their pants when they peed. We lived in a tract called Woodlawn—neat one and two story houses painted optimistic colors. The tract bordered a cemetery. Behind our back yard was a gully choked with

"White Angel," by Michael Cunningham, reprinted from *The New Yorker*, July 25, 1988, Brandt & Brandt Literary Agents.

brush and beyond that, the field of smooth, polished stones. I grew up with the cemetery and didn't mind it. It could be beautiful. A single stone angel, small-breasted and determined, rose amid the more conservative markers close to our house. Farther away, in a richer section, miniature mosques and Parthenons spoke silently to Cleveland of man's enduring accomplishments. Carlton and I played in the cemetery as children and, with a little more age, smoked joints and drank Southern Comfort there. I was, thanks to Carlton, the most criminally advanced nine-year-old in my fourth grade class. I was going places. I made no move without his counsel.

Here is Carlton several months before his death, in an hour so alive with snow that earth and sky are identically white. He labors among the markers, and I run after him stung by snow, following the light of his red knitted cap. Carlton's hair is pulled back into a ponytail, neat and economical, a perfect pinecone of hair. He is thrifty, in his way.

We have taken hits of acid with our breakfast juice. Or, rather, Carlton has taken a hit, and I, in consideration of my youth, have been allowed half. This acid is called windowpane. It is for clarity of vision, as Vicks is for decongestion of the nose. Our parents are at work, earning the daily bread. We have come out into the cold so that the house, when we reenter it, will shock us with its warmth and righteousness. Carlton believes in shocks.

"I think I'm coming on to it," I call out. Carlton has on his buckskin jacket, which is worn down to the shine. On the back, across his shoulder blades, his girlfriend has stitched an electric blue eye. As we walk I speak into the eye. "I think I feel something," I say.

"Too soon," Carlton calls back. "Stay loose, Frisco. You'll know when the time comes."

I am excited and terrified. We are into serious stuff. Carlton has done acid a half dozen times before, but I am new at it. We slipped the tabs into our mouths at breakfast, while our mother paused over the bacon. Carlton likes taking risks.

Snow collects in the engraved letters on the headstones. I lean into the wind trying to decide whether everything around me seems strange because of the drug or just because everything truly is strange. Three weeks earlier, a family across town had been sitting at home, watching television, when a single engine plane fell on them. Snow swirls around us, seeming to fall up as well as down.

Carlton leads the way to our spot, the pillared entrance to a society tomb. This tomb is a palace. Stone cherubs cluster on the peaked roof, with their stunted, frozen wings and matrons' faces. Under the roof is a veranda, backed by cast-iron doors that lead to the house of the dead proper. In summer this veranda is cool. In winter it blocks the wind. We keep a bottle of Southern Comfort here.

Carlton finds the bottle, unscrews the cap, and takes a good, long draw. He is studded with snowflakes. He hands me the bottle, and I take a more conservative drink. Even in winter, the tomb smells mossy. Dead leaves and a yellow M & M's wrapper, worried by the wind, scrape on the marble floor.

"Are you scared?" Carlton asks me.

I nod. I never think of lying to him.

"Don't be, man," he says. "Fear will screw you right up. Drugs can't hurt you if you feel no fear."

I nod.

We stand sheltered, passing the bottle. I lean into Carlton's certainty as if it gave off heat.

"We can do acid all the time at Woodstock," I say.

"Right on. Woodstock Nation. Yow!"

"Do people really *live* there?" I ask.

"Man, you've got to stop asking that. The concert's over, but people are still there. It's the new nation. Have faith."

I nod again, satisfied. There is a different country for us to live in. I am already a new person, renamed Frisco. My old name was Robert.

"We'll do acid all the time," I say.

"You better believe we will." Carlton's face, surrounded by snow and marble, is lit. His eyes are vivid as neon. Something in them tells me he can see the future, a ghost that hovers over everybody's head. In Carlton's future we all get released from our jobs and schooling. Awaiting us all, and soon, is a bright perfect simplicity. A life among the trees by the river.

"How are you feeling, man?" he asks me.

"Great," I tell him, and it is purely the truth. Doves clatter up out of a bare tree and turn at the same instant, transforming themselves from steel to silver in the snow-blown light. I know then that the drug is working. Everything before me has become suddenly radiantly itself. How could Carlton have known this was about to happen?

"Oh," I whisper. His hand settles on my shoulder.

"Stay loose, Frisco," he says.

"There's not a thing in this pretty world to be afraid of. I'm here."

I am not afraid. I am astonished. I had not realized until this moment how real everything is. A twig lies on the marble at my feet, bearing a cluster of hard brown berries. The broken-off end is raw, white, fleshy. Trees are alive.

"I'm here," Carlton says again, and he is.

Hours later, we are sprawled on the sofa in front of the television, ordinary as Wally and the Beav. Our mother makes dinner in the kitchen. A pot lid clangs. We are undercover agents. I am trying to conceal my amazement.

Our father is building a grandfather clock from a kit. He wants to have something to leave us, something for us to pass along. We can hear him in the basement, sawing and pounding. I know what is laid out on his sawhorses—a long, raw wooden box, onto which he glues fancy moldings. A pearl of sweat meanders down his forehead as he works. Tonight I discovered my ability to see every room of the house at once, to know every single thing that goes on. A mouse nibbles inside the wall. Electrical wires curl behind the plaster, hidden and patient as snakes.

"Sh-h-h," I say to Carlton, who has not said anything. He is watching television through his splayed fingers. Gunshots ping. Bullets raise chalk dust on a concrete wall. I have no idea what we are watching.

"Boys?" our mother calls from the kitchen. I can, with my new ears, hear her slap hamburgers into patties. "Set the table like good citizens," she calls.

"O.K., Ma," Carlton replies, in a gorgeous imitation of normality. Our father hammers in the basement. I can feel Carlton's heart ticking. He pats my hand, to assure me that everything's perfect.

We set the table, fork knife spoon, paper napkins triangled to one side. We know the moves cold. After we are done I pause to notice the dining room wallpaper: a golden farm, backed by mountains. Cows graze, autumn trees cast golden shade. This scene repeats itself three times, on three walls.

"Zap," Carlton whispers. "Zzzz-zoom."

"Did we do it right?" I ask him.

"We did everything perfect, little son. How are you doing in there, anyway?" He raps lightly on my head.

"Perfect, I guess." I am staring at the wallpaper as if I were thinking of stepping into it.

"You guess. You guess? You and I are going to other planets, man. Come over here."

"Where?"

"Here. Come here." He leads me to the window. Outside snow skitters under the street lamps. Ranch-style houses hoard their warmth but bleed light into the gathering snow.

"You and I are going to fly, man," Carlton whispers, close to my ear. He opens the window. Snow blows in, sparking on the carpet. "Fly," he says and we do. For a moment we strain up and out, the black night wind blowing in our faces—we raise ourselves up off the cocoa-colored deep-pile wool-and-polyester-carpet by a sliver of an inch. I swear it to this day. Sweet glory. The secret of flight is this: You have to do it immediately, before your body realizes it is defying the laws.

We both know we have taken momentary leave of the earth. It does not strike either of us as remarkable, any more than does the fact that airplanes sometimes fall from the sky, or that we have always lived in Ohio and will soon leave for a new nation. We settle back down. Carlton touches my shoulder.

"You wait, Frisco," he says. "Miracles are happening. Goddam miracles."

I nod. He pulls down the window, which reseals itself with a sucking sound. Our own faces look back at us from the cold dark glass. Behind us, our mother drops the hamburgers into the skillet. Our father bends to his work under a hooded light bulb, preparing the long box into which he will lay clockwork, pendulum, a face. A plane drones by overhead, invisible in the clouds. I glance nervously at Carlton. He smiles his assurance and squeezes the back of my neck.

March. After the thaw. I am walking through the cemetery, thinking about my endless life. One of the beauties of living in Cleveland is that any direction feels like progress. I've memorized the map. We are by my calculations three hundred and fifty miles shy of Woodstock, New York. On this raw new day I am walking east, to the place where Carlton and I keep our bottle. I am going to have an early nip, to celebrate my bright future.

When I get to our spot, I hear low moans coming from behind the tomb. I freeze, considering my options. The sound is a long, drawn-out agony with a whip at the end, a final high C, something like "OooooOw," a wolf's cry run backward. What decides me on investigation rather than flight is the need to create a story. In the stories Carlton likes best, people always do the foolish risky thing. I find I can reach decisions this way—by thinking of myself as a character in a story told by Carlton.

I creep around the side of the monument, cautious as a badger, pressed up close to the marble. I peer over a cherub's girlish shoulder. What I find is Carlton on the ground with his girlfriend, in a jumble of clothes and bare flesh. Carlton's jacket, the one with the embroidered eye, is draped over the stone, keeping watch.

I hunch behind the statue. I can see the girl's naked arms, and the familiar bones of Carlton's spine. The two of them moan together in the brown winter grass. Though I can't make out the girl's expression, Carton's face is twisted and grimacing, the cords of his neck pulled tight. I had never thought the experience might be painful. I watch, trying to learn. I hold onto the cherubs cold wings.

It isn't long before Carlton catches sight of me. His eyes rove briefly, ecstatically skyward, and what do they light on but his brother's small head sticking up next to a cherub's. We lock eyes and spend a moment in mutual decision. The girl keeps on clutching at Carlton's skinny back. He decides to smile at me. He decides to wink.

I am out of there so fast I tear up divots. I dodge among the stones, jump the gully, clear the fence into the swing-set-and-picnic-table sanctity of the back yard. Something about that wink. My heart beats as fast as a sparrow's. I go into the kitchen and find our mother washing fruit. She asks what's going on. I tell her nothing is. Nothing at all.

She sighs over an apple's imperfection. The curtains sport blue teapots. Our mother works the apple with a scrub brush. She believes they come coated with poison.

"Where's Carlton?" she asks.

"Don't know," I tell her.

"Bobby?"

"Huh?"

"What exactly is going on?"

"Nothing," I say. My heart works itself up to a hummingbird rate, more buzz than beat.

"I think something is. Will you answer a question?"

"O.K."

"Is your brother taking drugs?"

I relax a bit. It's only drugs. I know why she is asking. Lately police cars have been cruising past our house like sharks. They pause, take note, glide on. Some neighborhood crackdown. Carlton is famous in these parts.

"No," I tell her.

She faces me with the brush in one hand, an apple in the other. "You wouldn't lie to me would you?" She knows something is up. Her nerves run through this house. She can feel dust settling on the tabletops, milk starting to turn in the refrigerator.

"No," I say.

"Something's going on," she sighs. She is a small efficient woman who looks at things as if they gave off a painful light. She grew up on a farm in Wisconsin and spent her girlhood tying up bean rows, worrying over the sun and rain. She is still trying to overcome her habit of modest expectations.

I leave the kitchen, pretending sudden interest in the cat. Our mother follows, holding her brush. She means to scrub the truth out of me. I follow the cat, his erect black tail and pink anus.

"Don't walk away when I'm talking to you," our mother says.

I keep walking, to see how far I'll get, calling "Kittykittykitty." In the front hall, our father's homemade clock chimes the half hour. I make for the clock. I get as far as the rubber plant before she collars me.

"I told you not to walk away," she says, and cuffs me a good one with the brush. She catches me on the ear and sets it ringing. The cat is out of there quick as a quarter note.

I stand for a minute, to let her know I've received the message. Then I resume walking. She hits me again, this time on the back of the head, hard enough to make me see colors. "Will you *stop?*" she screams. Still I keep walking. Our house runs west to east. With every step I get closer to Yasgur's farm.

Carlton comes home whistling. Our mother treats him like a guest who's overstayed. He doesn't care. He is lost in optimism. He pats her cheek and calls her "Professor." He treats her as if she were harmless and so she is.

She never hits Carlton. She suffers him the way farm girls suffer a thieving crow, with a grudge so old it borders on reverence. She gives him a scrubbed apple and tells him what she'll do if he tracks mud on the carpet.

I am waiting in our room. He brings the smell of the cemetery with him—its old snow and wet pine needles. He rolls his eyes at me, takes a crunch of his apple. "What's happening, Frisco?" he says.

I have arranged myself loosely on my bed trying to pull a Dylan riff out of my harmonica. I have always figured I can bluff my way into wisdom. I offer Carlton a dignified nod.

He drops onto his own bed. I can see a crushed crocus stuck to the black rubber sole of his boot.

"Well Frisco," he says, "today you are a man."

I nod again. Is that all there is to it?

"Yow," Carlton says. He laughs, pleased with himself and the world. "That was so perfect."

I pick out what I can of "Blowin' in the Wind."

Carlton says, "Man when I saw you out there spying on us I thought to myself, *Yes*. Now *I'm* really here. You know what I'm saying?" He waves his apple core.

"Uh-huh," I say.

"Frisco, that was the first time her and I ever did it. I mean, we'd talked. But when we finally got down to it, there you were. My brother. Like you *knew*."

I nod, and this time for real. What happened was an adventure we had togeth-er. All right. The story is beginning to make sense.

"Aw, Frisco," Carlton says. "I'm gonna find you a girl too. You're nine. You been a virgin too long."

"Really?" I say.

"*Man.* We'll find you a woman from the sixth grade, somebody with a little ex-perience. We'll get stoned and all make out under the trees in the boneyard. I want to be present at your deflowering man. You're gonna need a brother there."

I am about to ask, as casually as I can manage, about the relationship between love and bodily pain, when our mother's voice cuts into the room. "You did it," she screams. "You tracked mud all over the rug."

A family entanglement follows. Our mother brings our father who comes and stands in the doorway with her, taking in evidence. He is a formerly handsome man. His face has been worn down by too much patience. He has lately taken up some sporty touches—a goatee, a pair of calfskin boots.

Our mother points out the trail of muddy half-moons that lead from the door to Carlton's bed. Dangling over the end of the bed are the culprits themselves, volup-tuously muddy, with Carlton's criminal feet still in them.

"You see?" she says. "You see what he thinks of me?"

Our father, a reasonable man, suggested that Carlton clean it up. Our mother finds that too small a gesture. She wants Carlton not to have done it in the first place. "I don't ask for much," she says. "I don't ask where he goes. I don't ask why the police are sud-denly so interested in our house. I ask that he not track mud all over the floor. That's all." She squints in the glare of her own outrage.

"Better clean it right up," our father says to Carlton.

"And that's it?" Our mother says. "He cleans up the mess and all's forgiven?"

"Well, what do you want him to do? Lick it up?"

"I want some consideration," she says, turning helplessly to me. "That's what I want."

I shrug, at a loss. I sympathize with our mother but am not on her team.

"All right," she says. " I just won't bother cleaning the house anymore. I'll let you men handle it. I'll sit and watch television and throw my candy wrappers on the floor."

She starts out, cutting the air like a blade. On her way out, she picks up a jar of pencils, looks at it, and tosses the pencils on the floor. They fall like fortune-telling sticks, in pairs and crisscrosses.

Our father goes after her, calling her name. Her name is Isabel. We can hear them making their way across the house, our father calling, "Isabel, Isabel," while our mother, pleased with the way the pencils looked, dumps more things onto the floor.

"I hope she doesn't break the TV," I say.

"She'll do what she needs to do," Carlton tells me.

"I hate her," I say. I am not certain about that. I want to test the sound of it, to see if it's true.

"She's got more balls than any of us, Frisco," he says. "Better watch what you say about her."

I keep quiet. Soon I get up and start gathering pencils because I prefer that to lying around trying to follow the shifting lines of allegiance. Carlton goes for a sponge and starts in on the mud.

"You get shit on the carpet, you clean it up," he says. "Simple."

The time for all my questions about love has passed, and I am not so unhip as to force a subject. I know it will come up again. I make a neat bouquet of pencils. Our mother rages through the house.

Later, after she has thrown enough and we three have picked it all up, I lie on my bed thinking things over. Carlton is on the phone with his girlfriend, talking low. Our mother, becalmed but still dangerous, cooks dinner. She sings as she cooks, some slow forties number that must have been all over the jukes when her first husband's plane went down in the Pacific. Our father plays his clarinet in the basement. That is where he goes to practice, down among his woodworking tools, the neatly hung hammers and awls that throw oversized shadows in the light of the single bulb. If I put my ear to the floor I can hear him, pulling a long, low tomcat moan out of that horn. There is some strange comfort in pressing my ear to the carpet and hearing our father's music leaking up through the floorboards. Lying down, with my ear to the floor, I join in on my harmonica.

That spring our parents have a party to celebrate the sun's return. It has been a long, bitter winter, and now the first wild daisies are poking up on the lawns and among the graves.

Our parents' parties are mannerly affairs. Their friends, schoolteachers all, bring wine jugs and guitars. They are Ohio hip. Though they hold jobs and meet mortgages, they think of themselves as independent spirits on a spying mission. They have agreed to impersonate teachers until they write their novels, finish their dissertations, or just save up enough money to set themselves free.

Carlton and I are the lackeys. We take coats, fetch drinks. We have done this at every party since we were small, trading on our precocity, doing a brother act. We know the moves. A big, lipsticked woman who has devoted her maidenhood to ninth-grade math calls me Mr. Right. An assistant vice-principal in a Russian fur hat asks us both whether we expect to vote Democratic or Socialist. By sneaking sips I manage to get myself semi-crocked.

The reliability of the evening is derailed halfway through, however, by a half-dozen of Carlton's friends. They rap on the door and I go for it, anxious as a carnival sharp to see who will step up next and swallow the illusion that I'm a kindly sober nine-year-old child. I'm expecting callow adults, and what do I find but a pack of young outlaws, big-booted and wild-haired. Carlton's girlfriend stands in front, in an outfit made up almost entirely of fringe.

"Hi, Bobby," she says confidently. She comes from New York, and is more than just locally smart.

"Hi," I say. I let them all in despite a retrograde urge to lock the door and phone the police. Three are girls, four boys. They pass me in a cloud of dope smoke and sly-eyed greeting.

What they do is invade the party. Carlton is standing on the far side of the rumpus room, picking the next album, and his girl cuts straight through the crowd to his side. She has the bones and the loose, liquid moves that some people consider beautiful. She walks through that room as if she'd been sent to teach the whole party a lesson.

Carlton's face tips me off that this was planned. Our mother demands to know what's going on here. She is wearing a long, dark-red dress that doesn't interfere with her shoulders. When she dresses up, you can see what it is about her, or what it was. She is the source of Carlton's beauty. I have our father's face.

Carlton does some quick talking. Though it is against our mother's better judgement, the invaders are suffered to stay. One of them, an Eddie Haskell for all his leather and hair, tells her she is looking good. She is willing to hear it.

So the outlaws, house-sanctioned, start to mingle. I work my way over to Carlton's side, the side unoccupied by his girlfriend. I would like to say something ironic and wised-up, something that will band Carlton and me against every other person in the room. I can feel the shape of the comment I have in mind but, being a tipsy nine-year-old, can't get my mouth around it. What I say is "Shit, man."

Carlton's girl laughs. I would like to tell her what I have figured out about her but I am nine, and three-quarters gone on Tom Collinses. Even sober, I can only imagine a sharp-tongued wit.

"Hang on, Frisco," Carlton tells me. "This could turn into a real party."

I can tell by the light in his eyes what is going down. He has arranged a blind date between our parents friends and his own. It's a Woodstock move—he is plotting a future in which young and old have business together. I agree to hang on, and go to the kitchen, hoping to sneak a few knocks of gin.

There I find our father leaning up against the refrigerator. A line of butterfly-shaped magnets hovers around his head. "Are you enjoying this party?" he asks, touching his goatee. He is still getting used to being a man with a beard.

"Uh-huh."

"I am, too," he says sadly. He never meant to be a high school music teacher. The money question caught up with him.

"What do you think of this music?" he asks. Carlton has put the Stones on the turntable. Mick Jagger sings "19th Nervous Breakdown." Our father gestures in an openhanded way that takes in the room, the party, the whole house—everything the music touches.

"I like it," I say.

"So do I." He stirs his drink with his finger and sucks on the finger.

"I *love* it," I say, too loud. Something about our father leads me to raise my voice. I want to grab handfuls of music out of the air and stuff them into my mouth.

"I'm not sure I could say I love it," he says. "I'm not sure if I could say that, no. I would say I'm friendly to its intentions. I would say that if this is the direction music is going in, I won't stand in its way."

"Uh-huh," I say. I am already anxious to get back to the party but don't want to hurt his feelings. If he senses he's being avoided, he can fall into fits of apology more terrifying than our mother's rages.

"I think I may have been too rigid with my students," our father says. "Maybe over the summer you boys could teach me a few things about the music young people are listening to these days."

"Sure," I say loudly. We spend a minute waiting for the next thing to say.

"You boys are happy, aren't you?" he asks. "Are you enjoying this party?"

"We're having a great time," I say.

"I thought you were. I am, too."

I have by this time gotten myself to within jumping distance of the door. I call out, "Well, goodbye" and dive back into the party.

Something has happened in my absence. The party has started to roll. Call it an accident of history and the weather. Carlton's friends are on decent behavior, and our parents' friends have decided to give up some of their wine-and-folk-song propriety to see what they can learn. Carlton is dancing with a vice-principal's wife. Carlton's friend Frank, with his ancient child face, and I.Q. in the low sixties, dances with our mother. I see that our father has followed me out of the kitchen. He positions himself at the party's edge; I leap into its center. I invite the fuchsia-lipped math teacher to dance. She is only too happy. She is big and graceful as a parade float and I steer her effortlessly out into the middle of everything. My mother, who is known around school for Sicilian discipline, dances freely, which is news to everybody. There is no getting around her beauty.

The night rises higher and higher. A wildness sets in. Carlton throws new music on the turntable—Janis Joplin, the Doors, the Dead. The future shines for everyone, rich with the possibility of more nights exactly like this, even our father is pressed into dancing, which he does like a flightless bird, all flapping arms and potbelly. Still he dances. Our mother has a kiss for him.

Finally I nod out on the sofa, blissful under the drinks. I am dreaming of flight when our mother comes and touches my shoulder. I smile up into her flushed, smiling face.

"Its hours past your bedtime," she says, all velvet motherliness. I nod. I can't dispute the fact.

She keeps on nudging my shoulder. I am a moment or two apprehending the fact that she actually wants me to leave the party and go to bed. "No," I tell her.

"Yes," she smiles.

"No," I say cordially, experimentally. This new mother can dance, and flirt. Who knows what else she might allow.

"Yes." The velvet motherliness leaves her voice. She means business, business of the usual kind. I get myself off the sofa and I run to Carlton for protection. He is laughing with his girl, a sweaty question mark of hair plastered to his forehead. I plow into him so hard he nearly goes over.

"Whoa, Frisco," he says. He takes me up under the arms and swings me a half turn. Our mother plucks me out of his hands and sets me down, with a good, farm-style hold on the back of my neck.

"Say goodnight, Bobby," she says. She adds, for the benefit of Carlton's girl. "He should have been in bed before this party started."

"No," I holler. I try to twist loose, but our mother has a grip that could crack walnuts.

Carlton's girl tosses her hair and says, "Good night, baby." She smiles a victor's smile. She smooths the stray hair off Carlton's forehead.

"No," I scream again. Something about the way she touches his hair. Our mother calls our father, who comes and scoops me up and starts out of the room with me, holding me like a live bomb. Before I go, I lock eyes with Carlton. He shrugs and says, "Night, man." Our father hustles me out. I do not take it bravely. I leave flailing, too furious to cry, dribbling a thread of spittle.

Later I lie alone on my narrow bed, feeling the music hum in the coiled springs. Life is cracking open right there in our house. People are changing. By tomorrow, no one will be quite the same. How can they let me miss it? I dream up revenge against our parents, and worse for Carlton. He is the one who could have saved me. He could have banded with me against them. What I can't forgive is his shrug, his mild-eyed, "Night, man." He has joined the adults. He has made himself bigger and taken size from me. As the Doors thump "Strange Days," I hope something awful happens to him. I say so to myself.

Around midnight, dim-witted Frank announces he has seen a flying saucer hovering over the back yard. I can hear his deep, excited voice all the way in my room. He says it is like a blinking, luminous cloud. I hear half the party struggling out through the sliding glass door in a disorganized whooping knot. By that time everyone is so delirious a flying saucer would be just what they expected. That much celebration would logically attract an answering happiness from across the stars.

I get out of bed and sneak down the hall. I will not miss alien visitors for anyone, not even at the cost of our mother's wrath or our father's disappointment. I stop at the end of the hallway, though, embarrassed to be in pajamas. If there really are aliens, they will think I am the lowest member of the house. While I hesitate over whether to go back to my room to change, people start coming back inside, talking about a trick of the mist and an airplane. People resume their dancing.

Carlton must have jumped the back fence. He must have wanted to be there, alone, singular, in case they decided to take somebody with them. A few nights later I will go out and stand where he would have been standing. On the far side of the gully, now a river swollen with melted snow, the cemetery will gleam like a lost city. The moon will be full. I will hang around just as Carlton must have, hypnotized by the silver light on the stones, the white angel raising her arms up across the river.

According to our parents, the mystery is why he ran back into the house full tilt. Something in the graveyard may have scared him, he may have needed to break its spell, but I think it's more likely that when he came back to himself he just couldn't wait to return to the music and the people, the noisy disorder of continuing life.

Somebody has shut the sliding glass door. Carlton's girlfriend looks lazily out, touching base with her own reflection. I look, too. Carlton is running toward the house. I hesitate. Then I figure he can bump his nose. It will be a good joke on him.

I let him keep coming. His girlfriend sees him through her own reflection, starts to scream a warning just as Carlton hits the glass.

It is an explosion. Triangles of glass fly brightly through the room. I think that for him it must be more surprising than painful, like hitting water from a great height. He stands blinking for a moment. The whole party stops, stares, getting its bearing. Bob Dylan sings "Just Like a Woman." Carlton reaches up curiously to take out the shard of glass that is stuck in his neck, and that is when the blood starts. It shoots out of him. Our mother screams. Carlton steps forward into his girlfriend's arms and the two of them fall together. Our mother throws herself down on top of him and the girl. People shout their accident wisdom. Don't lift him. Call an ambulance. I watch from the hallway. Carlton's blood spurts, soaking into the carpet, spattering people's clothes. Our mother and father both try to plug the wound with their hands, but the blood just shoots between their fingers. Carlton looks more puzzled than anything, as if he can't quite follow this turn of events. "It's all right," our father tells him, trying to stop the blood. "It's all right, just don't move, it's all right." Carlton nods, and holds our father's hand. His eyes take on an astonished light. Our mother screams, "Is anybody *doing* anything?" What comes out of Carlton grows darker, almost black. I watch. Our father tries to get a hold on Carlton's neck while Carlton keeps trying to take his hand. Our mother's hair is matted with blood. It runs down her face. Carlton's girl holds him to her breasts, touches his hair, whispers in his ear.

He is gone by the time the ambulance gets there. You can see the life drain out of him. When his face goes slack, our mother wails. A part of her flies wailing through the house, where it will wail and rage forever. I feel our mother pass through me on her way out. She covers Carlton's body with her own.

He is buried in the cemetery out back. Years have passed—we are living in the future, and it has turned out differently from what we'd planned. Our mother has established her life of separateness behind the guest room door. Our father mutters his greetings to the door as he passes.

One April night, almost a year to the day after Carlton's accident, I hear cautious footsteps shuffling across the living-room floor after midnight. I run out eagerly, thinking of ghosts, but find only our father in moth-colored pajamas. He looks unsteadily at the dark air in front of him.

"Hi, Dad," I say from the doorway.

He looks in my direction. "Yes?"

"It's me, Bobby."

"Oh, Bobby," he says. "What are you doing up, young man?"

"Nothing," I tell him. "Dad?"

"Yes, son."

"Maybe you'd better come back to bed. O.K.?"

"Maybe I had," he says. "I just came out here for a drink of water, but I seem to have gotten turned around in the darkness. Yes, maybe I better had."

I take his hand and lead him down the hall to his room. The grandfather clock chimes the quarter-hour.

"Sorry," our father says.

I get him into bed. "There," I say. "O.K.?"

"Perfect. Could not be better."

"O.K. Good night."

"Good night. Bobby?"

"Uh-huh?"

"Why don't you stay a minute?" he says. "We could have ourselves a talk, you and me. How would that be?"

"O.K.," I say. I sit on the edge of his mattress. His bedside clock ticks off the minutes.

I can hear the low rasp of his breathing. Around our house, the Ohio night chirps and buzzes. The small gray finger of Carlton's stone pokes up among the others, within sight of the angel's white eyes. Above us, airplanes and satellites sparkle. People are flying even now toward New York or California, to take up lives of risk and invention.

I stay until our father has worked his way into a muttering sleep.

Carlton's girlfriend moved to Denver with her family a month before. I never learned what it was she'd whispered to him. Though she'd kept her head admirably during the accident, she lost it afterward. She cried so hard at the funeral that she had to be taken away by her mother—an older, redder-haired version of her. She started seeing a psychiatrist three times a week. Everyone, including my parents, talked about how hard it was for her, to have held a dying boy in her arms at that age. I'm grateful to her for holding my brother while he died, but I never once heard her mention the fact that though she had been through something terrible, at least she was still alive and going places. At least she had protected herself by trying to warn him. I can appreciate the intricacies of her pain. But as long as she was in Cleveland, I could never look her straight in the face. I couldn't talk about the wounds she suffered. I can't even write her name.

Fiesta, 1980

Junot Díaz

Junot Díaz was born in Santo Domingo in the Dominican Republic and moved to Central New Jersey with his family when he was still a boy. He attended Rutgers University in New Brunswick, N.J. where he received his Bachelor's degree, which he followed with a Master of Fine Arts degree from Cornell University. His short stories have appeared in such publications as The Paris Review, *the* New Yorker, African Voices, *and* Best American Short Stories 1996, *and they are collected in* Drown, *published by Riverhead Books in 1996. "Fiesta, 1980" is included in* Drown *and first appeared in* Story *magazine.*

Mami's youngest sister—my tía Yrma—finally made it to the United States that year. She and tío Miguel got themselves an apartment in the Bronx, off the Grand Concourse and everybody decided that we should have a party. Actually, my pops decided, but everybody—meaning Mami, tía Yrma, tío Miguel and their neighbors—thought it a dope idea. On the afternoon of the party Papi came back from work around six. Right on time. We were all dressed by then, which was a smart move on our part. If Papi had walked in and caught us lounging around in our underwear, he would have kicked our asses something serious.

He didn't say nothing to nobody, not even my moms. He just pushed past her, held up his hand when she tried to talk to him and headed right into the shower. Rafa gave me the look and I gave it back to him; we both knew Papi had been with that Puerto Rican woman he was seeing and wanted to wash off the evidence quick.

Mami looked really nice that day. The United States had finally put some meat on her; she was no longer the same flaca who had arrived here three years before. She had cut her hair short and was wearing tons of cheap-ass jewelry which on her

---

"Fiesta," by Junot Díaz, reprinted from *Drown,* 1996, Riverhead Books.

didn't look too lousy. She smelled like herself, like the wind through a tree. She always waited until the last possible minute to put on her perfume because she said it was a waste to spray it on early and then have to spray it on again once you got to the party.

We—meaning me, my brother, my little sister and Mami—waited for Papi to finish his shower. Mami seemed anxious, in her usual dispassionate way. Her hands adjusted the buckle of her belt over and over again. That morning, when she had gotten us up for school, Mami told us that she wanted to have a good time at the party. I want to dance, she said, but now, with the sun sliding out of the sky like spit off a wall, she seemed ready just to get this over with.

Rafa didn't much want to go to no party either, and me, I never wanted to go anywhere with my family. There was a baseball game in the parking lot outside and we could hear our friends, yelling, Hey, and, Cabrón, to one another. We heard the pop of a ball as it sailed over the cars, the clatter of an aluminum bat dropping to the concrete. Not that me or Rafa loved baseball; we just liked playing with the local kids, thrashing them at anything they were doing. By the sounds of the shouting, we both knew the game was close, either of us could have made a difference. Rafa frowned and when I frowned back, he put up his fist. Don't you mirror me, he said.

Don't you mirror me, I said.

He punched me—I would have hit him back but Papi marched into the living room with his towel around his waist, looking a lot smaller than he did when he was dressed. He had a few strands of hair around his nipples and a surly closed-mouth expression, like maybe he'd scalded his tongue or something.

Have they eaten? he asked Mami.

She nodded. I made you something.

You didn't let him eat, did you?

Ay, Dios mío, she said, letting her arms fall to her side.

Ay, Dios mío is right, Papi said.

I was never supposed to eat before our car trips, but earlier, when she had put out our dinner of rice, beans and sweet platanos, guess who had been the first one to clean his plate? You couldn't blame Mami really, she had been busy—cooking, getting ready, dressing my sister Madai. I should have reminded her not to feed me but I wasn't that sort of son.

Papi turned to me. Coño, muchacho, why did you eat?

Rafa had already started inching away from me. I'd once told him I considered him a low-down chickenshit for moving out of the way every time Papi was going to smack me.

Collateral damage, Rafa had said. Ever heard of it?

No.

Look it up.

Chickenshit or not, I didn't dare glance at him. Papi was old-fashioned; he expected your undivided attention when you were getting your ass whupped. You couldn't look him in the eye either—that wasn't allowed. Better to stare at his belly button, which was perfectly round and immaculate. Papi pulled me to my feet by my ear.

74

If you throw up—

I won't, I cried, tears in my eyes, more out of reflex than pain.

Ya, Ramón, ya. It's not his fault, Mami said.

They've known about this party forever. How did they think we were going to get there? Fly?

He finally let go of my ear and I sat back down. Madai was too scared to open her eyes. Being around Papi all her life had turned her into a major-league wuss. Anytime Papi raised his voice her lip would start trembling, like some specialized tuning fork. Rafa pretended that he had knuckles to crack and when I shoved him, he gave me a *Don't start* look. But even that little bit of recognition made me feel better.

I was the one who was always in trouble with my dad. It was like my God-given duty to piss him off, to do everything the way he hated. Our fights didn't bother me too much. I still wanted him to love me, something that never seemed strange or contradictory until years later, when he was out of our lives.

By the time my ear stopped stinging Papi was dressed and Mami was crossing each one of us, solemnly, like we were heading off to war. We said, in turn, Bendición, Mami, and she poked us in our five cardinal spots while saying, Que Dios te bendiga.

This was how all our trips began, the words that followed me every time I left the house.

None of us spoke until we were inside Papi's Volkswagen van. Brand-new, lime-green and bought to impress. Oh, we were impressed, but me, every time I was in that VW and Papi went above twenty miles an hour, I vomited. I'd never had trouble with cars before—that van was like my curse. Mami suspected it was the upholstery. In her mind, American things—appliances, mouthwash, funny-looking upholstery—all seemed to have an intrinsic badness about them. Papi was careful about taking me anywhere in the VW, but when he had to, I rode up front in Mami's usual seat so I could throw up out a window.

¿Cómo te sientas? Mami asked over my shoulder when Papi pulled onto the turnpike. She had her hand on the base of my neck. One thing about Mami, her palms never sweated.

I'm OK, I said, keeping my eyes straight ahead. I definitely didn't want to trade glances with Papi. He had this one look, furious and sharp, that always left me feeling bruised.

Toma. Mami handed me four mentas. She had thrown three out her window at the beginning of our trip, an offering to Eshú; the rest were for me.

I took one and sucked it slowly, my tongue knocking it up against my teeth. We passed Newark Airport without any incident. If Madai had been awake she would have cried because the planes flew so close to the cars.

How's he feeling? Papi asked.

Fine, I said. I glanced back at Rafa and he pretended like he didn't see me. That was the way he was, at school and at home. When I was in trouble, he didn't know me. Madai was solidly asleep, but even with her face all wrinkled up and drooling she looked cute, her hair all separated into twists.

I turned around and concentrated on the candy. Papi even started to joke that we might not have to scrub the van out tonight. He was beginning to loosen up, not checking his watch too much. Maybe he was thinking about that Puerto Rican woman or maybe he was just happy that we were all together. I could never tell. At the toll, he was feeling positive enough to actually get out of the van and search around under the basket for dropped coins. It was something he had once done to amuse Madai, but now it was habit. Cars behind us honked their horns and I slid down in my seat. Rafa didn't care; he grinned back at the other cars and waved. His actual job was to make sure no cops were coming. Mami shook Madai awake and as soon as she saw Papi stooping for a couple of quarters she let out this screech of delight that almost took off the top of my head.

That was the end of the good times. Just outside the Washington Bridge, I started feeling woozy. The smell of the upholstery got all up inside my head and I found myself with a mouthful of saliva. Mami's hand tensed on my shoulder and when I caught Papi's eye, he was like, No way. Don't do it.

The first time I got sick in the van Papi was taking me to the library. Rafa was with us and he couldn't believe I threw up. I was famous for my steel-lined stomach. A third-world childhood could give you that. Papi was worried enough that just as quick as Rafa could drop off the books we were on our way home. Mami fixed me one of her honey-and-onion concoctions and that made my stomach feel better. A week later we tried the library again and on this go-around I couldn't get the window open in time. When Papi got me home, he went and cleaned out the van himself, an expression of *askho* on his face. This was a big deal, since Papi almost never cleaned anything himself. He came back inside and found me sitting on the couch feeling like hell.

It's the car, he said to Mami. It's making him sick.

This time the damage was pretty minimal, nothing Papi couldn't wash off the door with a blast of the hose. He was pissed, though; he jammed his finger into my cheek, a nice solid thrust. That was the way he was with his punishments: imaginative. Earlier that year I'd written an essay in school called "My Father the Torturer," but the teacher made me write a new one. She thought I was kidding.

We drove the rest of the way to the Bronx in silence. We only stopped once, so I could brush my teeth. Mami had brought along my toothbrush and a tube of toothpaste and while every car known to man sped by us she stood outside with me so I wouldn't feel alone.

Tío Miguel was about seven feet tall and had his hair combed up and out, into a demi-fro. He gave me and Rafa big spleen-crushing hugs and then kissed Mami and finally ended up with Madai on his shoulder. The last time I'd seen Tío was at the airport, his first day in the United States. I remembered how he hadn't seemed all that troubled to be in another country.

He looked down at me. Carajo, Yunior, you look horrible!

He threw up, my brother explained.

I pushed Rafa. Thanks a lot, ass-face.

Hey, he said. Tío asked.

Tío clapped a bricklayer's hand on my shoulder. Everybody gets sick sometimes, he said. You should have seen me on the plane over here. Dios mio! He rolled his Asian-looking eyes for emphasis. I thought we were all going to die.

Everybody could tell he was lying. I smiled like he was making me feel better.

Do you want me to get you a drink? Tío asked. We got beer and rum.

Miguel, Mami said. He's young.

Young? Back in Santo Domingo, he'd be getting laid by now.

Mami thinned her lips, which took some doing.

Well, it's true, Tío said.

So, Mami, I said. When do I get to go visit the D.R.?

That's enough, Yunior.

It's the only pussy you'll ever get, Rafa said to me in English.

Not counting your girlfriend, of course.

Rafa smiled. He had to give me that one.

Papi came in from parking the van. He and Miguel gave each other the sort of handshakes that would have turned my fingers into Wonder bread.

Coño, compa'i, ¿cómo va todo? they said to each other.

Tía came out then, with an apron on and maybe the longest Lee Press-On Nails I've ever seen in my life. There was this one guru motherfucker in the *Guinness Book of World Records* who had longer nails, but I tell you, it was close. She gave everybody kisses, told me and Rafa how guapo we were—Rafa, of course, believed her—told Madai how bella she was, but when she got to Papi, she froze a little, like maybe she'd seen a wasp on the tip of his nose, but then kissed him all the same.

Mami told us to join the other kids in the living room. Tío said, Wait a minute, I want to show you the apartment. I was glad Tía said, Hold on, because from what I'd seen so far, the place had been furnished in Contemporary Dominican Tacky. The less I saw, the better. I mean, I liked plastic sofa covers but damn, Tío and Tía had taken it to another level. They had a disco ball hanging in the living room and the type of stucco ceilings that looked like stalactite heaven. The sofas all had golden tassels dangling from their edges. Tía came out of the kitchen with some people I didn't know and by the time she got done introducing everybody, only Papi and Mami were given the guided tour of the four-room third-floor apartment. Me and Rafa joined the kids in the living room. They'd already started eating. We were hungry, one of the girls explained, a pastelito in hand. The boy was about three years younger than me but the girl who'd spoken, Leti, was my age. She and another girl were on the sofa together and they were cute as hell.

Leti introduced them: the boy was her brother Wilquins and the other girl was her neighbor Mari. Leti had some serious tetas and I could tell that my brother was going to gun for her. His taste in girls was predictable. He sat down right between Leti and Mari and by the way they were smiling at him I knew he'd do fine. Neither of the girls gave me more than a cursory one-two, which didn't bother me. Sure, I liked girls but I was always too terrified to speak to them unless we were arguing or I was calling them stupidos, which was one of my favorite words that year. I turned to Wilquins and asked him what there was to do around here. Mari, who had the lowest voice I'd ever heard, said, He can't speak.

What does that mean?

He's mute.

I looked at Wilquins incredulously. He smiled and nodded, as if he'd won a prize or something.

Does he understand? I asked.

Of course he understands, Rafa said. He's not dumb.

I could tell Rafa had said that just to score points with the girls. Both of them nodded. Low-voice Mari said, He's the best student in his grade.

I thought, Not bad for a mute. I sat next to Wilquins. After about two seconds of TV Wilquins whipped out a bag of dominos and motioned to me. Did I want to play? Sure. Me and him played Rafa and Leti and we whupped their collective asses twice, which put Rafa in a real bad mood. He looked at me like maybe he wanted to take a swing, just one to make him feel better. Leti kept whispering into Rafa's ear, telling him it was OK.

In the kitchen I could hear my parents slipping into their usual modes. Papi's voice was loud and argumentative; you didn't have to be anywhere near him to catch his drift. And Mami, you had to put cups to your ears to hear hers. I went into the kitchen a few times—once so the tíos could show off how much bullshit I'd been able to cram in my head the last few years; another time for a bucket-sized cup of soda. Mami and Tía were frying tostones and the last of the pastelitos. She appeared happier now and the way her hands worked on our dinner you would think she had a life somewhere else making rare and precious things. She nudged Tía every now and then, shit they must have been doing all their lives. As soon as Mami saw me though, she gave me the eye. Don't stay long, that eye said. Don't piss your old man off.

Papi was too busy arguing about Elvis to notice me. Then somebody mentioned María Montez and Papi barked, María Montez? Let me tell *you* about María Montez, compa'i.

Maybe I was used to him. His voice—louder than most adults'—didn't bother me none, though the other kids shifted uneasily in their seats. Wilquins was about to raise the volume on the TV, but Rafa said, I wouldn't do that. Muteboy had balls, though. He did it anyway and then sat down. Wilquins's pop came into the living room a second later, a bottle of Presidente in hand. That dude must have had Spider-senses or something. Did you raise that? he asked Wilquins and Wilquins nodded.

Is this your house? his pops asked. He looked ready to beat Wilquins silly but he lowered the volume instead.

See, Rafa said. You nearly got your ass *kicked*.

I met the Puerto Rican woman right after Papi had gotten the van. He was taking me on short trips, trying to cure me of my vomiting. It wasn't really working but I looked forward to our trips, even though at the end of each one I'd be sick. These were the only times me and Papi did anything together. When we were alone he treated me much better, like maybe I was his son or something.

Before each drive Mami would cross me.

Bendición, Mami, I'd say.

She'd kiss my forehead. Que Dios te bendiga. And then she would give me a handful of mentas because she wanted me to be OK. Mami didn't think these excursions would cure anything, but the one time she had brought it up to Papi he had told her to shut up, what did she know about anything anyway?

Me and Papi didn't talk much. We just drove around our neighborhood. Occasionally he'd ask, How is it?

And I'd nod, no matter how I felt.

One day I was sick outside of Perth Amboy. Instead of taking me home he went the other way on Industrial Avenue, stopping a few minutes later in front of a light blue house I didn't recognize. It reminded me of the Easter eggs we colored at school, the ones we threw out the bus windows at other cars.

The Puerto Rican woman was there and she helped me clean up. She had dry papery hands and when she rubbed the towel on my chest, she did it hard, like I was a bumper she was waxing. She was very thin and had a cloud of brown hair rising above her narrow face and the sharpest blackest eyes you've ever seen.

He's cute, she said to Papi.

Not when he's throwing up, Papi said.

What's your name? she asked me. Are you Rafa?

I shook my head.

Then it's Yunior, right?

I nodded.

You're the smart one, she said, suddenly happy with herself. Maybe you want to see my books?

They weren't hers. I recognized them as ones my father must have left in her house. Papi was a voracious reader, couldn't even go cheating without a paperback in his pocket.

Why don't you go watch TV? Papi suggested. He was looking at her like she was the last piece of chicken on earth.

We got plenty of channels, she said. Use the remote if you want.

The two of them went upstairs and I was too scared of what was happening to poke around. I just sat there, ashamed, expecting something big and fiery to crash down on our heads. I watched a whole hour of the news before Papi came downstairs and said, Let's go.

About two hours later the women laid out the food and like always nobody but the kids thanked them. It must be some Dominican tradition or something. There was everything I liked—chicharrones, fried chicken, tostones, sancocho, rice, fried cheese, yuca, avocado, potato salad, a meteor-sized hunk of pernil, even a tossed salad which I could do without—but when I joined the other kids around the serving table, Papi said, Oh no you don't, and took the paper plate out of my hand. His fingers weren't gentle.

What's wrong now? Tía asked, handing me another plate.

He ain't eating, Papi said. Mami pretended to help Rafa with the pernil.

Why can't he eat?

Because I said so.

The adults who didn't know us made like they hadn't heard a thing and Tío just smiled sheepishly and told everybody to go ahead and eat. All the kids—about ten of them now—trooped back into the living room with their plates a-heaping and all the adults ducked into the kitchen and the dining room, where the radio was playing loud-ass bachatas. I was the only one without a plate. Papi stopped me before I could get away from him. He kept his voice nice and low so nobody else could hear him.

If you eat anything, I'm going to beat you. ¿Entiendes?

I nodded.

And if your brother gives you any food, I'll beat him too. Right here in front of everybody. ¿Entiendes?

I nodded again. I wanted to kill him and he must have sensed it because he gave my head a little shove.

All the kids watched me come in and sit down in front of the TV.

What's wrong with your dad? Leti asked.

He's a dick, I said.

Rafa shook his head. Don't say that shit in front of people.

Easy for you to be nice when you're eating, I said.

Hey, if I was a pukey little baby, I wouldn't get no food either.

I almost said something back but I concentrated on the TV. I wasn't going to start it. No fucking way. So I watched Bruce Lee beat Chuck Norris into the floor of the Colosseum and tried to pretend that there was no food anywhere in the house. It was Tía who finally saved me. She came into the living room and said, Since you ain't eating, Yunior, you can at least help me get some ice.

I didn't want to, but she mistook my reluctance for something else.

I already asked your father.

She held my hand while we walked; Tía didn't have any kids but I could tell she wanted them. She was the sort of relative who always remembered your birthday but who you only went to visit because you had to. We didn't get past the first-floor landing before she opened her pocketbook and handed me the first of three pastelitos she had smuggled out of the apartment.

Go ahead, she said. And as soon as you get inside make sure you brush your teeth.

Thanks a lot, Tía, I said.

Those pastelitos didn't stand a chance.

She sat next to me on the stairs and smoked her cigarette. All the way down on the first floor and we could still hear the music and the adults and the television. Tía looked a ton like Mami; the two of them were both short and light-skinned. Tía smiled a lot and that was what set them apart the most.

How is it at home, Yunior?

What do you mean?

How's it going in the apartment? Are you kids OK?

I knew an interrogation when I heard one, no matter how sugar-coated it was. I didn't say anything.

Don't get me wrong, I loved my tía, but something told me to keep my mouth shut. Maybe it was family loyalty, maybe I just wanted to protect Mami or I was afraid that Papi would find out—it could have been anything really.

Is your mom all right?

I shrugged.

Have there been lots of fights?

None, I said. Too many shrugs would have been just as bad as an answer. Papi's at work too much.

Work, Tía said, like it was somebody's name she didn't like.

Me and Rafa, we didn't talk much about the Puerto Rican woman. When we ate dinner at her house, the few times Papi had taken us over there, we still acted like nothing was out of the ordinary. Pass the ketchup, man. No sweat, bro. The affair was like a hole in our living room floor, one we'd gotten so used to circumnavigating that we sometimes forgot it was there.

By midnight all the adults were crazy dancing. I was sitting outside Tía's bedroom—where Madai was sleeping—trying not to attract attention. Rafa had me guarding the door; he and Leti were in there too, with some of the other kids, getting busy no doubt. Wilquins had gone across the hall to bed so I had me and the roaches to mess around with.

Whenever I peered into the main room I saw about twenty moms and dads dancing and drinking beers.

Every now and then somebody yelled, Quisqueya! And then everybody else would yell and stomp their feet. From what I could see my parents seemed to be enjoying themselves.

Mami and Tía spent a lot of time side by side, whispering, and I kept expecting something to come of this, a brawl maybe. I'd never once been out with my family when it hadn't turned to shit. We weren't even theatrical or straight crazy like other families. We fought like sixth-graders, without any real dignity. I guess the whole night I'd been waiting for a blowup, something between Papi and Mami. This was how I always figured Papi would be exposed, out in public, where everybody would know.

You're a cheater!

But everything was calmer than usual. And Mami didn't look like she was about to say anything to Papi.

The two of them danced every now and then but they never lasted more than a song before Mami joined Tía again in whatever conversation they were having.

I tried to imagine Mami before Papi. Maybe I was tired, or just sad, thinking about the way my family was. Maybe I already knew how it would all end up in a few years, Mami without Papi, and that was why I did it. Picturing her alone wasn't easy. It seemed like Papi had always been with her, even when we were waiting in Santo Domingo for him to send for us.

The only photograph our family had of Mami as a young woman, before she married Papi, was the one that somebody took of her at an election party that I found one day while rummaging for money to go to the arcade. Mami had it tucked into her immigration papers. In the photo, she's surrounded by laughing cousins I will never meet, who are all shiny from dancing, whose clothes are rumpled and loose. You can tell it's night and hot and that the mosquitos have been biting. She sits straight and even in a crowd she stands out, smiling quietly like maybe she's the one everybody's celebrating. You can't see her hands but I imagined they're knotting a straw or a bit of thread. This was the woman my father met a year later on the Malecón, the woman Mami thought she'd always be.

Mami must have caught me studying her because she stopped what she was doing and gave me a smile, maybe her first one of the night. Suddenly I wanted to go over and hug her, for no other reason than I loved her, but there were about eleven fat jiggling bodies between us. So I sat down on the tiled floor and waited.

I must have fallen asleep because the next thing I knew Rafa was kicking me and saying, Let's go. He looked like he'd been hitting those girls off; he was all smiles. I got to my feet in time to kiss Tía and Tío good-bye. Mami was holding the serving dish she had brought with her.

Where's Papi? I asked.

He's downstairs, bringing the van around. Mami leaned down to kiss me.

You were good today, she said.

And then Papi burst in and told us to get the hell downstairs before some pendejo cop gave him a ticket. More kisses, more handshakes and then we were gone.

I don't remember being out of sorts after I met the Puerto Rican woman, but I must have been because Mami only asked me questions when she thought something was wrong in my life. It took her about ten passes but finally she cornered me one afternoon when we were alone in the apartment. Our upstairs neighbors were beating the crap out of their kids, and me and her had been listening to it all afternoon. She put her hand on mine and said, Is everything OK, Yunior? Have you been fighting with your brother?

Me and Rafa had already talked. We'd been in the basement, where our parents couldn't hear us. He told me that yeah, he knew about her.

Papi's taken me there twice now, he said.

Why didn't you tell me? I asked.

What the hell was I going to say? *Hey, Yunior, guess what happened yesterday. I met Papi's sucia!*

I didn't say anything to Mami either. She watched me, very very closely. Later I would think, maybe if I had told her she would have confronted him, would have done something, but who can know these things? I said I'd been having trouble in school and like that everything was back to normal between us. She put her hand on my shoulder and squeezed and that was that.

We were on the turnpike, just past Exit 11, when I started feeling it again. I sat up from leaning against Rafa. His fingers smelled and he'd gone to sleep almost as soon as he got into the van. Madai was out too but at least she wasn't snoring.

In the darkness, I saw that Papi had a hand on Mami's knee and that the two of them were quiet and still. They weren't slumped back or anything; they were both wide awake, bolted into their seats. I couldn't see either of their faces and no matter how hard I tried I could not imagine their expressions. Neither of them moved. Every now and then the van was filled with the bright rush of somebody else's headlights. Finally I said, Mami, and they both looked back, already knowing what was happening.

Who Shot Johnny?

Debra Dickerson

A graduate of Harvard Law School, Debra Dickerson worked as a lawyer for the NAPC before deciding to become a full time writer. She contributes regularly to The Nation *while also publishing in* The Christian Science Monitor, The Boston Review, *and* Good Housekeeping. *She currently lives in Arlington, Virginia.*

Given my level of political awareness, it was inevitable that I would come to view the everyday events of my life through the prism of politics and the national discourse. I read *The Washington Post, The New Republic, The New Yorker, Harper's, The Atlantic Monthly, The Nation, National Review, Black Enterprise,* and *Essence* and wrote a weekly column for the Harvard Law School *Record* during my three years just ended there. I do this because I know that those of us who are not well-fed white guys in suits must not yield the debate to them, however well-intentioned or well-informed they may be. Accordingly, I am unrepentant and vocal about having gained admittance to Harvard through affirmative action; I am a feminist, stoic about my marriage chances as a well-educated, thirty-six-year-old black woman who won't pretend to need help taking care of herself. My strength flags, though, in the face of the latest role assigned to my family in the national drama. On July 27, 1995, my sixteen-year-old nephew was shot and paralyzed.

Talking with friends in front of his house, Johnny saw a car he thought he recognized. He waved boisterously—his trademark—throwing both arms in the air in a full-bodied, hop-hop Y. When he got no response, he and his friends sauntered down the walk to join a group loitering in front of an apartment building. The car followed. The driver got out, brandished a revolver, and fired into the air. Everyone scattered. Then he took aim and shot my running nephew in the back.

"Who Shot Johnny?" by Debra Dickerson, reprinted from *The Best American Essays,* 1998.

Johnny never lost consciousness. He lay in the road, trying to understand what had happened to him, why he couldn't get up. Emotionlessly, he told the story again and again on demand, remaining apologetically firm against all demands to divulge the missing details that would make sense of the shooting but obviously cast him in a bad light. Being black, male, and shot, he must apparently be involved with gangs or drugs. Probably both. Witnesses corroborate his version of events.

Nearly six months have passed since that phone call in the night and my nightmarish headlong drive from Boston to Charlotte. After twenty hours behind the wheel, I arrived haggard enough to reduce my mother to fresh tears and to find my nephew reassuring well-wishers with an eerie sang-froid.

I take the day shift in his hospital room; his mother and grandmother, a clerk and cafeteria worker, respectively, alternate nights there on a cot. They don their uniforms the next day, gaunt after hours spent listening to Johnny moan in his sleep. How often must his subconscious replay those events and curse its host for saying hello without permission, for being carefree and young while a would-be murderer hefted the weight of his uselessness and failure like Jacob Marley's* chains? How often must he watch himself lying stubbornly immobile on the pavement of his nightmares while the sound of running feet syncopate his attacker's taunts?

I spend these days beating him at gin rummy and Scrabble, holding a basin while he coughs up phlegm and crying in the corridor while he catheterizes himself. There are children here much worse off than he. I should be grateful. The doctors can't, or won't, say whether he'll walk again.

I am at once repulsed and fascinated by the bullet, which remains lodged in his spine (having done all the damage it can do, the doctors say). The wound is undramatic—small, neat, and perfectly centered—an impossibly pink pit surrounded by an otherwise undisturbed expanse of mahogany. Johnny has asked me several times to describe it but politely declines to look in the mirror I hold for him.

Here on the pediatric rehab ward, Johnny speaks little, never cries, never complains, works diligently to become independent. He does whatever he is told; if two hours remain until the next pain pill, he waits quietly. Eyes bloodshot, hands gripping the bed rails. During the week of his intravenous feeding, when he was tormented by the primal need to masticate, he never asked for food. He just listened while we counted down the days for him and planned his favorite meals. Now required to dress himself unassisted, he does so without demur, rolling himself back and forth valiantly on the bed and shivering afterward, exhausted. He "ma'am"s and "sir"s everyone politely. Before his "accident," a simple request to take out the trash could provoke a firestorm of teenage attitude. We, the women who have raised him, have changed as well; we've finally come to appreciate those boxer-baring, oversized pants we used to hate—it would be much more difficult to fit properly sized pants over his diaper.

He spends a lot of time tethered to rap music still loud enough to break my concentration as I read my many magazines. I hear him try to soundlessly mouth the

* Jacob Marley: The doomed ghost in Charles Dickens's *A Christmas Carol.*

85

obligatory "mothafuckers" overlaying the funereal dirge of the music tracks. I do not normally tolerate disrespectful music in my or my mother's presence, but if it distracts him now . . .

"Johnny," I ask later, "do you still like gangster rap?" During the long pause I hear him think loudly, I'm paralyzed Auntie, not stupid. "I mostly just listen to hip-hop," he says evasively into his *Sports Illustrated.*

Miserable though it is, time passes quickly here. We always seem to be jerking awake in our chairs just in time for the next pill, his every-other-night bowel program, the doctor's rounds. Harvard feels a galaxy away—the world revolves around Family Members Living with Spinal Cord Injury class, Johnny's urine output, and strategizing with my sister to find affordable, accessible housing. There is always another long-distance uncle in need of an update, another church member wanting to pray with us, or Johnny's little brother in need of some attention.

We Dickerson women are so constant a presence the ward nurses and cleaning staff call us by name and join us for cafeteria meals and cigarette breaks. At Johnny's birthday pizza party, they crack jokes and make fun of each other's husbands (there are no men here). I pass slices around and try not to think, Seventeen with a bullet.

Oddly, we feel little curiosity or specific anger toward the man who shot him. We have to remind ourselves to check in with the police. Even so, it feels pro forma, like sending in those $2 rebate forms that come with new pantyhose: you know your request will fall into a deep, dark hole somewhere, but still, it's your duty to try. We push for an arrest because we owe it to Johnny and to ourselves as citizens. We don't think about it otherwise—our low expectations are too ingrained. A Harvard aunt notwithstanding, for people like Johnny, Marvin Gaye was right that only three things are sure: taxes, death, and trouble. At least it wasn't the second.

We rarely wonder about or discuss the brother who shot him because we already know everything about him. When the call came, my first thought was the same one I'd had when I'd heard about Rosa Parks's beating: a brother did it. A non-job-having, middle-of-the-day malt-liquor-drinking, crotch-clutching, loud-talking brother with many neglected children born of many forgotten women. He lives in his mother's basement with furniture rented at an astronomical interest rate, the exact amount of which he does not know. He has a car phone, an $80 monthly cable bill, and every possible phone feature but no savings. He steals Social Security numbers from unsuspecting relatives and assumes their identities to acquire large TV sets for which he will never pay. On the slim chance that he is brought to justice, he will have a colorful criminal history and no coherent explanation to offer for his act. His family will raucously defend him and cry cover-up. Some liberal lawyer just like me will help him plea-bargain his way to yet another short stay in a prison pesthouse that will serve only to add another layer to the brother's sociopathology and formless, mindless nihilism. We know him. We've known and feared him all our lives.

As a teenager, he called, "Hey, baby, gimme somma that boodie!" at us from car windows. Indignant at our lack of response, he followed up with, "Fuck you, then, 'ho!" He called me a "white-boy-lovin' nigger bitch oreo" for being in the gifted program and loving it. At twenty-seven, he got my seventeen-year-old sister pregnant with Johnny and lost interest without ever informing her that he was married. He snatched my widowed mother's purse as she waited in predawn darkness for the bus to work and then broke into our house while she soldered on an assembly line. He chased all the small entrepreneurs from our neighborhood with his violent thievery and put bars on our windows. He kept us from sitting on our own front porch after dark and laid the foundation for our periodic bouts of self-hating anger and racial embarrassment. He made our neighborhood a ghetto. He is the poster fool behind the maddening community knowledge that there are still some black mothers who raise their daughters but merely love their sons. He and his cancerous carbon copies eclipse the vast majority of us who are not sociopaths and render us invisible. He is the Siamese twin who has died but cannot be separated from his living, vibrant sibling; which of us must attract more notice? We despise and disown this anomalous loser, but for many he *is* black America. We know him, we know that he is outside the fold, and we know that he will only get worse. What we didn't know is that, because of him, my little sister would one day be the latest hysterical black mother wailing over a fallen child on TV.

Alone, lying in the road bleeding and paralyzed but hideously conscious, Johnny had lain helpless as he watched his would-be murderer come to stand over him and offer this prophecy: "Betch'ou won't be doin' nomo' wavin', mothafucker."

Fuck you, asshole. He's fine from the waist up. You just can't do anything right, can you?

I Heard a Fly Buzz When I Died (XLVLI)

Emily Dickinson

Emily Dickinson was born on December 10, 1830 in Amherst, Massachusetts, USA. She attended Amherst Academy and Mount Holyoke Female Seminary (now Mount Holyoke College). Only ten of her poems were published in her lifetime. Like most women in that time period, she excelled at domestic activities and led a rather isolated life. After her death on May 15, 1886 over 1700 poems, which she had bound into booklets, were discovered. The fame of her poetry has spread and now she is acclaimed throughout the world.

1.

I heard a fly buzz when I died;
   The stillness round my form
Was like the stillness in the air
   Between the heaves of storm.

The eyes beside had wrung them dry,
   And breaths were gathering sure
For that last onset, when the king
   Be witnessed in his power.

I willed my keepsakes, signed away
   What portion of me I
Could make assignable,—and then
   There interposed a fly,

With blue, uncertain, stumbling buzz,
   Between the light and me;
And then the windows failed, and then
   I could not see to see.

September, 1973

Ariel Dorfman

*Ariel Dorfman was born in Argentina, the son of Jewish parents
who grew up speaking Yiddish and Russian as well as Spanish. In
1943, his father left Argentina and began working for the United
Nations in New York. Soon after, Dorfman learned to speak English and refused to speak any other language with his parents. In
1954, his parents moved to Chile, where he continued to speak English but he was again attracted to Spanish. In 1968, Dorfman,
who had married a Chilean and had a son, came back to the US
to teach at Berkeley. After a year and a half of cultural experi-
mentation, he returned to Chile and became involved with the
effort of bringing Salvador Allende to power. In 1973 he narrowly
missed being killed during the military coup against Allende. After
the coup, Dorfman left Chile and now lives in exile in the US. His
works include* Death and the Maiden *and* Konfidenz, *both dealing
with terrorism and its consequences on the personal lives of people.
The following story is part of a memoir and refers to the events surrounding the military coup that overthrew Allende's government.*

It is late in September.

I have taken refuge in the house of the Israeli Ambassador.

You have said goodbye to me, my love, and now you are going down the stairs.
Soon the sound of the door to the Embassy will be heard closing, your small figure
will pass to the other side of the gates, and then you will cross the street. That's
where the two men come up to speak to you. The conversation hardly lasts as long
as it takes for a cigarette to be lit by the smaller man, the one with the checked jacket. The other one looks you in the eyes and your eyes must feel distant and startled

"September, 1973," by Ariel Dorfman, reprinted from *Granta: The Magazine of New Writing*,
Volume 60, 1998, John Wiley/The Wiley Agency.

at that instant. Then they invite you to get into the car. One of them takes your arm, but he does so with discretion, almost courteously. The motor is running, humming like a well-fed cat, but the car does not move. Now you're getting in, you and the smaller man in the back, and the other one in front. His strong, decisive shoulders form a contrast to his apologetic lips, to the thin impoverished wisp of his moustache. It will not be possible to see you. Only, all of a sudden, your hand which accepts a cigarette and then cups the flickering flame of the lighter. Your other hand can only be seen on one occasion, for a moment fluttering on the top of the back seat, fingers that hesitate, the shine of a wedding ring. Then it withdraws. The man in the front, seated next to the empty driver's seat, is the one asking the questions. Now, with his left hand, he turns off the engine and pockets the keys. That means they do not plan to leave right away. He will remain half-hunched up against the door, one leg raised, the shoe pushing against the upholstery, fingers intertwined at the knee. Once in a while, he scratches under his sock, rubs the skin compressed by his sock. They will not be in a hurry. Children will pass by on bikes calling each other by the names their parents gave them many years ago; the mailman will cross this spring day that seems like summer bringing news and ads and maybe letters from lost loves; mothers will go for a morning stroll and teach their kids how to stand up on two feet, take a step or two instead of crawling. Now a bird perches itself on the warm roof of the car and, without even a trill, flies off like an arrow. Maybe, inside, you've detected that slight presence, that slighter absence, like a leaf that falls from a tree out of season, a bit too late; maybe you've understood that a pair of wings opened up and then was gone. The man extracts a small notebook from a pocket in his jacket, and then a pencil. He passes it to you. During the briefest wave of time, your hand can be seen receiving the pencil, the notebook. Then, as if you were not really there in the back seat of the car, that extension of your body disappears and nothing more can be seen. The man tosses his keys up into the air and catches them neatly. He smiles. He points a key at you and says something, it must be a question. Impossible to know what you answered. A beggar woman stumbles down the street, a flock of ragtag kids in her wake. She approaches the car to ask for something, and then she backs off, half-understanding or not wanting to understand. Now the car window opens and the swarthy face of the smaller man appears, the man who has been sitting next to you. He hasn't slept much, hasn't slept well: there are bags under his eyes and his features are puffy. He blinks under that implacable daylight. Then he looks towards the Embassy for a while, giving the windows the once-over to see if there is somebody watching, if there is somebody behind half-drawn curtains trying to register and remember each movement, each gesture. He stays like that for a good while, motionless, as if he could guess what is happening behind those walls. He takes out a handkerchief and wipes it across his forehead, cleans the sweat from the rest of his face. He needs to shave, he needs to get home for a good shave. Maybe all night while he waited he's been thinking of the bath full of hot water. The air dances with white spores; he blinks his heavy eyelids. The breeze has begun to fall asleep under the spell of the day's heat. He emerges from the car quickly. A stream of sunlight slides down his body. Now he gets back into the car, into the driver's seat. He holds his hand out so the other man can give him the keys. The sound of the back door that opened and closed, the front door that opened and closed, does not disturb the quiet. It's almost like a sound of harmony, sweet metal. The car moves off, passes the house, passes the curtained windows, for an eternal white instant your petite face can be seen, the way your shoulders breathe, that dress which presses to your body like the skin of a lover. You will pass without looking towards the house, your face will pass, your eyes sinking into the abrupt horizon of the street which connects with other streets. But they will not take you away. Now the car brakes a bit further on, sheltered under the generous shade of that tree you have come to know so well, that you have heard moaning and dancing its branches below the weight of the wind last night. All that can be seen is the back of the car, and in a hollow opened by the leaves gently swaying with the rays of this spring that has quickened into summer, a blur of colour that could be your hair or your neck trembling under your hair. If it were not for the leisurely and merciless progress of the minute hand on your wristwatch, where the slow blood inside your arm finds and flows with the mysterious blood inside your hand, if it were not for the imperceptible rotation of this planet, it might be thought that time had stagnated, that all movement is paralysed, that silence is definitive, and that you will stay here for ever, you, the men, the car, the street. No beggar will pass. The mailman will not come back again. The children will have to put away their bicycles and go and eat lunch. When the sun begins to invade the top of the car, when midday has finally concluded and the afternoon has finally begun, when the intolerable heat forces the driver to seek a new refuge, nothing in the world, neither the buzzing of bees nor the yellow cheerful burst of the flowers, will be able to stop that engine from being started up again, that car from inching away from the kerb, and this time it will not pause under the shade or in the sun, this time the car will go on and on and on, nothing can stop it from losing itself there, far away, down the street which connects with other streets, taking you to that place from where you will never return.

This story, seemingly fictitious, really happened. It happened to us, to Angélica and to me, exactly as written here, exactly as I wrote it many years later. Except for the ending. They did not take her away, not for a day, not for a month, not for all time. But the rest is true: by the end of September I had taken temporary refuge in the residence of one of my mother's friends, the wife of the Israeli Ambassador, waiting during the next week for a chance to slip into one of the heavily guarded Latin American Embassies that could guarantee me safe conduct out of the country. And when Angélica had come to visit me and spend the night, the next morning she had been detained by two of Pinochet's secret policemen who had been watching the house under the impression that Senator Carlos Altamirano, the fugitive head of the Socialist party, thin and bespectacled like me, had sought refuge there. An absurd notion, given his pro-Palestinian sympathies. But Angélica managed to outwit those detectives without discussing international affairs and escaped the fate the character in the story was unable to avoid.

When many years later I came to write the experience, I ended it differently, tragically, partly because that is the way most episodes like this one do end, but mainly, I think, because that was the only way of transmitting to myself and others the horror of what went on in my mind during that hour when the woman I loved was in the hands of men who could do anything they wanted to her, anything they wanted and I could do nothing to stop them. That ending did not happen in reality but it did repeat itself over and over in my imagination as I watched from a window, praying I would not have to watch it over and over in the days and years to come in my memory, praying that I would not have to imagine a world without Angélica.

Discovering, after so many days obsessed with my ever-increasing distance from the country, that I would rather lose Chile than lose Angélica, that I could live without Chile but that I could not live without Angélica, beginning to understand that the private home I had built with her was more important and would outlast the public home I had sought to build with Chile and its people.

It was then, I think, that for the first time in my life I clearly separated my wife from the country where she had been born.

Ever since I had met her, Angélica had been confused, in my mind, with Chile. All the readings and all the trips and all the protests and all the snow on all the mountains did less to attach me to that country than this one frail human being.

There I was in early 1961, a stranger in a land that I had inhabited for seven years without finding a real gateway, whose songs and customs and people I hardly knew, no matter how much I had come to admire them, regard them as a potential avenue for liberation. And then, one day, Angélica. To be quite frank, what enchanted me about her to begin with were her dazzling looks and fiery spirit and extreme joy of life, the hot sexual thought of a lithe *moreno* body under her dress, that enchanting smile of hers that the gods of advertising couldn't have coached out of a woman if they had been given a thousand years and a ton of Max Factor make-up. How much of this I identified with the exotic Chile or Latin America that I had been secretly and transgressively hungering for all these years is anybody's guess. I experienced love with the metaphors available to males in Latin America—and elsewhere—at that time, no matter how suspect and gendered I may consider them now, more than thirty years later: the woman as the earth and earth-goddess to be excavated, a territory to be explored by a pioneer, a land in which to root your manhood like a tree, those were the images that surged inside me as we made love. I could never entirely rid myself of the feeling that I was somehow making mine something more than an individual woman, that I was making love to a community that was inside her, that through her body and her life I was binding myself to a permanent place on this planet.

Now that I write this, I have come to understand that it was ultimately not Chile that I desired in her. What attracted me most deeply in the woman who would become my wife were qualities that transcended national origins or boundaries, things I would have treasured in her life if she had been Lithuanian or from Mars. Her fierce loyalty, her amazing ability to see through people, her stubborn (and often exasperating) tendency to speak without minding the consequences, her almost animal loyalty, her fearlessness, her unpredictability—none of these were necessarily typical of Chile and some of them, such as her undiplomatic directness or her rejection of compromises, could even be construed as extremely un-Chilean.

And yet, if it was not Chile that finally ended up joining us, without Chile, nevertheless, the Chile I imagined inside her, it is probable that our love would not have lasted. Angélica is wonderful, but she was not then and certainly is not now, in spite of her name, an angel. Not that I was that easy either. We were attracted to each other precisely because we were opposites and if life was never boring and never will be while she is around, it was a constant clash. Given these circumstances and our immaturity, it is quite possible that we wouldn't have made it to marriage and beyond merely sustained by the dim intuition that each of us had found the long-lost half of their soul. An additional something was necessary for our love to survive those rough and desperate break-ups that all young lovers flounder through, and that something, for me, frequently seemed the vast Chile that I felt Angélica contained within herself. I could feel the country bringing me back for more, my need for this identity she gave me fastening me to her, Chile secretly gluing us together. It is the perverse logic of love that the reverse was true for Angélica: what kept her by my side when things didn't seem to work out was, she has told me, the very fact that I came from some other place, her intuition that I would not treat her the way Chilean males treat women, that I could be entirely trusted, that I was transparent, that I was naïve: in other words, that I was a gringo. A gringo who happened to be frantically searching for a country that would answer his loneliness and transience.

Angélica possessed that country merely by virtue of having been born here, simply because her forefathers and foremothers had made love under these mountains and mingled their many races and interbred their Iberian and Mediterranean and Indian and African stock at a time when mine had never even dreamed of emigrating; she possessed it in the nursery rhymes in Spanish she had sung when I had been reciting Old Mother Hubbard; she possessed it in the peasant proverbs she had absorbed in the dusty plaza of the small countryside town in the Aconcagua Valley where she had been brought up; she possessed it in every Chilean spice, every Chilean fruit, every Chilean meal that had nurtured her. That was Chile, all of that and more. She had been accumulating every drop of experience inside herself like a reservoir. At some point early in our fumbling and fearful and expectant movement towards one another, I sensed that reservoir, sensed that I could drink from its waters, drink Chile in her waters.

How vast were those waters and how insatiable my thirst was brought home to me the first night we became *'pololos'*—a word with which Chileans designate boys and girls who are going steady, a word that comes from a butterfly-like insect that goes from flower to flower making itself dizzy with sweetness. We had slunk into a sort of discotheque and started timidly to explore one another the way you do when you are under twenty and the universe has everything to teach you and an orchestra is remotely playing a bolero, *Bésame, bésame mucho, come si fuera esta noche la última vez,* kiss me, keep on kissing me, as if tonight were the last night, and then Angélica took her mouth from mine and began to sing (a bit off-key, but who cared) the words to that song of Latin American love that I had bypassed so often on the radio as I rushed to hum along with Frankie Avalon. A tango followed, which she also knew by heart, and inside that brain of hers, behind those freckles, was the whole repertoire of popular Latin America that I had despised and that I now wanted to learn by heart to prove my new-found identity. It may have been that very night when I asked her if she danced *cueca,* the Chilean national dance, and she smiled mischievously and grabbed a napkin from the table and waved it a bit in the air and hid her face behind it and suggested that she could teach me some steps, that it was a matter of imagining a rooster out courting. That I had to try and corral her, corner her, that this was the game. She was the treasure and I was the hunter. She would hide and I would seek.

It may have been the next day, when we went down to the centre of Santiago together, that I realized that Angélica had within herself a treasure she barely knew about, a treasure that I was seeking and that she was not even trying to hide. Her presence by my side as we strolled through the centre of the city I had lived in for seven years suddenly transformed me into a tourist arriving at this foreign destination for the first time. I had often passed this café, for instance, and it meant absolutely nothing to me, but for Angélica it was the place where in the Forties her journalist father, after he had put the paper to bed, would meet her mother and a group of Popular Front friends and drink and talk till dawn. As Angélica casually told me the story of the night her father had waited for the news of the Allied landing in Normandy, we were interrupted by a pretty young woman. She came up to us, pecked Angélica's cheek and was introduced to me as the daughter of her 'Mami Lolo', the woman who had brought up Angélica when she was a little girl in the countryside. The two of them chatted for a while about people I did not know and places I had never been. When the young woman said goodbye and we continued on our way, Angélica sketched out the story of her nanny, who had been brought very young into the family house as a helper and later on had cared for the grandchildren, and who, it would turn out, was in fact the illegitimate daughter of Angélica's grandfather. 'You have to come to Santa Maria,' Angélica said, 'where I was raised, and meet my Mami Lolo.' Half a block later, Angélica was greeted by someone else and so it went and so it would go. So many people and so many conversations and so many stories, stories, stories. Perhaps it was then that I began to understand that Angélica was a network of stories, a lineage of stories, a wellspring of stories that had made her, that she was full to the brim with people, with *Chileans,* who had made her. It may have been then or it may have been later, but at some point rather early in our relationship, I realized that Angélica's connection to Chile was the opposite of mine, that it was not and never could be voluntary, that she could not discard it as I was in the process of discarding the United States, that it was as much part of her as her lungs or her skin. In the months and years to come, as she guided me into her life and her body, she also guided me into the mysteries of a continent that should have been mine by birthright but from which I had cut myself off, a country I had seen for years as nothing more than a stop on the road to somewhere else.

And when I had been faced with the loss of that country after the coup, when I had finally agreed that yes, I would seek refuge in an embassy, what had ultimately made that decision tolerable like a secret silhouette inside me was the promise of

Angélica, the certainty that I could wander the earth for ever if the woman who had taught Chile to me was by my side.

Now she was in that car with those two men and I had come face to face with the possibility that she would not accompany me in my wanderings, that she would not be there at all. I told myself that maybe this was the cruel and hidden reason behind my miraculous survival: death had spared me, because all along it was going to take Angélica instead. Death was going to punish me for having refused its gift and stayed in this country all this September. I was going to be punished for not having left immediately and sent my family away; this was what I deserved for pretending that I was untouchable and immortal.

But again I was given a reprieve.

When those two men released her and she came back into the residence and we trembled against each other, when I was able to hold my love, my best friend, my companion for life, in these arms that had already despaired of ever touching her again, my hand going through her hair over and over, closing my eyes and then opening them again to make sure that it was still true, that she was still here, I was finally ready to learn the lesson that death had sent me one more time, perhaps one last time. It was then that the coup finally caught up with me, that it descended on me as it had descended on La Moneda and exploded silently inside me like the bombs had exploded all over the city and made me understand, for the first time since Allende's overthrow, the full and irreversible reality of the evil that was visiting us and that would not go away. When I had anticipated my own death, I thought I had discovered what the Inferno is: the place where you suffer for ever without being able to escape. Now I knew I had been wrong: the Inferno is the one place in the world where the person you most love will suffer for all eternity while you are forced to watch, unable to intervene, responsible for having put her there.

And that Inferno was here, the country I had associated with Paradise.

It was time to leave Chile.

Indians on the Shelf

Michael Dorris

Michael Dorris, who sometimes wrote under the pseudonym Milou North, is known as an activist for the rights of American Indians as well as a talented writer. Born in Louisville, Kentucky, he is of Modoc Indian as well as English and French descent. He founded the Native American Studies Program at Dartmouth, and in 1971 became one of the first American bachelors to adopt a child, a boy with fetal alcohol syndrome. The trials and tribulations of raising his adopted son are described in his most famous book, The Broken Cord *(1989).*

In 1981, Dorris married Louise Erdrich and together they adopted two more American Indian children and had three of their own. In 1997, when the couple were about to divorce, Michael Dorris committed suicide in a motel in New Hampshire. It is unclear whether the cause of the suicide may have been the divorce or his chronic depression. When he died, Dorris was working on a book about fetal alcohol effect, a less debilitating condition that affected his other adopted children. He also wrote children's books and novels.

While on my way to do fieldwork in New Zealand several years ago, I stopped in Avarua, capital of the Cook Islands. To my tourist's eye it was a tropical paradise right out of Michener: palm trees, breadfruit and pineapples, crashing surf, and a profusion of flowers. Most people spoke Maori, and traditional Polynesian music and dance were much in evidence; there was no television, one movie theatre, one radio station, and a few private telephones.

There were, of course, gift shops, aimed primarily at people like myself who wanted to take with them some mememto of days spent sitting in the sun, eating arrowroot pudding and smelling frangipani in every breeze. And so I browsed, past the

------

"Indians on the Shelf," by Michael Dorris, reprinted from *The American Indian and the Problem of History,* edited by Calvin Martin, 1987, Georges Borchardt, Inc., Literary Agents.

Fijian tapa cloth, past the puka shell necklaces, past the coconut oil perfume, and came face to face with an all-too-familiar sight: perched in a prominent position on a shelf behind the cash register was an army of stuffed monkeys, each wearing a turkey-feather imitation of a Sioux war bonnet and clasping in right paw a plywood toma-hawk. "The Indians" had beaten *this* Indian to Rarotonga.

The salesperson replied to my startled question that, yes, indeed, these simian braves were a hot item, popular with tourist and native alike. She herself, she added with a broad smile, had played cowboys and Indians as a child.

More recently, I entertained in my home a young man from Zaire who was spending the summer at Dartmouth College in order to teach Swahili to students who would travel the next winter in Kenya on a foreign study program. My guest spoke very little English, a good deal more French, and three East African languages.

He was homesick for his tiny village on the west shore of Lake Tanganyika, and the Santa Clara pueblo chili I served reminded him of the spicy stews he ate as a child. We compared tribes, his and mine, and he listened with rare appreciation to recordings of southwestern Indian music. He had never met "real" Indians before, he reported, and was interested and curious about every detail. But it was not until I brought out an old eagle-feather headdress, a family treasure, that his eyes lit up with true recognition. Sweeping it out of my hand, and with an innocent and ingenuous laugh, he plopped it on his head, assumed a fierce expression and, patting his hand over his mouth, said "woo woo woo." He, too, in his radioless, roadless, remote village, had played cowboys and Indians; it was part of his culture, and he knew how to behave.

Generations of Germans have learned to read with Karl May's romanticized Indian novels; Hungarian intellectuals dressed in cultural drag cavort in imitation buckskin each summer, playing Indians for a week on a Danube island; and an un-pleasant, right-wing student newspaper at the college where I teach tries to make some symbolic "conservative" point by peddling "Indian-head" doormats for fifteen dol-lars each. Far from vanishing, as some once forecast, the First American seems if any-thing to be gaining ground as a cultural icon.

As folklore, Indians seem infinitely flexible; they can be tough and savage, as in the Washington Redskins football team, or, starring in environmental commercials, turn maudlin and weepy at the sight of litter. In advertising they are inextricably linked with those products (corn oil, tobacco) the general public acknowledges as indigenous to the Americas. Ersatz Indians have inspired hippies, Ralph Lauren designs, and boy scouts. But flesh and blood Native Americans have rarely participated in or benefit-ed from the creation of these imaginary Indians, whose recognition factor, as they say on Madison Avenue, outranks, on a world scale, that of Santa Claus, Mickey Mouse, and Coca Cola combined.

For most people, the myth has become real and a preferred substitute for ethno-graphic reality. The Indian mystique was designed for mass consumption by a European audience, the fulfillment of old and deep-seated expectations for "the Other." It is lit-tle wonder, then, that many non-Indians literally would not know a real Native Amer-ican if they fell over one, for they have prepared for a well-defined, carefully honed legend. Ordinary human beings, with widely variable phenotypes and personalities, fall short of the mold. Unless they talk "Indian" (a kind of metaphoric mumbo jumbo pidgin of English), ooze nostalgia for bygone days, and come bedecked with metallic or beaded jewelry, many native people who hold positions of respect and authority within their own communities are disappointments to non-Indians whose standards of ethnic validity are based on Pocahontas, Squanto, or Tonto.

In a certain sense, for five hundred years Indian people have been measured and have competed against a fantasy over which they have had no control. They are compared with beings who never really *were*, yet the stereotype is taken for truth. Last week my local mail carrier knocked at my door and announced that he was taking a group of little boys in the woods where they intended to live "like real Iroquois" for two days; did I have any advice, he wondered? In reply I suggested simply that they bring along their mommies, pointing out that in a matrilineal society children of that age would be entirely bound by the dictates of their associated clan mothers. This was not what he wanted to hear; it ran counter to his assumption of a macho, male-bonded Indian culture where men were dominant and women were "squaws," retiring and ineffectual unless there was a travois to pull. He and his group did not want to live like "real" Iroquois, and he was chagrined that the Six Nations did not conform to his version of proper savage behavior.

Such attitudes are difficult to rebut successfully, grounded as they are in long traditions of unilateral definitions. In the centuries since Columbus got lost in 1492, a plethora of European social philosophers have attempted to "place" Indians within the context of a Western intellectual tradition that never expected a Western Hemisphere, much less an inhabited one, to exist. It has been the vogue for hundreds of years for Europeans to describe Native Americans not in terms of themselves, but only in terms of who they are (or are not) vis-à-vis non-Indians. Hardly a possible explanation, from Lost Tribes of Israel to outer space or Atlantis refugees, has been eschewed in the quest for a properly rationalized explanation. Puritans viewed Indians as temptations from the devil; Frederick Jackson Turner, when he noticed them at all, saw them as obstacles to be overcome on the frontier; and expansionists, from President Andrew Jackson to Interior Secretary James Watt, have regarded them as simply and annoyingly in the way.

Popular American history, as taught in the schools, omits mention of the large precontact Indian population and its rapid decline due to the spread of European diseases. Instead, students are given the erroneous impression that the few indigenous people who did live in the Americas were dispatched to the Happy Hunting Ground due to conflict with stalwart pioneers and cavalrymen. Such a view of history, clearly at odds with well-documented facts, only serves to reinforce the myth of Indian aggressiveness and bellicosity and further suggests that they got what they deserved. In addition, by picturing Indians as a warlike and dangerous foe, Euro-American ancestors reap honor by having been victorious.

The pattern of Indian-European negotiation for land title in the seventeenth, eighteenth, and nineteenth centuries is also misrepresented; though students learn about the fifty states, they remain unaware of the existence of close to two hundred "domestic, dependent nations" within the country, and regard reservations, if they are conscious of them at all, as transitory poverty pockets "given" to the Indians by philanthropic bureaucrats. In many respects living Native Americans remain as mysterious, exotic, and unfathomable to their contemporaries in the 1980s as Powhatan appeared to John Smith over three hundred fifty years ago. Native rights, motives, customs, languages, and aspirations are misunderstood out of an ignorance that is both self-serving and self-righteous.

Part of the problem may well stem from the long-standing tendency of European or Euro-American thinkers to regard Indians as so "Other," so fundamentally and profoundly different, that they fail to extend to native peoples certain traits commonly regarded as human. A survey of literature dealing with Indians over the past two or three hundred years would seem to imply that Indians are motivated more often by mysticism than by ambition, are charged more by unfathomable visions than by intelligence or introspection, and in effect derive their understandings of the world more from an appeal to the irrational than to empiricism. Since the whys and wherefores of Native American society are not easily accessible to those culture-bound by Western traditional values, there is a tendency to assume that Indians are creatures either of instinct or whimsy.

This idea is certainly not new; Rousseau's noble savages wandered, pure of heart, through a preconcupiscent world, never having had so much as a bite of the fruit from the "tree of the knowledge of good and evil" (Genesis 2:17). Romantics, most of whom had never seen a living specimen, patronized Indians by eulogizing them, and thus denied them a common bond of humanity with other men and women. Since native people were assumed a priori to be incomprehensible, they were seldom comprehended; their societies were simply beheld, often through cloudy glasses, and rarely penetrated by the tools of logic and deductive analysis automatically reserved for cultures prejudged to be "civilized."

And on those occasions when Europeans did attempt to relate themselves to native societies, it was not, ordinarily, on a human being to human being basis, but rather through an ancestor-descendant model. Indians, though obviously contemporary with their observers, were somehow regarded as ancient, as examples of what Stone Age Europeans were like. In the paradigm of European confusion, Indians have been objects of mystery and speculation, not people.

It makes a great story, a real international crowd-pleaser that spans historical ages and generations, but there is a difficulty: Indians were, and are, *Homo sapiens sapiens.* Unless the presence of a shovel-shaped incisor, an epicanthic fold or an extra molar cusp (or the absence of Type B blood) affords one an extra toe in the metaphysical door, native people have had to cope, for the last 40,000 or so years, just like everyone else. Their cultures have had to make internal sense, their medicines have had to work consistently and practically, their philosophical explanations have had to be reasonably satisfying and dependable, or else the ancestors of those we call Indians really would have vanished long ago.

In other words, Native American societies rested upon intelligence. They developed and maintained usable, pragmatic views of the world. Those of their systems that had survived long enough to have been observed by fifteenth-century Europeans were certainly dynamic but clearly had worked for millennia.

The difficulty in accepting this almost tautological fact comes from the Euro-centric conviction that the West holds a virtual monopoly on "science," logic, and clear-thinking. To admit that other, culturally divergent viewpoints are equally plausible is to cast doubt on the monolithic center of Judeo-Christian belief: that there is but *one* of everything—God, right way, truth—and Europeans alone knew what that was. If Indian cultures were admitted to be possibly viable, then European societies were not the exclusive club they had always maintained they were.

It is little wonder, therefore, that Indian peoples were perceived not as they were but as they *had* to be, from a European point of view. They were whisked out of the realm of the real and into the land of make-believe. Indians became variably super and subhuman, never ordinary. They dealt in magic, not judgment. They were imagined to be stuck in their past, not guided by its precedents.

Such a situation argues strongly for the development and dissemination of a more accurate, more objective historical account of native people, but this is easier said than done. Inasmuch as the Indian peoples of North America were, before and during much of their contact period with Europe, non-literate, the requirements for recounting an emic native history are particularly demanding and, by the standards of most traditional methodology, unorthodox. There do not exist the familiar and reassuring kinds of written documentation that one finds in European societies of equivalent chronological periods, and the forms of tribal record preservation that are available—oral history, tales, mnemonic devices, and religious rituals—strike the average, university-trained academic as inexact, unreliable, and suspect. Culture-bound by their own approach to knowledge, they are apt to throw up their hands in despair and exclaim that *nothing* can be known of Indian history. By this logic, an absolute void is more acceptable than a reasonable, educated guess, and "evidence" is defined in only the most narrow sense.

Furthermore, it is naive to assume that most historians can view their subject without certain impediments to objectivity. Every professor in the last three hundred years, whether he or she was enculturated in Rarotonga or Zaire, in Hanover, New Hampshire or Vienna, was exposed at an early age to one or another form of folklore about Indians. For some it may well be that the very ideas about Native American cultures that initially attracted them to the field of American history are the items most firmly rooted in myth. They may have come to first "like" Indians because they believed them to be more honest, stoic, and brave than other people, and forever after have to strive against this bias in presenting their subjects as real, complicated people. Or they may discover to their disillusionment that all Indians are not pure of heart and have to suppress, consciously or unconsciously, their abiding resentment and disenchantment.

For most people, serious learning about Native American culture and history is different from acquiring knowledge in other fields, for it requires an initial, abrupt, and wrenching demythologizing. One does not start from point zero, but from minus ten, and is often required to abandon cherished childhood fantasies of super-heroes and larger-than-life villains.

There would seem to be a certain starting advantage here for historians or anthropologists who also happen to be ethnically Native American, especially if they grew up in the context of tribal society. For them, at least, Indians have always been and are real, and they may have less difficulty in establishing links of continuity between contemporary and historical populations. They may have access to traditionally-kept records and escape some of the prejudice against non-Western methods. They may be more comfortable with taking analytical risks in hypothesizing explanations for traditional practices, basing their assumptions upon subtle but persuasive clues surviving in their own cultural experience.

Native scholars, of course, have their own special problems. For one thing, few of them have avoided exposure to the media blitz on folkloric or fantasy Indians. Indian children are as often tempted to "play Indian" as are their non-native contemporaries. They may be expected to live up to their mythic counterparts and feel like failures when they cry at pain or make noise in the woods. American Indians who deal as scholars with Indian materials are assumed by some non-natives to be hopelessly subjective and biased, and as such their work is dismissed as self-serving. Certainly it is true that most Native American scholarship could be termed "revisionist," but that in itself does not prove illegitimacy. Europeans and Euro-Americans have not felt shy in writing about their respective ancestors and are not automatically accused of aggrandizing them; why should native scholars be less capable of relatively impartial retrospection?

Whoever attempts to write Native American history must admit in advance to fallibility. There is not and never will be any proof, no possibility of "hard evidence" to support a conjecture based on deduction. David Bradley, in *The Chaneysville Incident,* writes wistfully of a firmly fixed chamber in Historian's Heaven in which all things are clear. "And we believe," he says, "if we have been good little historians, just before they do whatever it is they finally do with us, they'll take us in there and show us what was *really* going on. It's not that we want so much to know we were right. We *know* we're not right (although it would be nice to see exactly how close we came). It's just that we want to, really, truly, utterly, absolutely, completely, finally *know*" (1982:277).

Indian history hardly even offers purgatory. It depends on the imperfect evidence of archeology; the barely-disguised, self-focused testimony of traders, missionaries, and soldiers, all of whom had their own axes to grind and viewed native peoples through a narrow scope; and, last and most suspect of all, common sense. The making of cross-cultural, cross-temporal assumptions is enough to send every well-trained Western academic into catatonia, but there is no avoiding it. If we stipulate only a few givens—that Indian societies were composed of people of the normal range of intelligence; that human beings *qua* human beings, where and whenever they may live, share some traits; that Indians were and are human beings—then we have at least a start. We can dare, having amassed and digested all the hard data we can lay our hands on, to leap into the void and attempt to see the world through the eyes of our historical subjects. We can try to make sense out of practices and beliefs and reactions that do not conform to a Western model but must, within the configurations of their own cultures, have an explanation. We can stop treating Indians like sacred, one-dimensional European myths and begin the hard, terribly difficult and unpredictable quest of regarding them as human beings.

What Makes Superman
So Darned American?

Gary Engle

Gary Engle is a professor of English at Cleveland State University. He specializes in popular culture and has written numerous magazine and journal articles. He has also published a book The Grotesque Essence: Plays from American Minstrel Style *(1978). The following essay was published in a collection entitled* Superman at Fifty! *co-authored with Dennis Dooley.*

When I was young I spent a lot of time arguing with myself about who would win in a fight between John Wayne and Superman. On days when I wore my cowboy hat and cap guns, I knew the Duke would win because of his pronounced superiority in the all-important matter of swagger. There were days, though, when a frayed army blanket tied cape-fashion around my neck signalled a young man's need to believe there could be no end to the potency of his being. Then the Man of Steel was the odds-on favorite to knock the Duke for a cosmic loop. My greatest childhood problem was that the question could never be resolved because no such battle could ever take place. I mean, how would a fight start between the only two Americans who never started anything, who always fought only to defend their rights and the American way?

Now that I'm older and able to look with reason on the mysteries of childhood, I've finally resolved the dilemma. John Wayne was the best older brother any kid could ever hope to have, but he was no Superman.

Superman is *the* great American hero. We are a nation rich with legendary figures. But among the Davy Crocketts and Paul Bunyans and Mike Finks and Pecos Bills and all the rest who speak for various regional identities in the pantheon of American folklore, only Superman achieves truly mythic stature, interweaving a pattern of beliefs, literary conventions, and cultural traditions of the American people more

"What Makes Superman So Darned American?," by Gary Engle, reprinted from *Superman at Fifty,* 1987, Octavia Press.

powerfully and more accessibly than any other cultural symbol of the twentieth century, perhaps of any period in our history.

The core of the American myth in *Superman* consists of a few basic facts that remain unchanged throughout the infinitely varied ways in which the myth is told—facts with which everyone is familiar, however marginal their knowledge of the story. Superman is an orphan rocketed to Earth when his native planet Krypton explodes; he lands near Smallville and is adopted by Jonathan and Martha Kent, who inculcate in him their American middle-class ethic; as an adult he migrates to Metropolis where he defends America—no, the world! no, the Universe!—from all evil and harm while playing a romantic game in which, as Clark Kent, he hopelessly pursues Lois Lane, who hopelessly pursues Superman, who remains aloof until such time as Lois proves worthy of him by falling in love with his feigned identity as a weakling. That's it. Every narrative thread in the mythology, each one of the thousands of plots in the fifty-year stream of comics and films and TV shows, all the tales involving the demigods of the Superman pantheon—Superboy, Supergirl, even Krypto the Superdog—every single one reinforces by never contradicting this basic set of facts. That's the myth, and that's where one looks to understand America.

It is impossible to imagine Superman being as popular as he is and speaking as deeply to the American character were he not an immigrant or an orphan. Immigration, of course, is the overwhelming fact in American history. Except for the Indians, all Americans have an immediate sense of their origins elsewhere. No nation on Earth has so deeply embedded in its social consciousness the imagery of passage from one social identity to another: the Mayflower of the New England separatists, the slave ships from Africa and the subsequent underground railroads toward freedom in the North, the sailing ships and steamers running shuttles across two oceans in the nineteenth century, the freedom airlifts in the twentieth. Somehow the picture just isn't complete without Superman's rocketship.

Like the peoples of the nation whose values he defends, Superman is an alien, but not just any alien. He's the consummate and totally uncompromised alien, an immigrant whose visible difference from the norm is underscored by his decision to wear a costume of bold primary colors so tight as to be his very skin. Moreover, Superman the alien is real. He stands out among the hosts of comic book characters (Batman is a good example) for whom the superhero role is like a mask assumed when needed, a costume worn over their real identities as normal Americans. Superman's powers—strength, mobility, x-ray vision and the like—are the comic-book equivalents of ethnic characteristics, and they protect and preserve the vitality of the foster community in which he lives in the same way that immigrant ethnicity has sustained American culture linguistically, artistically, economically, politically, and spiritually. The myth of Superman asserts with total confidence and a childlike innocence the value of the immigrant in American culture.

From this nation's beginnings Americans have looked for ways of coming to terms with the immigrant experience. This is why, for example, so much of American literature and popular culture deals with the theme of dislocation, generally focused in characters devoted or doomed to constant physical movement. Daniel Boone became an

American legend in part as a result of apocryphal stories that he moved every time his neighbors got close enough for him to see the smoke of their cabin fires. James Fenimore Cooper's Natty Bumppo spent the five long novels of the Leatherstocking saga drifting ever westward, like the pioneers who were his spiritual offspring, from the Mohawk Valley of upstate New York to the Great Plains where he died. Huck Finn sailed through the moral heart of America on a raft. Melville's Ishmael, Wister's Virginian, Shane, Gatsby, the entire Lost Generation, Steinbeck's Okies, Little Orphan Annie, a thousand fiddlefooted cowboy heroes of dime novels and films and television—all in motion, searching for the American dream or stubbornly refusing to give up their innocence by growing old, all symptomatic of a national sense of rootlessness stemming from an identity founded on the experience of immigration.

Individual mobility is an integral part of America's dreamwork. Is it any wonder, then, that our greatest hero can take to the air at will? Superman's ability to fly does more than place him in a tradition of mythic figures going back to the Greek messenger god Hermes or Zetes the flying Argonaut. It makes him an exemplar in the American dream. Take away a young man's wheels and you take away his manhood. Jack Kerouac and Charles Kurault go on the road; William Least Heat Moon looks for himself in a van exploring the veins of America in its system of blue highways; legions of gray-haired retirees turn Air Stream trailers and Winnebagos into proof positive that you can, in the end, take it with you. On a human scale, the American need to keep moving suggests a neurotic aimlessness under the surface of adventure. But take the human restraints off, let Superman fly unencumbered when and wherever he will, and the meaning of mobility in the American consciousness begins to reveal itself. Superman's incredible speed allows him to be as close to everywhere at once as it is physically possible to be. Displacement is, therefore, impossible. His sense of self is not dispersed by his life's migration but rather enhanced by all the universe that he is able to occupy. What American, whether an immigrant in spirit or in fact, could resist the appeal of one with such an ironclad immunity to the anxiety of dislocation?

In America, physical dislocation serves as a symbol of social and psychological movement. When our immigrant ancestors arrived on America's shores they hit the ground running, some to homestead on the Great Plains, others to claw their way up the socioeconomic ladder in coastal ghettos. Upward mobility, westward migration, Sunbelt relocation—the wisdom in America is that people don't, can't, mustn't end up where they begin. This belief has the moral force of religious doctrine. Thus the American identity is ordered around the psychological experience of forsaking or losing the past for the opportunity of reinventing oneself in the future. This makes the orphan a potent symbol of the American character. Orphans aren't merely free to reinvent themselves. They are obliged to do so.

When Superman reinvents himself, he becomes the bumbling Clark Kent, a figure as immobile as Superman is mobile, as weak as his alter ego is strong. Over the years commentators have been fond of stressing how Clark Kent provides an illusory image of wimpiness onto which children can protect their insecurities about their own personal (and, hopefully, equally illusory) weaknesses. But I think the role of Clark Kent is far more complex than that.

During my childhood, Kent contributed nothing to my love for the Man of Steel. If left to contemplate him for too long, I found myself changing from cape back into cowboy hat and guns. John Wayne, at least, was no sissy that I could ever see. Of course, in all the Westerns that the Duke came to stand for in my mind, there were elements that left me as confused as the paradox between Kent and Superman. For example, I could never seem to figure out why cowboys so often fell in love when there were obviously better options: horses to ride, guns to shoot, outlaws to chase, and savages to kill. Even on the days when I became John Wayne, I could fall victim to a never-articulated anxiety about the potential for poor judgment in my cowboy heroes. Then, I generally drifted back into a worship of Superman. With him, at least, the mysterious communion of opposites was honest and on the surface of things.

What disturbed me as a child is what I now think makes the myth of Superman so appealing to an immigrant sensibility. The shape-shifting between Clark Kent and Superman is the means by which this mid-twentieth-century, urban story—like the pastoral, nineteenth-century Western before it—addresses in dramatic terms the theme of cultural assimilation.

At its most basic level, the Western was an imaginative record of the American experience of westward migration and settlement. By bringing the forces of civilization and savagery together on a mythical frontier, the Western addressed the problem of conflict between apparently mutually exclusive identities and explored options for negotiating between them. In terms that a boy could comprehend, the myth explored the dilemma of assimilation—marry the school marm and start wearing Eastern clothes or saddle up and drift further westward with the boys.

The Western was never a myth of stark moral authority. Pioneers fled civilization by migrating west, but their purpose in the wilderness was to rebuild civilization. So civilization was both good and bad, what Americans fled from and journeyed toward. A similar moral ambiguity rested at the heart of the wilderness. It was an Eden in which innocence could be achieved through spiritual rebirth, but it was also the anarchic force that most directly threatened the civilized values America wanted to impose on the frontier. So the dilemma arose: In negotiating between civilization and the wilderness, between the old order and the new, between the identity the pioneers carried with them from wherever they came and the identity they sought to invent, Americans faced an impossible choice. Either they pushed into the New World wilderness and forsook the ideals that motivated them or they clung to their origins and polluted Eden.

The myth of the Western responded to this dilemma by inventing the idea of the frontier in which civilized ideals embodied in the institutions of family, church, law, and education are revitalized by the virtues of savagery: independence, self-reliance, personal honor, sympathy with nature, and ethical uses of violence. In effect, the mythical frontier represented an attempt to embody the perfect degree of assimilation in which both the old and new identities came together, if not in a single self-image, then at least in idealized relationships, like the symbolic marriage of reformed cowboy and displaced school marm that ended Owen Wister's prototypical *The Virginian,* or the mystical masculine bonding between representatives of an ascendant and a vanishing America—Natty Bumppo and Chingachgook, the Lone Ranger and Tonto. On the Western frontier, both the old and new identities equally mattered.

As powerful a myth as the Western was, however, there were certain limits to its ability to speak directly to an increasingly common twentieth-century immigrant sensibility. First, it was pastoral. Its imagery of dusty frontier towns and breathtaking mountainous desolation spoke most affectingly to those who conceived of the American dream in terms of the nineteenth-century immigrant experience of rural settlement. As the twentieth century wore on, more immigrants were, like Superman, moving from rural or small-town backgrounds to metropolitan environments. Moreover, the Western was historical, often elegiacally so. Underlying the air of celebration in even the most epic and romantic of Westerns—the films of John Ford, say, in which John Wayne stood tall for all that any good American boy could ever want to be—was an awareness that the frontier was less a place than a state of mind represented in historic terms by a fleeting moment glimpsed imperfectly in the rapid wave of westward migration and settlement. Implicitly, then, whatever balance of past and future identities the frontier could offer was itself tenuous or illusory.

Twentieth-century immigrants, particularly the Eastern European Jews who came to America after 1880 and who settled in the industrial and mercantile centers of the Northeast—cities like Cleveland where Jerry Siegel and Joe Shuster grew up and created Superman—could be entertained by the Western, but they developed a separate literary tradition that addressed the theme of assimilation in terms closer to their personal experience. In this tradition issues were clear-cut. Clinging to an Old World identity meant isolation in ghettos, confrontation with a prejudiced mainstream culture, second-class social status, and impoverishment. On the other hand, forsaking the past in favor of total absorption into the mainstream, while it could result in socioeconomic progress, meant a loss of the religious, linguistic, even culinary traditions that provided a foundation for psychological well-being. Such loss was particularly tragic for the Jews because of the fundamental role played by history in Jewish culture.

Writers who worked in this tradition—Abraham Cahan, Daniel Fuchs, Henry Roth, and Delmore Schwarz, among others—generally found little reason to view the experience of assimilation with joy or optimism. Typical of the tradition was Cahan's early novel *Yekl*, on which Joan Micklin Silver's film *Hester Street* was based. A young married couple, Jake and Gitl, clash over his need to be absorbed as quickly as possible into the American mainstream and her obsessive preservation of their Russian-Jewish heritage. In symbolic terms, their confrontation is as simple as their choice of headgear—a derby for him, a babushka for her. That the story ends with their divorce, even in the context of their gradual movement toward mutual understanding of one another's point of view, suggests the divisive nature of the pressures at work in the immigrant communities.

Where the pressures were perhaps most keenly felt was in the schools. Educational theory of the period stressed the benefits of rapid assimilation. In the first decades of this century, for example, New York schools flatly rejected bilingual education—a common response to the plight of non-English-speaking immigrants even today—and there were conscientious efforts to indoctrinate the children of immigrants with American values, often at the expense of traditions within the ethnic community. What resulted was a generational rift in which children were openly embarrassed by and even contemptuous of their parents' values, setting a pattern in American life in which second-generation immigrants migrate psychologically if not physically from their parents, leaving it up to the third generation and beyond to rediscover their ethnic roots.

Under such circumstances, finding a believable and inspiring balance between the old identity and the new, like that implicit in the myth of the frontier, was next to impossible. The images and characters that did emerge from the immigrant communities were often comic. Seen over and over in the fiction and popular theater of the day was the figure of the *yiddische Yankee,* a jingoistic optimist who spoke heavily accented American slang, talked baseball like an addict without understanding the game, and dressed like a Broadway dandy on a budget—in short, one who didn't understand America well enough to distinguish between image and substance and who paid for the mistake by becoming the butt of a style of comedy bordering on pathos. So engrained was this stereotype in popular culture that it echoes today in TV situation comedy.

Throughout American popular culture between 1880 and the Second World War the story was the same. Oxlike Swedish farmers, German brewers, Jewish merchants, corrupt Irish ward healers, Italian gangsters—there was a parade of images that reflected in terms often comic, sometimes tragic, the humiliation, pain, and cultural insecurity of people in a state of transition. Even in the comics, a medium intimately connected with immigrant culture, there simply was no image that presented a blending of identities in the assimilation process in a way that stressed pride, self-confidence, integrity, and psychological well-being. None, that is, until Superman.

The brilliant stroke in the conception of Superman—the sine qua non that makes the whole myth work—is the fact that he has two identities. The myth simply wouldn't work without Clark Kent, mild-mannered newspaper reporter and later, as the myth evolved, bland TV newsman. Adopting the white-bread image of a wimp is first and foremost a moral act for the Man of Steel. He does it to protect his parents from nefarious sorts who might use them to gain an edge over the powerful alien. Moreover, Kent adds to Superman's powers the moral guidance of a Smallville upbringing. It is Jonathan Kent, fans remember, who instructs the alien that his powers must always be used for good. Thus does the myth add a mainstream white Anglo-Saxon Protestant ingredient to the American stew. Clark Kent is the clearest stereotype of a self-effacing, hesitant, doubting, middle-class weakling ever invented. He is the epitome of visible invisibility, someone whose extraordinary ordinariness makes him disappear in a crowd. In a phrase, he is the consummate figure of total cultural assimilation, and significantly, he is not real. Implicit in this is the notion that mainstream cultural norms, however useful, are illusions.

Though a disguise, Kent is necessary for the myth to work. This uniquely American hero has two identities, one based on where he comes from in life's journey, one on where is going. One is real, one an illusion, and both are necessary for the myth of balance in the assimilation process to be complete. Superman's powers make the hero capable of saving humanity; Kent's total immersion in the American heartland makes him want to do it. The result is an improvement on the Western: an optimistic myth of assimilation but with an urban, technocratic setting.

One must never underestimate the importance to a myth of the most minute elements which do not change over time and by which we recognize the story. Take Superman's cape, for example. When Joe Shuster inked the first Superman stories, in the early thirties when he was still a student at Cleveland's Glenville High School, Superman was strictly beefcake in tights, looking more like a circus acrobat than the ultimate Man of Steel. By June of 1938 when *Action Comics* no. 1 was issued, the image had been altered to include a cape, ostensibly to make flight easier to render in the pictures. But it wasn't the cape of Victorian melodrama and adventure fiction, the kind worn with a clasp around the neck. In fact, one is hard-pressed to find any precedent in popular culture for the kind of cape Superman wears. His emerges in a seamless line from either side of the front yoke of his tunic. It is a veritable growth from behind his pectorals and hangs, when he stands at ease, in a line that doesn't so much drape his shoulders as stand apart from them and echo their curve, like an angel's wings.

In light of this graphic detail, it seems hardly coincidental that Superman's real, Kryptonic name is Kal-El, an apparent neologism by George Lowther, the author who novelized the comic strip in 1942. In Hebrew, *el* can be both root and affix. As a root, it is the masculine singular word for God. Angels in Hebrew mythology are called *benei Elohim* (literally, sons of the Gods), or *Elyonim* (higher beings). As an affix, *el* is most often translated as "of God," as in the plenitude of Old Testament given names: Ishma-el, Dani-el, Ezeki-el, Samu-el, etc. It is also a common form for named angels in most Semitic mythologies: Israf-el, Aza-el, Uri-el, Yo-el, Rapha-el, Gabri-el and—the one perhaps most like Superman—Micha-el, the warrior angel and Satan's principal adversary.

The morpheme *Kal* bears a linguistic relation to two Hebrew roots. The first, *kal,* means "with lightness" or "swiftness" (faster than a speeding bullet in Hebrew?). It also bears a connection to the root *hal,* where *h* is the guttural *ch* of *chutzpah. Hal* translates roughly as "everything" or "all." *Kal-el,* then, can be read as "all that is God," or perhaps more in the spirit of the myth of Superman, "all that God is." And while we're at it, *Kent* is a form of the Hebrew *kana.* In its *k-n-t* form, the word appears in the Bible, meaning "I have found a son."

I'm suggesting that Superman raises the American immigrant experience to the level of religious myth. And why not? He's not just some immigrant from across the waters like all our ancestors, but a real alien, an extraterrestrial, a visitor from heaven if you will, which fact lends an element of the supernatural to the myth. America has no national religious icons nor any pilgrimage shrines. The idea of a patron saint is ludicrous in a nation whose Founding Fathers wrote into the founding documents the fundamental if not eternal separation of church and state. America, though, is pretty much as religious as other industrialized countries. It's just that our tradition of religious diversity precludes the nation's religious character from being embodied in objects or persons recognizably religious, for such are immediately identified by their attachment to specific sectarian traditions and thus contradict the eclecticism of the American religious spirit.

In America, cultural icons that manage to tap the national religious spirit are of necessity secular on the surface and sufficiently generalized to incorporate the diversity of American religious traditions. Superman doesn't have to be seen as an angel to be appreciated, but in the absence of a tradition of national religious iconography, he can serve as a safe, nonsectarian focus for essentially religious sentiments, particularly among the young.

In the last analysis, Superman is like nothing so much as an American boy's fantasy of a messiah. He is the male, heroic match for the Statue of Liberty, come like an immigrant from heaven to deliver humankind by sacrificing himself in the service of others. He protects the weak and defends truth and justice and all the other moral virtues inherent in the Judeo-Christian tradition, remaining ever vigilant and ever chaste. What purer or stronger vision could there possibly be for a child? Now that I put my mind to it, I see that John Wayne never had a chance.

The Red Convertible

Louise Erdrich

Louise Erdrich and her husband, Michael Dorris, also a writer, lived with their children in New Hampshire and collaborated on everything they wrote. The Crown of Columbus, *1991, is their most recent work. Born in 1954, Erdrich grew up in Wahpeton, North Dakota, near the Turtle Mountain Chippewa Reservation. Her mother was a member of the Chippewa tribe; both parents worked for the Bureau of Indian Affairs.*

Erdrich was the first to attend coeducational classes at Dartmouth in 1972 where she met her husband, also part Indian (Modoc) and chair of Dartmouth's Native American Studies Department. She graduated with a B.A. in 1976 and earned her M.A. in creative writing at Johns Hopkins University in 1977. She has attended MacDowell and Yaddo writers' colonies. Her first novel, Love Medicine *(1984), won the 1984 National Book Critics' Circle Award for the Best Work of Fiction. The first book of a trilogy,* Love Medicine *was followed by* The Beet Queen *and* Tracks. *All three are set in North Dakota and involve interrelated narratives detailing the lives of a number of families, both Indian and non-Indian, who live on and off an Indian reservation.*

Erdrich's poetry has been collected in Jacklight *(1984) and* Baptism of Desire *(1991).*

I was the first one to drive a convertible on my reservation. And of course it was red, a red Olds. I owned that car along with my brother Henry Junior. We owned it together until his boots filled with water on a windy night and he bought out my share.

"The Red Convertible," by Louise Erdrich, reprinted from *Love Medicine* (new and expanded version), 1995, Henry Holt and Company.

Now Henry owns the whole car, and his younger brother Lyman (that's myself), Lyman walks everywhere he goes.

How did I earn enough money to buy my share in the first place? My one talent was I could always make money. I had a touch for it, unusual in a Chippewa. From the first I was different that way, and everyone recognized it. I was the only kid they let in the American Legion Hall to shine shoes, for example, and one Christmas I sold spiritual bouquets for the mission door to door. The nuns let me keep a percentage. Once I started, it seemed the more money I made the easier the money came. Everyone encouraged it. When I was fifteen I got a job washing dishes at the Joliet Cafe, and that was where my first big break happened.

It wasn't long before I was promoted to busing tables, and then the short-order cook quit and I was hired to take her place. No sooner than you know it I was managing the Joliet. The rest is history. I went on managing. I soon became part owner, and of course there was no stopping me then. It wasn't long before the whole thing was mine.

After I'd owned the Joliet for one year, it blew over in the worst tornado ever seen around here. The whole operation was smashed to bits. A total loss. The fryalator was up in a tree, the grill torn in half like it was paper. I was only sixteen. I had it all in my mother's name, and I lost it quick, but before I lost it I had every one of my relatives, and their relatives, to dinner, and I also bought that red Olds I mentioned, along with Henry.

The first time we saw it! I'll tell you when we first saw it. We had gotten a ride up to Winnipeg, and both of us had money. Don't ask me why, because we never mentioned a car or anything, we just had all our money. Mine was cash, a big bankroll from the Joliet's insurance. Henry had two checks—a week's extra pay for being laid off, and his regular check from the Hewel Bearing Plant.

We were walking down Portage anyway, seeing the sights, when we saw it. There it was, parked, large as life. Really as *if* it was alive. I thought of the word *repose,* because the car wasn't simply stopped, parked, or whatever. That car reposed, calm and gleaming, a FOR SALE sign in its left front window. Then, before we had thought it over at all, the car belonged to us and our pockets were empty. We had just enough money for gas back home.

We went places in that car, me and Henry. We took off driving all one whole summer. We started off toward the Little Knife River and Mandaree in Fort Berthold and then we found ourselves down in Wakpala somehow, and then suddenly we were over in Montana on the Rocky Boy, and yet the summer was not even half over. Some people hang on to details when they travel, but we didn't let them bother us and just lived our everyday lives here to there.

I do remember this one place with willows. I remember I laid under those trees and it was comfortable. So comfortable. The branches bent down all around me like a tent or a stable. And quiet, it was quiet, even though there was a powwow close enough so I could see it going on. The air was not too still, not too windy either. When the dust rises up and hangs in the air around the dancers like that, I feel good.

Henry was asleep with his arms thrown wide. Later on, he woke up and we started driving again. We were somewhere in Montana, or maybe on the Blood Reserve—it could have been anywhere. Anyway it was where we met the girl.

All her hair was in buns around her ears, that's the first thing I noticed about her. She was posed alongside the road with her arm out, so we stopped. That girl was short, so short her lumber shirt looked comical on her, like a nightgown. She had jeans on and fancy moccasins and she carried a little suitcase.

"Hop on in," says Henry. So she climbs in between us.

"We'll take you home," I says. "Where do you live?"

"Chicken," she says.

"Where the hell's that?" I ask her.

"Alaska."

"Okay," says Henry, and we drive.

We got up there and never wanted to leave. The sun doesn't truly set there in summer, and the night is more a soft dusk. You might doze off, sometimes, but before you know it you're up again, like an animal in nature. You never feel like you have to sleep hard or put away the world. And things would grow up there. One day just dirt or moss, the next day flowers and long grass. The girl's name was Susy. Her family really took to us. They fed us and put us up. We had our own tent to live in by their house, and the kids would be in and out of there all day and night. They couldn't get over me and Henry being brothers, we looked so different. We told them we knew we had the same mother, anyway.

One night Susy came in to visit us. We sat around in the tent talking of this and that. The season was changing. It was getting darker by that time, and the cold was even getting just a little mean. I told her it was time for us to go. She stood up on a chair.

"You never seen my hair," Susy said.

That was true. She was standing on a chair, but still, when she unclipped her buns the hair reached all the way to the ground. Our eyes opened. You couldn't tell how much hair she had when it was rolled up so neatly. Then my brother Henry did something funny. He went up to the chair and said, "Jump on my shoulders." So she did that, and her hair reached down past his waist, and he started twirling, this way and that, so her hair was flung from side to side.

"I always wondered what it was like to have long pretty hair," Henry says. Well we laughed. It was a funny sight, the way he did it. The next morning we got up and took leave of those people.

On to greener pastures, as they say. It was down through Spokane and across Idaho then Montana and very soon we were racing the weather right along under the Canadian border through Columbus, Des Lacs, and then we were in Bottineau County and soon home. We'd made most of the trip, that summer, without putting up the car hood at all. We got home just in time, it turned out, for the army to remember Henry had signed up to join it.

I don't wonder that the army was so glad to get my brother that they turned him into a Marine. He was built like a brick outhouse anyway. We liked to tease him that they really wanted him for his Indian nose. He had a nose big and sharp as a hatchet, like the nose on Red Tomahawk, the Indian who killed Sitting Bull, whose profile is on signs all along the North Dakota Highways. Henry went off to training camp, came home once during Christmas, then the next thing you know we got an overseas letter from him. It was 1970, and he said he was stationed up in the northern hill country. Whereabouts I did not know. He wasn't such a hot letter writer, and only got off two before the enemy caught him. I could never keep it straight, which direction those good Vietnam soldiers were from.

I wrote him back several times, even though I didn't know if those letters would get through. I kept him informed all about the car. Most of the time I had it up on blocks in the yard or half taken apart, because that long trip did a hard job on it under the hood.

I always had good luck with numbers, and never worried about the draft myself. I never even had to think about what my number was. But Henry was never lucky in the same way as me. It was at least three years before Henry came home. By then I guess the whole war was solved in the government's mind, but for him it would keep on going. In those years I'd put his car into almost perfect shape. I always thought of it as his car while he was gone, even though when he left he said, "Now it's yours," and threw me his key.

"Thanks for the extra key," I'd said. "I'll put it up in your drawer just in case I need it." He laughed.

When he came home, though, Henry was different, and I'll say this: the change was no good. You could hardly expect him to change for the better, I know. But he was quiet, so quiet, and never comfortable sitting anywhere but always up and moving around. I thought back to times we'd sat still for whole afternoons, never moving a muscle, just shifting our weight along the ground, talking to whoever sat with us, watching things. He'd always had a joke, then, too, and now you couldn't get him to laugh, or when he did it was more the sound of a man choking, a sound that stopped up the throats of other people around him. They got to leaving him alone most of the time, and I didn't blame them. It was a fact: Henry was jumpy and mean.

I'd bought a color TV set for my mom and the rest of us while Henry was away. Money still came very easy. I was sorry I'd ever bought it though, because of Henry. I was also sorry I'd bought color, because with black-and-white the pictures seem older and farther away. But what are you going to do? He sat in front of it, watching it, and that was the only time he was completely still. But it was the kind of stillness that you see in a rabbit when it freezes and before it will bolt. He was not easy. He sat in his chair grabbing the armrests with all his might, as if the chair itself was moving at a high speed and if he let go at all he would rocket forward and maybe crash right through the set.

Once I was in the room watching TV with Henry and I heard his teeth click at something. I looked over, and he'd bitten through his lip. Blood was going down his chin. I tell you right then I wanted to smash that tube to pieces. I went over to it but

Henry must have known what I was up to. He rushed from his chair and shoved me out of the way, against the wall. I told myself he didn't know what he was doing.

My mom came in, turned the set off real quiet, and told us she had made something for supper. So we went and sat down. There was still blood going down Henry's chin, but he didn't notice it and no one said anything, even though every time he took a bite of his bread his blood fell onto it until he was eating his own blood mixed with the food.

While Henry was not around we talked about what was going to happen to him. There were no Indian doctors on the reservation, and my mom couldn't come around to trusting the old man, Moses Pillager, because he courted her long ago and was jealous of her husbands. He might take revenge through her son. We were afraid that if we brought Henry to a regular hospital they would keep him.

"They don't fix them in those places," Mom said; "they just give them drugs."

"We wouldn't get him there in the first place," I agreed, "so let's just forget about it."

Then I thought about the car.

Henry had not even looked at the car since he'd gotten home, though like I said, it was in tip-top condition and ready to drive. I thought the car might bring the old Henry back somehow. So I bided my time and waited for my chance to interest him in the vehicle.

One night Henry was off somewhere. I took myself a hammer. I went out to that car and I did a number on its underside. Whacked it up. Bent the tail pipe double. Ripped the muffler loose. By the time I was done with the car it looked worse than any typical Indian car that has been driven all its life on reservation roads, which they always say are like government promises—full of holes. It just about hurt me, I'll tell you that! I threw dirt in the carburetor and I ripped all the electric tape off the seats. I made it look just as beat up as I could. Then I sat back and waited for Henry to find it.

Still it took him over a month. That was all right, because it was just getting warm enough, not melting, but warm enough to work outside.

"Lyman," he says, walking in one day, "that red car looks like shit."

"Well it's old," I says, "You got to expect that."

"No way!" says Henry. "That car's a classic! But you went and ran the piss right out of it, Lyman, and you know it don't deserve that. I kept that car in A-one shape. You don't remember. You're too young. But when I left, that car was running like a watch. Now I don't even know if I can get it to start again, let alone get it anywhere near its old condition."

"Well you try," I said, like I was getting mad, "but I say it's a piece of junk."

Then I walked out before he could realize I knew he'd strung together more than six words at once.

After that I thought he'd freeze himself to death working on that car. He was out there all day, and at night he rigged up a little lamp, ran a cord out the window, and had himself some light to see by while he worked. He was better than he had been before, but that's still not saying much. It was easier for him to do the things the rest of us did. He ate more slowly and didn't jump up and down during the meal to get this or that or look out the window. I put my hand on the back of the TV set, I admit, and fiddled around with it good, so that it was almost impossible now to get a clear picture. He didn't look at it very often anyway. He was always out with that car or going off to get parts for it. By the time it was really melting outside, he had it fixed.

I had been feeling down in the dumps about Henry around this time. We had always been together before. Henry and Lyman. But he was such a loner now that I didn't know how to take it. So I jumped at the chance one day when Henry seemed friendly. It's not that he smiled or anything. He just said, "Let's take that old shitbox for a spin." Just the way he said it made me think he could be coming around.

We went out to the car. It was spring. The sun was shining very bright. My only sister, Bonita, who was just eleven years old, came out and made us stand together for a picture. Henry leaned his elbow on the red car's windshield, and he took his other arm and put it over my shoulder, very carefully, as though it was heavy for him to lift and he didn't want to bring the weight down all at once.

"Smile," Bonita said, and he did.

That picture. I never look at it anymore. A few months ago, I don't know why, I got his picture out and tacked it on the wall. I felt good about Henry at the time, close to him. I felt good having his picture on the wall, until one night when I was looking at television. I was a little drunk and stoned. I looked up at the wall and Henry was staring at me. I don't know what it was, but his smile had changed, or maybe it was all gone. All I know is I couldn't stay in the same room with that picture. I was shaking. I got up, closed the door, and went into the kitchen. A little later my friend Ray came over and we both went back into that room. We put the picture in a brown bag, folded the bag over and over tightly, then put it way back in a closet.

I still see that picture now, as if it tugs at me, whenever I pass that closet door. The picture is very clear in my mind. It was so sunny that day Henry had to squint against the glare. Or maybe the camera Bonita held flashed like a mirror, blinding him, before she snapped the picture. My face is right out in the sun, big and round. But he might have drawn back, because the shadows on his face are deep as holes. There are two shadows curved like little hooks around the ends of his smile, as if to frame it and try to keep it there—that one, first smile that looked like it might have hurt his face. He has his field jacket on and the worn-in clothes he'd come back in and kept wearing ever since. After Bonita took the picture, she went into the house and we got into the car. There was a full cooler in the trunk. We started off, east, toward Pembina and the Red River because Henry said he wanted to see the high water.

The trip over there was beautiful. When everything starts changing, drying up, clearing off, you feel like your whole life is starting. Henry felt it, too. The top was down and the car hummed like a top. He'd really put it back in shape, even the tape on the seats was very carefully put down and glued back in layers. It's not that he smiled again or even joked, but his face looked to me as if it was clear, more peaceful. It looked as though he wasn't thinking of anything in particular except the bare fields and windbreaks and houses we were passing.

The river was high and full of winter trash when we got there. The sun was still out, but it was colder by the river. There were still little clumps of dirty snow here and there on the banks. The water hadn't gone over the banks yet, but it would, you could tell. It was just at its limit, hard swollen, glossy like an old gray scar. We made ourselves a fire, and we sat down and watched the current go. As I watched it I felt something squeezing inside me and tightening and trying to let go all at the same time. I knew I was just not feeling it myself; I knew I was feeling what Henry was going through at that moment. Except that I couldn't stand it, the closing and opening. I jumped to my feet. I took Henry by the shoulders and I started shaking him. "Wake up," I says, "wake up, wake up, wake up!" I didn't know what had come over me. I sat down beside him again.

His face was totally white and hard. Then it broke, like stones break all of a sudden when water boils up inside them.

"I know it," he says. "I know it. I can't help it. It's no use."

We start talking. He said he knew what I'd done with the car. It was obvious it had been whacked out of shape and not just neglected. He said he wanted to give the car to me for good now, it was no use. He said he'd fixed it just to give it back and I should take it.

"No way," I says. "I don't want it."

"That's okay," he says, "you take it."

"I don't want it, though," I says back to him, and then to emphasize, just to emphasize, you understand, I touch his shoulder. He slaps my hand off.

"Take that car," he says.

"No," I say. "Make me," I say and then he grabs my jacket and rips the arm loose. The jacket is a class act, suede with tags and zippers. I push Henry backwards, off the log. He jumps up and bowls me over. We go down in a clinch and come up swinging hard, for all we're worth, with our fists. He socks my jaw so hard I feel like it swings loose. Then I'm at his rib cage and land a good one under his chin so his head snaps back. He's dazzled. He looks at me and I look at him and then his eyes are full of tears and blood and at first I think he's crying. But no, he's laughing. "Ha! Ha!" he says. "Ha! Ha! Take good care of it."

"Okay," I says. "Okay, no problem. Ha! Ha!"

I can't help it, and I start laughing too. My face feels fat and strange, and after a while I get a beer from the cooler in the trunk, and when I hand it to Henry he takes his shirt and wipes my germs off. "Hoof-and-mouth disease," he says. For some reason this cracks me up, and so we're really laughing for a while, and then we drink all the rest of the beers one by one and throw them in the river and see how far, how fast, the current takes them before they fill up and sink.

"You want to go on back?" I ask after a while. "Maybe we could snag a couple nice Kashpaw girls."

He says nothing. But I can tell his mood is turning again.

"They're all crazy, the girls up here, every damn one of them."

"You're crazy too," I say, to jolly him up. "Crazy Lamartine boys!"

He looks as though he will take this wrong at first. His face twists, then clears and he jumps on his feet. "That's right!" he says. "Crazier 'n hell. Crazy Indians!"

I think its the old Henry again. He throws off his jacket and starts springing his legs up from the knees like a fancy dancer. He's down doing something between a grass dance and a bunny hop, no kind of dance I ever saw before, but neither has anyone else on all this green growing earth. He's wild. He wants to pitch whoopee! He's up and at me and all over. All this time I'm laughing so hard, so hard my belly is getting tied up in a knot.

"Got to cool me off!" he shouts all of a sudden. Then he runs over to the river and jumps in.

There's boards and other things in the current. It's so high. No sound comes from the river after the splash he makes, so I run right over. I look around. It's getting dark. I see he's halfway across the water already, and I know he didn't swim there because the current took him. It's far. I hear his voice, though, very clearly across it.

"My boots are filling," he says.

He says this in a normal voice, like he just noticed and he doesn't know what to think of it. Then he's gone. A branch comes by. Another branch. And I go in.

By the time I get out of the river, off the snag I pulled myself onto, the sun is down. I walk back to the car, turn on the high beams, and drive it up the bank. I put it in first gear and then I take my foot off the clutch. I get out, close the door, and watch it plow softly into the water. The headlights reach in as they go down, searching, still lighted even after the water swirls over the back end. I wait. The wires short out. It is all finally dark. And then there is only the water, the sound of it going and running and going and running and running.

The Hunting Years

Tom Franklin

Tom Franklin was born in Southern Alabama. He worked as a heavy equipment operator in a grit factory, a construction inspector in a chemical plant, and a clerk in a hospital morgue. His first book, Poachers *(1999), from which the following story has been excerpted, has attracted considerable attention. The title story, a novella, won the 1999 Edgar Allan Poe Award and was included in* New Stories From the South, Best American Mystery Stories *and* Best Mystery Stories of the Century.

The stories in Poachers *are set in southwest Alabama—an area where snake-infested swamps, polluting factories, and junked-up trailer parks pose equal challenges to people. The characters work in grit factories, drink a lot, spoil their marriages, or daydream of taking off for Alaska. Violence boils in their blood. As the following autobiographical piece shows, the violence and the drunkenness are all integral to an ideal of masculinity perverted by postindustrial life.*

Standing on a trestle in south Alabama, I look down into the coffee-brown water of the Blowout, a fishing hole I loved as a boy. It's late December, cold. A stiff wind rakes the water, swirls dead leaves and nods the tall brown cattails along the bank. Farther back in the woods it's very still, cypress trees and knees, thick vines, an abandoned beaver's lodge. Buzzards float overhead, black smudges against the gray clouds. Once, on this trestle, armed with only fishing rods, my brother Jeff and I heard a panther scream. It's a sound I've never forgotten, like a madwoman's shriek. After that, we brought guns when we came to fish. But today I'm unarmed, and the only noise is the groan and hiss of bulldozers and trucks on a new-cut logging road a quarter-mile away.

"Introduction: The Hunting Years," by Tom Franklin, reprinted from *Poachers*, 1999, HarperPerennial.

I left the south four years ago, when I was thirty, to go to graduate school in Fayetteville, Arkansas, where among transplanted Yankees and westerners I realized how lucky I was to have been raised here in these southern woods among poachers and storytellers. I know, of course, that most people consider Arkansas the south, but it's not *my* south. My south—the one I haven't been able to get out of my blood or my imagination, the south where these stories take place—is lower Alabama, lush and green and full of death, the wooded counties between the Alabama and Tombigbee Rivers.

Yesterday at five A.M. I left Fayetteville and drove seven hundred miles south to my parents' new house in Mobile, and this morning I woke early and drove two more hours, past the grit factory and the chemical plants where I worked in my twenties, to Dickinson, the community where we lived until I was eighteen. It's a tiny place, one store (now closed) and a post office in the same building, a kudzu-netted graveyard, railroad tracks. I've been finishing a novella that takes place in these woods—in the story, a man is killed right beneath where I'm standing—and I'm here looking for details of the landscape, for things I might've forgotten.

To get to the Blowout, I picked through a half-mile of pine trees that twelve years ago had been one of my family's cornfields. I hardly recognized the place. I walked another half-mile along the new logging road, then climbed onto the railroad track, deep woods on both sides, tall patchwork walls of briar and tree, brown thrashers hopping along unseen like something pacing me. My father and aunts and uncles used to own this land. It was ours. When my grandfather died, he divided almost six hundred acres among his five children. He expected them to keep it in the family, but one by one they sold it for logging or to hunting dubs. Today none of it is ours.

I'm about to leave when I notice that fifty yards down the track something big is disentangling itself from the trees. For a moment I reexperience the shock I used to feel whenever I saw a deer, but this is only a hunter. I see that he's spotted me, is climbing onto the tracks and coming this way. Because I lived in these parts for eighteen years, I expect to know him, and for a moment I feel foolish: What am I doing here at the Blowout, during hunting season, without a gun?

It's a familiar sensation, this snag of guilt, because when I was growing up, a boy who didn't hunt was branded as a pussy. For some reason, I never wanted to kill things, but I wasn't bold enough to say so. Instead, I did the expected: went to church on Sundays and on Wednesday nights, said "Yes ma'am" and "No sir" to my elders. And I hunted.

Though I hated (and still hate) to get up early, I rose at four A.M. Though I hated the cold, I made my way through the icy woods, climbing into one of our family's deer stands or sitting at the base of a thick live oak to still hunt, which simply means waiting for a buck to walk by so you can shoot him. And because I came to hunting for the wrong reasons, and because I worried that my father, brother and uncles might see through my ruse, I became the most zealous hunter of us all.

I was the one who woke first in the mornings and shook Jeff awake. The first in the truck. The first to the railroad track, where we climbed the rocky hill and crept toward the Blowout, our splitting-up point. On those mornings, the stars still out, it would be too dark to see our breath, the cross ties creaking beneath our boots, and

I would walk the quietest, holding my double-barrel sixteen-gauge shotgun against my chest, my bare thumb on the safety and my left trigger finger on the first of its two triggers. When we got to the Blowout, I'd go left, without a word, and Jeff right. I'd creep down the loose rocks, every sound amplified in the still morning, and I'd step quietly over the frozen puddles below and into the dark trees.

In the woods, the stars disappeared overhead as if swiped away, and I inched forward with my hand before my face to feel for briars, my eyes watering from the cold. When I got far enough, I found a tree to sit beneath, shivering and miserable, thinking of the stories I wanted to write and hoping for something to shoot. Because at sixteen, I'd never killed a deer, which meant I was technically still a pussy.

Of course there were a lot of real hunters in my family, including my father. Though he no longer hunted, Gerald Franklin commanded the respect of the most seasoned woodsman because as a young man he'd been a legendary killer of turkeys (and we all knew that turkey hunters consider themselves the only serious sportsmen, disdaining deer or any other game the way fly fishermen look down on bait fishermen). Dad never bragged about the toms he'd shot, but we heard everything from our uncles. According to them, my father had been the wildest of us all, getting up earlier and staying in the woods later than any man in the county.

There's a story he tells where he woke on a spring Sunday to go hunting—he never used a clock, relying instead on his "built-in" alarm. Excited because he knew which tree a gobbler had roosted in the evening before, he dressed in the dark so he wouldn't wake my mother, pregnant with me. When he got to the woods it was still pitch black, so he settled down to wait for daylight. An hour passed, and no sign of light. Instead of going back home, though, he laid his gun aside, lit a cigarette and continued to wait for a dawn that wouldn't arrive for three more hours. Later, laughing, he told my uncles he'd gotten to the woods around one A.M.

But at some point, before I started first grade, he quit hunting. I always figured it was because he'd found religion. I grew up going to the Baptist church every Sunday with a father who was a deacon, not a hunter. Ours was a godly household—to this day I've never heard Dad curse—and we said grace at every meal (even if we ate out) and prayed as a family each night, holding hands. After church on Sunday mornings, Dad sat in our living room and read his Bible, wearing his tie all day, then loaded us in the big white Chrysler to head back to church in the evening.

If we passed the three Wiggins brothers, dressed in old clothes and carrying hand-cut fishing poles, Dad shook his head and gave us all a minisermon on the perils of fishing on the Lord's day. Though neither he nor anyone else has ever confirmed it, I've always thought that by not hunting he was paying a kind of self-imposed penance for the Saturday nights in his youth he'd spent in pool halls, and for the Sundays he'd skipped church to chase turkeys.

Sometimes, in my own hunting years, huddled against a sweet gum, waiting for noon or dusk to give me permission to leave the woods, I'd imagine my father as a younger man, slipping through the trees, still wearing his blue mechanic's shirt with his name stitched across the chest, grease from his garage under his fingernails, carrying in his callused hands the same sixteen-gauge shotgun he would later give me. He was heading toward where he'd heard a gobbler that morning before work.

When he got to the spot, he knelt and, cradling the shotgun, removed from the pocket of his old army jacket the little box turkey caller he would give my brother years later. It was wooden and hollow like a tiny guitar box. You drew a peg over its green surface as gently as you could, the way you'd peel an apple without breaking the skin. If you knew what you were doing, it made a quiet, perfect hen's cluck, something a man could barely hear, but a sound that would snap a gobbler's head around half a mile away. After Dad had clucked a time or two, he waited, and when he heard the distant answer—that mysterious lovely cry, half a rooster's crow and half the whinny of a horse—he worked his jaw like a man shifting his chewing tobacco, and from under his tongue he moved his "yepper" to the roof of his mouth.

Year after year, in our stockings for Christmas, he'd been giving Jeff and me our own yeppers, tiny plastic turkey callers the size of a big man's thumbnail, and he would try to teach us to "yep" the way turkeys do. Jeff caught on quickly, but it made me gag.

It was this kind of gift that let me know my father wanted me to hunt, though he never pressed, and let me know he was bothered by the fact that, until I was fifteen years old, I played with dolls. Not girls' dolls, but "action figures." The original G.I. Joe with his fuzzy crew cut and a scar on his chin, Johnny West with his painted-on clothes, Big Jim with his patented karate chop: I had them all. I loved playing with them, and because Jeff was two years younger than I was, he did whatever I did. But while he would wrench off G.I. Joe's head and hands to examine how the doll was put together, I would imagine that my G.I. Joe was Tarzan of the Apes. One of my sister's Barbie dolls, stripped to a skimpy jungle bikini, became Jane. A foot-tall Chewbacca was Kerchak, an ape. In the lush green summer afternoons, Jeff and I built African villages out of sticks and vines. We dug a wide trench across our backyard and with the garden hose made a muddy brown river filled with rubber snakes and plastic crocodiles.

When the Wiggins brothers pedaled up on their rusty bicycles—they were stringy, sun-yellowed boys who smelled like sweat and fish and never wore shirts or shoes in summer, who lived a mile away down a dirt road in the woods—Jeff and I would toss our dolls into the bushes and pretend to be cleaning up a mess in the backyard.

"Wanna go fishin'?" Kent Wiggins would ask, stuffing his lower lip with Skoal. His father worked for the lumber mill, and Kent would get a job there when he turned eighteen. I envied them the ease with which they accepted and handled their lives, the way they spit between their teeth, flicked a rod, fired a rifle.

Jeff and I always went wherever they asked us to go—I was afraid of being laughed at and being called a mama's boy for saying no, and Jeff enjoyed the fishing. And sitting on the trestle over the Blowout, watching the Wigginses and my little brother pull in catfish after catfish, I'd long for my G.I. Joe, and hate the longing.

Once, when I was newly fifteen in Kmart with ten birthday dollars to spend, Dad came up beside me.

"You could buy a hunting knife," he whispered.

"Gerald . . ." my mother warned.

He let go of my shoulders, put his hands in his pockets.

"He wants to get a new outfit for his G.I. Joe," Mom said to Dad.

I'd never felt more like a pussy.

So the hell with it, I thought, and headed for the tall line of fishing rods I could see beyond the toy aisle. Dad fell into step beside me. He let me shave the bristly hairs off his wrist in search of the sharpest knife while Mom stood with her arms folded near the stink bait, glaring into space. At the checkout counter, I watched Dad add another five to my ten dollars for the Old Timer Sharpfinger I'd picked. When we left the store, he had his arm around me.

As Dad drove us home, I asked him if he wished I didn't play with G.I. Joes. Mom sat far across the long seat, looking out her window. At my question, her head jerked toward Dad, who stopped whistling. He glanced at her before catching my eye in the rearview mirror.

"No," he said. "I'm real proud of you, son. I'm glad you've got . . . imagination."

When Jeff killed his first buck, a spike, I was there.

Despite being younger, Jeff has always been a much better shot than I am. I'd gotten Dad's sixteen-gauge at Christmas, but Jeff had unwrapped a Marlin thirty-thirty lever-action rifle. The fact that I was eighteen and still using a shotgun didn't go unnoticed—the boy with the weakest aim always gets the scattergun because its spray of buckshot gives more chances for a hit than a single bullet. Never mind that my sixteen-gauge was an antique that had belonged to my grandfather, a rare Foxboro crafted of blued Sterlingworth steel, a side-by-side model that broke open behind the walnut stock. The shells slid in and the breech closed with a muffled snap, a sound more like cloth than metal. It's a gun I can take apart—barrel, forearm, stock—and reassemble in thirty seconds. A gun worth over two thousand dollars. Yet in the woods, I was ashamed of it.

The high school closed on opening day of deer season, and on that first morning in 1980, Jeff and I sat in opposite tree stands—small seats built overlooking a wide field where deer came to graze—and from mine I watched my brother sight me with the scope of his rifle. I sat rigid, silent, ready for a deer, while a hundred yards away, Jeff waved at me. Gave me the finger. He pissed from off his stand, *twice.* He yawned. Slept. But as one hour became two, I stayed stock-still—I didn't have Jeff's instinct for knowing when to be ready, for being relaxed until it was time to raise your gun and aim. My limbs began to tingle, the blood slowing in my veins like a creek icing up. I didn't blink for so long that the woods blurred, and I began to feel that I was part of them, the trees and the leaves taking on a buzzing resonance and losing their sharp edges, the buzzing increasing like a hornet loose inside my head, and for an instant I hung there, the center of something, seeing from my ears, hearing from my eyes, the world around me a tangible glow of brindle noise. Then I blinked.

And from across the field came Jeff's gunshot.

From then on, I insisted on sitting in Jeff's lucky stand. A year later, early in the 1981 season, the sixteen-gauge in my lap, I was there, waiting. Tense. It was dusk, and I was losing hope again. I'd been hunting like a fanatic—once or twice a day. I'd stopped taking books with me. I'd seen deer and even missed a doe, the fabled buck fever claiming me with violent seizures, my gun barrel shaking, teeth clacking.

Now, on the lucky stand, I didn't see the deer when it walked into the field. You seldom do: they just appear. And if it's a buck, like this one, you notice the antlers first, the sleekest, sharpest things in the world, not bone but blood vessels dried and hard as stone. On the stand, I lifted the jittering shotgun, slowly, thumbing the safety, the buck less than twenty yards from where I sat trembling.

I aimed, blood roaring in my ears, and fired, not feeling the kick.

The buck raised his head, still chewing. His antlers seemed to unwind as he looked around, wondering where that blast had come from. At some point, I remembered that I had another barrel, and I began pulling the trigger again, before finally realizing that I had to pull the *second* trigger. When I fired, the deer buckled and recovered, then vanished, replaced by the noise of something tearing through the dead leaves behind me, a painful sound hacking down the gully.

From across the field, Jeff's voice: "Kill anything?"

I descended the ladder, my hands shaking. At the bottom, I struggled to break open the gun, and shells from my pocket fell to the ground. I reloaded, and, nearly crying, slid to the bottom of the gully.

The deer—thank God—was there. Still alive, but down. His side caving in and out and a hind leg quivering. Approaching him, I counted his points—six, seven, eight—an eight-point! What I was supposed to do now, what Dad and my uncles had drilled into me, was to cautiously approach the buck, draw my knife and cut his throat, watch him bleed to death. But in my excitement, I forgot this. Instead, I moved to within three feet of the deer's flagging side and flipped the sixteen-gauge's safety off. I put a finger on each of the shotgun's triggers, and, holding the gun at my hip, pulled them at the same time.

That night, my entire family admired the deer lying in the back of Dad's pickup, its black eyes turning foggy. It's traditional to rub blood on a boy's face when he kills his first deer, but Dad had a lesson to teach. I'd gut-shot the buck so badly that a lot of meat had been ruined. The hole I'd blown in his side was big enough to put my head in, and Dad came up behind me and did exactly that. When he pulled me out by my neck, I was almost sick, but I managed to hold it, like a man. That was when everyone gathered around me, my uncles and Jeff clapping my back, Mom and my aunts hugging me, trying not to get blood on their blouses.

When I tell this story, I end by saying that nothing except Beth Ann accepting my marriage proposal on a warm wine-and-cheese afternoon in Paris has surpassed the feeling I had that night. As Dad guided me through cleaning the deer, peeling down its skin, trimming away the small white pockets of fat, my eight-year-old cousin approached us. When the boy saw the buck's bloody, empty body cavity, he tumbled away, gagging. Dad rolled his eyes at me. Then we began to quarter the red meat, my face and neck still bloody, my hair stiff with gore.

Near the close of the same season, I sat on a wooded hill in a plot of land on which my father, when he sold it, had been wise enough to retain the mineral and hunting rights. It was only two months after I'd killed my eight-point, but now things were different because Jeff had bragged about the buck at school. Whenever I told the story, I always made myself seem foolish by giving the deer both barrels at such close range. People seemed to like that. I was discovering the power of self-depreciation and didn't mind being laughed at as long as everyone knew I'd killed the deer. And they did: Coach Horn had led me to his office behind the gym and shown me the antlers on his walls. For the first time in my life, I wasn't a pussy. No. Sitting on the hillside that evening, I was a man who'd enjoyed his first taste of blood and who wanted more.

It was a mild January day, the leaves crisp, stirred by the wind to an almost constant rustle. Suddenly, an even bigger eight-point buck had materialized at the bottom of the ravine, stealing among the live oaks. First I saw his rack of antlers as he nosed along the ground, eating acorns. Then his shoulders. His flat tail. The color of dead leaves, he blended so well into the hillside that I only saw him when he moved. My heart began to rattle, and, as if he heard it, the buck raised his head and looked right at me. He lifted his nose and snorted, his nostrils gleaming. For a moment he seemed to vanish, to have never been there, but before I could panic I saw him again as he took a step away from me.

Somehow, I did everything right—aimed when he put his head down, squeezed instead of jerked the trigger—and *still* damn near missed. My buckshot pellets sprayed the deer across his neck, face and antlers, chipping them, bringing bloody beads across his cheeks, putting out one eye and—we saw this later—injuring his spine so that he only had use of his front legs, the back two paralyzed. I stood and watched him drag himself through the leaves, trying to get away, pawing and stumbling down the gullyside.

From the next hollow over, Jeff called, "Kill anything?"

I half fell to the bottom of the ravine. The deer lay still, just a slight rippling of his big leathery sides, blood glistening on his black nose. While I circled him, gun ready, he watched me, his head up, turning to keep me in sight. One eye was red and bleeding, but the other remained bright and clear. From over the hill, I heard Jeff crashing through the leaves. I knew he'd heard my shot—my single shot—and I didn't want him to hear another.

Why didn't I cut the deer's throat? There was no shame in that, and it was the safest way to avoid the buck's deadly antlers. But instead I did something that shocks me to this day. I dropped the sixteen-gauge and drew my Sharpfinger. I approached the deer, watching him follow me with his good eye. Carefully, the way you'd reach to pin a snake with your foot, I stuck out my leg and put my boot on the buck's neck, forcing his head down. I knelt on top of him, straddled his back. Now I heard his ragged breathing, felt his heat on my thighs. I took one thick tine of his antlers in my right hand and turned his good eye away so he couldn't see. He didn't resist. I raised the knife and began to stab him in the shoulder where I knew his heart was. The buck barely moved beneath me, and the blade cut cleanly, as if I were sticking soft dirt. I stabbed him twelve times, in what I thought a buckshot pattern would be. Then I laid my hand on the deer's hot shoulder, over the wounds I'd made, and felt that his heart had stopped.

By the time Jeff came running down the hill, I'd begun my first solo act of field dressing. It was—and still is—the biggest buck anyone in my family had killed, weighing over 220, seventy pounds more than I weighed at the time.

Later, as we hoisted the deer up beneath our skinning tree, Dad noticed the holes in the buck's side. He nodded to Jeff and me. "Now boys," he said, "*that* was a good shot." With my knife, I made a series of cuts along the deer's hind legs, and Jeff and Dad helped me peel down the buck's fur—a noise like Velcro makes—to reveal the nearly purple carcass beneath.

Night had fallen, and with a flashlight Dad looked at the deer's side. He bent, examining it more closely, working his finger into one of the knife slits. Then he stared me down.

"Son," he said, "is that what I think it is?"

I didn't answer.

He reached for the deer's head and lifted it by the giant, chipped, eight-point rack, a set of antlers so big I could step into it like pants. He grabbed me by the small of my back and jammed me into my dead deer. He brought the antlers against my stomach and pushed the points in so hard they hurt.

"Do you know what 'eviscerate' means?" he asked me.

Now, at the Blowout, the hunter approaches me on the trestle. I expect it's one of the Wiggins brothers, and here I am again, as gunless and guilty and foolish as if I'm holding a doll. But as the man draws closer, a scoped rifle in the crook of his arm, I see from his expensive camouflage, fluorescent orange hat and face paint that he's not from around here. The men who live in these parts hunt in work clothes, old boots and faded camo jackets passed down from their fathers or grandfathers. They would never wear face paint or an orange hat. When I hunted I used to carry such a cap in my pocket in case I ran into a game warden, but most of the hunters I grew up admiring simply never ran into game wardens. These men raise their own coon and squirrel dogs. Their rifles have taped stocks. Although they often kill out of season or at night, they usually eat what they kill. I admire them, and so I feel a flicker of distaste for this outsider.

"Hello," I say to the fellow, probably a lawyer from Mobile. "Kill anything?"

"Get out of here," he says.

I cock my head. "I'm sorry?"

"You heard me. This is private property. You're trespassing on our hunting club." He swings his gun barrel toward the woods on the right, as if pointing to his buddies lurking in the shadows, their faces green and black, twigs in their hair, expensive ri-fles aimed at my head.

I spit through my teeth. I don't tell him that this used to be my family's land, that I've dragged deer over this very track, spent hours on this goddamn trestle. Instead I say, "The railroad's not private property."

"The hell it's not," he says. And raises the rifle, aims at me.

We stand facing one another. It will be dark soon, and from the left side of the track comes the distant snarl of a logger's power saw. I try to see myself through the hunter's eyes: my ragged jeans, my leather jacket and hiking boots. To him I proba-bly look like a hippie, like the last thing you'd expect to find out here.

Meanwhile, the hunter is edgy, glancing behind him in the woods. "I'm not gonna tell you again," he says.

The saw rattles to a stop, then revs up again.

"You hear that?" I ask. "That'll ruin your hunting more than I will."

I know I should leave, but instead I sit on the cold rail and look away from the hunter, at the woods. I recall a story my father told me. He was turkey hunting down here early on a Sunday morning. Creeping along, he heard a wavering voice, and it spooked him. He followed it through the trees until, in the distance, he saw an old black preacher standing on a stump, practicing his sermon. He had a giant white Bible in one hand and a red handkerchief for face-mopping in the other. Despite the forty-degree weather, his shirtsleeves were rolled up. Dad stopped and listened to the man's tremulous voice, knowing that every turkey for miles was gone, that his hunting was spoiled. He might as well have gone home. When I asked him if he was angry he said no, just spooked.

I turn and look at the hunter's camouflaged face. "You ever hunt turkeys?"

"Go to hell," he says, and walks away. He doesn't look back, just heads into the woods. When he's gone I stand up and close my coat. Take a last long look at the Blowout, then make my way carefully down the side of the tracks. I duck under the dark-ening magnolia branches on the other side and start back toward the logging road.

I know, as I walk, that I'm not the fancy-rifled lawyer in face paint and new cam-ouflage, yet neither am I the dedicated native hunter I pretended to be all those years. Now when I return here, to Dickinson, it's as a kind of stranger—after all, I've left, got-ten educated, lost some of my drawl. I even married a Yankee. And coming back like this to hunt for details for my stories feels a bit like poaching on land that used to be mine. But I've never lost the need to tell of my Alabama, to reveal it, lush and green and full of death. So I return, knowing what I've learned. I come back, where life is slow dying, and I poach for stories. I poach because I want to recover the paths while there's still time, before the last logging trucks rumble through and the old, dark ways are at last forever hewn.

Imperial Bedroom

Jonathan Franzen

Jonathan Franzen is a writer for New York Times. *He has also written two novels* The Twenty-Seventh City *(1988) and* Strong Motion *(1991) that have enjoyed success with readers and critics alike. Franzen was selected by* Granta *magazine as one of its 20 Best Young American Novelists.*

Our privacy panic isn't merely exaggerated. It's founded on a fallacy. Ellen Alderman and Caroline Kennedy, in "The Right to Privacy," sum up the conventional wisdom of privacy advocates like this: "There is less privacy than there used to be." The claim has been made or implied so often, in so many books and editorials and talk-show dens, that Americans, no matter how passive they are in their behavior, now dutifully tell pollsters that they're very much worried about privacy. From almost any historical perspective, however, the claim seems bizarre.

In 1890, an American typically lived in a small town under conditions of near-panoptical surveillance. Not only did his every purchase "register" but it registered in the eyes and in the memory of shopkeepers who knew him, his parents, his wife, and his children. He couldn't so much as walk to the post office without having his movements tracked and analyzed by neighbors. Probably he grew up sleeping in a bed with his siblings and possibly with his parents, too. Unless he was well-off, his transportation—a train, a horse, his own two feet—either was communal or exposed him to the public eye.

In the suburbs and exurbs where the typical American lives today, tiny nuclear families inhabit enormous houses, in which each person has his or her own bedroom and, sometimes, bathroom. Compared even with suburbs in the sixties and seventies, when I was growing up, the contemporary condominium development or gated community offers a striking degree of anonymity. It's no longer the rule that you know your neighbors. Communities increasingly tend to be virtual, the participants either faceless or firmly in control of the faces they present. Transportation is largely private: the latest S.U.V.s are the size of living rooms and come with onboard telephones, CD players, and TV screens; behind the tinted windows of one of these high-riding, I-see-you-but-you-can't-see-me mobile PrivacyGuard® units, a person can be wearing pajamas or a licorice bikini, for all anybody knows or cares. Maybe the government intrudes on the family a little more than it did a hundred years ago (social workers look in on the old and the poor, health officials require inoculations, the police inquire about spousal battery), but from a privacy perspective these intrusions don't begin to make up for the small-town snooping they've replaced.

"The right to be left alone"? Far from disappearing, it's exploding. It's the essence of modern American architecture, landscape, transportation, communications, and mainstream political philosophy. The real reason that Americans are passive about privacy is so big as to be almost invisible: we're flat-out *drowning* in privacy.

What's threatened isn't the private sphere. It's the public sphere. Much has been made of the discouraging effect that the Starr investigation may have on future aspirants to public office (only zealots and zeros need apply), but that's just half of it. The public world of Washington, because it's public, belongs to everyone. We're all invited to participate with our votes, our patriotism, our campaigning, and our opinions. The collective weight of a population makes possible our faith in the public world as something larger and more enduring and more dignified than any messy individual can be in private. But, just as one sniper in a church tower can keep the streets of an entire town empty, one real gross-out scandal can undermine that faith.

If privacy depends upon an expectation of invisibility, the expectation of *visibility* is what defines a public space. My "sense of privacy" functions to keep the public out of the private *and* to keep the private out of the public. A kind of mental Border collie yelps in distress when I feel that the line between the two has been breached. This is why the violation of a public space is so similar, as an experience, to the violation of privacy. I walk past a man taking a leak on a sidewalk in broad daylight (delivery-truck drivers can be especially self-righteous in their "Ya gotta go, ya gotta go" philosophy of bladder management), and although the man with the yawning fly is ostensibly the one whose privacy is compromised by the leak, I'm the one who feels the impingement. Flashers and sexual harassers and fellators on the pier and self-explainers on the cross-town bus all similarly assault our sense of the public by exposing themselves.

Since really serious exposure in public today is assumed to be synonymous with being seen on television, it would seem to follow that televised space is the premier public space. Many things that people say to me on television, however, would never be tolerated in a genuine public space—in a jury box, for example, or even on a city sidewalk. TV is an enormous, ramified extension of the billion living rooms and bedrooms in which it's consumed. You rarely hear a person on the subway talking loudly about, say, incontinence, but on television it's been happening for years. TV is devoid of shame, and without shame there can be no distinction between public and private. Last winter, an anchorwoman looked me in the eye and, in the tone of a close female relative, referred to a litter of babies in Iowa as "America's seven little darlin's." It was strange enough, twenty-five years ago, to get Dan Rather's reports on Watergate between spots for Geritol and Bayer aspirin, as if Nixon's impending resignation were somehow situated in my medicine chest. Now, shelved between ads for Promise margarine and Celebrity Cruises, the news itself is a soiled cocktail dress—TV the wardrobe and nothing but.

Reticence, meanwhile, has become an almost obsolete virtue. People now readily name their diseases, rents, and antidepressants. Sexual histories get spilled on first dates, Birkenstocks and cutoffs infiltrate the office on casual Fridays, telecommuting puts the boardroom in the bedroom, the "softer" modern office design puts the bedroom in the boardroom, salespeople unilaterally address customers by their first names, waiters won't bring me food until I've established a personal relationship with them, voice-mail machinery stresses the "I" in "I'm sorry, but I don't understand what you dialled," and cyberenthusiasts, in a particularly grotesque misnomer, designate as "public forums" pieces of etched silicon with which a forum's unshaved "participant" may communicate while sitting cross-legged in tangled sheets and wearing gym shorts. The networked world as a threat to privacy? It's the ugly spectacle of a privacy triumphant.

A genuine public space is a place where every citizen is welcome to be present, and where the purely private is excluded or restricted. One reason that attendance at art museums has soared in recent years is that museums still feel public in this way. After those tangled sheets, how delicious the enforced decorum and the hush, the absence of in-your-face consumerism. How sweet the promenading, the seeing and being seen. Everybody needs a promenade sometimes—a place to go when you want to announce to the world (not the little world of friends and family but the big world, the real world) that you have a new suit, or are in love, or suddenly realize that you stand a full inch taller when you don't hunch your shoulders.

Unfortunately, the fully public place is a nearly extinct category. We still have courtrooms and the jury pool, commuter trains and bus stations, here and there a small-town Main Street that really is a main street rather than a strip mall, certain coffee bars, and certain city sidewalks. Otherwise, for American adults the only halfway public space is the world of work. Here, especially in the upper echelons of business, codes of dress and behavior are routinely enforced, personal disclosures are penalized, and formality is still the rule. But these rituals extend only to the employees of the firm, and even they, when they become old, disabled, obsolete, or outsourceable, are liable to be expelled and thereby relegated to the tangled sheets.

The last big, steep-walled bastion of public life in America is Washington, D.C. Hence the particular violation I felt when the Starr report crashed in. Hence the feeling of being intruded on. It was privacy invasion, all right: private life brutally invading the most public of public spaces. I don't want to see sex on the news from Washington. There's sex everywhere else I look—on sitcoms, on the Web, on dust jackets, on the billboards in Times Square. Can't there be one thing in the national landscape that isn't about the bedroom? We all know there's sex in the cloakrooms of power, sex behind the pomp and circumstance, sex beneath the robes of justice; but can't we act like grownups and pretend otherwise? Pretend not that "no one is looking" but that *everyone* is looking?

For two decades now, business leaders and politicians across much of the spectrum, both Gingrich Republicans and Clinton Democrats, have extolled the virtues of privatizing public institutions. But what better word can there be for Lewinskygate and the ensuing irruption of disclosures (the infidelities of Helen Chenoweth, of Dan Burton, of Henry Hyde) than "privatization"? Anyone who wondered what a privatized Presidency might look like may now, courtesy of Mr. Starr, behold one.

In Denis Johnson's short story "Beverly Home," the young narrator spends his days working at a nursing home for the hopelessly disabled, where there is a particularly unfortunate patient whom no one visits:

> He was only thirty-three, I believe he said, but it was hard to guess what he told about himself because he really couldn't talk anymore, beyond clamping his lips repeatedly around his protruding tongue while groaning.
>
> No more pretending for him! He was completely and openly a mess. Meanwhile the rest of us go on trying to fool each other.

In a coast-to-coast, shag-carpeted imperial bedroom, we could all just be messes and save ourselves the trouble of pretending. But who wants to live in a pajama-party world? Privacy loses its value unless there's something it can be defined against. "Meanwhile the rest of us go on trying to fool each other"—and a good thing, too. The need to put on a public face is as basic as the need for the privacy in which to take it off. We need both a home that's not like a public space and a public space that's not like home.

Walking up Third Avenue on a Saturday night, I feel bereft. All around me, attractive young people are hunched over their StarTacs and Nokias with preoccupied expressions, as if probing a sore tooth, or adjusting a hearing aid, or squeezing a pulled muscle: personal technology has begun to look like a personal handicap. What I really want from a sidewalk is that people see me and let themselves be seen, but even this modest ideal is thwarted by cell-phone users and their unwelcome privacy. They say things like "Should we have couscous with that?" and "I'm on my way to Blockbuster." They aren't breaking any law by broadcasting these dining-nook conversations. There's no Publicity-Guard® that I can buy, no expensive preserve of public life to which I can flee. Seclusion, whether in a suite at The Plaza or in a cabin in the Catskills, is comparatively effortless to achieve. Privacy is protected as both commodity and right; public forums are protected as neither. Like old-growth forests, they're few and irreplaceable and should be held in trust by everyone. The work of maintaining them only gets harder as the private sector grows ever more demanding,

130

distracting, and disheartening. Who has the time and energy to stand up for the public sphere? What rhetoric can possibly compete with the American love of "privacy"?

When I return to my apartment after dark, I don't immediately turn my lights on. Over the years, it's become a reflexive precaution on my part not to risk spooking exposed neighbors by flooding my living room with light, although the only activity I ever seem to catch them at is watching TV.

My skin-conscious neighbor is home with her husband tonight, and they seem to be dressing for a party. The woman, a vertical strip of whom is visible between the Levolors and the window frame, is wearing a bathrobe and a barrette and sitting in front of a mirror. The man, slick-haired, wearing suit pants and a white T-shirt, stands by a sofa in the other room and watches television in a posture that I recognize as uncommitted. Finally, the woman disappears into the bedroom. The man puts on a white shirt and a necktie and perches sidesaddle on an arm of the sofa, still watching television, more involved with it now. The woman returns wearing a strapless yellow dress and looking like a whole different species of being. Happy the transformation! Happy the distance between private and public! I see a rapid back-and-forth involving jewelry, jackets, and a clutch purse, and then the couple, dressed to the nines, ventures out into the world.

Dearly Disconnected

Ian Frazier

An Ohio native, Frazier attended Harvard, where he wrote for the Lampoon *and earned national attention with their parody of* Cosmo, *featuring Henry Kissinger as centerfold. Frazier graduated from Harvard in 1973, and he joined the staff of* The New Yorker, *where his pieces appeared for two decades. His first book,* Dating Your Mom, *started a career that got him critical and public acclaim. Frazier has been compared to such well-known humorists as Mark Twain and James Thurber. Among his best-known books are* Nobody Better, Better than Nobody, Great Plains, On the Rez, *and* Coyote v. Acme. *As research for* Great Plains, *he drove 25,000 miles, spanning and crisscrossing the region between Montana and Texas.*

Before I got married I was living by myself in an A-frame cabin in northwestern Montana. The cabin was a single high-ceilinged room, and at the center of the room, mounted on the rough-hewn log that held up the ceiling beam, was a telephone. I knew no one in the area or indeed the whole state, so my entire social life came to me through that phone. The woman I would marry was living in Sarasota, Florida, and the distance between us suggests how well we were getting along at the time. We had not been in touch for several months; she had no phone. One day she decided to call me from a pay phone. We talked for a while, and after her coins ran out I jotted the number on the wood beside my phone and called her back. A day or two later, thinking about the call, I wanted to talk to her again. The only number I had for her was the pay-phone number I'd written down.

The pay phone was on the street some blocks from the apartment where she stayed. As it happened, though, she had just stepped out to do some errands a few minutes before I called, and she was passing by on the sidewalk when the phone rang. She had no reason to think that a public phone ringing on a busy street would be for her.

Excerpt from "Dearly Disconnected," by Ian Frazier, reprinted from *Mother Jones,* 2000.

She stopped, listened to it ring again, and picked up the receiver. Love is pure luck; somehow I had known she would answer, and she had known it would be me.

Long afterward, on a trip to Disney World in Orlando with our two kids, then aged six and two, we made a special detour to Sarasota to show them the pay phone. It didn't impress them much. It's just a nondescript Bell Atlantic pay phone on the cement wall of a building. But its ordinariness and even boringness only make me like it more; I have a fondness for ordinary places where extraordinary events have occurred. On my mental map of Florida, that pay phone is a landmark looming above the city it occupies—and a notable, if private, historic site.

I'm interested in pay phones in general these days, especially because I get the feeling that they are about to disappear. Technology, in the form of sleek little phones in our pockets, has swept them by, and they're beginning to seem antique. When I was young they were just there, a given, often as stubborn and uncongenial as the curbstone underfoot. They were instruments of torture sometimes, requiring fistfuls of change in those pre-phone-card days, and the operator was a real person who stood maddeningly between you and whomever you were trying to call. And when the call went wrong, as communication often does, the pay phone provided a focus for your rage. Pay phones were always getting smashed, the receivers shattered to bits against the booth, the coin slots jammed with chewing gum, the cords yanked out and unraveled to the floor.

You used to hear people standing at pay phones and cursing them. I remember the sound of my own frustrated shouting confined by the glass walls of a phone booth—the kind you don't see much anymore, with a little ventilating fan in the ceiling that turned on when you shut the double-hinged glass door. The noise that fan made in the silence of a phone booth was for me the essence of romantic melancholy. Certain pay phones I still resent for the unhappiness they caused me; others I will never forgive.

There was always a touch of seediness and sadness to pay phones, and a sense of transience. Drug dealers made calls from them, and shady types who did not want their whereabouts known, and people too poor to have phones of their own, and otherwise respectable people planning assignations. In the movies, any character who used a pay phone was either in trouble or contemplating a crime. Pay phones came with their own special atmospherics and even, sometimes, accessories—the predictable bad smells and graffiti, of course, as well as cigarette butts, soda cans, scattered pamphlets from the Jehovah's Witnesses, and single bottles of beer (empty) still in their individual, street-legal paper bags. Mostly, pay phones evoked the mundane: "Honey, I'm just leaving. I'll be there soon." But you could tell that a lot of undifferentiated humanity had flowed through these places, and that in the muteness of each pay phone's little space, wild emotion had howled.

Once, when I was living in Brooklyn, I read in the newspaper that a South American man suspected of dozens of drug-related contract murders had been arrested at a pay phone in Queens. Police said that the man had been on the phone setting up a murder at the time of his arrest. The newspaper story gave the address of the pay phone, and out of curiosity one afternoon I took a long walk to Queens to look at it.

It was on an undistinguished street in a middle-class neighborhood, by a florist's shop. By the time I saw it, however, the pay phone had been blown up, firebombed. I had never before seen a pay phone so damaged; explosives had blasted pieces of the phone itself wide open in metal shreds like frozen banana peels, and flames had blackened everything and melted the plastic parts and burned the insulation off the wires. Soon after, I read that police could not find enough evidence against the suspected murderer and so had let him go.

The phone on the wall of the concession stand at Redwood Pool, where I used to stand dripping and call my mom to come and pick me up; the sweaty phones used almost only by men in the hallway outside the maternity ward at Lenox Hill Hospital in New York; the phone by the driveway of the Red Cloud Indian School in South Dakota where I used to talk with my wife while priests in black slacks and white socks chatted on a bench nearby; the phone in the old wood-paneled booth with leaded glass windows in the drugstore in my Ohio hometown—each one is as specific as a birthmark, a point on earth unlike any other.

It's the cell phone, of course, that's putting the pay phone out of business. The pay phone is to the cell phone as the troubled and difficult older sibling is to the cherished newborn. People even treat their cell phones like babies, cradling them in their palms and beaming down upon them lovingly as they dial. You sometimes hear people yelling on their cell phones, but they almost never yell at them. Cell phones are toylike, nearly magic; when I see a cell-phone user gently push the little antenna and fit the phone back into its brushed-vinyl carrying case and tuck the case inside his jacket beside his heart, I feel sorry for the beat-up pay phone standing in the rain.

And yet I don't think that pay phones will disappear completely. Probably they will survive for a long while as clumsy old technology still of some use to those lagging behind, and as a backup if ever the superior systems should temporarily fail. Before pay phones became endangered I never thought of them as public spaces, which of course they are. They suggest a human average; they belong to anybody who has a couple of coins. Now I see that, like public schools and public transportation, pay phones belong to a former commonality our culture is no longer quite so sure it needs.

I have a weakness for places—old battlefields, car-crash sites, houses where famous authors lived. Bygone passions should always have an address, it seems to me. Ideally, the world would be covered with plaques and markers listing the notable events that occurred at each particular spot. A sign on every pay phone would describe how a woman broke up with her fiancé here, how a young ballplayer learned that he had made the team. Unfortunately, the world itself is fluid and changes out from under us; the rocky islands Mark Twain was careful to avoid in the Mississippi are now stone outcroppings in a soybean field. Meanwhile, our passions proliferate into illegibility, and the places they occur can't hold them. Eventually pay phones will become relics of an almost vanished landscape, and of a time when there were fewer of us and our stories were on an earlier page. Romantics like me will have to reimagine our passions as they are—unmoored to earth, like an infinitude of cell-phone messages flying through the atmosphere.

Departmental

Robert Frost

Although he was born in San Francisco, Robert Frost (1874–1963) had long been associated with the New England that became his home at the age of ten. He briefly attended Dartmouth in New Hampshire and Harvard in Massachusetts, but disliked academic culture and dropped out of both universities to work in a mill, edit a country newspaper, teach school, and farm. After many years as a farmer, Frost moved to England and published his first collection of poetry, A Boy's Will, *in 1913 at the age of 39. When he published* North of Boston *in 1914, which includes such poems as "The Wood-Pile," "Mending Wall," and "The Death of the Hired Man," he established his reputation as an important voice in American poetry, and he returned to the US to settle on a farm in New Hampshire. His next volume,* Mountain Interval *(1916) included "The Road Not Taken," and he won the Pulitzer Prize for poetry in 1923 for the collection* New Hampshire, *which includes the poem "Stopping by Woods on a Snowy Evening." More Pulitzers were awarded for his* Collected Poems *in 1930,* A Further Range *in 1936, and* A Witness Tree *in 1942. Frost is considered one of the most influential voices in twentieth-century American poetry, and he is one of America's best-loved poets.*

An ant on the tablecloth
Ran into a dormant moth
Of many times his size.
He showed not the least surprise.

"Departmental," by Robert Frost, reprinted from *Poetry and Prose,* edited by Lantham and Thompson, 1972, Holt, Rinehart and Winston.

His business wasn't with such.
He gave it scarcely a touch,
And was off on his duty run.
Yet if he encountered one
Of the hive's enquiry squad
Whose work is to find out God
And the nature of time and space,
He would put him onto the case.
Ants are a curious race;
One crossing with hurried tread
The body of one of their dead
Isn't given a moment's arrest—
Seems not even impressed.
But he no doubt reports to any
With whom he crosses antennae,
And they no doubt report
To the higher-up at court.
Then word goes forth in Formic:
"Death's come to Jerry McCormic,
Our selfless forager Jerry.
Will the special Janizary
Whose office it is to bury
The dead of the commissary
Go bring him home to his people.
Lay him in state on a sepal.
Wrap him for shroud in a petal.
Embalm him with ichor of nettle.
This is the word of your Queen."
And presently on the scene
Appears a solemn mortician;
And taking formal position,
With feelers calmly atwiddle,
Seizes the dead by the middle,
And heaving him high in air,
Carries him out of there.
No one stands round to stare.
It is nobody else's affair.

It couldn't be called ungentle.
But how thoroughly departmental.

On Friendship

Francine Du Plessix Gray

Born in 1930 in France, Francine DuPlessix Gray came to the United States when she was eleven. She attended Bryn Mawr College for two years and then in the early fifties attended Black Mountain College, an experimental school in North Carolina attended by numerous artists who eventually became well known. Among Gray's contemporaries at Black Mountain were the poets Robert Creeley and Charles Olson, the choreographer and dancer Merce Cunningham, and the artist Robert Motherwell.

Gray's novels include Lovers and Tyrants *(1976),* World Without End *(1981), and* October Blood *(1985). She is also a journalist and essayist, and has written for* The New Yorker, *the* New York Review of Books, Vogue, *the* Saturday Review, *and the* New Republic. *Her essays are collected in* Adam and Eve in the City *(1987) where "On Friendship" first appeared.*

I saw Madame Bovary at Bloomingdale's the other morning, or rather, I saw many incarnations of her. She was hovering over the cosmetic counters, clutching the current issue of *Cosmopolitan,* whose cover line read "New Styles of Coupling, Including Marriage." Her face already ablaze with numerous products advertised to make her irresistible to the opposite sex, she looked anguished, grasping, overwrought, and terribly lonely. And I thought to myself: Poor girl! With all the reams of literature that have analyzed her plight (victimized by double standards, by a materialistic middle-class glutting on the excesses of romantic fiction), notwithstanding all these diagnoses, one fact central to her tragic fate has never been stressed enough: Emma Bovary had a faithful and boring husband and a couple of boring lovers—not so intolerable a

"On Friendship," by Francine Du Plessix Gray, reprinted from *Adam and Eve in the City*, 1987, Simon & Schuster.

condition—but she did not have a friend in the world. And when I think of the great solitude which the original Emma and her contemporaries exude, one phrase jumps to my mind. It comes from an essay by Francis Bacon, and it is one of the finest statements ever penned about the human need for friendship: "Those who have no friends to open themselves unto are cannibals of their own hearts."

In the past years the theme of friendship has been increasingly prominent in our conversations, in our books and films, even in our college courses. It is evident that many of us are yearning with new fervor for this form of bonding. And our yearning may well be triggered by the same disillusionment with the reign of Eros that destroyed Emma Bovary. Emma was eating her heart out over a fantasy totally singular to the Western world, and only a century old at that: the notion that sexual union between men and women who believe that they are passionately in love, a union achieved by free choice and legalized by marriage, tends to offer a life of perpetual bliss and is the most desirable human bond available on earth. It is a notion bred in the same frenzied climate of the romantic epoch that caused countless young Europeans to act like the characters of their contemporary literature. Goethe's *Werther* is said to have triggered hundreds of suicides. Numerous wives glutted on the fantasies of George Sand's heroines demanded separations because their husbands were unpoetic. And Emma Bovary, palpitating from that romantic fiction which precurses our current sex manuals in its outlandish hopes for the satiation of desire, muses in the third week of her marriage: Where is "the felicity, the passion, the intoxication" that had so enchanted her in the novels of Sir Walter Scott?

This frenzied myth of love which has also led to the downfall of Cleopatra, Juliet, Romeo, and King Kong continues to breed, in our time, more garbled thinking, wretched verse, and nonsensical jingles than any emotion under the sun: "All You Need Is Love," or as we heard it in our high school days, "Tell me you'll love me forever, if only tonight." As Flaubert put it, we are all victims of romanticism. And if we still take for granted its cult of heterosexual passion, it is in part because we have been victimized, as Emma was, by the propaganda machine of the Western novel. It was the power and the genius of the novel form to fuse medieval notions of courtly love with the idealization of marriage that marked the rise of the eighteenth-century middle class. (By "romantic love," I mean an infatuation that involves two major ingredients: a sense of being "enchanted" by another person through a complex process of illusion, and a willingness to totally surrender to that person.)

One hardly needs a course in anthropology to realize that this alliance of marriage and romantic love is restricted to a small segment of the Western world, and would seem sheer folly in most areas of this planet. The great majority of humans—be it in China, Japan, Africa, India, the Moslem nations—still engage in marriages prearranged by their elders or dictated by pragmatic reasons of money, land, tribal politics, or (as in the Socialist countries) housing shortages. Romantically motivated marriage as the central ingredient of the good life is almost as novel in our own West. In popular practice, it remained restricted to a narrow segment of the middle class until the twentieth century. And on the level of philosophical reflection, it was always friendship between members of the same sex, never any bonding of sexual affection, which from Greek times to the Enlightenment was held to be the cornerstone of human happiness. Yet this central role allotted to friendship for two thousand years has been progressively eroded by such factors as the nineteenth-century exaltation of instinct; science's monopoly on our theories of human sentiment; the massive eroticizing of society; and that twentieth-century celebration of the body that reaches its peak in the hedonistic solitude of the multiple orgasm.

To Aristotle, friendship can be formed only by persons of virtue: a man's capacity for friendship is the most accurate measure of his virtue; it is the foundation of the state, for great legislators care even more for friendship than they care for justice. To Plato, as we know, passionate affection untainted by physical relations is the highest form of human bonding. To Cicero, *Amicitia* is more important than either money, power, honors, or health because each of these gifts can bring us only one form of pleasure, whereas the pleasures of friendship are marvelously manifold; and friendship being based on equity, the tyrant is the man least capable of forming that bond because of his need to wield power over others. Montaigne's essay, along with Bacon's, is the most famous of many that glorify our theme in the Renaissance. And like the ancients, he stresses the advantages of friendship over any kind of romantic and physical attachment. Love for members of the opposite sex, in Montaigne's words, is "an impetuous and fickle flame, undulating and variable, a fever flame subject to fits and lulls." Whereas the fire of friendship produces "a general and universal warmth, moderate and even," and will always forge bonds superior to those of marriage because marriage's continuance is "constrained and forced, depending on factors other than our free will."

A century later, even La Rouchefoucauld, that great cynic who described the imperialism of the ego better than any other precursor of Freud, finds that friendship is the only human bond in which the tyrannical cycle of our self-love seems broken, in which "we can love each other even more than we love ourselves." One of the last classic essays on friendship I can think of before it loses major importance as a philosophical theme is by Ralph Waldo Emerson. And it's interesting to note that by mid-nineteenth century, the euphoric absolutes which had previously described this form of bonding are sobered by many cautious qualifications. A tinge of modern pragmatism sets in. Emerson tends to distrust any personal friendship unless it functions for the purpose of some greater universal fraternity.

Yet however differently these thinkers focused on our theme, they all seemed to reach a consensus on the qualities of free will, equity, trust, and selflessness unique to the affection of friendship. They cannot resist comparing it to physical passion, which yearns for power over the other, seeks possession and the state of being possessed, seeks to devour, breeds on excess, can easily become demonic, is closely allied to the death wish, and is often a form of agitated narcissism quite unknown to the tranquil, balanced rule of friendship. And rereading the sagas of Tristan and Iseult, Madame Bovary, and many other romantic lovers, it is evident that their passions tend to breed as much on a masturbatory excitement as on a longing for the beloved. They are in love with love, their delirium is involved with a desire for self-magnification

139

through suffering, as evidenced in Tristan's words, "Eyes with joy are blinded. I myself am the world." There is confrontation, turmoil, aggression, in the often militaristic language of romantic love: Archers shoot fatal arrows or unerring shafts; the male enemy presses, pursues, and conquers; women surrender after being besieged by amorous assaults. Friendship on the other hand is the most pacifist species in the fauna of human emotions, the most steadfast and sharing. No wonder then that the finest pacifist ideology in the West was devised by a religious group—the Quakers—which takes as its official name the Religious Society of Friends; the same temperate principle of fraternal bonding informs that vow demanded by the Benedictine Order—the Oath of Stability—which remains central to the monastic tradition to this day. No wonder, also, that the kind of passionate friendship shared by David and Jonathan has inspired very few masterpieces of literature, which seem to thrive on tension and illicitness. For until they were relegated to dissecting rooms of the social sciences, our literary views of friendship tended to be expressed in the essay form, a cool, reflective mode that never provided friendship with the motive, democratic, propagandistic force found by Eros in novel, verse, and stage. To this day, friendship totally resists commercial exploitation, unlike the vast businesses fueled by romantic love that support the couture, perfume, cosmetic, lingerie, and pulp-fiction trades.

One should note, however, that most views of friendship expressed in the past twenty centuries of Western thought have dealt primarily with the male's capacity for affection. And they tend to be extremely dubious about the possibility of women ever being able to enjoy genuine friendship with members of their own sex, not to speak of making friends with male peers. Montaigne expressed a prejudice that lasts well into our day when he wrote, "The ordinary capacity of women is inadequate for that communion and fellowship which is the nurse of that sacred bond, nor does their soul feel firm enough to endure the strain of so tight and durable a knot." It is shocking, though not surprising, to hear prominent social scientists paraphrase that opinion in our own decades. Konrad Lorenz and Lionel Tiger, for instance, seem to agree that women are made eminently unsociable by their genetic programming; their bonding, in Lorenz's words, "must be considered weak imitations of the exclusively male associations." Given the current vogue for sociobiology, such assertions are often supported by carefully researched papers on the courtship patterns of Siberian wolves, the prevalence of eye contact among male baboons, and the vogue for gangbanging among chimpanzees.

Our everyday language reflects the same bias: "Fraternity" is a word that goes far beyond its collegiate context and embraces notions of honor, dignity, loyalty. "Sorority" is something we might have belonged to as members of the University of Oklahoma's bowling team in the early 1950s. So I think it is high time that the same feminist perspective that has begun to correct the biases of art history and psychoanalysis should be brought to bear on this area of anthropology. We have indeed been deprived of those official, dramatically visible rites offered to men in pub, poolroom, Elks, hunting ground, or football league. And having been brought up in a very male world, I'm ashamed to say it took me a decade of feminist consciousness

140

to realize that the few bonding associations left to twentieth century women—garden clubs, church suppers, sewing circles (often derided by men because they do not deal with power)—have been activities considerably more creative and life-enhancing than the competition of the poolroom, the machismo of beer drinking, or the bloodshed of hunting.

Among both sexes, the rites and gestures of friendship seemed to have been decimated in the Victorian era, which brought a fear of homosexuality unprecedented in the West. (They also tended to decrease as rites of heterosexual coupling became increasingly permissive.) Were Dr. Johnson and James Boswell[1] gay, those two men who constantly exhibited their affection for each other with kisses, tears, and passionate embraces? I suspect they were as rabidly straight as those tough old soldiers described by Tacitus begging for last kisses when their legion broke up. Since Freud, science has tended to dichotomize human affection along lines of deviance and normalcy, genitality and platonic love, instead of leaving it as a graduated spectrum of emotion in which love, friendship, sensuality, sexuality, can freely flow into each other as they did in the past. This may be another facet of modern culture that has cast coolness and self-consciousness on our gestures of friendship. The 1960s brought us some hope for change, both in its general emotional climate and in our scientists' tendency to relax their definitions of normalcy and deviance. For one of the most beautiful signs of that decade's renewed yearning for friendship and community, particularly evident among the groups who marched in civil-rights or antiwar demonstrations, was the sight of men clutching, kissing, embracing each other unabashedly as Dr. Johnson and James Boswell.

Which leads me to reflect on the reasons why I increasingly turn to friendship in my own life: In a world more and more polluted by the lying of politicians and the illusions of the media, I occasionally crave to hear and to tell the truth. To borrow a beautiful phrase from Friedrich Nietzsche, I look upon my friend as "the beautiful enemy" who alone is able to offer me total candor. I look for the kind of honest friend Emma Bovary needed: one who could have told her that her lover was a jerk.

Friendship is by its very nature freer of deceit than any other relationship we can know because it is the bond least affected by striving for power, physical pleasure, or material profit, most liberated from any oath of duty or of constancy. With Eros, the *body* stands naked, in friendship our *spirit* is denuded. Friendship, in this sense, is a human condition resembling what may be humanity's most beautiful and necessary lie—the promise of an afterlife. It is an almost celestial sphere in which we most resemble that society of angels offered us by Christian theology, in which we can sing the truth of our inner thoughts in relative freedom and abundance. No wonder then that the last contemporary writers whose essays on friendship may remain classics are those religiously inclined, scholars relatively unaffected by positivism or behaviorism, or by the general scientificization of human sentiment. That marvelous Christian maverick, C. S. Lewis, tells us: "Friendship is unnecessary, like philosophy, like art, like the universe itself (since God did not *need* to create). It has no survival value; rather it is one of those things that give value to survival." And the Jewish thinker Simone Weil focuses on the classic theme of free consent when she writes: "Friendship is a miracle by which a person consents to view from a certain distance, and without coming any nearer, the very being who is necessary to him as food."

The quality of free consent and self-determination inherent in friendship may be crucial to the lives of twentieth-century women beginning their vocations. But in order to return friendship to an absolutely central place in our lives, we might have to wean ourselves in part from the often submissive premises of romantic passion. I suspect that we shall always need some measure of swooning and palpitating, of ecstasy and trembling, of possessing and being possessed. But, I also suspect that we've been bullied and propagandized into many of these manifestations by the powerful modern organism that I call the sexual-industrial complex and that had an antecedent in the novels that fueled Emma Bovary's deceitful fantasies. For one of the most treacherous aspects of the cult of romantic love has been its complex idealization and exploitation of female sexuality. There is now a new school of social scientists who are militantly questioning the notion that Western romantic love is the best foundation for human bonding, and their criticism seems much inspired by feminist perspectives. The Australian anthropologist Robert Brain, for instance, calls romantic love "a lunatic relic of medieval passions . . . the handmaiden of a moribund capitalistic culture and of an equally dead Puritan ethic."

What exactly would happen if we women remodeled our concepts of ideal human bonding on the ties of friendship and abandoned the premises of enchantment and possession? Such a restructuring of our ideals of happiness could be extremely subversive. It might imply a considerable de-eroticizing of society. It could bring about a minor revolution against the sexual-industrial complex that brings billions of dollars to thousands of men by brainwashing us into the roles of temptress and seductress, and estranges us from the plain and beautiful Quaker ideal of being a sister to the world. How topsy-turvy the world would be! Dalliance, promiscuity, all those more sensationalized aspects of the Women's Movement that were once seen as revolutionary might suddenly seem most bourgeois and old fashioned activities. If chosen in conditions of rigorous self-determination, the following values, considered up to now as reactionary, could suddenly become the most radical ones at hand: Virginity, Celibacy. Monastic communities. And that most endangered species of all, fidelity in marriage, which has lately become so exotically rare that it might soon become very fashionable, and provide the cover story for yet another publication designed to alleviate the seldom-admitted solitude of swinging singles: "Mick Jagger Is into Fidelity."

ENDNOTE

[1] **Dr. Johnson and James Boswell:** Samuel Johnson (1709–1784), quintessential English man of letters, whose fast friendship with James Boswell (1740–1795) resulted in Boswell's *Life of Samuel Johnson,* which immortalized Johnson as a brilliant, witty conversationalist.

And What Would You Do, Ma?

Steve Hassett

*Steve Hasset is an assistant attorney general for the State of Wash-
ington specializing in child protection cases. But his way to becoming a lawyer took many turns. In 1966, he dropped out of college
in order to join the army as a paratrooper. For one year, he was a
machine gunner and First Air Cavalry squad leader in Vietnam.
He also spent a year in Korea as an intelligence analyst. In 1970 he
helped found the Buffalo chapter of the Vietnam Veterans against the
War. He went to law school after trying his hand at various blue-
collar jobs, and he specialized in family and Veteran's law.*

And what would you do, ma,
if eight of your sons step
out of the TV and begin
killing chickens and burning
hooches in the living room,
stepping on booby traps
and dying in the kitchen,
beating your husband and
taking him and shooting
skag and forgetting in
the bathroom?

would you lock up your daughter?

would you stash the apple pie?

would you change channels?

(1976)

"And What Would You Do, Ma?" by Steve Hassett, reprinted from *The Vietnam War in American
Stories, Songs and Poems*, edited by H. Bruce Franklin, 1976, Bedford/St. Martin's Press.

Christmas

Steve Hassett

See the headnote for Steve Hassett's "And What Would You Do, Ma?"
for biographical information.

The Hessian in his last letter home
said in part
"they are all rebels here
who will not stand to fight
but each time fade before us
as water into sand . . .

the children beg in their rude hamlets

the women stare with hate

the men flee into the barrens at our approach
to lay in ambush

some talk of desertion . . .
were it not for the hatred
they bear us, more would do so

There is no glory here.
Tell Hals he must evade the Prince's levy
through exile or deformity

Winter is hard upon us. On the morrow we enter
Trenton. There we rest till the New Year. . . ."

(1976)

"Christmas," by Steve Hassett, reprinted from *The Vietnam War in American Stories, Songs and Poems,* edited by H. Bruce Franklin, 1976, Bedford/St. Martin's Press.

Indian Camp

Ernest Hemingway

Considered one of the most influential and often-imitated American writers, Hemingway was influenced by Ezra Pound and Gertrude Stein, whose style he imitated. Born in 1899 in Illinois, Hemingway's writing was shaped by early experiences hunting and fishing in northern Michigan, and working as reporter for a Kansas City newspaper, as a member of a volunteer ambulance unit in Europe during World War I, as a reporter for the Toronto Star, and eventually as a foreign correspondent in Paris.

His early publications, Three Stories and Ten Poems *(Paris, 1923) and* In Our Time *(Scribners, 1925) reveal the clear prose style for which he became noted, and his preoccupations with understated violence, repressed states of feeling, and loss. As the leading figure of a group of writers that Gertrude Stein called the "lost generation," Hemingway invoked through his narratives the confusion and demoralization of post-World War I veterans and victims struggling to live in what appeared to be a valueless world. Disillusioned, traumatized characters in* In Our Time, *defeated by early childhood experiences and love and war, prefigure two of his most widely read novels,* The Sun Also Rises *(1926) and* A Farewell to Arms *(1929).*

Men Without Women *(1927) and* Winner Take Nothing *(1933) are collections of fine short stories. These were followed by a number of lesser works,* Death in the Afternoon *(1932) about bullfighting, and* The Green Hills of Africa *(1935) about game hunting.*

The Fifth Column and the First Forty-Nine Stories *(1938) contained two of his most popular stories, "The Short Happy Life of Francis Macomber" and "The Snows of Kilimanjaro." For Whom The Bell Tolls *(1940) is based on an incident that happened during the*

"Indian Camp," by Ernest Hemingway, reprinted from *In Our Time*, 1925, Simon & Schuster.

Spanish Civil War and echoes the loss and blunted feelings of earlier works.

In 1952 The Old Man and Sea, *a parable of man against the forces of nature, again won Hemingway critical approval, and in 1954 he was awarded the Nobel Prize. In 1961 Hemingway committed suicide by shotgun after many years of illness, alcoholism, and depression.*

Throughout his life, Hemingway presented himself as "a man's man," sportsman, fearless reporter, bullfighting aficionado, big-game-hunter, and hard-drinking lover of adventure. He was married four times. His life story is one of the most publicized of the twentieth century, with six biographies written of his life, TV movies, and many film adaptions of his works. Among other works, his letters were published posthumously, as were earlier poems, a novel, and A Moveable Feast, *vignettes of his years in Paris in the 1920s. He leaves behind a body of work that, although uneven, is characterized by elemental emotive patterns and some of the finest, most spare prose ever written.*

At the lake shore there was another rowboat drawn up. The two Indians stood waiting.

Nick and his father got in the stern of the boat and the Indians shoved it off and one of them got in to row. Uncle George sat in the stern of the camp rowboat. The young Indian shoved the camp boat off and got in to row Uncle George.

The two boats started off in the dark. Nick heard the oarlocks of the other boat quite a way ahead of them in the mist. The Indians rowed with quick choppy strokes. Nick lay back with his father's arm around him. It was cold on the water. The Indian who was rowing them was working very hard, but the other boat moved further ahead in the mist all the time.

"Where are we going, Dad?", Nick asked.

"Over to the Indian camp. There is an Indian lady very sick."

"Oh," said Nick.

Across the bay they found the other boat beached. Uncle George was smoking a cigar in the dark. The young Indian pulled the boat way up on the beach. Uncle George gave both the Indians cigars.

They walked up from the beach through a meadow that was soaking wet with dew, following the young Indian who carried a lantern. Then they went into the woods and followed a trail that led to the logging road that ran back into the hills. It was much lighter on the logging road as the timber was cut away on both sides. The young Indian stopped and blew out his lantern and they all walked on along the road.

They came around a bend and a dog came out barking. Ahead were the lights of the shanties where the Indian bark peelers lived. More dogs rushed out at them. The two Indians sent them back to the shanties. In the shanty nearest the road there was a light in the window. An old woman stood in the doorway holding a lamp.

Inside on a wooden bunk lay a young Indian woman. She had been trying to have her baby for two days. All the old women in the camp had been helping her. The men had moved off up the road to sit in the dark and smoke out of range of the noise she made. She screamed just as Nick and the two Indians followed his father and Uncle George into the shanty. She lay in the lower bunk, very big under a quilt. Her head was turned to one side. In the upper bunk was her husband. He had cut his foot very badly with an ax three days before. He was smoking a pipe. The room smelled very bad.

Nick's father ordered some water to be put on the stove, and while it was heating he spoke to Nick.

"This lady is going to have a baby, Nick," he said.

"I know," said Nick.

"You don't know," said his father, "Listen to me. What she is going through is called being in labor. The baby wants to be born and she wants it to be born. All her muscles are trying to get the baby born. That is what is happening when she screams."

"I see," Nick said.

Just then the woman cried out.

"Oh, Daddy, can't you give her something to make her stop screaming?" asked Nick.

"No. I haven't any anesthetic," his father said. "But her screams are not important. I don't hear them because they are not important."

The husband in the upper bunk rolled over against the wall.

The woman in the kitchen motioned to the doctor that the water was hot. Nick's father went into the kitchen and poured about half of the water out of the big kettle into a basin. Into the water left in the kettle he put several things he unwrapped from a handkerchief,

"Those must boil," he said, and began to scrub his hands in the basin of hot water with a cake of soap he had brought from the camp. Nick watched his father's hands scrubbing each other with the soap. While his father washed his hands very carefully and thoroughly, he talked.

"You see, Nick, babies are supposed to be born head first but sometimes they're not. When they're not they make a lot of trouble for everybody. Maybe I'll have to operate on this lady. We'll know in a little while."

When he was satisfied with his hands he went in and went to work.

"Pull back that quilt, will you, George?" he said. "I'd rather not touch it."

Later when he started to operate Uncle George and three Indian men held the woman still. She bit Uncle George on the arm and Uncle George said, "Damn squaw

147

bitch!" and the young Indian who had rowed Uncle George over laughed at him. Nick held the basin for his father. It all took a long time.

His father picked the baby up and slapped it to make it breathe and handed it to the old woman.

"See, it's a boy, Nick," he said, "How do you like being an interne?"

Nick said, "All right." He was looking away so as not to see what his father was doing.

"There. That gets it," said his father and put something into the basin.

Nick didn't look at it.

"Now," his father said, "there's some stitches to put in. You can watch this or not, Nick, just as you like. I'm going to sew up the incision I made."

Nick did not watch. His curiosity had been gone for a long time.

His father finished and stood up. Uncle George and the three Indian men stood up. Nick put the basin out in the kitchen.

Uncle George looked at his arm. The young Indian smiled reminiscently.

"I'll put some peroxide on that, George," the doctor said.

He bent over the Indian woman. She was quiet now and her eyes were closed. She looked very pale. She did not know what had become of the baby or anything.

"I'll be back in the morning," the doctor said, standing up. "The nurse should be here from St. Ignace by noon and she'll bring everything we need."

He was feeling exalted and talkative as football players are in the dressing room after a game.

"That's one for the medical journal, George," he said. "Doing a Caesarian with a jack-knife and sewing it up with nine-foot, tapered gut leaders."

Uncle George was standing against the wall, looking at his arm.

"Oh, you're a great man, all right," he said.

"Ought to have a look at the proud father. They're usually the worst sufferers in these little affairs," the doctor said. "I must say he took it all pretty quietly."

He pulled back the blanket from the Indian's head. His hand came away wet. He mounted on the edge of the lower bunk with the lamp in one hand and looked in. The Indian lay with his face toward the wall. His throat had been cut from ear to ear. The blood had flowed down into a pool where his body sagged the bunk. His head rested on his left arm. The open razor lay, edge up, in the blankets.

"Take Nick out of the shanty, George," the doctor said.

There was no need of that. Nick, standing in the door of the kitchen, had a good view of the upper bunk when his father, the lamp in one hand, tipped the Indian's head back.

It was just beginning to be daylight when they walked along the logging road back toward the lake.

"I'm terribly sorry I brought you along, Nickie," said his father, all his postoperative exhilaration gone. "It was an awful mess to put you through."

"Do ladies always have such a hard time having babies?" Nick asked.

"No, that was very, very exceptional."

"Why did he kill himself, Daddy?"

"I don't know, Nick. He couldn't stand things, I guess."

"Do many men kill themselves, Daddy?"

"Not very many, Nick."

"Do many women?"

"Hardly ever."

"Don't they ever?"

"Oh, yes. They do sometimes."

"Daddy?"

"Yes."

"Where did Uncle George go?"

"He'll turn up all right."

"Is dying hard, Daddy?"

"No, I think it's pretty easy, Nick. It all depends."

They were seated in the boat, Nick in the stern, his father rowing. The sun was coming up over the hills. A bass jumped, making a circle in the water. Nick trailed his hand in the water. It felt warm in the sharp chill of the morning.

In the early morning on the lake sitting in the stern of the boat with his father rowing, he felt quite sure that he would never die.

The Cast

Ted Hughes

Ted Hughes established his reputation as a poet in the mid-1950s with a series of poems about animals, distinctive through their harsh imagery. The volume of verse entitled Crow *retells the legend of creation and birth through the vision of a predatory mocking crow. He also produced several books of children's verse, plays, and translations. He was England's Poet Laureate up to the time of his death, but his achievement was overshadowed by the suicide of his wife, Sylvia Plath, an accomplished poet in her own right. Before he died, he published* Birthday Letters, *a volume of intensely emotional poems about their doomed love.*

Daddy had come back to hear
All you had against him. He
Could not believe it. Where
Did you get those words if not
in the tails of his bees? For others
The honey. For him, Cupid's bow
Modified in Peenemünde
Via Brueghel. Helpless
As weightless, voiceless as lifeless,
He had to hear it all
Driven into him up to the feathers,
Had to stand the stake
Not through his heart, but upright
In the town square, him tied to it
Stark naked full of those arrows
In the bronze of immortal poesy.

"The Cast," by Ted Hughes, reprinted from *Birthday Letters*, 1998, Farrar, Strauss & Giroux.

So your cry of deliverance
Materialized in his
Sacrificed silence. Every arrow
Nailing him there a star
In your constellation. The giant
Chunk of jagged weapon—
His whole distorted statue
Like a shard of shrapnel
Eased out of your old wound. Rejected
By your body. Daddy
No longer to be borne. Your words
Like phagocytes, ridding you with a roar
Of the heavy pain.

Healed you vanished
From the monumental
Immortal form
Of your injury: your Daddy's
Body full of your arrows. Though it was
Your blood that dried on him.

Adultery

Laura Kipnis

Laura Kipnis is a video maker and cultural critic. She holds a BFA from San Francisco Art Institute and a MFA from Nova Scotia College of Art. She has received grants and fellowships from the Guggenheim Foundation, the Rockefeller Foundation, and the National Endowment for the Arts for both production and media criticism. Her videotapes have been screened and broadcast in the US, Europe, Japan, and Australia. In addition to her two books Bound and Gagged: Pornography and the Politics of Fantasy in America *(Grove, 1996 paperback, Duke, 1999) and* Ecstasy Unlimited: On Sex, Capital, Gender & Aesthetics *(Minnesota, 1993), her essays and reviews have appeared in* Critical Inquiry, Social Text, Wide Angle, The Village Voice, *and* Harper's.

"Would you like to dance?" You've mustered all the studied casualness you can, momentarily convincing yourself (self-deception being the sine qua non of moments such as these) that your heart is as pure as the gold of your wedding band, your virtue as thick as your mortgage-payment booklet. Your torpid married body now pressed nervously against this person who's been casting winsome glances in your direction all night, a muffled but familiar feeling seems to be stirring deep within you, a distant rumbling getting louder and louder, like a herd of elephants massing on the bushveld. Oh God, it's your libido, once a noted freedom fighter, now a sorry shriveled thing—from Sixties outlaw to Nineties upstanding citizen, Janis Joplin to Tipper Gore, in just a few short decades.

Maybe it wasn't a party; it was a conference, an airplane, your health club, or, for those who like living on the edge, the office. The venue doesn't matter; what does

---

Excerpt from "Adultery," by Laura Kipnis, reprinted from *Critical Inquiry,* Winter 1997.

is finding yourself so voluptuously hurtled into a state of possibility, a might-be-the-start-of-something kind of moment. You feel transformed: suddenly so charming, so attractive, awakened from emotional deadness, and dumbstruck with all the stabbing desire you thought you'd outgrown. Then there's that first nervous phone call, coffee, or a drink, and that incredible marathon conversation; it's been so long since someone really listened to you like that. Somehow things quickly get a little more serious than you'd anticipated, which you secretly (all right, desperately) wanted, and now *emotions* are involved, vulnerability—emotions you didn't intend on having, vulnerability that thrills you to the core—and you shouldn't be feeling any of this, but you're also weirdly . . . is it elated?

Hard on the heels of that elation is a cold fusion of numbing anxiety and gnawing guilt. You seem to be sweating constantly; your conscience feels like an inflamed appendix, paining you, about to burst open with bile and flame. You decide to talk it out with the new love object, make the graceful exit. "I just can't," you explain mournfully, while realizing that, actually, you can. No reliable statistics are available on the average time lapse between the utterance "I just can't" and the commencement of foreplay, but psycholinguists should consider investigating that phrase's peculiar aphrodisiacal power. And, anyway, guilt is good homeopathic medicine: it reassures you that you're really not a bad person. A bad person wouldn't be feeling guilty.

Of course, adulterers do behave badly; deception rules in this land. But note the phraseology of the charges typically leveled against the adulterer: "immaturity" (failure to demonstrate the requisite degree of civilized repression); "selfishness" (failure to work for the collective good); "boorishness" (failure to achieve proper class behavior). Or the extra fillip of moral trumping: "People will get hurt!"

If adultery summons the shaming language of bad citizenship, this language also indicates the extent to which marriage is meant to function as a boot camp for citizenship instruction. Anything short of a full salute to existing conditions will be named bad ethics. Ambivalence, universal though it may be, is typically regarded as the ur-form of bad marital citizenship, and adultery has become the favored metonym for all broken promises, intimate and national, a transparent sign of tawdriness and bad behavior, an indication of moral laxity and lack of industriousness.

We all know that Good Marriages Take Work. But then work takes work, too. Wage labor, intimacy labor—are you ever not on the clock? If you're working at monogamy, you've already entered a system of exchange: an economy of intimacy governed, as such economies are, by scarcity, threat, and internalized prohibitions; secured ideologically, as such economies are, by incessant assurances that there are no viable alternatives. When monogamy becomes work, when desire is organized contractually, with accounts kept and fidelity extracted like labor from employees, with marriage a domestic factory policed by means of rigid shop-floor discipline designed to keep wives and husbands choke-chained to the reproduction machinery, this is a somewhat different state of affairs than the Happy Marriage.

Good marriages may take work, but unfortunately, in erotic life, trying is always trying too hard. Erotically speaking, work doesn't work; play is what works. Nevertheless, although labor and capital may have struck a temporary truce over the eight-hour workday (an advance crumbling around us as we speak), in our emotional culture it's double shifting for everyone. The work ethic long ago penetrated the sphere of leisure. Is intimacy already the next lost cause? Or do you labor happily under the conviction that intimacy is your haven from the brutalities of the marketplace and domestic labor a refuge from the grind of wage labor? Oh, it's a labor of love? But sentimentality about the work ethic is not exactly a new story, given how useful it is in heading off unsentimental inquiries about the frequently soul-crippling conditions of the factories, productive and reproductive.

It is also worth noting here that marriages bind couples together not just emotionally but juridically as well. Just as the role of the state in protecting dominant interests in the realm of wage labor is not neutral—meaning that on those occasions when, for example, federal troops fire on striking workers, we might not want to describe their return to work as precisely voluntary—so too in matters of domestic labor does the state make clear its compelling interest in promoting good marital citizenship. In many locales, having sex with someone who isn't your spouse means that you're betraying the state as well as your mate. Although divorce laws vary from state to state, currently twenty-four states still have adultery laws on the books. The state of Louisiana has even introduced something called "covenant marriage," which couples can elect over civil marriage and which will make divorces even more difficult to obtain (incompatibility isn't sufficient grounds, though adultery is). In the nation of marriage, adultery is traitorship, divorce means having your passport revoked, and who mediates your subjection to the state but your spouse? Infidelity makes you an infidel to the law, for which your spouse becomes an emblem, the hinge between the privacy of your desires and the power of the state installed right there in your master bedroom. . . .

Romance is, quite obviously, a socially sanctioned zone for wishing and desiring as well as a repository of excess. Mobilized by unconscious fantasy, it's potentially a profoundly antisocial form as well. So the state steps in and licenses its practices, as if couples were pharmacists dispensing controlled substances to each other. And when possibilities to transform everyday life do manage to force themselves into the open, like tiny, delicate sprouts struggling up through the hard dirt, what an array of sharp-bladed mechanisms stands ready to mow them into mulch.

What would it take to sustain the new forms of self and the world of gratified needs invented by your love affair—that is, if you hadn't been persuaded that a sheepish return to the emotional deadness you tried so desperately and so recently to escape now counts as a happy ending, or if you hadn't deluded yourself that your bittersweet love affair with your own unhappiness somehow protects those around you from misery? What would it take to install those newfound forms of optimism and desire into ordinary life in place of emotional fatigue and renunciation? At the very least, it would take an unembarrassed commitment to utopian thinking. It would mean forging connections between the myriad forms in which we do tentatively invent these possibilities in our everyday lives and larger questions about the social organization of work, love, shame, and pleasure. It would take fantasy, which is indispensable to this kind of social project. In our everyday practices, though, aren't we all quite dedicated to inventing beautiful, nascent worlds in which the realization of desire is possible? Do we not, at some level, know that these aren't banal questions, we avant-gardists of everyday life, we emergent utopians who experimentally construct different futures out of whatever we can, taking up residence in our ragtag inventions in starving, greedy ways, though barely able to imagine committing to them—tourists in the world of gratification armed with temporary visas. We have, after all, been born into social forms in which fighting for happiness looks like a base and selfish thing, and realization of desire is at best thwarted and fleeting, so often an affair of short duration.

The Ramble

Dika Lam

Dika Lam was born in Ontario, Canada. She attended Cornell University and taught creative writing at an East Village high school as a New York Times *Fellow in the MFA program at New York University. Her fiction has appeared in* Washington Square, The Green Hills Literary Lantern, *and* Dandelion. *Presently, she is working on a collection of short stories and a novel about the history of Central Park. The following piece was published in* Story *magazine in 1998.*

Thousands of miles away, in the most populous country in the world, an old man pushed off on a narrow raft fashioned from five bamboo poles. He was not alone. Ten cormorants rode the crests and swells of the river with him, ten elegant birds with pale throats and autumn in their cheeks. They laughed together with the old man, pumping their black wings. Around them rose the chilled smoke of mountains. In the distance, similar rafts could be seen, their silhouettes sharp against the gloaming—men and birds, a secret club.

Each spring and fall, millions of birds pass through New York along the Atlantic flyway—clouds of warblers and tree swallows, sapsuckers and gnatcatchers. That May, I caught a glimpse of the songbirds, some of whom racked up two thousand miles before dropping out of the Gotham sky for a rest.

After reading that Central Park was one of the top bird-watching sites in the country, I headed there every day. Sneaking out of the shop just after five, I quietly gathered my knapsack and headed for the back door.

As Ma bent down to adjust the Mao shirt on a gweilo customer, she shot me the usual dirty look that said, *where do you think you're going?*

Hip white girls had been snapping up her boxy satin bags with the bamboo handles. Off-duty models tried on the pajamas in accordioned cloth, humming along

---

to the Hong Kong pop songs that Ma piped through the speakers. At work in the shop, I was forced to wear one of my mother's creations, a white cotton tee with an embroidered dragon curving up the capped sleeve and along my neck.

"You're such a pretty girl," said Ma. "Why do you always wear such plain clothes?"

My mother wanted to be the next Josie Natori or Vivienne Tam or even Issey Miyake, the Japanese designer. Her talent was so much greater than my willingness to help her with the business. Truth was, I hated clothes. In the avian world, it's the males who present their dazzling feathers for approval while the females remain safe and unnoticed in the bush.

I was looking for a cormorant in New York City, concentrating on the Ramble: thirty-seven acres of potential bird land, 275 species to be spotted. The Binocularheads who frequented the park said that successful sightings were only a matter of being in the right place at the right time. Of seeing without being seen.

"Maybe you should check up by the reservoir," one of the birders recommended.

"You're better off at Jamaica Bay," said an old man, fishing his extra set of eyes from a hefty case: black, rubber-armored binocs that looked ready to sight an army.

At Willow Oven, I slunk past a group of Japanese tourists on a nature stroll, frightened that the Binocularheads would think I was one of them. Funny how birders could easily tell the difference between a Clark's grebe and a western grebe, but all yellow people looked the same to them.

At the Boathouse Café, I asked the maître d' for the "bird book"—the nature log where excited birders penned their latest sightings. When I told him what I was looking for, the maître d' added his own bit of advice: "The cormorant is a summer visitor. Perhaps you should come back in a few weeks."

The pages were disappointing:

May 1, 11, A.M., beautiful prothonotary warbler, emergency yellow, with blackish gray wings.—Cathy Jones.

Noon. Spotted a red-tailed hawk, swooping over Belvedere Castle.—Jerry Spink.

I looked past the maître d' at the Lake, with the sun setting in the background. On the terrace of the waterside bar, a group of Manhattan women sipped ice-thick drinks, their straws stained with lipstick. Although they were dressed in the New York uniform—black suits, black heels, black sunglasses—they did not speak to each other. Theirs was a lonely fashion.

The Statue of Liberty's torch once burned even brighter than it does now. The light was dimmed following a tragic incident, when a noted ornithologist posted himself at the top of the statue to observe the spring migration. As the fog rolled in, the birds lost track of their guiding stars. Disoriented by Lady Liberty's beacon, the flocks changed course and collided with the observation deck. That night, the huddled masses consisted of 271 dead birds.

I suppose I was a migrant of sorts. My parents and I had moved downstate the summer before, allowing me ample time to enjoy the urban camouflage. I quickly learned that if you want to remain incognito in Manhattan, it's easy to be absorbed, even ignored. The day before, I'd spotted a man in a gigantic canary suit, passing out flyers at Herald Square. He might have been a yellow cab, for all anyone cared.

This was good news for me. In the Finger Lakes region, where I grew up, I lived in an unwelcome state of local prominence. People wrongly assumed that my family ran the dry cleaners, or the China Bowl Buffet in the strip mall. Kids asked if I was a "commie." In class, whenever any reference to China was made, I ducked my head to avoid notice. Watching news footage of gray-clothed mainland Chinese, pedaling their loaded bikes across Tiananmen Square, I itched for the same kind of anonymity.

Thousands of miles away, in the most populous country in the world, an old man cried, "Ha ha ha." It was not laughter. He was asking his feathered family to dive deep into the cold waters and come up with fish, the bamboo rattling as the man's rubber boots thumped up and down on the raft. Imitating the call of the cormorants, he squawked as they sprang into the river, some of them surfacing already with fish in their mouths.

The old man lifted the birds from the water with a pole, their feet finding purchase as he swung them onto the raft. To prevent them from eating their catch, the old man had tied thick grasses around their necks. The birds' heads jerked as he pulled fish from their beaks, the silvery bodies falling into the basket that was anchored to the center of the raft. The dance continued as any number of birds were diving, or being scooped up, or surfacing in the water, lit by the lanterns of other crafts. At midnight, the old man pulled up to a nook that was like a second back, a rocky hollow that housed him and his birds and his brown pipe. As the old man struck a match and inhaled the first of the smoke, the great cormorants formed a circle around their leader with love and respect.

My father told me that in China, all the men brought their birds to the tea houses. The birdcages were so numerous, they decorated the open pavilions like strings of feathered lights.

"Tell me more, Ba-Ba," I said.

"Your grandfather knew a lot about birds. Your grandfather grew up in a family of cormorants."

On the rare occasion when Ba and I were home at the same time (my father worked late hours for a Chinese-American nonprofit group), he told me family stories. I couldn't get enough. Both sets of grandparents passed away long ago, and I never had the chance to know them.

I hesitated before asking the perennial question. "Are we finally going to China this summer?" What I'd seen of the Old World was confined to picture books and a slew of melodramatic Chinese movies where the heroine always got killed.

"You know, your mother is working very hard these days."

I sighed as my father lit his pipe against my window-view of moon. The cityscape loomed larger on account of my recent birthday present, a vintage pair of 1930 Bausch & Lomb 6 X 30 prism stereo binoculars that were used by the Army Signal Corps. My fingers curled around the leather, so smoothed by past hands that the housing over the lenses had worn thin. At night, I polished the brassy parts with some fine material that I borrowed from the back of Ma's shop. She would notice, but she wouldn't say much, only look at me strangely, as if I could not be her daughter.

Maybe I wasn't. I never dolled myself up in the latest fashions. I dropped out of college, something a good Chinese daughter was never supposed to do. Maybe I was born on a boat on a blue lake, thousands of miles away. Perhaps I missed my calling as a fisherman in Asia, where none of my cormorants would care how I looked.

When I was in high school, I permed my hair, I colored it crimson, I did everything I could to break away from the stereotypical China-doll bob. It only made me stand out even more. On my daily jaunts to the Ramble, I took care to hide myself under a dull hat.

Birds and people adapt to their surroundings in the most astonishing ways. Two specimens of the endangered peregrine falcon settled on a fifty-ninth-floor ledge of the Met Life Building. A pair of red-tailed hawks recently raised a family on Fifth Avenue.

As for my parents, they appeared to be adapting well to life in the West 30s. When we moved, Ma avoided the Chinese communities in Queens and the Lower East Side, opting for a fifth-floor walk-up near the Garment District. On the days when we worked closely together, the shop was hot with tension.

"Why don't you wear a little makeup?" said Ma, a safety pin between her teeth. "We've been in New York for a year and you never meet people. You always go out alone."

"It's not my fault I'm an only child," I said.

In the Ramble, I clattered over the wooden bridge spanning the Gill—a thousand feet of woodland stream. I restocked the bird feeders at Azalea Pond. Sometimes, I'd approach the Ramble from Cherry Hill and skirt the east side of the Lake, taking in the double-barrelled view of the San Remo Towers, the skyline of Central Park West. Dust-colored skyscrapers watched over this greenest of basins, its heavy-leaved trees that took their fullness from the Lake. There was a quiet here that came only from water.

From behind a curtain of willow, I spotted an old black man along the shore, teaching a little girl how to fish. She glanced up self-consciously as she yanked out a tiny catch. Banging its shiny flatness against the rocks, she screamed, "Grandpa! Look! Look!"

The little girl's grandfather wore a crushed hat and a navy blue jacket that reminded me of Ba's silk housecoat. As the sun flooded the Lake, making the fish look bigger and more golden, the girl laughed, her fingers bright with water. She danced in the winking light while her grandfather looped his left hand around the line, his right hand coming up to loosen the hook. He leaned down toward the Lake, the fish falling back in the water with a writhing plop. She noticed me looking at her and squealed with pride.

*   *   *

Not long after this, the visions began.

In the middle of the Lake drifted a raft made of five bamboo poles. Edged in sun-haze was an old Chinese man in rubber boots, yoking a pole behind his neck as if he were about to heft a barbell. Ten cormorants perched on either side of him, settling on the pole like crows on a telephone wire, a phalanx of companions who threw back their heads to bark at the sky. I could not have imagined anything more wonderful.

No one else seemed to notice. Rustling among the undergrowth were bird mavens who whispered about hidden nests. The old man smiled at me, and for the first time, I didn't mind being seen. I smiled back, truly happy in the glow of my secret. And then, just as suddenly, he was gone.

Thousands of miles away, in the most populous country in the world, the old man was born on an ancient lake, on a narrow houseboat crowded with the smells of fish and steamed rice.

One day, when he was barely four, he watched his father sneak a cormorant egg into the hen's nest to be incubated with the chicken's brood. Anyone could see that the cormorant egg was not like the others, not the color of dried white paint. It stood out like an alien orb. With patient obsession, the little boy watched the egg through its twenty-five days of a hen's strange heat.

On the morning when the cormorant had produced the egg, the boy's father had fished it out of the seaweed nest and said, "It is a male." As he wondered how his father could tell the difference, he was already learning the importance of observation. Keen sight became even more vital near hatching time, when the boy's father kept a strict watch. If the hen were to discover the foreigner, she would peck the newborn cormorant to death.

One night, the boy was roused by his parents.

"Your brother is about to be born," they whispered. His father had recently cupped the egg away from its foster home and placed it gently in a nest of his own making. The boy gaped at its radiance. With a long shuddering crack, the oval began to weaken under the force of invisible blows. Here and there, the boy caught the darting revelation of new beak, the shell collapsing into hairline shards. Between the fragments were the torn webs of membrane, the egg-house beating with the breath of life.

His father pulled the dead shell away and the little boy was no longer an only child.

A department store agreed to buy my mother's dresses. As Ma sprang into prominence, I scowled at the latest fashion magazines. An issue of *Vogue* featured shirts with embroidered loop buttons and a trio of Caucasian models in knockoffs of Chinese wedding garb.

A glamorous-looking blonde walked into the shop. With a pang, I remembered what it was like to grow up among whites—I suddenly felt short and deformed. Not surprisingly, it took her a while to notice me perched on a stool, surrounded by bolts of shantung.

"Hey, I'm here to see Mrs. Wong."

"Who shall I tell her is here?"

"Alameda Grossvogel, the model from the agency."

When I made my way to the sewing room, Ma and her assistants were buried in thread and cloth.

"Alameda Grossvogel is here, from the agency," I said.

Around my mother's neck was a pair of glasses attached to multicolored twists of rope.

"Tell her I'll be out in a couple of minutes." She didn't look up from her patterns, her diagrams, her renderings.

"You know, Grossvogel means 'big bird' in German," I volunteered. I contemplated using this bit of small talk on the model, but she didn't look very friendly. Lately, I'd been yearning for company, any kind at all.

As I turned to leave, my mother said, "You're not wearing that outfit to the park again, are you?"

I wondered why my mother never used Asian models.

For two exhausting months, the little boy's father fed the newborn chick every hour. He slept on a pallet under the baby cormorant's nest, waking like clockwork to the cry of a tiny beak. When the cormorant was old enough to walk, it chased the little boy around the shifting planks of the boat, the duo shrieking with brotherly love.

After sharing dinner with the bird, who gobbled down the translucent flakes of fish, the little boy went to sleep clutching a cormorant feather. Bird and boy tested their voices at the same time: it was only a matter of weeks before the little boy learned to speak the cormorant's language.

This was not extraordinary. Men and cormorants had fished together for one thousand years. Cormorants gathered up to ten pounds of fish a day, diving to mysteries of eighty feet. When the birds had fished and bred and grown old, their human fathers bid them farewell and put them to sleep with rice alcohol. I knew they must have missed them very much.

As I was on the phone with the New York Rare Bird Alert hotline, my mother walked into the room. "You're going to have to fill in for one of the models," she announced.

I shook my head, listening to a pleasant male voice update me on the latest sandpiper sighting.

"You're going to have to wear the cheongsam in the fashion show."

"Absolutely not." I visualized myself striding down the runway like a fool.

My mother's face flushed red, her throat swelling as a low sigh escaped her. "Why are you always so ashamed of yourself?" she asked. "You haven't even looked at the dress."

One afternoon, I saw my grandfather rising against the sky like King Arthur. Alone in the Ladies Pavilion, a wrought-iron shelter on the promontory called Hernshead, I spied his raft cutting out from behind a crag. On the lakeshore, a middle-aged couple was busy feeding swans and canvasbacks.

Against my usual instincts, I shouted, "Do you see that?"

The couple turned away from the swans, bread bags hanging limp in their fingers. "See what?"

I looked at the still, empty water. The raft was gone. "Nothing."

I had spied the cormorants hunched over, like vultures. Every time I saw the raft now, my grandfather got closer. Magnified through my lenses, the beads of water on his forehead looked like tiny amber eyes.

I left the pavilion and walked to the edge of the Lake. Lifting my binoculars, I saw the vision again—a man and his birds in constant watch. I jerked my head away, only to catch the couple looking at me. It was obvious that they didn't see him.

With a splash, my binoculars fell in the water. When I fished them out, they were slick and green and the sun caught on the lenses. The raft had disappeared yet again.

"Show yourself!" I said to the open air. "Why don't you show yourself!"

A chunk of bread hit me on the arm. The swan feeders were leaving.

When I got back to the shop, the lights were off. I pulled my sodden binocs out of their case and went to steal another scrap of cloth from the sewing room.

When I turned on the light, I tried not to scream. There, hanging on the dressmaker's dummy, was a cormorant. A dress in the guise of a bird—blackish feathers clinging to a skin of dark silk, a set of sequined eyes ringed with white, orange darts at the bust. I walked around to the rear of the mannequin and fingered the stitching that skirted the small of the back like a shoreline. The dress was gaudy and bold— the most beautiful thing I had ever seen. Pinned to one of the shoulder straps was a piece of paper that read "Xiao Feng" in Chinese characters.

My name.

I slipped out of my park-wear. As the army green pants pooled onto the concrete floor, I unzipped my mother's creation and gently lifted it off the form. Stepping into the soft cloth, I realized it had been a long time since I'd worn a dress. The zipper gathered the silk, closing me into an echo of my own body—my mother's vision. It struck me that she had never recorded my measurements, that she must have guessed every one of my vital numbers.

Parkgoers tittered as I strode past. A rollerblader skidded to a stop. A child in a stroller laughed and pointed as I pranced by in a traveling cloud of feathers. I hugged the path along the Lake, taking my place in the very center of Bow Bridge.

My grandfather was by the boathouse, drifting ever closer to me. I could see the birds with fish in their beaks and the old man's smile as he noticed what I was wearing. Forgoing my usual hat, I'd duck-slicked my hair with the stiffest gel.

The great blue heron, standing at four feet, is the tallest bird in the park. Not that day. I was the tallest, most conspicuous bird the Ramble had ever seen.

My grandfather's raft approached Bow Bridge. As he sailed under the arch, I leaned over as far as I could, absorbing each detail of his upturned face, moving to the other side before the raft drifted into view again.

The giggling died down as the picnickers and tourists concluded I was off to a fashion shoot or a coven meeting. Still, none of them noticed the Chinese man in rubber boots, or the ring of birds who dried their enormous unfurled wings in the light.

"I have chosen to show myself," I announced. The cormorants pumped their long, thin necks in applause.

I must have looked like just another madwoman, speaking to the white curve of the bridge, to the empty flow space under the arch.

"Show yourself!" I said to my grandfather. "It's time."

He glided past the willows and marsh grass and came to a stop in the middle of the Lake.

The black man lay down his fishing rod, his little granddaughter with the pigtails was curiously silent, the family in the rowboat lost an oar, and even the sun concentrated its yellow eye on the sight of a raft and a man and ten large birds.

It was a miracle that lasted for a blink, and in that snatch of time, I blew my grandfather a kiss so everyone could see I was a member of his family.

The First Snow

Daniel Lyons

Daniel Lyons has an MFA from the University of Michigan. His stories have appeared in Redbook *and* Playboy, *as well as literary magazines. He won first place in 1992 for the Playboy College Fiction contest. His first collection of stories,* The First Snow, *was published by the University of Massachusetts Press and won the 1992 Associated Writing Programs (AWP) Award in short fiction. His story "First Snow" was inspired by an article he read that reported on married men who were arrested for having sex in the woods in southern Michigan. The arrest caused quite a stir in the town. Gay rights advocates protested harassment and some of the men lost their jobs. Lyons imagined the plight of the families involved and immediately sat down to write his story after reading the article.*

The newspaper prints their names, and I admit that makes it worse. There are sixteen of them, and my father, whose name begins with A, is at the top of the list: Henry Abbott.

There was a rest area in Derry, apparently, and a path into the woods, and a giant hollow sycamore in the meeting place where they were arrested. The story in the *Gazette* says New Hampshire state troopers have been watching for weeks, camouflaged. They have videotapes.

The phone calls begin: more words for *fag* than I knew existed. Mom takes a call, listens, and slams down the phone. Her hair is matted to her head, her blouse is wrinkled, her eyes are bloodshot from not sleeping: she looks the way she did the time Jenny's appendix burst and we sat up all night in the hospital waiting room. She unplugs the phone.

"The First Snow," by Daniel Lyons, reprinted from *Story*, Winter 1993.

"Visiting his mother," she says, disgusted. That was the excuse Dad used when he went out yesterday. I'm trying to remember how long he's been visiting Nana on Sundays.

She lights a cigarette and then stubs it out, so hard that it snaps. "Bob, I'm sorry," she tells me, "but I won't live with this."

Dad spent the night in jail. Mom said she couldn't handle the police station, all the smirks and snickers. He was arraigned this morning, and now, six hours later, he's still at his lawyer's office. I imagine this is a first for Mr. Pangione. He's a contract man: wills, taxes, divorces—the last, I think, may be of use when the criminal case is finished. I picture the two of them in their big leather chairs: Mr. Pangione embarrassed and looking down at his desk, my father fidgeting, afraid to go home.

Dad does more than jump into strange cars in rest areas. The big surprise is that he has a steady. All I can gather from the conversation taking place behind the bedroom door upstairs is that the steady is married, and that he too is shocked about Dad's adventures in the woods.

"What, and do you love him? Do you love him? I can't believe I'm asking this! My husband! I'm going to be sick."

Dad starts to cry. I can hear his wet words, but I can't make them out. Oddly, the news of the steady doesn't seem so bad.

Jenny and Nelson are in the family room playing Chutes and Ladders, oblivious. Jenny is seven and Nelson is five—both, I hope, too young to remember this. I, however, am seventeen.

I spread the *Gazette* out on the kitchen table and read the list of names again, wondering which one was the one with my father. What an image: all those men, moving silently in the woods, my father among them.

I fold the paper and put it up on top of the refrigerator, where Jenny and Nelson won't find it. I think about stupid things: Should I still do my homework? Will we have Thanksgiving? What are we doing for dinner tonight?

Mom solves the last one: Kentucky Fried Chicken. We sit, the five of us, at what I suppose will be our own Last Supper. Jenny and Nelson make castles with their mashed potatoes and Mom doesn't scold them; Dad grips the drumstick Mom gave him—at least she's got her sense of humor—and makes fake small talk about school, where he did not teach today; Mom gives him polite fake responses between gulps from her tumbler of gin; I watch for a while, then stare straight into my plate, not wanting to meet any of their eyes.

Later, Mom packs suitcases and duffel bags and moves with Jenny and Nelson to the Driscolls' house. I tell her I'm going to stay at home.

Mom puts the kids in the car, then comes in to ask me once more to come with her. For a moment I am literally standing between them: Mom at the open door, angry; Dad by the fireplace, drumming his fingers on the mantel, looking away. He is a schoolteacher, a man accustomed to dignity, which he is now working hard to maintain.

"Well?" she says.

The fact is, I feel bad for my father. I'm not going to leave him here alone.

"You go on without me," I say.

Just like any other night, Dad sits slack-gutted in his recliner in the family room, watching television. I go in and sit on the couch. The show is NFL highlights.

"Look at that hit," he says. "Jesus Christ."

There is a slow-motion replay: the arms stretching for the pass, the safety spearing in from behind, the tiny moment when there is no motion, then the legs lifting up, the head snapping back like a car crash dummy's, the ball tumbling free.

"Jesus Christ," he says again. He grabs a handful of peanuts from the can, shakes them in his hand like dice, and looks at me."You going to stay for the game?" he says.

The air in the room feels over pressurized, like in a submarine that has surfaced too quickly.

"I don't know," I say.

"Well," he says, smiling, "I'm glad you decided to stay."

Suddenly I want to reach over and smack him for being so happy; I'd like to wipe that smile off his face.

"I'm glad you're in such a good mood," I say.

He sits up and says, "Bob, look—"

But I turn my back. I mumble something about homework and run upstairs to my room.

I'm on the phone with Drew—yes, everyone knows; some jerk has already started a joke—when another call comes in. It's Mr. Ryan, Dad's principal. I click back to Drew, tell him I've got to go, then call down to Dad.

"Well, I don't need to go to school tomorrow," he says when he arrives upstairs a few minutes later.

He tries to smile, then stands slope-shouldered in my doorway, looking old and paunchy in his cardigan sweater—more like an old fart at the Elks Club than some fairy running around in the woods. "I'm suspended," he says.

In homeroom there are eyes on me. I keep my head down. I write my name, over and over, in a spiral notebook. When Miss Moynihan calls my name there are snickers from the back of the room, but she stares them down. So she knows too, I think. We watch a video about nuclear weapons.

In the hall people make faces and whisper to each other, but they stay away, which is the best I can expect. It's not like I've got an army of friends who would rush to defend me. Drew comes up and fake punches me in the stomach—I guess to let me know that we're still manly men and to let everyone else know that he, at least, is on my side. He is five-foot-three and plays snare drum in the marching band. "So, Meester Elwood," he says. "You learn the Jetson's Theme?"

"The what?"

He pushes his glasses up the bridge of his nose. "Fuck you. The cartoon medley."

I make a face.

"For today? Rehearsal? The Turkey Day game?" He waves his hand back and forth in front of my face. "Hello? Hello?"

I explain that I am dropping band. Playing clarinet is just one of several things I will not do in public for a long, long time. Others: wear pink shirts, sharpen pencils, eat bananas. Beer in long-neck bottles. Anything to do with flowers.

On the door of my locker, in indelible black magic marker, is a drawing of a man, naked, kneeling down, with another man kneeling behind him, a giant third leg standing up from his abdomen. "Gee, Dad," the cartoon voice balloon says, "why can't we just go camping, like other families?"

The *Gazette* runs a front-page story about the arraignment. There is a priest, a banker, a man who runs a Sunoco station. Then there's my father, the menace of the J. G. Whittier Middle School.

A group of parents is calling for an investigation. "We want to know, has he ever chaperoned dances? Has he supervised gym?" a man named Ralph Leighton says.

A New Hampshire state trooper describes "the activities observed at the location." He uses words like "sodomy" and "fondling." During the arrest, he says, officers wore thick rubber gloves to keep from getting AIDS. Suddenly I think of our plates, our glasses, our toilet seat: but no, I think, that's ridiculous.

A Derry selectman says he doesn't care what these guys do as long as they do it in someone else's town. "I don't hate queers," he says.

After dinner, no kidding—Dad is cleaning his shotgun. He laughs when he sees the look on my face.

"For Christ's sake, Bob." He's wearing his most Dad outfit: corduroys from L. L. Bean, a polo shirt, and a golf sweater. "I thought we'd go down to Plum Island on Saturday. Ducks are open."

We really do hunt, he and I. Deer, ducks. But Jesus, I'm thinking—what's next? A pickup truck? Drinking contests? Washing whites with colors?

Dad is sunk so deep into his recliner that he and the chair look like all one piece, as if it grew out of his back. The remarkable thing is how much like a Dad he is. He is a little too fat in the belly and ass, and his brown hair is thin on top and shot with gray on the sides. He even wears brown tortoise-shell half-glasses when he reads the newspaper.

I study his face, looking for clues. For three days I've wondered how he managed to fool us all for so long. Wasn't there anything different about him? Yes, I realize now, there is a certain softness in his cheeks, a slackness at the edges of his mouth, which I hadn't noticed before.

"What?" he says, looking up from oiling the barrel.

"Nothing. Is that the Remington?"

He scowls. I turn back to the television and pretend to watch the commercial.

167

The phone rings. I jump up. "I'll unplug it."

"No," he says. He groans getting out of his chair. "Hello?" he says. Then, in a voice I've never heard: "Hi! Yes, I was hoping! I called this afternoon. Right. Oh, wait a minute." He hands me the phone. "Hang this up when I get upstairs?" Before I hang up I hear him say, "So, Mark."

In the night the phone rings. I reach, wondering how long it's been ringing.

A voice says, "You know how fags—"

I hang up. My breath rises in short, quick bursts. I think about school tomorrow. The phone rings again, and I unplug the cord, forgetting the other phones: the ringing continues in the kitchen, in the family room, in my father's room. My father says hello.

Then, groggy, he says, "Pardon me?"

I turn my face into my pillow. In the morning he pours me coffee and apologizes for the calls. "We'll get an answering machine," he says.

Mom says the Driscolls have room for me. I tell her I'm fine. "We're going hunting," I tell her. She rolls her eyes.

It's Wednesday. We're having dinner at Beshara's, a Lebanese place on South Union Street.

"Anyway, you can't all stay with the Driscolls," I say. "I mean, forever."

She says she is fully aware of what she can and can't do. She reminds me that she is my mother, I tell her I'm fully aware of that. I tell her that Dad is still Dad; that in most ways, nothing has changed. She uses words like "denial" and "trauma." She talks about lawyers and restraining orders. She pushes a cube of lamb back and forth on her plate.

"Are you going to eat that?" I say.

"Here." She slides her plate toward me.

I tell her my theory, which is that Dad has a brain tumor. Yesterday Drew told me about an uncle of his who one day at breakfast told his wife he was leaving her and the children to become a painter. And then did.

"That was Gauguin," she says.

"What?"

"Never mind."

"Anyway, something like a year later the guy had a seizure, and when they took him to the hospital they found out he had a tumor on his brain, the size of a grapefruit."

She lights a cigarette, "Why is it that tumors are always the size of a grapefruit? They're never the size of an orange. Or a cantaloupe."

This has been harder on her than I'd realized. I push on, though, explaining to her how Drew's uncle woke after surgery and didn't even know he'd left his family—the whole thing had been a mistake.

"And they all lived happily ever after," she says.

"Not really."

She raises an eyebrow. I shake my head.

"It doesn't matter. What *does* matter is that we get Dad in for a brain scan—fast." Finally, I make her laugh.

Our house leaks cold air through every joint, and the frame shudders and groans in the November wind. This house has been in the Abbott family since Ralph Waldo Emerson lived in our town. Emerson, in fact, ate dinner here, with my great-great-great uncle, Walter Henry Abbott.

I can't sleep. I lie still as a stone beneath two blankets and wonder whether my father fantasizes about me.

He must think about men. Young men: he must like the way we look. Does he think about me? Does he look at me? Has he ever? I cast back, but I can't remember any incidents. He sees me in the morning, though, scampering cold in a towel from the bathroom to my bedroom. I think about him eyeing me, wanting to take me in his mouth.

For a moment I wish him dead: I wonder what it would be like if he were gone. It is as if I have discovered that the man in the other room is not who he says he is; that he has been in a witness protection program and his real name is not Henry Abbott, but something else altogether, something sinister and Italian; that he is not my father at all.

I wonder if I will inherit this. I had a dream, once. But just once. And there was Art Brancato, a senior when I was a freshman: hairy-chested in the locker room, lounging naked, unafraid, a full-grown man at seventeen; I studied the way he squinted when he laughed, and for a while I tried to walk the way he did, rolling my shoulders. But no. That's not the same.

In the morning there is frost on the lawn and someone has spray-painted "Honk If You Love Men" on both sides of the Cutlass. The front of the house is spattered with eggs—it looks as if something big has sneezed on us.

Thanksgiving is a week away. Drew says I can come to his family's house, but I have to turn him down. Dad says he's going to cook dinner. He's counting on me. Secretly I'm hoping that someone will invite us—Aunt Marian, maybe—but I realize that's unlikely. We are pariahs, the unclean. So we will end up, the two of us, leaning over our little turkey and thanking God—for what? For not being run over by a train? For not being hit by lightning? "Well," I imagine Dad saying in his phony classroom voice, "we've still got two good arms and two good legs. That's more than some can say."

He calls the Driscolls to see if Mom and the kids will come home for the holiday. He has not spoken to her since she left. His hand shakes so much that he misses the number and has to hang up and dial again.

"Bill? Henry. Thanks," he says when Mr. Driscoll answers. "That means a lot right now. Right. I know. It's tough on all of us. I'm calling for Kate, actually. Oh. Well, I mean, you could tell her, all I want to do is talk. I mean, what harm—OK. All right. Maybe later, then."

But later she won't take his call, either.

He goes upstairs. I hear him on the phone with Mark. I imagine he's inviting him for Thanksgiving. Before our Norman Rockwell holiday scene can take form in my mind, I hear a sound like coughing from behind his door.

"For Christ's sake," he says. "For Christ's sake. All right then. I won't. I said I won't. Bye."

I dread gym but I don't ask to be excused. Afterward, in the locker room, I can't help it: I glance at their bodies. Not between their legs, but at the legs themselves. The long muscles of the thighs. The arms, the shoulders, the chests. The curved, wing-shaped backs.

I want to know if this excites me. I have always insisted that it doesn't, but I've never actually checked.

I look at their shapes, pink in the steam of the shower room. There is something, maybe. My looks are too furtive to tell. If I stared I might feel more. Or I might feel less.

It's Thursday afternoon. Walking home I hear the band practicing in the field behind the auditorium, and I hate my father for bringing me to this.

At home, Aunt Marian, Dad's sister, is sitting on the couch. She has brought a coffee cake; she makes them for funerals. She fidgets with the cellophane wrapping. Dad's family is pure Yankee, as tight with their feelings as they are with their money. They're not equipped for this.

"Well," she says.

He plants himself into his recliner. "So, yes," he says. "Nice of you."

Kindness lasts as long as a cup of tea. She avoids all references to Thanksgiving and instead chatters on about family gossip: which cousin got which piece of furniture from Grandmother Wilkinson's house in Gloucester, why Cousin Richard needed electroshock therapy. Then, her support shown, her duty endured, she rises to leave.

At the door she says, "Has Mom called?"

"Maybe I should call her."

"Poor dear Henry." She kisses his cheek. She turns to me and I get the same kiss. "Take care, Robert."

Twice that afternoon he starts to call, then hangs up. He putters. He fixes the leak in the roof in the back porch. He cleans leaves from the rain gutters.

Mom is taking Jenny and Nelson to spend Thanksgiving in Ohio with her sister. They might not come back, she says.

She and Dad are in the kitchen, Friday afternoon. I'm in the family room, wondering what we'll call this room now. Den, maybe.

Dad says she's using her children as bargaining chips.

"There's no bargaining going on here," she says. She tells him he should get a lawyer.

He sits at the kitchen table. He looks like a guy in a Vietnam movie, mumbling about all his dead friends, too shell-shocked to think straight.

She takes out a piece of paper and begins running down a list of what they own and what their debts are. Suddenly he interrupts her, slams his hand on the table, and says, "Look, you can't goddamn *do* this. You can't."

More and more he is angry. I take this as a good sign. At least he's acting like a man. In the scenario I dread, he slides the other way: he gets a fancy haircut, shrieks at jokes, flips his hands as he speaks.

Mom doesn't flinch. She folds the paper, puts it in her purse, and snaps it shut. "Good-bye, then," she says.

I walk her to the car. We sit in the driveway. She lights a new cigarette from the old one. Her hands tremble. She says, "I really don't think you should be staying here."

"Look," I say, "I'm not going to sleep on some couch in some basement."

"Does the other guy—" She drags, then exhales. "Does he come over?"

"I think they broke up."

"Broke up." She shakes her head. "Jesus Christ." She laughs. She seems fragile, as if she's grown old too fast, like the plants in those sped-up film clips. I can't look at her. "Bob," she says, "I want you to come with us to Ohio."

Don't do this, I'm thinking. Don't make me choose. In seven months I will finish school and then I will leave them all; but for now I want things to stay the same.

"I can get a court order," she says. "You're a minor."

Across the street, Mr. Gauthier is on his lawn, raking leaves and watching us. I wave at him. He looks away.

"Bob, please," she says.

"Reveille," Dad says. It's Saturday morning, still dark out. "Rise and shine."

We stop at Big Bear for coffee and cinnamon rolls. On the way to Plum Island I fall back to sleep, and when I wake up we are backing down the boat ramp. We have rented a Nissan Sentra while the Cutlass is being painted.

I winch out the boat, a twelve-foot Sears aluminum rowboat with a three-horse Evinrude motor, then drag it ashore with the bow line while Dad parks.

We sputter down the channel into the thick of the salt marsh, then sit and wait. The dawn sky is sick gray. I worry that it might rain. Dad loads five shells into the chamber of his gas-action Remington and hands me two for my over-and-under, the gun he used as a boy. We sit facing each other, barrels across our laps. We wait. We wait some more.

"Open those sardines," he says.

This is our hunting breakfast, a habit he got from his father. It's a tradition I don't plan to carry on.

The tin cover sticks at first. I take off my gloves to get a better grip, and when I pull harder the lid suddenly tears off in my hand and runs a long, curved slice across the meat of my thumb. "Fuck," I say, because we swear when we hunt. "Motherfucker," I say, as a line of blood fills the cut.

Dad reaches across and takes my hand. "Let's have a look," he says, but his touch is like a spark, and I pull away.

He stops. His eyes are wide open. He starts to say something, then doesn't. I look out over the marsh. There is nothing but water and sky, all gray. I imagine us from above, in black and white, so small on the water. I place the tin of sardines on the bench seat between us. I squeeze my thumb in the palm of my other hand. A drop of blood hits the bottom of the boat with a splat. Another falls; then another.

He reaches back to the first-aid box and takes out a Band-Aid. "Here," he says. I hold out my thumb, and he wraps the cut.

We sit. He doesn't say anything. He stares at me. I put my gloves back on. The wake from a boat crossing the marsh rocks us clumsily. He's still staring.

"I'm sorry," I say finally. "I just can't understand."

He fidgets with his wool cap. "I know."

"Maybe someday. I don't know."

"But you still love your old man, don't you?"

I kick my boots together. "Don't ask me things like that."

I look up. His eyes are reaching. I'm thinking that whatever happens, I don't want to see him cry.

"I need to know that," he says. "It's important."

He tries to take my hand again, but again I pull away.

"Stop it," I say. I sit back away from him. "Just don't."

He droops. I consider starting the engine and heading out of the marsh. But as awful as this moment is, I am unable to let it go. I feel on the edge of a discovery, as if some truth is about to reveal itself.

It doesn't. We sit and wait without talking. The water is calm, and now that the sun has come up, it's almost warm. We eat the sardines on crackers.

Suddenly shots are booming out over the water all around us—I realize now we're not alone here—and looking up I see the first line of ducks arcing down into the marsh. I point over his shoulder and he wheels and drops to one knee but already we're too late, they're past us and banking off, but he fires and fires anyway, long after the others have stopped. With each shot the recoil kicks his right shoulder back, as if it might spin him around. The spent shells leap from his chamber and hit the bottom of the boat still smoking, and he fires, fires, and fires into the empty sky.

He collapses into the curve of the bow. He turns his face away. I crawl over and kneel by him. "Dad," I say, "they're gone." He takes my hand, and this time I let him keep it.

Our new Code-A-Phone is chirping, and the message light blinks in time with it. Dad drops his hunting gear in the corner and, still in his plaid wool coat and right in front of me, he rushes to the machine like a schoolgirl. There is a man's voice, and I'm thinking, I really don't want to hear this.

But it's a man named Duncan Gardner, a lawyer. He represents Mom. "From now on, if you want to talk, I'd like you to talk to me," he says.

There are no other messages. Dad stands there, realizing, I guess, how foolish he looks. He takes a bottle to bed.

Later, past midnight, I lie awake in bed. Outside, the first snow of the season is falling against the night sky, tumbling through the tree branches and ticking against my window, and it's as if all the trouble in the world is coming down on us. Our old house creaks. I watch the snow toss and mingle in the air.

Dad is stirring in his room. Then his door opens and he pads down the stairs, through the hall and across the kitchen. I hold myself still, expecting—and I admit, half-hoping—to hear the crack of a muffled report from the garage. At least then we all could get over this. Instead there is the hum of the refrigerator, the clink of a bottle, a kitchen chair scraping on the linoleum floor. I cannot imagine why, but my poor father has decided to trudge on, and I know there are worse times ahead.

I think of him down there alone in the dark. I think of my mother, sleeping on a couch in someone's house. I think of Drew's uncle with the brain tumor, whose wife was so glad to have him back from the hospital that she decorated the house with balloons and streamers and threw a party for him. What they couldn't know, as they passed around the pieces of cake and danced to Ray Charles records, was that in three months his liver and lungs would be rotten with cancer, and that a month after that he'd be dead, leaving his friends to feel small and stupid—scared of the future, and stunned by the secrets life buries in us.

Lightning and the Lightning Bug:
The Craft of the Essay

Ved Mehta

*Ved Mehta was born in India in 1934, and at the age of four, he
lost his sight. He first came to the United States as a student at a
school for the blind in Arkansas, and continued his education at
Pomona College, Yale University, and finally, Oxford. He became
a US citizen in 1975. Ved Mehta was a staff writer for* The New
Yorker *from 1961 to 1994 and has taught literature and history at
half a dozen colleges and universities, including Williams, Vassar,
and Yale. He is the author of an autobiographical series of books
with the omnibus title* Continents of Exile, *of which the eighth book,*
Remembering Mr. Shawn's *New Yorker:* The Invisible Art of Editing,
has just been published. Among his other books are Portrait of India,
Mahatma Gandhi and His Apostles, *and* Rajiv Gandhi and Rama's
Kingdom, *all from Yale University Press.*

In 1956, when I was twenty-two, I graduated from Pomona College, in California, and
went up to Oxford. There I started working for a second bachelor's degree, for in
those days the best way to take full advantage of what Oxford offered and to enter
into the stream of English life was to work for an undergraduate degree at the university. I was reading history and was required to submit one or two essays a week
to the scrutiny of my tutors, most of whom were world-class scholars. While I was
reading aloud to my medieval tutor one of my first essays, on the Anglo-Saxons, he
stopped me after the word *motivation* and asked why I tended to reach for jargon
when a good English word was to hand.

"Lightning and the Lightning Bug: The Craft of the Essay," by Ved Mehta, reprinted from *The
American Scholar*, Spring 1998, Volume 67 Issue 2.

"But everyone uses *motivation*," I protested.

"Jargon is imprecise and encourages weak thought," said my tutor. "A careful writer would use a word like *impulse*."

Until then, I had thought I was a tolerably good writer and had believed that after working over a draft several times I was able to say what I wanted to say. Indeed, before going up to Oxford, I had completed an entire book, an autobiography, much of which had been set down two years earlier, in the course of a summer. But I was so deeply in awe of Oxford and its tutorial system, and so impressionable, that my tutor's questioning of one infelicitous word effectively unraveled my confidence in my writing even as it began to sensitize me to the nuances of words. For some time thereafter, whenever I wrote a sentence, I would read it as my tutor might, and conclude that almost everything was wrong with it. I was reminded of an accomplished pianist friend who was then undergoing intense psychoanalysis and had become in the course of her treatment so self-conscious that she could scarcely play a five-finger exercise. But I felt sure that, just as her treatment contained the promise of her becoming a better pianist, so my Oxford education contained the promise of my becoming a better writer. The road, however, turned out to be a long and arduous one—and to stretch far beyond Oxford.

I recall how daunting were my first steps along that road. They led me to a chaos of randomly assembled materials that had to be subjected first to the elusive formulation of ideas and then to the untamable nature of language itself. I was constantly tempted to put off writing. There was always more to read, more to reflect on. I found I had first to decide what, exactly, I wanted to say, even if in the course of writing I should find myself saying something totally different. (All ideas grow and develop as one writes, I learned, since one's memory expands through the process of association.) Nevertheless, that initial idea, though it might be only the germ of one, enabled me to overcome the terror of the blank page. So as not to feel constrained or constricted, I would write what I came to call a "vomit draft," in which I would pour out everything I could think of without worrying about sense or grammar. Then I would start the process of revision. Cutting and shaping my thoughts helped me learn what, if anything, I knew about the subject. As I pressed on with my essay, I would try to come up with the most telling arguments or examples to buttress whatever point I was making. To locate them required me to interrupt the writing and go searching through many books. In time, I learned to find my way around indexes, tables of contents, and library catalogues. Sometimes I would put aside the essay and return later to cast a cold eye on it. The process as I describe it here may sound simple, but, as every student knows, it is turbulent and involves a lot of angst.

I remember that I was struck by the elegance and luster of many of the essays written by my English contemporaries. Compared to theirs, my best efforts came across as dull and lame. (In England, writing well in one's chosen subject is the foundation of a good education.) Before long, I discovered that many of the undergraduates I admired had developed their writing styles as schoolboys by imitating the styles of great authors or, if they were studying to be classicists, by translating Latin or Greek prose and verse into the styles of contemporary English authors, and vice versa. Sometimes these students wrote with a certain archness and artificiality, but I envied the facility and grace of expression that the best of them had developed. To cultivate ear and eye, some of them played a game that consisted of picking out characteristic passages from ancient and modern authors and seeing who could identify them. I tried to play the game, too, but because my knowledge of classical texts was either shaky or nonexistent, I was hopeless at it.

I confided my doubts about my schooling to my medieval tutor, and he said that he thought I needed to read more widely. I told him that since the age of fifteen, when I first started speaking English (I had grown up speaking Punjabi), I had done little besides read—and that, like many foreigners whose mother tongue was not English, I was an autodidact.

"Ah," he said. "But have you studied what makes one author's work different from another's?" My tutor explained that no piece of writing could prove effective and memorable unless its author found the right voice and the right style. For the study of these matters, he directed me to *The Oxford Book of English Prose,* a collection of choice morsels, mostly by British authors, culled and introduced by Sir Arthur Quiller-Couch and published in 1925. It was a feast: Chaucer, Shakespeare, Milton, Swift, Samuel Johnson, Lamb, Coleridge, Jane Austen, De Quincey, the Brontë sisters, Melville, Dickens, Arnold, Shaw, and many others. Over the next months and years, I returned to the book again and again. Genius being, by definition, inimitable and transcendent, the selections certainly didn't encourage me to attempt similar feats, but rather made anything I did attempt seem insipid by comparison.

Some young writers might find a study of the works of genius harmful, because it would discourage them from writing. They would do well to go their merry way and, like Walt Whitman, discover their inner resources on their own. How often have I met a mother who told me that her daughter wrote beautiful letters and would write a book if she could only find the time! Perhaps so. But, in my experience, for every natural writer there are ten or more writers who have to labor over their craft. Mark Twain once said, "The difference between the right word and the almost right word is the difference between lightning and the lightning bug." Even so, it is hard to imagine Mark Twain, who made a virtue of seeming artless, studying the great writers of the past.

I myself found my study of the masters very helpful. Because I could savor only a few pages of *The Oxford Book of English Prose* at a sitting, I dipped into the volume whenever I had a little time, reading and rereading a selection to ponder its tone and cadence, its diction and imagery, its movement and structure. It gradually became clear to me that well-wrought sentences from different authors had a distinctive logic and beauty that could no more be tampered with than could the authors' signatures. Unquestionably, no two writers were alike, yet it took me a long time to discern just what stylistic characteristics made every writer different from every other and then to be able to put those differences into words.

The precision and finish of prose became a passion with me. It led me on to grammar books, most notably Fowler's *Modern English Usage,* and to essays, not only by authors in Quiller-Couch's anthology, which included nothing published after 1914, but also by twentieth-century authors: Virginia Woolf, of whose ardent prose it may be said, among other things, that it launched a whole new way of thinking and writing; Edmund Wilson, who encapsulated in sinewy prose the life, work, and critical value of great authors as if no one else had ever written about them; V. S. Pritchett, who never wrote a book review that didn't contain an unexpected image; and E. B. White, whose homey yet elegant turns of phrase made you think that no one could convey, for instance, the feel of the day better than he could. . . .

The House Fly

James Merrill

James Merrill, the son of a founding partner of Merrill Lynch was the author of twelve volumes of verse, a novelist, and an essayist. Merrill was especially skilled in classic poetic forms with difficult to accomplish design. He wrote sonnets and sestinas, haikus and epigrams; he worked in terza rima and the Rubaiyat stanza. However, he was most authentic when he made his own verse forms. Merrill's poetry is generally understated, pervaded by a fine sense of humor and a deep understanding of contemporary life.

Come October, if I close my eyes,
A self till then subliminal takes flight
Buzzing round me, settling upon the knuckle,
The lip to be explored not as in June
But with a sense of verging on micromania
Of wrong, of tiny, hazy, crying wrongs
Which quite undo her—look at that zigzag totter,
Proboscis blindly tapping like a cane.
Gone? If so, only to re-alight

Or else in a stray beam resume the grand toilette
(Eggs of next year's mischief long since laid):
Unwearying strigils taken to the frayed,
Still glinting wings; the dull-red lacquer head
Lifted from its socket, turned mechanically
This way and that, like a wristwatch being wound,
As if there would always be time . . .

"The House Fly," by James Merrill, reprinted from *Late Settings: Poems*, 1985, Atheneum Press.

Downstairs in this same house one summer night,
Founding the cult, her ancestress alit
On the bare chest of Strato Mouflouzélis
Who stirred in the lamp-glow but did not wake.
To say so brings it back on every autumn
Feebler wings, and further from that Sun,
That mist-white wafer she and I partake of
Alone this afternoon, making a rite
Distinct from both the blessing and the blight.

Hagar

Toni Morrison

Toni Morrison was born in Lorain, Ohio. After she earned a Master's degree in English, she started teaching at Howard University in 1957. Later, while she worked as an editor at Random House, she started writing fiction. Her first novel, The Bluest Eye, *an expansion of an earlier short story, was published in 1970, and she attracted immediate attention as a promising writer. Her other novels include* Sula *(1973),* Song of Solomon *(1977), and* Tar Baby *(1981).* Beloved *(1987)—which won the 1988 Pulitzer Prize—is regarded by many as Morrison's most successful novel. The book explores many complex themes, including black Americans' relationship to slavery. The novel* Jazz *(1992) and the nonfiction book* Playing in the Dark: Whiteness and the Literary Imagination *(1992 were also well received. In 1993, Morrison won the Nobel Prize in literature. Her latest book is* Paradise *(1998). The following is a chapter from* Song of Solomon.

It was a long time after he left, that warm September morning, that she was able to relax enough to drop the knife. When it clattered to the linoleum, she brought her arms down, oh, so slowly, and cradled her breasts as though they were two mangoes thumbed over in the marketplace and pushed aside. She stood that way in the little rented room with the sunshine pouring in until Guitar came home. He could not get her to speak or move, so he picked her up in his arms and carried her downstairs. He sat her on the bottom step while he went to borrow a car to drive her home.

Terrible as he thought the whole business was, and repelled as he was by mindlessness in love, he could not keep the deep wave of sorrow from engulfing him as

"Chapter 13 from Song of Solomon," by Toni Morrison, reprinted from *Song of Solomon*, 1987, Plume.

he looked at this really rather pretty woman sitting straight as a pole, holding her breasts, and staring in front of her out of hollow eyes.

The engine of the old car he'd borrowed roared, but Guitar spoke softly to her. "You think because he doesn't love you that you are worthless. You think because he doesn't want you anymore that he is right—that his judgment and opinion of you are correct. If he throws you out, then you are garbage. You think he belongs to you because you want to belong to him. Hagar, don't. It's a bad word, 'belong.' Especially when you put it with somebody you love. Love shouldn't be like that. Did you ever see the way the clouds love a mountain? They circle all around it; sometimes you can't even see the mountain for the clouds. But you know what? You go up top and what do you see? His head. The clouds never cover the head. His head pokes through, because the clouds let him; they don't wrap him up. They let him keep his head up high, free, with nothing to hide him or bind him. Hear me, Hagar?" He spoke to her as he would to a very young child. "You can't own a human being. You can't lose what you don't own. Suppose you did own him. Could you really love somebody who was absolutely nobody without you? You really want somebody like that? Somebody who falls apart when you walk out the door? You don't, do you? And neither does he. You're turning over your whole life to him. Your whole life, girl. And if it means so little to you that you can just give it away, hand it to him, then why should it mean any more to him? He can't value you more than you value yourself." He stopped. She did not move or give any sign that she had heard him.

Pretty woman, he thought. Pretty little black-skinned woman. Who wanted to kill for love, die for love. The pride, the conceit of these doormat women amazed him. They were always women who had been spoiled children. Whose whims had been taken seriously by adults and who grew up to be the stingiest, greediest people on earth and out of their stinginess grew their stingy little love that ate everything in sight. They could not believe or accept the fact that they were unloved; they believed that the world itself was off balance when it appeared as though they were not loved. Why did they think they were so lovable? Why did they think their brand of love was better than, or even as good as, anybody else's? But they did. And they loved their love so much they would kill anybody who got in its way.

He looked at her again. Pretty. Pretty little black girl. Pretty little black-skinned girl. What had Pilate done to her? Hadn't anybody told her the things she ought to know? He thought of his two sisters, grown women now who could deal, and the litany of their growing up. Where's your daddy? Your mama know you out here in the street? Put something on your head. You gonna catch your death a cold. Ain't you hot? Ain't you cold? Ain't you scared you gonna get wet? Uncross your legs. Pull up your socks. I thought you was goin to the Junior Choir. Your slip is showin. Your hem is out. Come back in here and iron that collar. Hush your mouth. Comb your head. Get up from there and make that bed. Put on the meat. Take out the trash. Vaseline get rid of that ash.

Neither Pilate nor Reba knew that Hagar was not like them. Not strong enough, like Pilate, nor simple enough, like Reba, to make up her life as they had. She needed what most colored girls needed: a chorus of mamas, grandmamas, aunts, cousins, sisters, neighbors, Sunday school teachers, best girl friends, and what all to give her the strength life demanded of her—and the humor with which to live it.

Still, he thought, to have the object of your love, worthy or not, despise you, or leave you . . .

"You know what, Hagar? Everything I ever loved in my life left me. My father died when I was four. That was the first leaving I knew and the hardest. Then my mother. There were four of us and she just couldn't cut it when my father died. She ran away. Just ran away. My aunt took care of us until my grandmother could get there. Then my grandmother took care of us. Then Uncle Billy came. They're both close to dead now. So it was hard for me to latch on to a woman. Because I thought if I loved anything it would die. But I did latch on. Once. But I guess once is all you can manage." Guitar thought about it and said, "But I never wanted to kill her. *Him,* yeah. But not her." He smiled, but Hagar wasn't looking, wasn't even listening, and when he led her out of the car into Reba's arms her eyes were still empty.

All they knew to do was love her and since she would not speak, they brought things to please her. For the first time in life Reba *tried* to win things. And, also for the first time, couldn't. Except for a portable television set, which they couldn't connect because they had no electricity, Reba won nothing. No raffle ticket, no Bingo, no policy slip, no clearing-house number, no magazine sweepstakes, no, nor any unpierced carnival balloon succumbed to her magic. It wore her down. Puzzled and luckless, she dragged herself home clutching stalks of anything that blossomed along the edges of lots and other people's gardens. These she presented to her daughter, who sat in a chair by the window or lay in bed fingering, fingering her hair.

They cooked special things for her; searched for gifts that they hoped would break the spell. Nothing helped. Pilate's lips were still and Reba's eyes full of panic. They brought her lipstick and chocolate milk, a pink nylon sweater and a fuchsia bed jacket. Reba even investigated the mysteries of making jello, both red and green. Hagar didn't even look at it.

One day Pilate sat down on Hagar's bed and held a compact before her granddaughter's face. It was trimmed in a goldlike metal and had a pink plastic lid.

"Look, baby. See here?" Pilate turned it all around to show it off and pressed in the catch. The lid sprang open and Hagar saw a tiny part of her face reflected in the mirror. She took the compact then and stared into the mirror for a long while.

"No wonder," she said at last. "Look at that. No wonder. No wonder."

Pilate was thrilled at the sound of Hagar's voice. "It's yours, baby," she said. "Ain't it pretty?"

"No wonder," said Hagar. "No wonder."

"No wonder what?" asked Pilate.

"Look at how I look. I look awful. No wonder he didn't want me. I look terrible." Her voice was calm and reasonable, as though the last few days hadn't been lived through at all. "I need to get up from here and fix myself up. No *wonder!*" Hagar threw back the bedcover and stood up. "Ohhh. I smell too. Mama, heat me some water. I need a bath. A long one. We got any bath salts left? Oh, Lord, my head. Look at that." She peered into the compact mirror again. "I look like a ground hog. Where's the comb?"

Pilate called Reba and together they flew through the house to find the comb, but when they found it Hagar couldn't get the teeth through her roped and matted hair.

"Wash it," said Reba. "Wash it and we'll comb it while it's wet."

"I need shampoo, then. Real shampoo. I can't use Mama's soap."

"I'll go get some." Reba was trembling a little. "What kind?"

"Oh, any kind. And get some hair oil, Reba. Posner's, and some . . . Oh, never mind. Just that. Mama? Have you seen my . . . Oh, my God. No wonder. No wonder."

Pilate pulled a piece of string from Hagar's bedspread and put it in her mouth. "I'll heat up the water," she said.

When Reba got back she washed Hagar's hair, brushed it, and combed it gently.

"Just make me two braids, Reba. I'm going to have to go to the beauty shop. Today. Oh, and I need something to wear." Hagar stood at the door of the little cardboard closet, running her hands over the shoulders of dresses. "Everything's a mess in here. A mess. All wrinkled . . ."

"Water's hot. Where you want the tub?"

"Bring it in here."

"You think you should be taking a bath so soon?" Reba asked. "You just got up."

"Hush, Reba," said Pilate. "Let the child take care of herself."

"But she's been in the bed three days."

"All the more reason."

"I can't put these things on. Everything's a mess." Hagar was almost in tears.

Reba looked at Pilate. "I hope you right. I don't approve of getting up too fast and jumping right in some water."

"Help me with this tub and stop grumbling."

"All wrinkled. What am I going to wear?"

"That ain't enough water to cover her feet."

"It'll grow when she sits down."

"Where's my yellow dress? The one that buttons all the way down?"

"Somewhere in there, I reckon."

"Find it for me and press it, would you? I know it's a mess. Everything's a mess."

Reba found and pressed the yellow dress. Pilate helped Hagar bathe. Finally a clean and clothed Hagar stood before the two women and said, "I have to buy some clothes. New clothes. Everything I have is a mess."

They looked at each other. "What you need?" asked Pilate.

"I need everything," she said, and everything is what she got. She shopped for everything a woman could wear from the skin out, with the money from Reba's diamond. They had seventy-five cents between them when Hagar declared her needs, and six dollars owed to them from customers. So the two-thousand-dollar two-carat diamond went to a pawnshop, where Reba traded it for thirty dollars at first and then, accompanied by a storming Pilate, she went back and got one hundred and seventy more for it. Hagar stuffed two hundred dollars and seventy-five cents into her purse and headed downtown, still whispering to herself every now and then, "No wonder."

She bought a Playtex garter belt, I. Miller No Color hose, Fruit of the Loom panties, and two nylon slips—one white, one pink—one pair of Joyce Fancy Free and one of Con Brio ("Thank heaven for little Joyce heels"). She carried an armful of skirts and an Evan-Picone two-piece number into the fitting room. Her little yellow dress that buttoned all the way down lay on the floor as she slipped a skirt over her head and shoulders, down to her waist. But the placket would not close. She sucked in her stomach and pulled the fabric as far as possible, but the teeth of the zipper would not join. A light sheen broke out on her forehead as she huffed and puffed. She was convinced that her whole life depended on whether or not those aluminum teeth would meet. The nail of her forefinger split and the balls of her thumbs ached as she struggled with the placket. Dampness became sweat and her breath came in gasps. She was about to weep when the saleswoman poked her head through the curtain and said brightly, "How are you doing?" But when she saw Hagar's gnarled and frightened face, the smile froze.

"Oh, my," she said, and reached for the tag hanging from the skirt's waist. "This is a five. Don't force it. You need, oh, a nine or eleven, I should think. Please. Don't force it. Let me see if I have that size."

She waited until Hagar let the plaid skirt fall down to her ankles before disappearing. Hagar easily drew on the skirt the woman brought back, and without further search, said she would take it and the little two-piece Evan-Picone.

She bought a white blouse next and a nightgown—fawn trimmed in sea foam. Now all she needed was make-up.

The cosmetics department enfolded her in perfume, and she read hungrily the labels and the promise. Myrurgia for primeval woman who creates for him a world of tender privacy where the only occupant is you, mixed with Nina Ricci's L'Air du Temps. Yardley's Flair with Tuvaché's Nectaroma and D'Orsay's Intoxication. Robert Piguet's Fracas, and Calypso and Visa and Bandit. Houbigant's Chantilly. Caron's Fleurs de Rocaille and Bellodgia. Hagar breathed deeply the sweet air that hung over the glass counters. Like a smiling sleepwalker she circled. Round and round the diamond-clear counters covered with bottles, wafer-thin disks, round boxes, tubes, and phials. Lipsticks in soft white hands darted out of their sheaths like the shiny red penises of puppies. Peachy powders and milky lotions were grouped in front of poster after cardboard poster of gorgeous grinning faces. Faces in ecstasy. Faces somber with achieved seduction. Hagar believed she could spend her life there among the cut glass, shimmering in peaches and cream, in satin. In opulence. In luxe. In love.

It was five-thirty when Hagar left the store with two shopping bags full of smaller bags gripped in her hands. And she didn't put them down until she reached Lilly's Beauty Parlor.

"No more heads, honey." Lilly looked up from the sink as Hagar came in.

Hagar stared. "I have to get my hair done. I have to hurry," she said.

Lilly looked over at Marcelline. It was Marcelline who kept the shop prosperous. She was younger, more recently trained, and could do a light press that lasted.

Lilly was still using red-hot irons and an ounce of oil on every head. Her customers were loyal but dissatisfied. Now she spoke to Marcelline. "Can you take her? I can't, I know."

Marcelline peered deeply into her customer's scalp. "Hadn't planned on any late work. I got two more coming. This is my eighth today."

No one spoke. Hagar stared.

"Well," said Marcelline. "Since it's you, come on back at eight-thirty. Is it washed already?"

Hagar nodded.

"Okay," said Marcelline. "Eight-thirty. But don't expect nothing fancy."

"I'm surprised at you," Lilly chuckled when Hagar left. "You just sent two people away."

"Yeah, well, I don't feel like it, but I don't want no trouble with that girl Hagar. No telling what she might do. She jump that cousin of hers, no telling what she might do to me."

"That the one going with Macon Dead's boy?" Lilly's customer lifted her head away from the sink.

"That's her. Ought to be shamed, the two of them. *Cousins.*"

"Must not be working out if she's trying to kill him."

"I thought he left town."

"Wouldn't you?"

"Well, I know I don't want to truck with her. Not me."

"She don't bother nobody but him."

"Well, Pilate, then. Pilate know I turned her down, she wouldn't like it. They spoil that child something awful."

"Didn't you order fish from next door?"

"All that hair. I hope she don't expect nothing fancy."

"Call him up again. I'm getting hungry."

"Be just like her. No appointment. No nothing. Come in here all late and wrong and want something fancy."

She probably meant to wait somewhere. Or go home and return to Lilly's at eight-thirty. Yet the momentum of the thing held her—it was all of a piece. From the moment she looked into the mirror in the little pink compact she could not stop. It was as though she held her breath and could not let it go until the energy and busyness culminated in a beauty that would dazzle him. That was why, when she left Lilly's, she looked neither right nor left but walked on and on, oblivious of other people, street lights, automobiles, and a thunderous sky. She was thoroughly soaked before she realized it was raining and then only because one of the shopping bags split. When she looked down, her Evan-Picone white-with-a-band-of-color skirt was lying in a neat half fold on the shoulder of the road, and she was far far from home. She put down both bags, picked the skirt up and brushed away the crumbs of gravel that stuck to it. Quickly she refolded it, but when she tried to tuck it back into the shopping bag, the bag collapsed altogether. Rain soaked her hair and poured down her neck as she stooped to repair the damage. She pulled out the box of Con Brios, a smaller package of Van Raalte gloves, and another containing her fawn-trimmed-in-seafoam shortie nightgown. These she stuffed into the other bag. Retracing her steps, she found herself unable to carry the heavier bag in one hand, so she hoisted it up to her stomach and hugged it with both arms. She had gone hardly ten yards when the bottom fell out of it. Hagar tripped on Jungle Red (Sculptura) and Youth Blend, and to her great dismay, saw her box of Sunny Glow toppling into a puddle. She collected Jungle Red and Youth Blend safely, but Sunny Glow, which had tipped completely over and lost its protective disk, exploded in light peach puffs under the weight of the raindrops. Hagar scraped up as much of it as she could and pressed the wilted cellophane disk back into the box.

Twice before she got to Darling Street she had to stop to retrieve her purchases from the ground. Finally she stood in Pilate's doorway, limp, wet, and confused, clutching her bundles in whatever way she could. Reba was so relieved to see her that she grabbed her, knocking Chantilly and Bandit to the floor. Hagar stiffened and pulled away from her mother.

"I have to hurry," she whispered. "I have to hurry."

Loafers sluicing, hair dripping, holding her purchases in her arms, she made it into the bedroom and shut the door. Pilate and Reba made no move to follow her.

Hagar stripped herself naked there, and without taking time to dry her face or hair or feet, she dressed herself up in the white-with-a-band-of-color skirt and matching bolero, the Maidenform brassiere, the Fruit of the Loom panties, the no color hose, the Playtex garter belt and the Joyce con brios. Then she sat down to attend to her face. She drew charcoal gray for the young round eye through her brows, after which she rubbed mango tango on her cheeks. Then she patted sunny glow all over her face. Mango tango disappeared under it and she had to put it on again. She pushed out her lips and spread jungle red over them. She put baby clear sky light to outwit the day light on her eyelids and touched bandit to her throat, earlobes, and wrists. Finally she poured a little youth blend into her palm and smoothed it over her face.

At last she opened the door and presented herself to Pilate and Reba. And it was in their eyes that she saw what she had not seen before in the mirror: the wet ripped hose, the soiled white dress, the sticky, lumpy face powder, the streaked rouge, and the wild wet shoals of hair. All this she saw in their eyes, and the sight filled her own with water warmer and much older than the rain. Water that lasted for hours, until the fever came, and then it stopped. The fever dried her eyes up as well as her mouth.

She lay in her little Goldilocks'-choice bed, her eyes sand dry and as quiet as glass. Pilate and Reba, seated beside the bed, bent over her like two divi-divi trees beaten forward by a wind always blowing from the same direction. Like the trees, they offered her all they had: love murmurs and a protective shade.

"Mama." Hagar floated up into an even higher fever.

"Hmmm?"

"Why don't he like my hair?"

"Who, baby? Who don't like your hair?"

"Milkman."

"Milkman does too like your hair," said Reba.

"No. He don't. But I can't figure out why. Why he never liked my hair."

"Of course he likes it. How can he not like it?" asked Pilate.

"He likes silky hair." Hagar was murmuring so low they had to bend down to hear her.

"Silky hair? Milkman?"

"He doesn't like hair like mine."

"Hush, Hagar."

"Silky hair the color of a penny."

"Don't talk, baby."

"Curly, wavy, silky hair. He don't like mine."

Pilate put her hand on Hagar's head and trailed her fingers through her grand-daughter's soft damp wool. "How can he not love your hair? It's the same hair that grows out of his own armpits. The same hair that crawls up out his crotch on up his stomach. All over his chest. The very same. It grows out of his nose, over his lips, and if he ever lost his razor it would grow all over his face. It's all over his head, Hagar. It's his hair too. He got to love it."

"He don't love it at all. He hates it."

"No he don't. He don't know what he loves, but he'll come around, honey, one of these days. How can he love himself and hate your hair?"

"He loves silky hair."

"Hush, Hagar."

"Penny-colored hair."

"Please, honey."

"And lemon-colored skin."

"Shhh."

"And gray-blue eyes."

"Hush now, hush."

"And thin nose."

"Hush, girl, hush."

"He's never going to like my hair."

"Hush. Hush. Hush, girl, hush."

The neighbors took up a collection because Pilate and Reba had spent everything getting Hagar the things needed to fix herself up. It didn't amount to much, though, and it was touch and go whether she'd have a decent funeral until Ruth walked down to Sonny's Shop and stared at Macon without blinking. He reached into his cash drawer and pulled out two twenty-dollar bills and put them down on the desk. Ruth didn't stretch out her hand to pick them up, or even shift her feet. Macon hesitated, then wheeled around in his chair and began fiddling with the combination to his safe. Ruth waited. Macon dipped into the safe three separate times before Ruth unclasped her hands and reached for the money. "Thank you," she said, and marched off to Linden Chapel Funeral Home to make the fastest arrangements possible.

Two days later, halfway through the service, it seemed as though Ruth was going to be the lone member of the bereaved family there. A female quartet from Linden Baptist Church had already sung "Abide with Me"; the wife of the mortician had read the condolence cards and the minister had launched into his "Naked came ye into this life and naked shall ye depart" sermon, which he had always believed suitable for the death of a young woman; and the winos in the vestibule who came to pay their respects to "Pilate's girl," but who dared not enter, had begun to sob, when the door swung open and Pilate burst in, shouting, "Mercy!" as though it were a command. A young man stood up and moved toward her. She flung out her right arm and almost knocked him down. "I want mercy!" she shouted, and began walking toward the coffin, shaking her head from side to side as though somebody had asked her a question and her answer was no.

Halfway up the aisle she stopped, lifted a finger, and pointed. Then slowly, although her breathing was fast and shallow, she lowered her hand to her side. It was strange, the languorous, limp hand coming to rest at her side while her breathing was coming so quick and fast. "Mercy," she said again, but she whispered it now. The mortician scurried toward her and touched her elbow. She moved away from him and went right up to the bier. She tilted her head and looked down. Her earring grazed her shoulder. Out of the total blackness of her clothes it blazed like a star. The mortician tried to approach her again, and moved closer, but when he saw her inky, berry-black lips, her cloudy, rainy eyes, the wonderful brass box hanging from her ear, he stepped back and looked at the floor.

"Mercy?" Now she was asking a question. "Mercy?"

It was not enough. The word needed a bottom, a frame. She straightened up, held her head high, and transformed the plea into a note. In a clear bluebell voice she sang it out—the one word held so long it became a sentence—and before the last syllable had died in the corners of the room, she was answered in a sweet soprano: "I hear you."

The people turned around. Reba had entered and was singing too. Pilate neither acknowledged her entrance nor missed a beat. She simply repeated the word "Mercy," and Reba replied. The daughter standing at the back of the chapel, the mother up front, they sang.

> *In the nighttime.*
> *Mercy.*
> *In the darkness.*
> *Mercy.*
> *In the morning.*
> *Mercy.*
> *At my bedside.*
> *Mercy.*
> *On my knees now.*
> *Mercy. Mercy. Mercy. Mercy.*

They stopped at the same time in a high silence. Pilate reached out her hand and placed three fingers on the edge of the coffin. Now she addressed her words to the woman bordered in gray satin who lay before her. Softly, privately, she sang to Hagar the very same reassurance she had promised her when she was a little girl.

> *Who's been botherin my sweet sugar lumpkin?*
> *Who's been botherin my baby?*
> *Who's been botherin my sweet sugar lumpkin?*
> *Who's been botherin my baby girl?*
>
> *Somebody's been botherin my sweet sugar lumpkin.*
> *Somebody's been botherin my baby.*
> *Somebody's been botherin my sweet sugar lumpkin.*
> *Somebody's been botherin my baby girl.*
>
> *I'll find who's botherin my sweet sugar lumpkin.*
> *I'll find who's botherin my baby.*
> *I'll find who's botherin my sweet sugar lumpkin.*
> *I'll find who's botherin my baby girl.*

"My baby girl." The three words were still pumping in her throat as she turned away from the coffin. Looking about at the faces of the people seated in the pews, she fastened on the first pair of eyes that were directed toward her. She nodded at the face and said, "My baby girl." She looked for another pair of eyes and told him also, "My baby girl," Moving back down the aisle, she told each face turned toward her the same piece of news. "My baby girl. That's my baby girl. My baby girl. My baby girl. My baby girl."

Conversationally she spoke, identifying Hagar, selecting her away from everybody else in the world who had died. First she spoke to the ones who had the courage to look at her, shake their heads, and say, "Amen." Then she spoke to those whose nerve failed them, whose glances would climb no higher than the long black fingers at her side. Toward them especially she leaned a little, telling in three words the full story of the stumped life in the coffin behind her. "My baby girl." Words tossed like stones into a silent canyon.

Suddenly, like an elephant who has just found his anger and lifts his trunk over the heads of the little men who want his teeth or his hide or his flesh or his amazing strength, Pilate trumpeted for the sky itself to hear, "And she was *loved!*"

It startled one of the sympathetic winos in the vestibule and he dropped his bottle, spurting emerald glass and jungle-red wine everywhere.

Pet Fly

Walter Mosley

Walter Mosley was born in Los Angeles in 1952, but after high school he moved to Vermont, where he worked several jobs and attended several colleges before settling down to computer programming. From Vermont he moved to Boston and then, in 1982, to New York. He also moved from programming to establishing a consultancy in computer work with a partner.

Later he entered a writing workshop that led to his enrolling at City College to study with Frederic Tuten, the head of the college's writing program. While he was taking courses there, he wrote his first detective story, which eventually became Devil in a Blue Dress. *Walter Mosley is the author of the best selling* Easy Rawlins *series of mysteries, the novel* R.L.'s Dream, *and the story collection* Always Outnumbered, Always Outgunned, *for which he received the Anisfield-Wolf Book Award.*

Walter Mosley's novels are now published in eighteen countries. He is the president of the Mystery Writers of America, a member of the executive board of the PEN American Center and founder of its Open Book Committee, and is on the board of directors of the National Book Awards.

I had been seeing Mona Donelli around the building since my first day working in interoffice mail. Mona laughing, Mona complaining about her stiff new shoes or the air conditioning or her boyfriend refusing to take her where she wanted to go. She's very pretty. Mona wears short skirts and giggles a lot. She's not serious at all. When silly Mona comes in she says hello and asks how you are, but before you get a chance

---

"Pet Fly," by Walter Mosley, reprinted from *The New Yorker*, December 13, 1999.

to answer she's busy talking about what she saw on TV last night or something funny that happened on the ferry from Staten Island that morning.

I would see Mona almost every day on my delivery route—at the coffee-break room on the fifth floor or in a hallway, never at a desk. So when I made a rare delivery to the third-floor mortgage department and saw her sitting there, wearing a conservative sweater buttoned all the way up to her throat, I was surprised. She was so subdued, not sad but peaceful, looking at the wall in front of her and holding a yellow pencil with the eraser against her chin.

"Air conditioning too high again?" I asked, just so she'd know that I paid attention to the nonsense she babbled about.

She looked at me and I got a chill, because it didn't feel like the same person I saw flitting around the office. She gave me a silent and friendly smile, even though her eyes seemed to be wondering what my question meant.

I put down the big brown envelope addressed to her department and left without saying anything else.

Back in the basement, I asked my boss, Ernie, what was wrong with Mona.

"Nothing," he said. "I think she busted up with some guy or something. No, no, I'm a liar. She went out with her boyfriend's best friend without telling him. Now she doesn't get why the boyfriend's mad. That's what she said. Bitch. What she think?"

Ernie didn't suffer fools, as my mother would say. He was an older black man who had moved to New York from Georgia thirty-three years ago. He had come to work at Carter's Home Insurance three days after he arrived. "I would have been here on day one," he told me, "but my bus got in on Friday afternoon."

I'd been there for only three weeks. After I graduated from Hunter College, I didn't know what to do. I had a B.A. in poli sci, but I didn't really have any skills. Couldn't type or work a computer. I wrote all my papers in longhand and used a typing service. I didn't know what I wanted to do, but I had to pay the rent. When I applied for a professional-trainee position that Carter's Home had advertised at Hunter, the personnel officer told me that there was nothing available, but maybe if I took the mailroom position something might open up.

"They hired two white P.T.s the day after you came," Ernie told me at the end of the first week. I decided to ignore that. Maybe those people had applied before me, or maybe they had skills with computers or something.

I didn't mind my job. Big Linda Washington and Little Linda Brown worked with me. The Lindas had earphones and listened to music while they wheeled around their canvas mail carts. Big Linda liked rap and Little Linda liked R & B. Neither one talked to me much.

My only friend at work was Ernie. He was the interoffice mail director. He and I would sit in the basement and talk for hours sometimes. Ernie was proud of his years at Carter's Home. He liked the job and the company, but he had no patience for most of the bosses.

"Workin' for white people is always the same thing," Ernie would say.

"But Mr. Drew's black," I said the first time I heard his perennial complaint. Drew was the supervisor for all postal and interoffice communication. He was a small man with hard eyes and breath that smelled of vitamins.

"Used to be," Ernie said. "Used to be. But ever since he got promoted he forgot all about that. Used to be he'd come down here and we'd talk like you 'n' me doin'. But now he just stands at the door and grins and nods. Now he's so scared I'm gonna pull him down that he won't even sit for a minute."

"I don't get it," I once said to Ernie. "How can you like the job and the company if you don't like the people you work for?"

"It's a talent," he replied.

"Why 'on't you tuck in your shirt?" Big Linda Washington said, sneering at me on the afternoon after I had seen Mona Donelli at her third-floor desk. "You look like some kinda fool, hangin' out all over the place."

Big Linda was taller than I, broader, too, and I'm pretty big. Her hair was straightened and frosted in gold. She wore dresses in primary colors, as a rule. Her skin was berry black. Her face, unless it was contorted from appraising me, was pretty.

We were in the service elevator, going up to the fifth floor. I tucked the white shirttails into my black jeans.

"At least you could make it even so the buttons go straight down," she remarked. "Just 'cause you light-skinned you can't go 'round lookin' like a mess."

I would have had to open up my pants to do it right, and I didn't want Big Linda to get any more upset than she already was.

She grunted and sucked a tooth.

The elevator opened, and she rolled out her cart. We had parallel routes, but I went in the opposite direction, deciding to take mail from the bottom of the stack rather than let her humiliate me.

The first person I ran into was Mona. Now she was wearing a one-piece deep red dress held up by spaghetti straps. Her breasts were free under the thin fabric, and her legs were bare. Mona was short, with thick black hair and green eyes. Her skin had a hint of olive but not so deep as what you think of as a Sicilian complexion.

"I can see why you were wearing that sweater at your desk," I said.

"What?" she replied, in a very unfriendly tone.

"That white sweater you were wearing," I said.

"What's wrong with you? I don't even own a white sweater."

She turned abruptly and clicked away on her red high heels. I wondered what had happened. I kept thinking that it was because of my twisted-up shirt. Maybe that's what made people treat me badly, maybe it was my appearance.

I continued along my route, pulling files from the bottom and placing them in the right "in" boxes.

"If the boxes ain't side by side, just drop it anywhere and pick up whatever you want to," Ernie had told me on my first day. "That's what I do. Mr. Averill put down the rules thirteen years ago, just before they kicked him upstairs."

Bernard Averill was the vice president in charge of all non-professional employees. He administered the cafeteria workers, the maintenance staff, secretarial services, and both the inter-office and postal mail departments. He was Ernie's hero because he was the only V.P. who had worked his way up from an entry level position.

When I'd finished the route, I went through the exit door at the far end of the hall to get a drink of water. I planned to wait there long enough for Big Linda to have gone back down. While I was at the water fountain, a fly buzzed by my head. It caught my attention because not many flies made it into the air-conditioned buildings around Wall Street, even in summer.

The fly landed on my hand, then flew to the cold aluminum bowl of the water fountain. He didn't have enough time to drink before zooming up to the ceiling. From there he lit on the doorknob, then landed on the baby finger of my left hand. After that he buzzed down to the floor. He took no more than a second to enjoy each perch.

"You sure jumpy, Mr. Fly," I said, as I might have when I was a child. "But you might be a Miss Fly, huh?"

The idea that the neurotic fly could be a female brought Mona to mind. I hustled my cart toward the elevator, passing Big Linda on the way. She was standing in the hall, talking to another young black woman.

"I got to wait for a special delivery from, um, investigations," Big Linda explained.

"I got to go see a friend on three," I replied.

"Oh." Big Linda seemed relieved.

I realized that she was afraid I'd tell Ernie that she was idling with her friends. Somehow that stung more than her sneers.

She was still wearing the beaded sweater, but instead of the eraser she had a tiny Wite-Out brush in her hand, half an inch from a sheet of paper on her violet blotter.

"I bet that blotter used to be blue, huh?"

"What?" She frowned at me.

"That blotter—it looks violet, purple, but that's because it used to be blue but the sun shined on it, from the window."

She turned her upper torso to look out the window. I could see the soft contours of her small breasts against the white fabric.

"Oh," she said, turning back to me. "I guess."

"Yeah," I said. "I notice things like that. My mother says that's why I never finish anything. She says I get distracted all the time and don't keep my eye on the job."

"Do you have more mail for me?"

"No, uh-uh, I was just thinking."

She looked at the drying Wite-Out brush and then jammed it back into the small bottle that was in her other hand.

"I was thinking about when I saw you this morning," I continued. "About when I saw you and asked about the air conditioning and your sweater and you looked at me like I was crazy."

"Yes," she said, "why did you ask that?"

"Because I thought you were Mona Donelli," I said triumphantly.

"Oh." She sounded disappointed. "Most people figure out that I'm not Mona because my nameplate says Lana Donelli."

"Oh," I said, suddenly crushed. I could notice a blotter turning violet, but I couldn't read a nameplate.

Lana was amused.

"Don't look so sad," she said. "I mean, even when they see the name some people still call me Mona."

"They do?"

"Yeah. It's a problem having an identical twin. They see the name and think that Mona's a nickname or something. Isn't that dumb?"

"I didn't know you had a sister, but I saw Mona on the fifth floor in a red dress, and then I saw a fly that couldn't sit still, and then I knew that you had to be somebody else," I said.

"You're funny," Lana said, crinkling up her nose, as if she were trying to identify a scent. "What's your name?"

"Rufus Coombs."

"Hi, Rufus," she said.

"Hey," I said.

My apartment is on 168th Street, in Washington Heights. It's pretty much a Spanish-speaking neighborhood. I don't know many people there, but the rent is all I can afford. My apartment—living room with a kitchen alcove, a small bedroom, and a toilet with a shower—is on the eighth floor and looks out over the Hudson. The $458 a month includes heat and gas, but I pay my own electric. I took it because of the view. There was a cheaper unit on the second floor, but it had windows that look out on a brick wall and I was afraid I'd be burglarized.

"Do you own a TV or a stereo?" my mother asked when I was trying to decide which apartment to take.

"You know I don't."

"Then you ain't got nuthin' to burgle," she said. I had called her in California, where she lives with my uncle.

"But they don't know that," I said. "I might have a color TV with VCR and a bad sound system."

"Lord," my mother prayed.

I didn't own much; she was right about that. Single mattress on the floor, an old oak chair that I found on the street, and kitchen shelving that I bought from a liquidator, four bookshelves, propped up in the corner. I also have a rice pot, a frying pan, and a kettle, with cutlery and enough plates for two.

I have Rachel, an ex-girlfriend living in the East Village, who will call me back at work if I don't call her too often. My two other friends are Eric Chen and Willy Jones. They both live in Brooklyn and still go to school.

That evening, I climbed the seven flights up to my apartment. The elevator had stopped working a month ago. I sat in my chair and looked at the water. It was peaceful and relaxing. A fly was buzzing against the glass, trying to get out.

I got up to kill him. But up close I hesitated. His coloring was unusual, a metallic green. The dull red eyes seemed too large for the body, as though he were an intelligent mutant fly from some far-flung future on late-night television.

He buzzed against the pane, trying to get away from me. When I returned to my chair, he settled. The red sun was hovering above the cliffs of New Jersey. The green fly watched. I thought of the fly I'd seen at work. That bug had been black and fairly small by fly standards. Then I thought about Mona and then Lana. The smallest nudge of an erection stirred. I thought of calling Rachel, but I didn't have the heart to walk the three blocks to a phone booth. So I watched the sunset gleaming around the fly, who was now just a black spot on the window. I fell asleep in the chair.

At three A.M. I woke up and made macaroni and cheese from a mix. The fly came into the cooking alcove, where I stood eating my meal. He lit on the big spoon I'd used to stir the dinner and joined me for supper.

Ernie told me that mortgaging didn't get much interoffice mail.

"Most of their correspondence comes by regular mail," he explained.

"Aren't they on the newsletter list?"

"She a white girl?"

"So?"

"Nuthin'. But I want you to tell me what it's like if you get it."

I didn't answer him.

I began delivering invitations to office parties, sales force newsletters, and productivity tips penned by Mr. Averill to Lana Donelli. We made small talk for thirty seconds or so, then she'd pick up the phone to make a call. I always looked back as I rounded the corner to make sure she really had a call to make. She always did.

The following Monday, I bought a glass paperweight with the image of a smiling Buddha's face etched in the bottom. When I got to Lana's desk, she wasn't there. I waited around for a while but she didn't appear, so I wrote her a note that said "From Rufus to Lana" and put the leaded-glass weight on it.

I went away excited and half scared. What if she didn't see my note? What if she did and thought it was stupid? I was so nervous that I didn't go back to her desk that day.

"I really shouldn't have left it," I said that night to the green fly. He was perched peacefully on the rim of a small saucer. I had filled the inner depression with a honey-and-water solution. I was eating a triple cheeseburger with bacon and fries from Wendy's. My pet fly seemed happy with his honey water and buzzed my sandwich only a few times before settling down to drink.

"Maybe she doesn't like me," I said. "Maybe it's just that she was nice to me because she feels sorry for me. But how will I know if I don't try and see if she likes me?"

"Hi," I said to Lana the next morning. She was wearing a jean jacket over a white T-shirt. She smiled and nodded. I handed her Mr. Averill's productivity tips newsletter.

"Did you see the paperweight?"

"Oh, yeah," she said without looking me in the eye. "Thanks." Then she picked up the phone and began pressing buttons. "Hi, Tristan? Lana. I wanted to know if . . ." She put her hand over the receiver and looked at me. "Can I do something else for you?"

"Oh," I said. "No. No," and I wheeled away in a kind of euphoria.

It's only now, when I look back on that moment, that I can see the averted eyes, the quick call, and the rude dismissal for what they were. All I heard then was "Thanks." I even remember a smile. Maybe she did smile for a brief moment, maybe not.

On Tuesday and Wednesday, I left three presents for her. I left them when she was away from her desk. I got her a small box of four Godiva chocolates, a silk rose, and a jar of fancy rose-petal jelly. I didn't leave any more notes. I was sure that she'd know who it was.

On Thursday evening, I went to a nursery on the East Side, just south of Harlem proper. There I bought a bonsai, a crab apple tree, for $347.52. I figured I'd leave it during Lana's Friday lunch break, and then she'd be so happy that on Monday she'd have to have lunch with me, no matter what.

I suspected that something was wrong when my pet fly went missing. He didn't even show up when I started eating a Beef Burrito Supreme from Taco Bell. I checked the big spiderweb near the bathroom window, but there were no little bundles that I could see.

That evening I was on edge, thinking I saw flies flitting into every corner.

"What's that?" Ernie asked me the next morning when I came in with the tiny crab apple tree.

"It's a tree."

"Tree for what?"

"My friend Willy wanted me to pick it up for him. He wants it for his new apartment, and the only place he could get it is up near me. I'm gonna meet him at lunch and give it to him."

"Uh-huh," Ernie said.

"You got my cart loaded?" I asked him.

Just then the Lindas came out of the service elevator. Big Linda looked at me and shook her head, managing to express contempt and pity at the same time.

"There's your carts," Ernie said to them.

They attached their earphones and rolled back to the service elevator. Little Linda was looking me in the eye as the slatted doors closed. She was still looking at me as the lift rose.

"What about me?"

"That's all I got right now. Why don't you sit here with me?"

"Okay." I sat down, expecting Ernie to bring up one of his regular topics, either something about Georgia, white bosses, or the horse races, which he followed but never wagered on. But instead of saying anything he just started reading the *Post*.

After a few minutes I was going to say something, but the big swinging door opened. Our boss, Mr. Drew, leaned in. He smiled and nodded at Ernie and then pointed at me.

"Rufus Coombs?"

"Yeah?"

"Come with me."

I followed the dapper little man through the messy service hall to the passenger elevator, which the couriers rarely took. It was a two-man elevator, so Drew and I had to stand very close to each other. He wore too much cologne, but otherwise he was perfect for his supervisory job, wearing a light gray suit with a shirt that hinted at yellow. I knew that he must have been in his forties, but he could have passed for a graduate student. He was light-skinned, like me, with what my mother called good hair. There were freckles around his eyes. I could see all of that because Mr. Drew avoided my gaze. He wouldn't engage me in any way.

We got out on the second floor and went to his office, which was at the far end of the mail-sorting room.

I looked around the room as Drew was entering his office. I saw Mona looking at me from the crevice of a doorway. I knew it was Mona because she was wearing a skimpy dress that could nave been worn on a hot date. I got only a glimpse of her before she ducked away.

"Come on in, Coombs," Drew said.

The office was tiny. Drew actually had to stand on the tips of his toes and hug the wall to get behind his desk. There was a stool in front of the desk, not a chair.

By the time he said, "Sit down," I had lost my nervousness. I gauged the power of Mr. Leonard Drew by the size of his office.

"You're in trouble, Rufus," he said, looking as somber as he could.

"I am?"

He lifted a pink sheet of paper and shook it at me.

"Do you recognize this?" he asked.

"No."

"This is a sexual-harassment complaint form."

"Yeah?"

"It names you on the complaint."

"I don't get it."

"Lana Donelli . . ." He went on to explain everything that I had been doing and feeling for the last week as if they were crimes. Going to Lana's desk, talking to her, leaving gifts. Even remarking on her clothes had been construed as if there was a sexual innuendo attached. By the time he was finished, I was worried that the police might be called in.

"Lana says that she's afraid to come in to work," Drew said, his freckles disappearing into angry lines around his eyes.

197

I wanted to say that I didn't mean to scare her, but I could see that my intentions didn't matter, that a small woman like Lana would be afraid of a big, sloppy mail clerk hovering over her and leaving notes and presents.

"I'm sorry," I said.

"Sorry doesn't mean much when it's got to this point," he said. "If it was up to me, I'd send you home right now. But Mr. Averill says he wants to talk to you."

"Aren't you supposed to give me a warning?" I asked.

Drew twisted up his lips, as if he had tasted something so foul that he just had to spit it out. "You haven't been here a month. You're on probation."

"Oh," I said.

"Well?" he asked after a few moments.

"What?"

"Go back to the mailroom and stay down there. Tell Ernie that I don't want you in the halls. You're supposed to meet Mr. Averill at one-forty-five, in his office. I've given him my recommendation to let you go. After something like this, there's really no place for you here. But he can still refer the matter to the police. Lana might want a restraining order."

I wanted to tell him that a restraining order was ridiculous. I wanted to go to Lana and tell her the same thing. I wanted to tell her that I bought her a rose because she wore rose toilet water, that I bought her the tree because the sun on her blotter could support a plant. I really liked her. But even while I was imagining what I could say, I knew that it didn't matter.

"Well?" Drew said. "Go."

Ernie made busywork for us that morning. He told me that he was upset about what had happened, that he'd told Drew to go easy.

"You know if you was white this wouldn't never have happened," Ernie said. "That girl just scared you some Mandingo gonna rape her. You know that's a shame."

I went up to the third floor a little before twelve. Lana was sitting at her desk, writing on a yellow legal pad. I walked right up to her and started talking so she couldn't ignore what I had to say.

"I just wanted to tell you that I'm sorry if you think I was harassing you. I didn't mean it, but I can see how you might have thought I was. . . ."

Lana's face got hard.

". . . but I'm gonna get fired right after lunch and I just wanted to ask you one thing."

She didn't say anything, so I said, "Is it because I'm black that you're so scared'a me?"

"You're black?" she said. "I thought you were Puerto Rican or Spanish or something. I didn't know you were black. My boyfriend is black. You just give me the creeps. That's why I complained. I didn't think they were going to fire you."

She didn't care if I lived or died. She wasn't even scared, just disgusted. I thought I was in love, and I was about to be fired, and she'd never even looked close enough to see me.

I was so embarrassed that I went away without saying another word. I went down to the mailroom and sorted rubber bands until one-thirty-five.

Vice President Bernard Averill's office was on the forty-eighth floor of the Carter's Home Building. His secretary's office was larger by far than Mr. Drew's cubbyhole. The smiling blonde led me into Averill's airy room. Behind him was a giant window looking out over Battery Park, Ellis Island, and the Statue of Liberty. I would have been impressed if I wasn't empty inside.

Averill was on the phone.

"Sorry, Nick," he said into the receiver. "My one-forty-five is here."

He stood up, tall and thin. His gray suit looked expensive. His white shirt was crisp and bright under a rainbow tie. His gray hair was combed back, and his mustache was sharp enough to cut bread, as my mother is known to say.

"Sit down, Mr. Coombs."

He sat also. In front of him were two sheets of paper. At his left hand was the pink harassment form, at his right was a white form. Outside, the Budweiser blimp hovered next to Lady Liberty.

Averill brought his fingertips to just under his nose and gazed at a spot above my head.

"How's Ernie?" he asked.

"He's good," I said. "He's a great boss."

"He's a good man. He likes you."

I didn't know what to say to that.

Averill looked down at his desk. "This does not compute."

"What?"

He patted the white page. "This says that you're a college graduate, magna cum laude in political science, that you came here to be a professional trainee." He patted the pink sheet. "This says that you're an interoffice-mail courier who harasses secretaries in the mortgage department."

Averill reached into his vest pocket and came out with an open package of cigarettes. At orientation they'd told us that there was absolutely no smoking anywhere in the building, but he took one out anyway. He lit up and took a deep drag, holding the smoke in his lungs for a long time before exhaling.

"Is there something wrong with you?" he asked.

"I don't think so," I said, swallowing hard.

Averill examined me through the tobacco haze. He seemed disgusted.

Staring directly into my eyes, he said, "Do you see this desk?"

The question petrified me, but I couldn't say why. Maybe it was the intensity of his gaze.

"I could call five or six women into this office right now and have them right here on this desk. Right here." He jabbed the desk with his middle finger.

My heart was racing. I had to open my mouth to get enough air.

"They're not going to fill out any pink slips," he said. "Do you know why?"

I shook my head.

"Because I'm a man. I don't go running around leaving chocolates on empty desks like bait. I don't fake reasons to come skulking around with newsletters."

Averill seemed angry as well as offended. I wondered if he knew Lana, or maybe her family. Maybe he wanted to fight me. I wanted to quit right then, to stand up and walk out before anything else happened. I was already thinking of where I could apply for another job when Averill sat back and smiled.

"Why are you in the interoffice-mail room?" he asked, suddenly much friendlier.

"No P.T. positions were open when I applied," I said.

"Nonsense. We don't have a limit on P.T s."

"But Ms. Worth said —"

"Oh." Averill held up his hand. "Reena. You know, Ernie helped me out when I got here, twenty-three years ago. I was just a little older than you. They didn't have the P.T. program back then, just a few guys like Ernie. He never even finished high school, but he showed me the ropes."

Averill drummed the fingers of his free hand between the two forms that represented me.

"I know this Lana's sister," he said. "Always wearing those cocktail dresses in to work. Her boss is afraid to say anything, otherwise he might get a pink slip, too." He paused to ponder some more. "How would you like to be a P.T. floater?"

"What's that?" I asked.

"Bumps you up to a grade seven and lets you move around in the different departments until you find a fit."

I was a grade B1.

"I thought you were going to fire me."

"That's what Drew suggested, but Ernie says that it's just a mixup. What if I talked to Lana? What if I asked her to hold this back, to give you a second chance?"

"I'd like that," I said. "Thanks."

"Probably be better if I let Drew fire you, you know," he said, standing up. I stood, too. "I mean if you fuck up once you'll probably just do it again, right?"

He held out his hand.

Watching the forbidden smoke curl around his head, I imagined that Averill was some kind of devil. When I thanked him and shook his hand, something inside me wanted to scream.

I found six unused crack vials a block from the subway stop near my apartment. I knew they were unused because they still had the little plastic stoppers in them.

When I got upstairs, I spent hours searching my place. I looked under the mattress and behind the toilet, under the radiator, and even down under the burners on the stove. Finally, after midnight, I decided to open the windows.

The fly had crawled down into the crack between the window frame and the sill in my bedroom. His green body had dried out, which made his eyes even bigger. He'd gone down there to die, or maybe, I thought, he was trying to get away from me.

Maybe I had killed him. Later, I found out that flies have a very short life span. He probably died of old age.

I took his small, dried-out corpse and put it in one of the crack vials. I stoppered him in the tiny glass coffin and buried him among the roots of the bonsai crab apple.

"So you finally bought something nice for your house," my mother said after I told her about the changes in my life. "Maybe next you'll get a real bed."

The Man I Killed

Tim O'Brien

Tim O'Brien was born in Minnesota. He was drafted soon after he graduated from college, became an infantry sergeant in Vietnam, and received a Purple Heart. His literary works draw upon his Vietnam experiences. Among his books are If I Died in the Combat Zone, Box Me Up and Ship Me Home *(1973),* Northern Lights *(1975),* The Nuclear Age *(1981).* Going after Cacciato *(1978) won the National Book Award in 1979. His most recent works are:* Lake in the Woods *(1994), and* Off the Beaten Path in Tennessee *(1996). "The Man I Killed" is part of his volume of interconnected stories* The Things They Carried *(1990).*

His jaw was in his throat, his upper lip and teeth were gone, his one eye was shut, his other eye was a star-shaped hole, his eyebrows were thin and arched like a woman's, his nose was undamaged, there was a slight tear at the lobe of one ear, his clean black hair was swept upward into a cowlick at the rear of his skull, his forehead was lightly freckled, his fingernails were clean, the skin at his left cheek was peeled back in three ragged strips, his right cheek was smooth and hairless, there was a butterfly on his chin, his neck was open to the spinal cord and the blood there was thick and shiny and it was this wound that had killed him. He lay face-up in the center of the trail, a slim, dead, almost dainty young man. He had bony legs, a narrow waist, long shapely fingers. His chest was sunken and poorly muscled—a scholar, maybe. His wrists were the wrists of a child. He wore a black shirt, black pajama pants, a gray ammunition belt, a gold ring on the third finger of his right hand. His rubber sandals had been blown off. One lay beside him, the other a few meters up the trail. He had been born, maybe, in 1946 in the village of My Khe near the central coastline of Quang Ngai Province, where his parents farmed, and where his family had lived for several cen-

"The Man I Killed," by Tim O'Brien, from *The Things They Carried,* 1990, Houghton Mifflin Company.

turies, and where, during the time of the French, his father and two uncles and many neighbors had joined in the struggle for independence. He was not a Communist. He was a citizen and a soldier. In the village of My Khe, as in all of Quang Ngai, patriotic resistance had the force of tradition, which was partly the force of legend, and from his earliest boyhood the man I killed would have listened to stories about the heroic Trung sisters and Tran Hung Dao's famous rout of the Mongols and Le Loi's final victory against the Chinese at Tot Dong.[1] He would have been taught that to defend the land was a man's highest duty and highest privilege. He had accepted this. It was never open to question. Secretly, though, it also frightened him. He was not a fighter. His health was poor, his body small and frail. He liked books. He wanted someday to be a teacher of mathematics. At night, lying on his mat, he could not picture himself doing the brave things his father had done, or his uncles, or the heroes of the stories. He hoped in his heart that he would never be tested. He hoped the Americans would go away. Soon, he hoped. He kept hoping and hoping, always, even when he was asleep.

"Oh, man, you fuckin' trashed the fucker," Azar said. "You scrambled his sorry self, look at that, you *did*, you laid him out like Shredded fuckin' Wheat."

"Go away," Kiowa said.

"I'm just saying the truth. Like oatmeal."

"Go," Kiowa said.

"Okay, then, I take it back," Azar said. He started to move away, then stopped and said, "Rice Krispies, you know? On the dead test, this particular individual gets A-plus."

Smiling at this, he shrugged and walked up the trail toward the village behind the trees.

Kiowa kneeled down.

"Just forget that crud," he said. He opened up his canteen and held it out for a while and then sighed and pulled it away. "No sweat, man. What else could you do?"

Later, Kiowa said, "I'm serious. Nothing *anybody* could do. Come on, stop staring."

The trail junction was shaded by a row of trees and tall brush. The slim young man lay with his legs in the shade. His jaw was in his throat. His one eye was shut and the other was a star-shaped hole.

Kiowa glanced at the body.

"All right, let me ask a question," he said. "You want to trade places with him? Turn it all upside down—you *want* that? I mean, be honest."

The star-shaped hole was red and yellow. The yellow part seemed to be getting wider, spreading out at the center of the star. The upper lip and gum and teeth were gone. The man's head was cocked at a wrong angle, as if loose at the neck, and the neck was wet with blood.

"Think it over," Kiowa said.

[1]In A.D. 40, the Trung sisters led an insurrection against Chinese occupation that freed Vietnam for three years. In 1285 and 1287, General Tran Hung Dao led the Vietnamese in defeating two massive invasions by the Mongol armies of Kublai Khan that had already conquered China and much of Europe. Between 1418 and 1427, the Vietnamese under Le Loi drove out the Chinese occupiers, leading to the establishment of an independent Vietnam. [Ed.]

Then later he said, "Tim, it's a *war.* The guy wasn't Heidi—he had a weapon, right? It's a tough thing, for sure, but you got to cut out that staring."

Then he said, "Maybe you better lie down a minute."

Then after a long empty time he said, "Take it slow. Just go wherever the spirit takes you."

The butterfly was making its way along the young man's forehead, which was spotted with small dark freckles. The nose was undamaged. The skin on the right cheek was smooth and fine-grained and hairless. Frail-looking, delicately boned, the young man would not have wanted to be a soldier and in his heart would have feared performing badly in battle. Even as a boy growing up in the village of My Khe, he had often worried about this. He imagined covering his head and lying in a deep hole and closing his eyes and not moving until the war was over. He had no stomach for violence. He loved mathematics. His eyebrows were thin and arched like a woman's, and at school the boys sometimes teased him about how pretty he was, the arched eyebrows and long shapely fingers, and on the playground they mimicked a woman's walk and made fun of his smooth skin and his love for mathematics. The young man could not make himself fight them. He often wanted to, but he was afraid, and this increased his shame. If he could not fight little boys, he thought, how could he ever become a soldier and fight the Americans with their airplanes and helicopters and bombs? It did not seem possible. In the presence of his father and uncles, he pretended to look forward to doing his patriotic duty, which was also a privilege, but at night he prayed with his mother that the war might end soon. Beyond anything else, he was afraid of disgracing himself, and therefore his family and village. But all he could do, he thought, was wait and pray and try not to grow up too fast.

"Listen to me," Kiowa said. "You feel terrible, I know that."

Then he said, "Okay, maybe I *don't* know."

Along the trail there were small blue flowers shaped like bells. The young man's head was wrenched sideways, not quite facing the flowers, and even in the shade a single blade of sunlight sparkled against the buckle of his ammunition belt. The left cheek was peeled back in three ragged strips. The wounds at his neck had not yet clotted, which made him seem animate even in death, the blood still spreading out across his shirt.

Kiowa shook his head.

There was some silence before he said, "Stop *staring.*"

The young man's fingernails were clean. There was a slight tear at the lobe of one ear, a sprinkling of blood on the forearm. He wore a gold ring on the third finger of his right hand. His chest was sunken and poorly muscled—a scholar, maybe. His life was now a constellation of possibilities. So, yes, maybe a scholar. And for years, despite his family's poverty, the man I killed would have been determined to continue his education in mathematics. The means for this were arranged, perhaps, through the village liberation cadres, and in 1964 the young man began attending classes at the university in Saigon, where he avoided politics and paid attention to the problems of calculus. He devoted himself to his studies. He spent his nights alone, wrote romantic poems in his journal, took pleasure in the grace and beauty of differential equations. The war, he knew, would finally take him, but for the time being he would not let himself think about it. He had stopped praying; instead, now he waited. And as he waited, in his final year at the university he fell in love with a classmate, a girl of seventeen, who one day told him that his wrists were like the wrists of a child, so small and delicate, and who admired his narrow waist and the cowlick that rose up like a bird's tail at the back of his head. She liked his quiet manner; she laughed at his freckles and bony legs. One evening, perhaps, they exchanged gold rings.

Now one eye was a star.

"You okay?" Kiowa said.

The body lay almost entirely in shade. There were gnats at the mouth, little flecks of pollen drifting above the nose. The butterfly was gone. The bleeding had stopped except for the neck wounds.

Kiowa picked up the rubber sandals, clapping off the dirt, then bent down to search the body. He found a pouch of rice, a comb, a fingernail clipper, a few soiled piasters, a snapshot of a young woman standing in front of a parked motorcycle. Kiowa placed these items in his rucksack along with the gray ammunition belt and rubber sandals.

Then he squatted down.

"I'll tell you the straight truth," he said. "The guy was dead the second he stepped on the trail. Understand me? We all had him zeroed. A good kill—weapon, ammunition, everything." Tiny beads of sweat glistened at Kiowa's forehead. His eyes moved from the sky to the dead man's body to the knuckles of his own hands. "So listen, you best pull your shit together. Can't just sit here all day."

Later he said, "Understand?"

Then he said, "Five minutes, Tim. Five more minutes and we're moving out."

The one eye did a funny twinkling trick, red to yellow. His head was wrenched sideways, as if loose at the neck, and the dead young man seemed to be staring at some distant object beyond the bell-shaped flowers along the trail. The blood at the neck had gone to a deep purplish black. Clean fingernails, clean hair—he had been a soldier for only a single day. After his years at the university, the man I killed returned with his new wife to the village of My Khe, where he enlisted as a common rifleman with the 48th Vietcong Battalion. He knew he would die quickly. He knew he would see a flash of light. He knew he would fall dead and wake up in the stories of his village and people.

Kiowa covered the body with a poncho.

"Hey, you're looking better," he said. "No doubt about it. All you needed was time—some mental R&R."

Then he said, "Man, I'm sorry."

Then later he said, "Why not talk about it?"

Then he said, "Come on, man, talk."

He was a slim, dead, almost dainty young man of about twenty. He lay with one leg bent beneath him, his jaw in his throat, his face neither expressive nor inexpressive. One eye was shut. The other was a star-shaped hole.

"Talk," Kiowa said.

(1990)

A Good Man Is Hard to Find

Flannery O'Connor

Flannery O'Connor was the only child of Edward Francis O'Connor and Regina Cline O'Connor. After graduation from Georgia State College for Women in Milledgeville in 1945, she went to Iowa City and became a graduate student in the Writers' Workshop at the State University of Iowa. In 1947 she earned her master's degree at Iowa and went by invitation to the Yaddo, a writer's colony near Saratoga Springs, New York. She left there and moved to Ridgefield, Connecticut, where she lived with Robert Fitzgerald and his family. Then she received a severe setback. Her health declined. She discovered she had lupus erythematosus, like her father. When she had a reoccurrence her doctor suggested she move back to Georgia, where she lived with her mother and continued to write until her death in 1964. She left behind two novels, Wise Blood *(1952) and* The Violent Bear It Away *(1960), and two collections of short stories,* A Good Man Is Hard to Find *(1955) and* Everything that Rises Must Converge *(1965).*

The grandmother didn't want to go to Florida. She wanted to visit some of her connections in east Tennessee and she was seizing at every chance to change Bailey's mind. Bailey was the son she lived with, her only boy. He was sitting on the edge of his chair at the table, bent over the orange sports section of the *Journal.* "Now look here, Bailey," she said, "see here, read this," and she stood with one hand on her thin hip and the other rattling the newspaper at his bald head. "Here this fellow that calls himself The Misfit is aloose from the Federal Pen and headed toward Florida and you read here what it says he did to these people. Just you read it. I wouldn't take

"A Good Man Is Hard to Find," by Flannery O'Connor, reprinted from *A Good Man Is Hard to Find and Other Stories*, 1969, Harcourt Brace & Company.

my children in any direction with a criminal like that aloose in it. I couldn't answer to my conscience if I did."

Bailey didn't look up from his reading so she wheeled around then and faced the children's mother, a young woman in slacks, whose face was as broad and innocent as a cabbage and was tied around with a green head-kerchief that had two points on the top like rabbit's ears. She was sitting on the sofa, feeding the baby his apricots out of a jar. "The children have been to Florida before," the old lady said. "You all ought to take them somewhere else for a change so they would see different parts of the world and be broad. They never have been to east Tennessee."

The children's mother didn't seem to hear her but the eight-year-old boy, John Wesley, a stocky child with glasses, said, "If you don't want to go to Florida, why dontcha stay at home?" He and the little girl, June Star, were reading the funny papers on the floor.

"She wouldn't stay at home to be queen for a day," June Star said without raising her yellow head.

"Yes and what would you do if this fellow, The Misfit, caught you?" the grandmother asked.

"I'd smack his face," John Wesley said.

"She wouldn't stay at home for a million bucks," June Star said. "Afraid she'd miss something. She has to go everywhere we go."

"All right, Miss," the grandmother said. "Just remember that the next time you want me to curl your hair."

June Star said her hair was naturally curly.

The next morning the grandmother was the first one in the car, ready to go. She had her big black valise that looked like the head of a hippopotamus in one corner, and underneath it she was hiding a basket with Pitty Sing, the cat, in it. She didn't intend for the cat to be left alone in the house for three days because he would miss her too much and she was afraid he might brush against one of the gas burners and accidentally asphyxiate himself. Her son, Bailey, didn't like to arrive at a motel with a cat.

She sat in the middle of the back seat with John Wesley and June Star on either side of her. Bailey and the children's mother and the baby sat in front and they left Atlanta at eight forty-five with the mileage on the car at 55890. The grandmother wrote this down because she thought it would be interesting to say how many miles they had been when they got back. It took them twenty minutes to reach the outskirts of the city.

The old lady settled herself comfortably, removing her white cotton gloves and putting them up with her purse on the shelf in front of the back window. The children's mother still had on slacks and still had her head tied up in a green kerchief, but the grandmother had on a navy blue straw sailor hat with a bunch of white violets on the brim and a navy blue dress with a small white dot in the print. Her collars and cuffs were white organdy trimmed with lace and at her neckline she had pinned a purple spray of cloth violets containing a sachet. In case of an accident, anyone seeing her dead on the highway would know at once that she was a lady.

She said she thought it was going to be a good day for driving, neither too hot nor too cold, and she cautioned Bailey that the speed limit was fifty-five miles an hour and that the patrolmen hid themselves behind billboards and small clumps of trees and sped out after you before you had a chance to slow down. She pointed out interesting details of the scenery: Stone Mountain; the blue granite that in some places came up to both sides of the highway; the brilliant red clay banks slightly streaked with purple, and the various crops that made rows of green lace-work on the ground. The trees were full of silver-white sunlight and the meanest of them sparkled. The children were reading comic magazines and their mother had gone back to sleep.

"Let's go through Georgia fast so we won't have to look at it much," John Wesley said.

"If I were a little boy," said the grandmother, "I wouldn't talk about my native state that way. Tennessee has the mountains and Georgia has the hills."

"Tennessee is just a hillbilly dumping ground," John Wesley said, "and Georgia is a lousy state too."

"You said it," June Star said.

"In my time," said the grandmother, folding her thin veined fingers, "children were most respectful of their native states and their parents and everything else. People did right then. Oh look at the cute little pickaninny!" she said and pointed to a Negro child standing in the door of a shack. "Wouldn't that make a picture, now?" she asked and they all turned and looked at the little Negro out of the back window. He waved.

"He didn't have any britches on," June Star said.

"He probably didn't have any," the grandmother explained. "Little niggers in the country don't have things like we do. If I could paint, I'd paint that picture," she said.

The children exchanged comic books.

The grandmother offered to hold the baby and the children's mother passed him over the front seat to her. She set him on her knee and bounced him and told him about the things they were passing. She rolled her eyes and screwed up her mouth and stuck her leathery thin face into his smooth bland one. Occasionally he gave her a faraway smile. They passed a large cotton field with five or six graves fenced in the middle of it, like a small island. "Look at the graveyard!" the grandmother said, pointing it out. "That was the old family burying ground. That belonged to the plantation."

"Where's the plantation?" John Wesley asked.

"Gone With the Wind," said the grandmother. "Ha. Ha."

When the children finished all the comic books they had brought, they opened the lunch and ate it. The grandmother ate a peanut butter sandwich and an olive and would not let the children throw the box and the paper napkins out the window. When there was nothing else to do they played a game by choosing a cloud and making the other two guess what shape it suggested. John Wesley took one the shape of a cow and June Star guessed a cow and John Wesley said, no, an automobile, and June Star said he didn't play fair, and they began to slap each other over the grandmother.

The grandmother said she would tell them a story if they would keep quiet. When she told a story, she rolled her eyes and waved her head and was very dramatic. She said once when she was a maiden lady she had been courted by a Mr. Edgar Atkins Teagarden from Jasper, Georgia. She said he was a very good-looking man and a gentleman and that he brought her a watermelon every Saturday afternoon with his initials cut in it, E. A. T. Well, one Saturday, she said, Mr. Teagarden brought the watermelon and there was nobody at home and he left it on the front porch and returned in his buggy to Jasper, but she never got the watermelon, she said, because a nigger boy ate it when he saw the initials, E. A. T.! This story tickled John Wesley's funny bone and he giggled and giggled but June Star didn't think it was any good. She said she wouldn't marry a man that just brought her a watermelon on Saturday. The grandmother said she would have done well to marry Mr. Teagarden because he was a gentleman and had bought Coca-Cola stock when it first came out and that he had died only a few years ago, a very wealthy man.

They stopped at The Tower for barbecued sandwiches. The Tower was a part stucco and part wood filling station and dance hall set in a clearing outside of Timothy. A fat man named Red Sammy Butts ran it and there were signs stuck here and there on the building and for miles up and down the highway saying, TRY RED SAMMY'S FAMOUS BARBECUE. NONE LIKE FAMOUS RED SAMMY'S! RED SAM! THE FAT BOY WITH THE HAPPY LAUGH. A VETERAN! RED SAMMY'S YOUR MAN!

Red Sammy was lying on the bare ground outside The Tower with his head under a truck while a gray monkey about a foot high, chained to a small chinaberry tree, chattered nearby. The monkey sprang back into the tree and got on the highest limb as soon as he saw the children jump out of the car and run toward him.

Inside, The Tower was a long dark room with a counter at one end and tables at the other and dancing space in the middle. They all sat down at a board table next to the nickelodeon and Red Sam's wife, a tall burnt-brown woman with hair and eyes lighter than her skin, came and took their order. The children's mother put a dime in the machine and played "The Tennessee Waltz," and the grandmother said that tune always made her want to dance. She asked Bailey if he would like to dance but he only glared at her. He didn't have a naturally sunny disposition like she did and trips made him nervous. The grandmother's brown eyes were very bright. She swayed her head from side to side and pretended she was dancing in her chair. June Star said play something she could tap to so the children's mother put in another dime and played a fast number and June Star stepped out onto the dance floor and did her tap routine.

"Ain't she cute?" Red Sam's wife said, leaning over the counter. "Would you like to come be my little girl?"

"No I certainly wouldn't," June Star said. "I wouldn't live in a broken-down place like this for a million bucks!" and she ran back to the table.

"Ain't she cute?" the woman repeated, stretching her mouth politely.

"Aren't you ashamed?" hissed the grandmother.

Red Sam came in and told his wife to quit lounging on the counter and hurry up with these people's order. His khaki trousers reached just to his hip bones and his stomach hung over them like a sack of meal swaying under his shirt. He came over and sat down at a table nearby and let out a combination sigh and yodel. "You can't win," he said. "You can't win," and he wiped his sweating red face off with a gray handkerchief. "These days you don't know who to trust," he said. "Ain't that the truth?"

"People are certainly not nice like they used to be," said the grandmother.

"Two fellers come in here last week," Red Sammy said, "driving a Chrysler. It was a old beat-up car but it was a good one and these boys looked all right to me. Said they worked at the mill and you know I let them fellers charge the gas they bought? Now why did I do that?"

"Because you're a good man!" the grandmother said at once.

"Yes'm, I suppose so," Red Sam said as if he were struck with this answer.

His wife brought the orders, carrying the five plates all at once without a tray, two in each hand and one balanced on her arm. "It isn't a soul in this green world of God's that you can trust," she said. "And I don't count nobody out of that, not nobody," she repeated, looking at Red Sammy.

"Did you read about that criminal, The Misfit, that's escaped?" asked the grandmother.

"I wouldn't be a bit surprised if he didn't attact this place right here," said the woman. "If he hears about it being here, I wouldn't be none surprised to see him. If he hears it's two cent in the cash register, I wouldn't be a tall surprised if he . . ."

"That'll do," Red Sam said. "Go bring these people their Co'-Colas," and the woman went off to get the rest of the order.

"A good man is hard to find," Red Sammy said. "Everything is getting terrible. I remember the day you could go off and leave your screen door unlatched. Not no more."

He and the grandmother discussed better times. The old lady said that in her opinion Europe was entirely to blame for the way things were now. She said the way Europe acted you would think we were made of money and Red Sam said it was no use talking about it, she was exactly right. The children ran outside into the white sunlight and looked at the monkey in the lacy chinaberry tree. He was busy catching fleas on himself and biting each one carefully between his teeth as if it were a delicacy.

They drove off again into the hot afternoon. The grandmother took cat naps and woke up every few minutes with her own snoring. Outside of Toombsboro she woke up and recalled an old plantation that she had visited in this neighborhood once when she was a young lady. She said the house had six white columns across the front and that there was an avenue of oaks leading up to it and two little wooden trellis arbors on either side in front where you sat down with your suitor after a stroll in the garden. She recalled exactly which road to turn off to get to it. She knew that Bailey would not be willing to lose any time looking at an old house, but the more she talked about it, the more she wanted to see it once again and find out if the little twin arbors were still standing. "There was a secret panel in this house," she said craftily, not telling the truth but wishing that she were, "and the story went that all the family silver was hidden in it when Sherman came through but it was never found . . ."

"Hey!" John Wesley said. "Let's go see it! We'll find it! We'll poke all the woodwork and find it! Who lives there? Where do you turn off at? Hey Pop, can't we turn off there?"

"We never have seen a house with a secret panel!" June Star shrieked. "Let's go to the house with the secret panel! Hey Pop, can't we go see the house with the secret panel!"

"It's not far from here, I know," the grandmother said. "It wouldn't take over twenty minutes."

Bailey was looking straight ahead. His jaw was as rigid as a horseshoe. "No," he said.

The children began to yell and scream that they wanted to see the house with the secret panel. John Wesley kicked the back of the front seat and June Star hung over her mother's shoulder and whined desperately into her ear that they never had any fun even on their vacation, that they could never do what THEY wanted to do. The baby began to scream and John Wesley kicked the back of the seat so hard that his father could feel the blows in his kidney.

"All right!" he shouted and drew the car to a stop at the side of the road. "Will you all shut up? Will you all just shut up for one second? If you don't shut up, we won't go anywhere."

"It would be very educational for them," the grandmother murmured.

"All right," Bailey said, "but get this: this is the only time we're going to stop for anything like this. This is the one and only time."

"The dirt road that you have to turn down is about a mile back," the grandmother directed. "I marked it when we passed."

"A dirt road," Bailey groaned.

After they had turned around and were headed toward the dirt road, the grandmother recalled other points about the house, the beautiful glass over the front doorway and the candle-lamp in the hall. John Wesley said that the secret panel was probably in the fireplace.

"You can't go inside this house," Bailey said. "You don't know who lives there."

"While you all talk to the people in front, I'll run around behind and get in a window," John Wesley suggested.

"We'll stay in the car," his mother said.

They turned onto the dirt road and the car raced roughly along in a swirl of pink dust. The grandmother recalled the times when there were no paved roads and thirty miles was a day's journey. The dirt road was hilly and there were sudden washes in it and sharp curves on dangerous embankments. All at once they would be on a hill, looking down over the blue tops of trees for miles around, then the next minute, they would be in a red depression with the dust-coated trees looking down on them.

"This place had better turn up in a minute," Bailey said, "or I'm going to turn around."

The road looked as if no one had traveled on it in months.

"It's not much farther," the grandmother said and just as she said it, a horrible thought came to her. The thought was so embarrassing that she turned red in the face and her eyes dilated and her feet jumped up, upsetting her valise in the corner. The instant the valise moved, the newspaper top she had over the basket under it rose with a snarl and Pitty Sing, the cat, sprang onto Bailey's shoulder.

The children were thrown to the floor and their mother, clutching the baby, was thrown out the door onto the ground; the old lady was thrown into the front seat. The car turned over once and landed right-side-up in a gulch off the side of the road. Bailey remained in the driver's seat with the cat—gray-striped with a broad white face and an orange nose—clinging to his neck like a caterpillar.

As soon as the children saw they could move their arms and legs, they scrambled out of the car, shouting, "We've had an ACCIDENT!" The grandmother was curled up under the dashboard, hoping she was injured so that Bailey's wrath would not come down on her all at once. The horrible thought she had had before the accident was that the house she had remembered so vividly was not in Georgia but in Tennessee.

Bailey removed the cat from his neck with both hands and flung it out the window against the side of a pine tree. Then he got out of the car and started looking for the children's mother. She was sitting against the side of the red gutted ditch, holding the screaming baby, but she only had a cut down her face and a broken shoulder. "We've had an ACCIDENT!" the children screamed in a frenzy of delight.

"But nobody's killed," June Star said with disappointment as the grandmother limped out of the car, her hat still pinned to her head but the broken front brim standing up at a jaunty angle and the violet spray hanging off the side. They all sat down in the ditch, except the children, to recover from the shock. They were all shaking.

"Maybe a car will come along," said the children's mother hoarsely

"I believe I have injured an organ," said the grandmother, pressing her side, but no one answered her. Bailey's teeth were clattering. He had on a yellow sport shirt with bright blue parrots designed in it and his face was as yellow as the shirt. The grandmother decided that she would not mention that the house was in Tennessee.

The road was about ten feet above and they could see only the tops of the trees on the other side of it. Behind the ditch they were sitting in there were more woods, tall and dark and deep. In a few minutes they saw a car some distance away on top of a hill, coming slowly as if the occupants were watching them. The grandmother stood up and waved both arms dramatically to attract their attention. The car continued to come on slowly, disappeared around a bend and appeared again, moving even slower, on top of the hill they had gone over. It was a big black battered hearse-like automobile. There were three men in it.

It came to a stop just over them and for some minutes, the driver looked down with a steady expressionless gaze to where they were sitting, and didn't speak. Then he turned his head and muttered something to the other two and they got out. One was a fat boy in black trousers and a red sweat shirt with a silver stallion embossed on the front of it. He moved around on the right side of them and stood staring, his mouth partly open in a kind of loose grin. The other had on khaki pants and a blue striped coat and a gray hat pulled down very low, hiding most of his face. He came around slowly on the left side. Neither spoke.

The driver got out of the car and stood by the side of it, looking down at them. He was an older man than the other two. His hair was just beginning to gray and he wore silver-rimmed spectacles that gave him a scholarly look. He had a long creased face and didn't have on any shirt or undershirt. He had on blue jeans that were too tight for him and was holding a black hat and a gun. The two boys also had guns.

"We've had an ACCIDENT!" the children screamed.

The grandmother had the peculiar feeling that the bespectacled man was someone she knew. His face was as familiar to her as if she had known him all her life but she could not recall who he was. He moved away from the car and began to come down the embankment, placing his feet carefully so that he wouldn't slip. He had on tan and white shoes and no socks, and his ankles were red and thin. "Good afternoon," he said. "I see you all had you a little spill."

"We turned over twice!" said the grandmother.

"Oncet," he corrected. "We seen it happen. Try their car and see will it run, Hiram," he said quietly to the boy with the gray hat.

"What you got that gun for?" John Wesley asked. "Whatcha gonna do with that gun?"

"Lady," the man said to the children's mother, "would you mind calling them children to sit down by you? Children make me nervous. I want all you all to sit down right together there where you're at."

"What are you telling US what to do for?" June Star asked.

Behind them the line of woods gaped like a dark open mouth. "Come here," said their mother.

"Look here now," Bailey began suddenly, "we're in a predicament! We're in . . ."

The grandmother shrieked. She scrambled to her feet and stood staring. "You're The Misfit!" she said. "I recognized you at once!"

"Yes'm," the man said, smiling slightly as if he were pleased in spite of himself to be known, "but it would have been better for all you, lady, if you hadn't of reckernized me."

Bailey turned his head sharply and said something to his mother that shocked even the children. The old lady began to cry and The Misfit reddened.

"Lady," he said, "don't you get upset. Sometimes a man says things he don't mean. I don't reckon he meant to talk to you thataway."

"You wouldn't shoot a lady, would you?" the grandmother said and removed a clean handkerchief from her cuff and began to slap at her eyes with it.

The Misfit pointed the toe of his shoe into the ground and made a little hole and then covered it up again. "I would hate to have to," he said.

"Listen," the grandmother almost screamed, "I know you're a good man. You don't look a bit like you have common blood. I know you must come from nice people!"

"Yes mam," he said, "finest people in the world." When he smiled he showed a row of strong white teeth. "God never made a finer woman than my mother and my daddy's heart was pure gold," he said. The boy with the red sweat shirt had come around behind them and was standing with his gun at his hip. The Misfit squatted down on the ground. "Watch them children, Bobby Lee," he said. "You know they make me nervous." He looked at the six of them huddled together in front of him and he seemed to be embarrassed as if he couldn't think of anything to say. "Ain't a cloud in the sky," he remarked, looking up at it. "Don't see no sun but don't see no cloud either."

"Yes, it's a beautiful day," said the grandmother. "Listen," she said, "you shouldn't call yourself The Misfit because I know you're a good man at heart. I can just look at you and tell."

"Hush!" Bailey yelled. "Hush! Everybody shut up and let me handle this!" He was squatting in the position of a runner about to sprint forward but he didn't move.

"I pre-chate that, lady," The Misfit said and drew a little circle on the ground with the butt of his gun.

"It'll take a half a hour to fix this here car," Hiram called, looking over the raised hood of it.

"Well, first you and Bobby Lee get him and that little boy to step over yonder with you," The Misfit said, pointing to Bailey and John Wesley. "The boys want to ast you something," he said to Bailey. "Would you mind stepping back in them woods there with them?"

"Listen," Bailey began, "we're in a terrible predicament! Nobody realizes what this is," and his voice cracked. His eyes were as blue and intense as the parrots in his shirt and he remained perfectly still.

The grandmother reached up to adjust her hat brim as if she were going to the woods with him but it came off in her hands. She stood staring at it and after a second she let it fall on the ground. Hiram pulled Bailey up by the arm as if he were assisting an old man. John Wesley caught hold of his father's hand and Bobby Lee followed. They went off toward the woods and just as they reached the dark edge, Bailey turned and supporting himself against a gray naked pine trunk, he shouted, "I'll be back in a minute, Mamma, wait on me!"

"Come back this instant!" his mother shrilled but they all disappeared into the woods.

"Bailey Boy!" the grandmother called in a tragic voice but she found she was looking at The Misfit squatting on the ground in front of her. "I just know you're a good man," she said desperately. "You're not a bit common!"

"Nome, I ain't a good man," The Misfit said after a second as if he had considered her statement carefully, "but I ain't the worst in the world neither. My daddy said I was a different breed of dog from my brothers and sisters. 'You know,' Daddy said, 'it's some that can live their whole life out without asking about it and it's others has to know why it is, and this boy is one of the latters. He's going to be into everything!'" he put on his black hat and looked up suddenly and then away deep into the woods as if he were embarrassed again. "I'm sorry I don't have on a shirt before you ladies," he said, hunching his shoulders slightly. "We buried our clothes that we had on when we escaped and we're just making do until we can get better. We borrowed these from some folks we met," he explained.

"That's perfectly all right," the grandmother said.

"Maybe Bailey has an extra shirt in his suitcase."

"I'll look and see terrectly," The Misfit said.

"Where are they taking him?" the children's mother screamed.

"Daddy was a card himself," The Misfit said. "You couldn't put anything over on him. He never got in trouble with the Authorities though. Just had the knack of handling them."

"You could be honest too if you'd only try," said the grandmother. "Think how wonderful it would be to settle down and live a comfortable life and not have to think about somebody chasing you all the time."

The Misfit kept scratching in the ground with the butt of his gun as if he were thinking about it. "Yes'm, somebody is always after you," he murmured.

The grandmother noticed how thin his shoulder blades were just behind his hat because she was standing up looking down at him. "Do you ever pray?" she asked.

He shook his head. All she saw was the black hat wiggle between his shoulder blades. "Nome," he said.

There was a pistol shot from the woods, followed closely by another. Then silence. The old lady's head jerked around. She could hear the wind move through the tree tops like a long satisfied insuck of breath. "Bailey Boy!" she called.

"I was a gospel singer for a while," The Misfit said. "I been most everything. Been in the arm service, both land and sea, at home and abroad, been twict married, been an undertaker, been with the railroads, plowed Mother Earth, been in a tornado, seen a man burnt alive oncet," and he looked up at the children's mother and the little girl who were sitting close together, their faces white and their eyes glassy; "I even seen a woman flogged," he said.

"Pray, pray," the grandmother began, "pray, pray . . ."

"I never was a bad boy that I remember of," The Misfit said in an almost dreamy voice, "but somewheres along the line I done something wrong and got sent to the penitentiary. I was buried alive," and he looked up and held her attention to him by a steady stare.

"That's when you should have started to pray," she said. "What did you do to get sent to the penitentiary that first time?"

"Turn to the right, it was a wall," The Misfit said, looking up again at the cloudless sky. "Turn to the left, it was a wall. Look up it was a ceiling, look down it was a floor. I forget what I done, lady. I set there and set there, trying to remember what it was I done and I ain't recalled it to this day. Oncet in a while, I would think it was coming to me, but it never come."

"Maybe they put you in by mistake," the old lady said vaguely.

"Nome," he said. "It wasn't no mistake. They had the papers on me."

"You must have stolen something," she said.

The Misfit sneered slightly. "Nobody had nothing I wanted," he said. "It was a head-doctor at the penitentiary said what I had done was kill my daddy but I known that for a lie. My daddy died in nineteen ought nineteen of the epidemic flu and I never had a thing to do with it. He was buried in the Mount Hopewell Baptist churchyard and you can go there and see for yourself."

"If you would pray," the old lady said, "Jesus would help you."

"That's right," The Misfit said.

"Well then, why don't you pray?" she asked trembling with delight suddenly.

"I don't want no hep," he said. "I'm doing all right by myself."

Bobby Lee and Hiram came ambling back from the woods. Bobby Lee was dragging a yellow shirt with bright blue parrots in it.

"Thow me that shirt, Bobby Lee," The Misfit said. The shirt came flying at him and landed on his shoulder and he put it on. The grandmother couldn't name what the shirt reminded her of. "No, lady," The Misfit said while he was buttoning it up, "I found out the crime don't matter. You can do one thing or you can do another, kill a man or take a tire off his car, because sooner or later you're going to forget what it was you done and just be punished for it."

The children's mother had begun to make heaving noises as if she couldn't get her breath. "Lady," he asked, "would you and that little girl like to step off yonder with Bobby Lee and Hiram and join your husband?"

"Yes, thank you," the mother said faintly. Her left arm dangled helplessly and she was holding the baby, who had gone to sleep, in the other. "Hep that lady up, Hiram," The Misfit said as she struggled to climb out of the ditch, "and Bobby Lee, you hold onto that little girl's hand."

"I don't want to hold hands with him," June Star said. "He reminds me of a pig."

The fat boy blushed and laughed and caught her by the arm and pulled her off into the woods after Hiram and her mother.

Alone with The Misfit, the grandmother found that she had lost her voice. There was not a cloud in the sky nor any sun. There was nothing around her but woods. She wanted to tell him that he must pray. She opened and closed her mouth several times before anything came out. Finally she found herself saying, "Jesus. Jesus," meaning, Jesus will help you, but the way she was saying it, it sounded as if she might be cursing.

"Yes'm," The Misfit said as if he agreed. "Jesus thown everything off balance. It was the same case with Him as with me except He hadn't committed any crime and they could prove I had committed one because they had the papers on me. Of course," he said, "they never shown me my papers. That's why I sign myself now. I said long ago, you get you a signature and sign everything you do and keep a copy of it. Then you'll know what you done and you can hold up the crime to the punishment and see do they match and in the end you'll have something to prove you ain't been treated right. I call myself The Misfit," he said, "because I can't make what all I done wrong fit what all I gone through in punishment."

There was a piercing scream from the woods, followed closely by a pistol report. "Does it seem right to you, lady, that one is punished a heap and another ain't punished at all?"

"Jesus!" the old lady cried. "You've got good blood! I know you wouldn't shoot a lady! I know you come from nice people! Pray! Jesus, you ought not to shoot a lady. I'll give you all the money I've got!"

"Lady," The Misfit said, looking beyond her far into the woods, "there never was a body that give the undertaker a tip."

There were two more pistol reports and the grandmother raised her head like a parched old turkey hen crying for water and called, "Bailey Boy, Bailey Boy!" as if her heart would break.

"Jesus was the only One that ever raised the dead," The Misfit continued, "and He shouldn't have done it. He thown everything off balance. If He did what He said, then it's nothing for you to do but thow away everything and follow Him, and if He didn't, then it's nothing for you to do but enjoy the few minutes you got left the best way you can—by killing somebody or burning down his house or doing some other meanness to him. No pleasure but meanness," he said and his voice had become almost a snarl.

"Maybe He didn't raise the dead," the old lady mumbled, not knowing what she was saying and feeling so dizzy that she sank down in the ditch with her legs twisted under her.

"I wasn't there so I can't say He didn't," The Misfit said. "I wisht I had of been there," he said, hitting the ground with his fist. "It ain't right I wasn't there because if I had of been there I would of known. Listen lady," he said in a high voice, "if I had of been there I would of known and I wouldn't be like I am now." His voice seemed about to crack and the grandmother's head cleared for an instant. She saw the man's face twisted close to her own as if he were going to cry and she murmured, "Why you're one of my babies. You're one of my own children!" She reached out and touched him on the shoulder. The Misfit sprang back as if a snake had bitten him and shot her three times through the chest. Then he put his gun down on the ground and took off his glasses and began to clean them.

Hiram and Bobby Lee returned from the woods and stood over the ditch, looking down at the grandmother who half sat and half lay in a puddle of blood with her legs crossed under her like a child's and her face smiling up at the cloudless sky.

Without his glasses, The Misfit's eyes were red-rimmed and pale and defenseless-looking. "Take her off and thow her where you thown the others," he said, picking up the cat that was rubbing itself against his leg.

"She was a talker, wasn't she?" Bobby Lee said, sliding down the ditch with a yodel.

"She would have been a good woman," The Misfit said, "if it had been somebody there to shoot her every minute of her life."

"Some fun!" Bobby Lee said.

"Shut up, Bobby Lee," The Misfit said. "It's no real pleasure in life."

Orientation

Daniel Orozco

Daniel Orozco was raised in San Francisco and studied at the University of Washington, Seattle. He has published stories in The Santa Clara Review, Story *magazine and others. His story "The Bridge" was included in* Pushcart Prize XXI *(1997), and "Orientation," which appeared in* The Seattle Review, *was selected for inclusion in* The Best American Short Stories *1995. Presently, he teaches writing at San Francisco State University and is a Stegner Fellow in fiction at Stanford University.*

Those are the offices and these are the cubicles. That's my cubicle there, and this is your cubicle. This is your phone. Never answer your phone. Let the Voicemail System answer it. This is your Voicemail System Manual. There are no personal phone calls allowed. We do, however, allow for emergencies. If you must make an emergency phone call, ask your supervisor first. If you can't find your supervisor, ask Phillip Spiers, who sits over there. He'll check with Clarissa Nicks, who sits over there. If you make an emergency phone call without asking, you may be let go.

These are your IN and OUT boxes. All the forms in your IN box must be logged in by the date shown in the upper left-hand corner, initialed by you in the upper right-hand corner, and distributed to the Processing Analyst whose name is numerically coded in the lower left-hand corner. The lower right-hand corner is left blank. Here's your Processing Analyst Numerical Code Index. And here's your Forms Processing Procedures Manual.

You must pace your work. What do I mean? I'm glad you asked that. We pace our work according to the eight-hour workday. If you have twelve hours of work in your IN box, for example, you must compress that work into the eight-hour day. If you have one hour of work in your IN box, you must expand that work to fill the eight-hour day. That was a good question. Feel free to ask questions. Ask too many questions, however, and you may be let go.

That is our receptionist. She is a temp. We go through receptionists here. They quit with alarming frequency. Be polite and civil to the temps. Learn their names, and invite them to lunch occasionally. But don't get close to them, as it only makes it more difficult when they leave. And they always leave. You can be sure of that.

The men's room is over there. The women's room is over there. John LaFountaine, who sits over there, uses the women's room occasionally. He says it is accidental. We know better, but we let it pass. John LaFountaine is harmless, his forays into the forbidden territory of the women's room simply a benign thrill, a faint blip on the dull flat line of his life.

Russell Nash, who sits in the cubicle to your left, is in love with Amanda Pierce, who sits in the cubicle to your right. They ride the same bus together after work. For Amanda Pierce, it is just a tedious bus ride made less tedious by the idle nattering of Russell Nash. But for Russell Nash, it is the highlight of his day. It is the highlight of his life. Russell Nash has put on forty pounds, and grows fatter with each passing month, nibbling on chips and cookies while peeking glumly over the partitions at Amanda Pierce, and gorging himself at home on cold pizza and ice cream while watching adult videos on TV.

Amanda Pierce, in the cubicle to your right, has a six-year-old son named Jamie, who is autistic. Her cubicle is plastered from top to bottom with the boy's crayon artwork—sheet after sheet of precisely drawn concentric circles and ellipses, in black and yellow. She rotates them every other Friday. Be sure to comment on them. Amanda Pierce also has a husband, who is a lawyer. He subjects her to an escalating array of painful and humiliating sex games, to which Amanda Pierce reluctantly submits. She comes to work exhausted and freshly wounded each morning, wincing from the abrasions on her breasts, or the bruises on her abdomen, or the second-degree burns on the backs of her thighs.

But we're not supposed to know any of this. Do not let on. If you let on, you may be let go.

Amanda Pierce, who tolerates Russell Nash, is in love with Albert Bosch, whose office is over there. Albert Bosch, who only dimly registers Amanda Pierce's existence, has eyes only for Ellie Tapper, who sits over there. Ellie Tapper, who hates Albert Bosch, would walk through fire for Curtis Lance. But Curtis Lance hates Ellie Tapper. Isn't the world a funny place? Not in the ha-ha sense, of course.

Anika Bloom sits in that cubicle. Last year, while reviewing quarterly reports in a meeting with Barry Hacker, Anika Bloom's left palm began to bleed. She fell into a trance, stared into her hand, and told Barry Hacker when and how his wife would die. We laughed it off. She was, after all, a new employee. But Barry Hacker's wife is dead. So unless you want to know exactly when and how you'll die, never talk to Anika Bloom.

Colin Heavey sits in that cubicle over there. He was new once, just like you. We warned him about Anika Bloom. But at last year's Christmas Potluck, he felt sorry for her when he saw that no one was talking to her. Colin Heavey brought her a drink.

He hasn't been himself since. Colin Heavey is doomed. There's nothing he can do about it, and we are powerless to help him. Stay away from Colin Heavey. Never give any of your work to him. If he asks to do something, tell him you have to check with me. If he asks again, tell him I haven't gotten back to you.

This is the Fire Exit. There are several on this floor, and they are marked accordingly. We have a Floor Evacuation Review every three months, and an Escape Route Quiz once a month. We have our Biannual Fire Drill twice a year, and our Annual Earthquake Drill once a year. These are precautions only. These things never happen.

For your information, we have a comprehensive health plan. Any catastrophic illness, any unforeseen tragedy is completely covered. All dependents are completely covered. Larry Bagdikian, who sits over there, has six daughters. If anything were to happen to any of his girls, or to all of them, if all six were to simultaneously fall victim to illness or injury—stricken with a hideous degenerative muscle disease or some rare toxic blood disorder, sprayed with semiautomatic gunfire while on a class field trip, or attacked in their bunk beds by some prowling nocturnal lunatic—if any of this were to pass, Larry's girls would all be taken care of. Larry Bagdikian would not have to pay one dime. He would have nothing to worry about.

We also have a generous vacation and sick leave policy. We have an excellent disability insurance plan. We have a stable and profitable pension fund. We get group discounts for the symphony, and block seating at the ballpark. We get commuter ticket books for the bridge. We have Direct Deposit. We are all members of Costco.

This is our kitchenette. And this, this is our Mr. Coffee. We have a coffee pool, into which we each pay two dollars a week for coffee, filters, sugar, and CoffeeMate. If you prefer Cremora or half-and-half to CoffeeMate, there is a special pool for three dollars a week. If you prefer Sweet'n Low to sugar, there is a special pool for two-fifty a week. We do not do decaf. You are allowed to join the coffee pool of your choice, but you are not allowed to touch the Mr. Coffee.

This is the microwave oven. You are allowed to *heat* food in the microwave oven. You are not, however, allowed to *cook* food in the microwave oven.

We get one hour for lunch. We also get one fifteen-minute break in the morning, and one fifteen-minute break in the afternoon. Always take your breaks. If you skip a break, it is gone forever. For your information, your break is a privilege, not a right. If you abuse the break policy, we are authorized to rescind your breaks. Lunch, however, is a right, not a privilege. If you abuse the lunch policy, our hands will be tied, and we will be forced to look the other way. We will not enjoy that.

This is the refrigerator. You may put your lunch in it. Barry Hacker, who sits over there, steals food from this refrigerator. His petty theft is an outlet for his grief. Last New Year's Eve, while kissing his wife, a blood vessel burst in her brain. Barry Hacker's wife was two months pregnant at the time, and lingered in a coma for half a year before dying. It was a tragic loss for Barry Hacker. He hasn't been himself since. Barry Hacker's wife was a beautiful woman. She was also completely covered. Barry Hacker did not have to pay one dime. But his dead wife haunts him. She haunts all of us. We have seen her, reflected in the monitors of our computers, moving past our cubicles. We have seen the dim shadow of her face in our photocopies. She pencils herself in in the receptionist's appointment book, with the notation: To see Barry Hacker. She has left messages in the receptionist's Voicemail box, messages garbled by the electronic chirrups and buzzes in the phone line, her voice echoing from an immense distance within the ambient hum. But the voice is hers. And beneath her voice, beneath the tidal *whoosh* of static and hiss, the gurgling and crying of a baby can be heard.

In any case, if you bring a lunch, put a little something extra in the bag for Barry Hacker. We have four Barrys in this office. Isn't that a coincidence?

This is Matthew Payne's office. He is our Unit Manager, and his door is always closed. We have never seen him, and you will never see him. But he is here. You can be sure of that. He is all around us.

This is the Custodian's Closet. You have no business in the Custodian's Closet.

And this, this is our Supplies Cabinet. If you need supplies, see Curtis Lance. He will log you in on the Supplies Cabinet Authorization Log, then give you a Supplies Authorization Slip. Present your pink copy of the Supplies Authorization Slip to Ellie Tapper. She will log you in on the Supplies Cabinet Key Log, then give you the key. Because the Supplies Cabinet is located outside the Unit Manager's office, you must be very quiet. Gather your supplies quietly. The Supplies Cabinet is divided into four sections. Section One contains letterhead stationery, blank paper and envelopes, memo and note pads, and so on. Section Two contains pens and pencils and typewriter and printer ribbons, and the like. In Section Three we have erasers, correction fluids, transparent tapes, glue sticks, et cetera. And in Section Four we have paper clips and push pins and scissors and razor blades. And here are the spare blades for the shredder. Do not touch the shredder, which is located over there. The shredder is of no concern to you.

Gwendolyn Stich sits in that office there. She is crazy about penguins, and collects penguin knickknacks: penguin posters and coffee mugs and stationery, penguin stuffed animals, penguin jewelry, penguin sweaters and T-shirts and socks. She has a pair of penguin fuzzy slippers she wears when working late at the office. She has a tape cassette of penguin sounds which she listens to for relaxation. Her favorite colors are black and white. She has personalized license plates that read PEN GWEN. Every morning, she passes through all the cubicles to wish each of us a *good* morning. She brings Danish on Wednesdays for Hump Day morning break, and doughnuts on Fridays for TGIF afternoon break. She organizes the Annual Christmas Potluck, and is in charge of the Birthday List. Gwendolyn Stich's door is always open to all of us. She will always lend an ear, and put in a good word for you; she will always give you a hand, or the shirt off her back, or a shoulder to cry on. Because her door is always open, she hides and cries in a stall in the women's room. And John LaFountaine—who, enthralled when a woman enters, sits quietly in his stall with his knees to his chest— John LaFountaine has heard her vomiting in there. We have come upon Gwendolyn Stich huddled in the stairwell, shivering in the updraft, sipping a Diet Mr. Pibb and hugging her knees. She does not let any of this interfere with her work. If it interfered with her work, she might have to be let go.

221

Kevin Howard sits in that cubicle over there. He is a serial killer, the one they call the Carpet Cutter, responsible for the mutilations across town. We're not supposed to know that, so do not let on. Don't worry. His compulsion inflicts itself on strangers only, and the routine established is elaborate and unwavering. The victim must be a white male, a young adult no older than thirty, heavyset, with dark hair and eyes, and the like. The victim must be chosen at random, before sunset, from a public place; the victim is followed home, and must put up a struggle; et cetera. The carnage inflicted is precise: the angle and direction of the incisions; the layering of skin and muscle tissue; the rearrangement of the visceral organs; and so on. Kevin Howard does not let any of this interfere with his work. He is, in fact, our fastest typist. He types as if he were on fire. He has a secret crush on Gwendolyn Stich, and leaves a red-foil-wrapped Hershey's Kiss on her desk every afternoon. But he hates Anika Bloom, and keeps well away from her. In his presence, she has uncontrollable fits of shaking and trembling. Her left palm does not stop bleeding.

In any case, when Kevin Howard gets caught, act surprised. Say that he seemed like a nice person, a bit of a loner, perhaps, but always quiet and polite.

This is the photocopier room. And this, this is our view. It faces southwest. West is down there, toward the water. North is back there. Because we are on the seventeenth floor, we are afforded a magnificent view. Isn't it beautiful? It overlooks the park, where the tops of those trees are. You can see a segment of the bay between those two buildings there. You can see the sun set in the gap between those two buildings over there. You can see this building reflected in the glass panels of that building across the way. There. See? That's you, waving. And look there. There's Anika Bloom in the kitchenette, waving back.

Enjoy this view while photocopying. If you have problems with the photocopier, see Russell Nash. If you have any questions, ask your supervisor. If you can't find your supervisor, ask Phillip Spiers. He sits over there. He'll check with Clarissa Nicks. She sits over there. If you can't find them, feel free to ask me. That's my cubicle. I sit in there.

Brownies

ZZ Packer

ZZ Packer is an emerging talented writer. She was born in Chicago but raised in Atlanta and Louisville, Kentucky. Currently a Stegner fellow at Stanford, she holds degrees from Johns Hopkins and from the University of Iowa. "Brownies" was inspired by her childhood in the suburbs of Atlanta, where newly middle class African Americans tried to give their children a "proper" education sending them to ballet and gymnastics lessons. At that early age, Packer and her friends realized that they were made to imitate white models and began to resent whites, particularly white girls. "In 'Brownies,'" she says, "I wanted to capture how such bitterness was inherited and incubated."

By the end of our first day at Camp Crescendo, the girls in my Brownie troop had decided to kick the asses of each and every girl in Brownie Troop 909. Troop 909 was doomed from the first day of camp; they were white girls, their complexions like a blend of ice cream: strawberry, vanilla. They turtled out from their bus in pairs, their rolled-up sleeping bags chromatized with Disney characters—Sleeping Beauty, Snow White, Mickey Mouse—or the generic ones cheap parents bought—washed-out rainbows, unicorns, curly-eyelashed frogs. Some clutched Igloo coolers and still others held on to stuffed toys like pacifiers, looking all around them like tourists determined to be dazzled.

Our troop wended its way past their bus, past the ranger station, past the colorful trail guide drawn like a treasure map, locked behind glass.

"Man, did you smell them?" Arnetta said, giving the girls a slow once-over. "They smell like Chihuahuas. *Wet* Chihuahuas." Although we had passed their troop by yards, Arnetta raised her nose in the air and grimaced.

"Brownies," by ZZ Packer, reprinted from *Harper's Magazine*, November 1999, Volume 299 Issue 1794.

Arnetta said this from the very rear of the line, far away from Mrs. Margolin, who strung our troop behind her like a brood of obedient ducklings. Mrs. Margolin even looked like a mother duck—she had hair cropped close to a small ball of a head, almost no neck, and huge, miraculous breasts. She wore enormous belts that looked like the kind weight lifters wear, except hers were cheap metallic gold or rabbit fur or covered with gigantic fake sunflowers. Often these belts would become nature lessons in and of themselves. "See," Mrs. Margolin once said to us, pointing to her belt. "This one's made entirely from the feathers of baby pigeons."

The belt layered with feathers was uncanny enough, but I was more disturbed by the realization that I had never actually seen a baby pigeon. I searched for weeks for one, in vain—scampering after pigeons whenever I was downtown with my father.

But nature lessons were not Mrs. Margolin's top priority. She saw the position of troop leader as an evangelical post. Back at the A.M.E. church where our Brownie meetings were held, she was especially fond of imparting religious aphorisms by means of acrostics—Satan was the "Serpent Always Tempting And Noisome"; she'd refer to the Bible as "Basic Instructions Before Leaving Earth." Whenever she occasionally quizzed us on these at the beginning of the Brownie meeting, expecting to hear the acrostics parroted back to her, only Arnetta's correct replies soared over our vague mumblings. "Jesus?" Mrs. Margolin might ask expectantly, and Arnetta alone would dutifully answer, "Jehovah's Example, Saving Us Sinners."

Arnetta made a point of listening to Mrs. Margolin's religious talk and giving her what she wanted to hear. Because of this, Arnetta could have blared through a megaphone that the white girls of Troop 909 were "wet Chihuahuas" without arousing so much as a blink from Mrs. Margolin. Once Arnetta killed the troop goldfish by feeding it a French fry covered in ketchup, and when Mrs. Margolin demanded an explanation, Arnetta claimed that the goldfish had been eyeing her meal for hours, until—giving in to temptation—it had leapt up and snatched the whole golden fry from her fingertips.

"*Serious* Chihuahua," Octavia added—though neither Arnetta nor Octavia could *spell* "Chihuahua" or had ever *seen* a Chihuahua. Trisyllabic words had gained a sort of exoticism within our fourth-grade set at Woodrow Wilson Elementary. Arnetta and Octavia, compelled to outdo each other, would flip through the dictionary, determined to work the vulgar-sounding ones like "Djibouti" and "asinine" into conversation.

"*Caucasian* Chihuahuas," Arnetta said.

That did it. Drema and Elise doubled up on each other like inextricably entwined kites; Octavia slapped the skin of her belly; Janice jumped straight up in the air, then did it again, just as hard, as if to slam-dunk her own head. No one had laughed so hard since a boy named Martez had stuck his pencil in the electric socket and spent the whole day with a strange grin on his face.

"Girls, girls," said our parent helper, Mrs. Hedy. Mrs. Hedy was Octavia's mother. She wagged her index finger perfunctorily, like a windshield wiper. "Stop it now. Be good." She said this loudly enough to be heard, but lazily, nasally, bereft of any feeling or indication that she meant to be obeyed, as though she would say these words again at the exact same pitch if a button somewhere on her were pressed.

But the girls didn't stop laughing; they only laughed louder. It was the word "Caucasian" that had got them all going. One day at school, about a month before the Brownie camping trip, Arnetta had turned to a boy wearing impossibly high-ankled floodwater jeans, and said "What are *you? Caucasian?*" The word took off from there, and soon everything was Caucasian. If you ate too fast, you ate like a Caucasian; if you ate too slow, you ate like a Caucasian. The biggest feat anyone at Woodrow Wilson could do was to jump off the swing in midair, at the highest point in its arc, and if you fell (like I had, more than once) instead of landing on your feet, knees bent Olympic-gymnast-style, Arnetta and Octavia were prepared to comment. They'd look at each other with the silence of passengers who'd narrowly escaped an accident, then nod their heads, and whisper with solemn horror and haughtiness, *"Caucasian."*

Even the only white kid in our school, Dennis, got in on the Caucasian act. That time when Martez stuck the pencil in the socket, Dennis had pointed, and yelled, "That was *so* Caucasian!"

Living in the south suburbs of Atlanta, it was easy to forget about whites. Whites were like those baby pigeons: real and existing, but rarely thought about. Everyone had been to Rich's to go clothes shopping, everyone had seen white girls and their mothers coocooing over dresses; everyone had gone to the downtown library and seen white businessmen swish by importantly, wrists flexed in front of them to check the time on their watches as though they would change from Clark Kent into Superman any second. But those images were as fleeting as cards shuffled in a deck, whereas the ten white girls behind us—*invaders,* Arnetta would later call them—were instantly real and memorable, with their long shampoo-commercial hair, as straight as spaghetti from the box. This alone was reason for envy and hatred. The only black girl most of us had ever seen with hair that long was Octavia, whose hair hung past her butt like a Hawaiian hula dancer's. The sight of Octavia's mane prompted other girls to listen to her reverentially, as though whatever she had to say would somehow activate their own follicles. For example, when, on the first day of camp, Octavia made as if to speak, a silence began. "Nobody," Octavia said, "calls us niggers."

At the end of that first day, when half of our troop made its way back to the cabin after tag-team restroom visits, Arnetta said she'd heard one of the girls in Troop 909 call Daphne a nigger. The other half of the girls and I were helping Mrs. Margolin clean up the pots and pans from the ravioli dinner. When we made our way to the restrooms to wash up and brush our teeth, we met up with Arnetta midway.

"Man, I completely heard the girl," Arnetta reported. "Right, Daphne?"

Daphne hardly ever spoke, but when she did her voice was petite and tinkly, the voice one might expect from a shiny new earring. She'd written a poem once, for Langston Hughes Day, a poem brimming with all the teacher-winning ingredients—trees and oceans, sunsets and moons—but what cinched the poem for the grown-ups, snatching the win from Octavia's musical ode to Grandmaster Flash and the Furious Five, were Daphne's last lines:

You are my father, the veteran
When you cry in the dark
It rains and rains and rains in my heart

She'd worn clean, though faded, jumpers and dresses when Chic jeans were the fashion, but when she went up to the dais to receive her prize journal, pages trimmed in gold, she wore a new dress with a velveteen bodice and a taffeta skirt as wide as an umbrella. All the kids clapped, though none of them understood the poem. I'd read encyclopedias the way others read comics, and I didn't get it. But those last lines pricked me, they were so eerie, and as my father and I ate cereal, I'd whisper over my Froot Loops, like a mantra, *"You are my father, the veteran. You are my father, the veteran, the veteran, the veteran,"* until my father, who acted in plays as Caliban and Othello and was not a veteran, marched me up to my teacher one morning, and said, "Can you tell me what the hell's wrong with this kid?"

I had thought Daphne and I might become friends, but she seemed to grow spooked by me whispering those lines to her, begging her to tell me what they meant, and I had soon understood that two quiet people like us were better off quiet alone.

"Daphne? Didn't you hear them call you a nigger?" Arnetta asked, giving Daphne a nudge.

The sun was setting through the trees, and their leafy tops formed a canopy of black lace for the flame of the sun to pass through. Daphne shrugged her shoulders at first, then slowly nodded her head when Arnetta gave her a hard look.

Twenty minutes later, when my restroom group returned to the cabin, Arnetta was still talking about Troop 909. My restroom group had passed by some of the 909 girls. For the most part, they had deferred to us, waving us into the restrooms, letting us go even though they'd gotten there first.

We'd seen them, but from afar, never within their orbit enough to see whether their faces were the way all white girls appeared on TV—ponytailed and full of energy, bubbling over with love and money. All I could see was that some rapidly fanned their faces with their hands, though the heat of the day had long passed. A few seemed to be lolling their heads in slow circles, half-purposefully, as if exercising the muscles of their necks, half-ecstatically, rolling their heads about like Stevie Wonder.

"We can't let them get away with that," Arnetta said, dropping her voice to a laryngitic whisper. "We can't let them get away with calling us niggers. I say we teach them a lesson." She sat down cross-legged on a sleeping bag, an embittered Buddha, eyes glimmering acrylic black. "We can't go telling Mrs. Margolin, either. Mrs. Margolin'll say something about doing unto others and the path of righteousness and all. Forget that shit." She let her eyes flutter irreverently till they half closed, as though ignoring an insult not worth returning. We could all hear Mrs. Margolin outside, gathering the last of the metal campware.

Nobody said anything for a while. Arnetta's tone had an upholstered confidence that was somehow both regal and vulgar at once. It demanded a few moments of silence in its wake, like the ringing of a church bell or the playing of taps. Sometimes Octavia would ditto or dissent whatever Arnetta had said, and this was the signal that others could speak. But this time Octavia just swirled a long cord of hair into pretzel shapes.

"*Well?*" Arnetta said. She looked as if she had discerned the hidden severity of the situation and was waiting for the rest of us to catch up. Everyone looked from Arnetta to Daphne. It was, after all, Daphne who had supposedly been called the name, but Daphne sat on the bare cabin floor, flipping through the pages of the Girl Scout handbook, eyebrows arched in mock wonder, as if the handbook were a catalogue full of bright and startling foreign costumes. Janice broke the silence. She clapped her hands to broach her idea of a plan.

"They gone be sleeping," she whispered conspiratorially, "then we gone sneak into they cabin, then we gone put daddy longlegs in they sleeping bags. Then they'll wake up. Then we gone beat 'em up till they flat as frying pans!" She jammed her fist into the palm of her hand, then made a sizzling sound.

Janice's country accent was laughable, her looks homely, her jumpy acrobatics embarrassing to behold. Arnetta and Octavia volleyed amused, arrogant smiles whenever Janice opened her mouth, but Janice never caught the hint, spoke whenever she wanted, fluttered around Arnetta and Octavia futilely offering her opinions to their departing backs. Whenever Arnetta and Octavia shooed her away, Janice loitered until the two would finally sigh, "What is it, Miss Caucasoid? What do you want?"

"Oh shut up, Janice," Octavia said, letting a fingered loop of hair fall to her waist as though just the sound of Janice's voice had ruined the fun of her hair twisting.

"All right," Arnetta said, standing up. "We're going to have a secret meeting and talk about what we're going to do."

The word "secret" had a built-in importance. Everyone gravely nodded her head. The modifier form of the word had more clout than the noun. A secret meant nothing; it was like gossip: just a bit of unpleasant knowledge about someone who happened to be someone other than yourself. A secret *meeting* or a secret *club*, was entirely different.

That was when Arnetta turned to me, as though she knew doing so was both a compliment and a charity.

"Snot, you're not going to be a bitch and tell Mrs. Margolin, are you?"

I had been called "Snot" ever since first grade, when I'd sneezed in class and two long ropes of mucus had splattered a nearby girl.

"Hey," I said. "Maybe you didn't hear them right—I mean—"

"Are you gonna tell on us or not?" was all Arnetta wanted to know, and by the time the question was asked, the rest of our Brownie troop looked at me as though they'd already decided their course of action, me being the only impediment. As though it were all a simple matter of patriotism.

*   *   *

Camp Crescendo used to double as a high school band and field hockey camp until an arching field hockey ball landed on the clasp of a girl's metal barrette, knifing a skull nerve, paralyzing the right side of her body. The camp closed down for a few years, and the girl's teammates built a memorial, filling the spot on which the girl fell with hockey balls, upon which they had painted—all in nail polish—get-well tidings, flowers, and hearts. The balls were still stacked there, like a shrine of ostrich eggs embedded in the ground.

On the second day of camp, Troop 909 was dancing around the mound of nail polish-decorated hockey balls, their limbs jangling awkwardly, their cries like the constant summer squeal of an amusement park. There was a stream that bordered the field hockey lawn, and the girls from my troop settled next to it, scarfing down the last of lunch: sandwiches made from salami and slices of tomato that had gotten waterlogged from the melting ice in the cooler. From the stream bank, Arnetta eyed the Troop 909 girls, scrutinizing their movements to glean inspiration for battle.

"Man," Arnetta said, "we could bum-rush them right now if that damn lady would *leave.*"

The 909 troop leader was a white woman with the severe pageboy hairdo of an ancient Egyptian. She lay sprawled on a picnic blanket, Sphinxlike, eating a banana, sometimes holding it out in front of her like a microphone. Beside her sat a girl slowly flapping one hand like a bird with a broken wing. Occasionally, the leader would call out the names of girls who'd attempted leapfrogs and flips, or of girls who yelled too loudly or strayed far from the circle.

"I'm just glad Big Fat Mama's not following us here," Octavia said. "At least we don't have to worry about her." Mrs. Margolin, Octavia assured us, was having her Afternoon Devotional, shrouded in mosquito netting, in a clearing she'd found. Mrs. Hedy was cleaning mud from her espadrilles in the cabin.

"I handled them." Arnetta sucked on her teeth and proudly grinned. "I told her we was going to gather leaves."

"Gather leaves," Octavia said, nodding respectfully. "That's a good one. They're so mad-crazy about this camping thing." She looked from ground to sky, sky to ground. Her hair hung down her back in two braids like a squaw's. "I mean, I really don't know why it's even called *camping*—all we ever do with Nature is find some twigs and say something like, 'Wow, this fell from a tree.'" She then studied her sandwich. With two disdainful fingers, she picked out a slice of dripping tomato, the sections congealed with red slime. She pitched it into the stream embrowned with dead leaves and the murky effigies of other dead things, but in the opaque water a group of small silver-brown fish appeared. They surrounded the tomato and nibbled.

"Look!" Janice cried. "Fishes! Fishes!" As she scrambled to the edge of the stream to watch, a covey of insects threw up tantrums from the wheatgrass and nettle, a throng of tiny electric machines, all going at once. Octavia snuck up behind Janice as if to push her in. Daphne and I exchanged terrified looks. It seemed as though only we knew that Octavia was close enough—and bold enough—to actually push Janice into the stream. Janice turned around quickly, but Octavia was already staring serenely into the still water as though she were gathering some sort of courage from it. "What's so funny?" Janice said, eyeing them all suspiciously.

Elise began humming the tune to "Karma Chameleon," all the girls joining in, their hums light and facile. Janice began to hum, against everyone else, the high-octane opening chords of "Beat It."

"I love me some Michael Jackson," Janice said when she'd finished humming, smacking her lips as though Michael Jackson were a favorite meal. "I will marry Michael Jackson."

Before anyone had a chance to impress upon Janice the impossibility of this, Arnetta suddenly rose, made a sun visor of her hand, and watched Troop 909 leave the field hockey lawn.

"Dammit!" she said. "We've got to get them *alone*."

"They won't ever be alone," I said. All the rest of the girls looked at me. If I spoke even a word, I could count on someone calling me Snot, but everyone seemed to think that we could beat up these girls; no one entertained the thought that they might fight *back*. "The only time they'll be unsupervised is in the bathroom."

"Oh shut up, Snot," Octavia said.

But Arnetta slowly nodded her head. "The bathroom," she said. "The bathroom," she said, again and again. "The bathroom! The bathroom!" She cheered so blissfully that I thought for a moment she was joking.

According to Octavia's watch, it took us five minutes to hike to the restrooms, which were midway between our cabin and Troop 909's. Inside, the mirrors above the sinks returned only the vaguest of reflections, as though someone had taken a scouring pad to their surfaces to obscure the shine. Pine needles, leaves, and dirty flattened wads of chewing gum covered the floor like a mosaic. Webs of hair matted the drain in the middle of the floor. Above the sinks and below the mirrors, stacks of folded white paper towels lay on a long metal counter. Shaggy white balls of paper towels sat on the sink tops in a line like corsages on display. A thread of floss snaked from a wad of tissues dotted with the faint red-pink of blood. One of those white girls, I thought, had just lost a tooth.

The restroom looked almost the same as it had the night before, but it somehow seemed stranger now. We had never noticed the wooden rafters before, coming together in great V's. We were, it seemed, inside a whale, viewing the ribs of the roof of its mouth.

"Wow. It's a mess," Elise said.

"You can say that again."

Arnetta leaned against the doorjamb of a restroom stall. "This is where they'll be again," she said. Just seeing the place, just having a plan, seemed to satisfy her. "We'll go in and talk to them. You know, 'How you doing? How long will you be here?' that sort of thing. Then Octavia and I are gonna tell them what happens when they call any one of us a nigger."

"I'm going to say something, too," Janice said.

Arnetta considered this. "Sure," she said. "Of course. Whatever you want."

Janice pointed her finger like a gun at Octavia and rehearsed the line she'd thought up, "'We're gonna teach you a *lesson.'* That's what I'm going to say." She narrowed her eyes like a TV mobster. "'We're gonna teach you little girls a lesson!'"

With the back of her hand, Octavia brushed Janice's finger away. "You couldn't teach me to shit in a toilet."

"But," I said, "what if they say, 'We didn't say that. We didn't call anyone a N-I-G-G-E-R'?"

"Snot," Arnetta sighed. "Don't think. Just fight. If you even know how."

Everyone laughed while Daphne stood there. Arnetta gently laid her hand on Daphne's shoulder. "Daphne. You don't have to fight. We're doing this for you."

Daphne walked to the counter, took a clean paper towel, and carefully unfolded it like a map. With this, she began to pick up the trash all around. Everyone watched.

"C'mon," Arnetta said to everyone. "Let's beat it." We all ambled toward the restroom doorway, where the sunshine made one large white rectangle of light. We were immediately blinded and shielded our eyes with our hands, our forearms.

"Daphne?" Arnetta asked. "Are you coming?"

We all looked back at the girl, who was bending, the thin of her back hunched like a maid caught in stage limelight. Stray strands of her hair were lit nearly transparent, thin fiber-optic threads. She did not nod yes to the question, nor did she shake her head no. She abided, bent. Then she began again, picking up leaves, wads of paper, the cotton fluff innards from a torn stuffed toy. She did it so methodically, so exquisitely, so humbly, she must have been trained. I thought of those dresses she wore, faded and old, yet so pressed and clean; I then saw the poverty in them, I then could imagine her mother, cleaning the houses of others, returning home, weary.

"I guess she's not coming."

We left her, heading back to our cabin, over pine needles and leaves, taking the path full of shade.

"What about our secret meeting?" Elise asked.

Arnetta enunciated in a way that defied contradiction: "We just had it."

Just as we caught sight of our cabin, Arnetta violently swerved away from Octavia. "You farted," she said.

Octavia began to sashay, as if on a catwalk, then proclaimed, in a Hollywood-starlet voice, "My farts smell like perfume."

It was nearing our bedtime, but in the lengthening days of spring, the sun had not yet set.

"Hey, your mama's coming," Arnetta said to Octavia when she saw Mrs. Hedy walk toward the cabin, sniffling. When Octavia's mother wasn't giving bored, parochial orders, she sniffled continuously, mourning an imminent divorce from her husband. She might begin a sentence, "I don't know what Robert will do when Octavia and I are gone. Who'll buy him cigarettes?" and Octavia would hotly whisper

"Mama" in a way that meant: Please don't talk about our problems in front of everyone. Please shut up.

But when Mrs. Hedy began talking about her husband, thinking about her husband, seeing clouds shaped like the head of her husband, she couldn't be quiet, and no one could ever dislodge her from the comfort of her own woe. Only one thing could perk her up—Brownie songs. If the rest of the girls were quiet, and Mrs. Hedy was in her dopey sorrowful mood, she would say, "Y'all know I like those songs, girls. Why don't you sing one?" Everyone would groan except me and Daphne. I, for one, liked some of the songs.

"C'mon, everybody," Octavia said drearily. "She likes 'The Brownie Song' best."

We sang, loud enough to reach Mrs. Hedy:

I've something in my pocket;
It belongs across my face.
And I keep it very close at hand in a most convenient place.
I'm sure you couldn't guess it
If you guessed a long, long while.
So I'll take it out and put it on—
It's a great big Brownie Smile!

"The Brownie Song" was supposed to be sung as though we were elves in a workshop, singing as we merrily cobbled shoes, but everyone except me hated the song and sang it like a maudlin record, played at the most sluggish of rpms.

"That was good," Mrs. Hedy said, closing the cabin door behind her. "Wasn't that nice, Linda?"

"Praise God," Mrs. Margolin answered without raising her head from the chore of counting out Popsicle sticks for the next day's session of crafts.

"Sing another one," Mrs. Hedy said, with a sort of joyful aggression, like a drunk I'd once seen who'd refused to leave a Korean grocery.

"God, Mama, get over it," Octavia whispered in a voice meant only for Arnetta, but Mrs. Hedy heard it and started to leave the cabin.

"Don't go," Arnetta said. She ran after Mrs. Hedy and held her by the arm. "We haven't finished singing." She nudged us with a single look. "Let's sing 'The Friends Song.' For Mrs. Hedy."

Although I liked some of the songs, I hated this one:

Make new friends
But keep the o-old,
One is silver
And the other gold.

If most of the girls in my troop could be any type of metal, they'd be bunched-up wads of tinfoil maybe, or rusty iron nails you had to get tetanus shots for.

231

"No, no, no," Mrs. Margolin said before anyone could start in on "The Friends Song." "An uplifting song. Something to lift her up and take her mind off all these earthly burdens."

Arnetta and Octavia rolled their eyes. Everyone knew what song Mrs. Margolin was talking about, and no one, no one, wanted to sing it.

"Please, no," a voice called out. "Not 'The Doughnut Song.'"

"Please not 'The Doughnut Song,'" Octavia pleaded.

"I'll brush my teeth twice if I don't have to sing 'The Doughnut—'"

"Sing!" Mrs. Margolin demanded.

We sang:

Life without Jesus is like a do-ough-nut!
Like a do-ooough-nut!
Like a do-ooough-nut!
Life without Jesus is like a do-ough-nut!
There's a hole in the middle of my soul!

There were other verses, involving other pastries, but we stopped after the first one and cast glances toward Mrs. Margolin to see if we could gain a reprieve. Mrs. Margolin's eyes fluttered blissfully, half-asleep.

"Awww," Mrs. Hedy said, as though giant Mrs. Margolin were a cute baby. "Mrs. Margolin's had a long day."

"Yes indeed," Mrs. Margolin answered. "If you don't mind, I might just go to the lodge where the beds are. I haven't been the same since the operation."

I had not heard of this operation, or when it had occurred, since Mrs. Margolin had never missed the once-a-week Brownie meetings, but I could see from Daphne's face that she was concerned, and I could see that the other girls had decided that Mrs. Margolin's operation must have happened long ago in some remote time unconnected to our own. Nevertheless, they put on sad faces. We had all been taught that adulthood was full of sorrow and pain, taxes and bills, dreaded work and dealings with whites, sickness, and death.

"Go right ahead, Linda," Mrs. Hedy said. "I'll watch the girls." Mrs. Hedy seemed to forget about divorce for a moment; she looked at us with dewy eyes, as if we were mysterious, furry creatures. Meanwhile, Mrs. Margolin walked through the maze of sleeping bags until she found her own. She gathered a neat stack of clothes and pajamas slowly, as though doing so were almost painful. She took her toothbrush, her toothpaste, her pillow. "All right!" Mrs. Margolin said, addressing us all from the threshold of the cabin. "Be in bed by nine." She said it with a twinkle in her voice, as though she were letting us know she was allowing us to be naughty and stay up till nine-fifteen.

"C'mon, everybody," Arnetta said after Mrs. Margolin left. "Time for us to wash up."

Everyone watched Mrs. Hedy closely, wondering whether she would insist on coming with us since it was night, making a fight with Troop 909 nearly impossible. Troop 909 would soon be in the bathroom, washing their faces, brushing their teeth—completely unsuspecting of our ambush.

"We won't be long," Arnetta said. "We're old enough to go to the restroom by ourselves."

Mrs. Hedy pursed her lips at this dilemma. "Well, I guess you Brownies are almost Girl Scouts, right?"

"Right"

"Just one more badge," Drema said.

"And about," Octavia droned, "a million more cookies to sell." Octavia looked at all of us. *Now's our chance,* her face seemed to say, but our chance to do *what* I didn't exactly know.

Finally, Mrs. Hedy walked to the doorway where Octavia stood, dutifully waiting to say good-bye and looking bored doing it. Mrs. Hedy held Octavia's chin. "You'll be good?"

"Yes, Mama."

"And remember to pray for me and your father? If I'm asleep when you get back?"

"Yes, Mama."

When the other girls had finished getting their toothbrushes and washcloths and flashlights for the group restroom trip, I was drawing pictures of tiny birds with too many feathers. Daphne was sitting on her sleeping bag, reading.

"You're not going to come?" Octavia asked.

Daphne shook her head.

"I'm also gonna stay, too," I said. "I'll go to the restroom when Daphne and Mrs. Hedy go."

Arnetta leaned down toward me and whispered so that Mrs. Hedy, who had taken over Mrs. Margolin's task of counting Popsicle sticks, couldn't hear. "No, Snot. If we get in trouble, you're going to get in trouble with the rest of us."

We made our way through the darkness by flashlight. The tree branches that had shaded us just hours earlier, along the same path, now looked like arms sprouting menacing hands. The stars sprinkled the sky like spilled salt. They seemed fastened to the darkness, high up and holy, their places fixed and definite as we stirred beneath them.

Some, like me, were quiet because we were afraid of the dark; others were talking like crazy for the same reason.

"Wow," Drema said, looking up. "Why are all the stars out here? I never see stars back on Oneida Street."

"It's a camping trip, that's why," Octavia said. "You're supposed to see stars on camping trips."

Janice said, "This place smells like the air freshener my mother uses."

"These woods are *pine,*" Elise said. "Your mother probably uses pine air freshener."

Janice mouthed an exaggerated "Oh," nodding her head as though she just then understood one of the world's great secrets.

No one talked about fighting. Everyone was afraid enough just walking through the infinite deep of the woods. Even without seeing anyone's face, I could tell this wasn't about Daphne being called a nigger. The word that had started it all seemed melted now into some deeper, unnameable feeling. Even though I didn't want to fight, was afraid of fighting, I felt as though I were part of the rest of the troop, as though I were defending something. We trudged against the slight incline of the path, Arnetta leading the way. I wondered, looking at her back, what she could be thinking.

"You know," I said, "their leader will be there. Or they won't even be there. It's dark already. Last night the sun was still in the sky. I'm sure they're already finished."

"Whose flashlight is this?" Arnetta said, shaking the weakening beam of the light she was holding. "It's out of batteries."

Octavia handed Arnetta her flashlight. And that's when I saw it. The bathroom was just ahead.

But the girls were there. We could hear them before we could see them.

"Octavia and I will go in first so they'll think there's just two of us. Then wait till I say, 'We're gonna teach you a lesson,'" Arnetta said. "Then bust in. That'll surprise them."

"That's what I was supposed to say," Janice said.

Arnetta went inside, Octavia next to her. Janice followed, and the rest of us waited outside.

They were in there for what seemed like whole minutes, but something was wrong. Arnetta hadn't given the signal yet. I was with the girls outside when I heard one of the Troop 909 girls say, "NO. That did NOT happen!"

That was to be expected, that they'd deny the whole thing. What I hadn't expected was *the voice* in which the denial was said. The girl sounded as though her tongue were caught in her mouth. "That's a BAD word!" the girl continued. "We don't say BAD words!"

"Let's go in," Elise said.

"No," Drema said. "I don't want to. What if we get beat up?"

"Snot?" Elise turned to me, her flashlight blinding. It was the first time anyone had asked my opinion, though I knew they were just asking because they were afraid.

"I say we go inside, just to see what's going on."

"But Arnetta didn't give us the signal," Drema said. "She's supposed to say, 'We're going to teach you a lesson,' and I didn't hear her say it."

"C'mon," I said. "Let's just go in."

We went inside. There we found the white girls, but about five girls were huddled up next to one big girl. I instantly knew she was the owner of the voice we'd heard. Arnetta and Octavia inched toward us as soon as we entered.

"Where's Janice?" Elise asked, then we heard a flush. "Oh."

"I think," Octavia said, whispering to Elise, "they're retarded."

"We ARE NOT retarded!" the big girl said, though it was obvious that she was. That they all were. The girls around her began to whimper.

"They're just pretending," Arnetta said, trying to convince herself. "I know they are."

Octavia turned to Arnetta. "Arnetta. Let's just leave."

234

Janice came out of a stall, happy and relieved, then she suddenly remembered her line, pointed to the big girl, and said, "We're gonna teach you a lesson."

"Shut up, Janice," Octavia said, but her heart was not in it. Arnetta's face was set in a lost, deep scowl. Octavia turned to the big girl, and said loudly, slowly, as if they were all deaf, "We're going to leave. It was nice meeting you, okay? You don't have to tell anyone that we were here. Okay?"

"Why not?" said the big girl, like a taunt. When she spoke, her lips did not meet, her mouth did not close. Her tongue grazed the roof of her mouth, like a little pink fish. "You'll get in trouble. I know. I know."

Arnetta got back her old cunning. "If you said anything, then you'd be a tattletale."

The girl looked sad for a moment, then perked up quickly. A flash of genius crossed her face: "I *like* tattletale."

"It's all right, girls. It's gonna be all right!" the 909 troop leader said. It was as though someone had instructed all of Troop 909 to cry at once. The troop leader had girls under her arm, and all the rest of the girls crowded about her. It reminded me of a hog I'd seen on a field trip, where all the little hogs would gather about the mother at feeding time, latching on to her teats. The 909 troop leader had come into the bathroom shortly after the big girl threatened to tell. Then the ranger came, then, once the ranger had radioed the station, Mrs. Margolin arrived with Daphne in tow.

The ranger had left the restroom area, but everyone else was huddled just outside, swatting mosquitoes.

"Oh. They *will* apologize," Mrs. Margolin said to the 909 troop leader, but Mrs. Margolin said this so angrily, I knew she was speaking more to us than to the other troop leader. "When their parents find out, every one a them will be on punishment."

"It's all right. It's all right," the 909 troop leader reassured Mrs. Margolin. Her voice lilted in the same way it had when addressing the girls. She smiled the whole time she talked. She was like one of those TV cooking show women who talk and dice onions and smile all at the same time.

"See. It could have happened. I'm not calling your girls fibbers or anything." She shook her head ferociously from side to side, her Egyptian-style pageboy flapping against her cheeks like heavy drapes. "It *could* have happened, see. Our girls are *not* retarded. They are *delayed* learners." She said this in a syrupy instructional voice, as though our troop might be delayed learners as well. "We're from the Decatur Children's Academy. Many of them just have special needs."

"Now we won't be able to walk to the bathroom by ourselves!" the big girl said.

"Yes you will," the troop leader said, "but maybe we'll wait till we get back to Decatur—"

"I don't want to wait!" the girl said. "I want my Independence patch!"

The girls in my troop were entirely speechless. Arnetta looked as though she were soon to be tortured but was determined not to appear weak. Mrs. Margolin pursed her lips solemnly and said, "Bless them, Lord. Bless them."

In contrast, the Troop 909 leader was full of words and energy. "Some of our girls are echolalic—" She smiled and happily presented one of the girls hanging on to her, but the girl widened her eyes in horror and violently withdrew herself from the center of attention, as though she sensed she were being sacrificed for the village sins. "Echolalic," the troop leader continued. "That means they will say whatever they hear, like an echo—that's where the word comes from. It comes from 'echo.'" She ducked her head apologetically. "I mean, not all of them have the most progressive of parents, so if they heard a bad word they might have repeated it. But I guarantee it would not have been *intentional*."

Arnetta spoke. "I saw her say the word. I heard her." She pointed to a small girl, smaller than any of us, wearing an oversized T-shirt that read: EAT BERTHA'S MUSSELS.

The troop leader shook her head and smiled. "That's impossible. She doesn't speak. She can, but she doesn't."

Arnetta furrowed her brow. "No. It wasn't her. That's right. It was *her*."

The girl Arnetta pointed to grinned as though she'd been paid a compliment. She was the only one from either troop actually wearing a full uniform: the mocha-colored A-line shift, the orange ascot, the sash covered with patches, though all the same one—the Try-It patch. She took a few steps toward Arnetta and made a grand sweeping gesture toward the sash. "See," she said, full of self-importance, "I'm a Brownie." I had a hard time imagining this girl calling anyone a "nigger"; the girl looked perpetually delighted, as though she would have cuddled up with a grizzly if someone had let her.

On the fourth morning, we boarded the bus to go home.

The previous day had been spent building miniature churches from Popsicle sticks. We hardly left the cabin. Mrs. Margolin and Mrs. Hedy guarded us so closely, almost no one talked for the entire day.

Even on the day of departure from Camp Crescendo, all was serious and silent. The bus ride began quietly enough. Arnetta had to sit beside Mrs. Margolin, Octavia had to sit beside her mother. I sat beside Daphne, who gave me her prize journal without a word of explanation.

"You don't want it?"

She shook her head no. It was empty.

Then Mrs. Hedy began to weep. "Octavia," Mrs. Hedy said to her daughter without looking at her, "I'm going to sit with Mrs. Margolin. All right?"

Arnetta exchanged seats with Mrs. Hedy. With the two women up front, Elise felt it safe to speak. "Hey," she said, then she set her face into a placid vacant stare, trying to imitate that of a Troop 909 girl. Emboldened, Arnetta made a gesture of mock pride toward an imaginary sash, the way the girl in full uniform had done. Then they all made a game of it, trying to do the most exaggerated imitations of the Troop 909 girls, all without speaking, all without laughing loud enough to catch the women's attention.

Daphne looked at her shoes, white with sneaker polish. I opened the journal she'd given me. I looked out the window, trying to decide what to write, searching for lines, but nothing could compare with the lines Daphne had written, *"My father, the veteran,"* my favorite line of all time. The line replayed itself in my head, and I gave up trying to write.

By then, it seemed as though the rest of the troop had given up making fun of the 909 girls. They were now quietly gossiping about who had passed notes to whom in school. For a moment the gossiping fell off, and all I heard was the hum of the bus as we sped down the road and the muffled sounds of Mrs. Hedy and Mrs. Margolin talking about serious things.

"You know," Octavia whispered, 'why did *we* have to be stuck at a camp with retarded girls? You know?"

"You know why," Arnetta answered. She narrowed her eyes like a cat. "My mama and I were in the mall in Buckhead, and this white lady just kept looking at us. I mean, like we were foreign or something. Like we were from China."

"What did the woman say?" Elise asked.

"Nothing," Arnetta said. "She didn't say nothing."

A few girls quietly nodded their heads.

"There was this time," I said, "when my father and I were in the mall and—"

"Oh, shut up, Snot," Octavia said.

I stared at Octavia, then rolled my eyes from her to the window. As I watched the trees blur, I wanted nothing more than to be through with it all: the bus ride, the troop, school—all of it. But we were going home. I'd see the same girls in school the next day. We were on a bus, and there was nowhere else to go.

"Go on, Laurel," Daphne said to me. It was the first time she'd spoken the whole trip, and she'd said my name. I turned to her and smiled weakly so as not to cry, hoping she'd remember when I'd tried to be her friend, thinking maybe that her gift of the journal was an invitation of friendship. But she didn't smile back. All she said was, "What happened?"

I studied the girls, waiting for Octavia to tell me to "shut up" again before I even had a chance to utter another word, but everyone was amazed that Daphne had spoken. I gathered my voice. "Well," I said. "My father and I were in this mall, but *I* was the one doing the staring." I stopped and glanced from face to face. I continued. "There were these white people dressed like Puritans or something, but they weren't Puritans. They were Mennonites. They're these people who, if you ask them to do a favor, like paint your porch or something, they have to do it. It's in their rules."

"That sucks," someone said.

"C'mon," Arnetta said. "You're lying."

"I am not."

"How do you know that's not just some story someone made up?" Elise asked, her head cocked, full of daring. "I mean, who's gonna do whatever you ask?"

"It's not made up. I know because when I was looking at them, my father said, "See those people. If you ask them to do something, they'll do it. Anything you want.'"

No one would call anyone's father a liar. Then they'd have to fight the person, but Drema parsed her words carefully. "How does your *father* know that's not just some story? Huh?"

237

"Because," I said, "he went up to the man and asked him would he paint our porch, and the man said, 'Yes.' It's their religion."

"Man, I'm glad I'm a Baptist," Elise said, shaking her head in sympathy for the Mennonites.

"So did the guy do it?" Drema asked, scooting closer to hear if the story got juicy.

"Yeah," I said. "His whole family was with him. My dad drove them to our house. They all painted our porch. The woman and girl were in bonnets and long, long skirts with buttons up to their necks. The guy wore this weird hat and these huge suspenders."

"Why," Arnetta asked archly, as though she didn't believe a word, "would someone pick a *porch*? If they'll do anything, why not make them paint the whole *house*? Why not ask for a hundred bucks?"

I thought about it, and I remembered the words my father had said about them painting our porch, though I had never seemed to think about his words after he'd said them.

"He said," I began, only then understanding the words as they uncoiled from my mouth, "it was the only time he'd have a white man on his knees doing something for a black man for free."

I remembered the Mennonites bending like Daphne had bent, cleaning the restroom. I remembered the dark blue of their bonnets, the black of their shoes. They painted the porch as though scrubbing a floor. I was already trembling before Daphne asked quietly, "Did he thank them?"

I looked out the window. I could not tell which were the thoughts and which were the trees. "No," I said, and suddenly knew there was something mean in the world that I could not stop.

Arnetta laughed. "If I asked them to take off their long skirts and bonnets and put on some jeans, they would do it?"

And Daphne's voice—quiet, steady: "Maybe they would. Just to be nice."

Daddy

Sylvia Plath

Sylvia Plath was born in Massachusetts in 1932 and died in England in 1963, by suicide. Plath's experiences as a student at Smith College, which included a nervous breakdown in 1953, are chronicled in her novel The Bell Jar, *published in 1963. After graduating from Smith in 1955, Plath went to England on a scholarship, where she met and married the British poet Ted Hughes. They moved to Massachusetts for a brief stay while Plath taught at Smith, but then returned to England where they settled down and had children. Plath is best known for her highly charged, personal, confessional and often angry poetry. The only US publication of her poetry in her lifetime was* The Colossus, *published in 1962. Posthumous publications of poetry collections include* Ariel *(1966),* Crossing the Water *(1971), and* Winter Trees *(1972). Her* Collected Poems *won the Pulitzer Prize for poetry in 1981. Her prose writing is collected in* Johnny Panic and the Bible of Dreams *(1977), her selected letters are gathered in* Letters Home *(1975), and her* Journals *were published in 1982.*

You do not do, you do not do
Any more, black shoe
In which I have lived like a foot
For thirty years, poor and white,
Barely daring to breathe or Achoo.

Daddy, I have had to kill you.
You died before I had time—

Marble-heavy, a bag full of God,
Ghastly statue with one grey toe
Big as a Frisco seal

And a head in the freakish Atlantic
Where it pours bean green over blue
In the waters of beautiful Nauset.
I used to pray to recover you.
Ach, du.

In the German tongue, in the Polish town
Scraped flat by the roller
Of wars, wars, wars.
But the name of the town is common.
My Polack friend

Says there are a dozen or two.
So I never could tell where you
Put your foot, your root,
I never could talk to you.
The tongue stuck in my jaw.

It stuck in a barb wire snare.
Ich, ich, ich, ich,
I could hardly speak.
I thought every German was you.
And the language obscene

An engine, an engine
Chuffing me off like a Jew.
A Jew to Dachau, Auschwitz, Belsen.
I began to talk like a Jew.
I think I may well be a Jew.

The snows of the Tyrol, the clear beer of Vienna
Are not very pure or true.
With my gypsy ancestress and my weird luck
And my Taroc pack and my Taroc pack
I may be a bit of a Jew.

I have always been scared of *you*,
With your Luftwaffe, your gobbledygoo.
And your neat moustache

And your Aryan eye, bright blue.
Panzer-man, panzer-man, O You—

Not God but a swastika
So black no sky could squeak through.
Every woman adores a Fascist,
The boot in the face, the brute
Brute heart of a brute like you.

You stand at the blackboard, daddy,
In the picture I have of you,
A cleft in your chin instead of your foot
But no less a devil for that, no not
Any less the black man who

Bit my pretty red heart in two.
I was ten when they buried you.
At twenty I tried to die
And get back, back, back to you.
I thought even the bones would do

But they pulled me out of the sack,
And they stuck me together with glue.
And then I knew what to do.
I made a model of you,
A man in black with a Meinkampf look

And a love of the rack and the screw.
And I said I do, I do.
So daddy, I'm finally through.
The black telephone's off at the root,
The voices just can't worm through.

If I've killed one man, I've killed two—
The vampire who said he was you
And drank my blood for a year,
Seven years, if you want to know.
Daddy, you can lie back now.

There's a stake in your fat black heart
And the villagers never liked you.
They are dancing and stamping on you.
They always *knew* it was you.
Daddy, daddy, you bastard, I'm through.

241

A Heretic's View on the New Bioethics

Jeremy Rifkin

*A social activist, Jeremy Rifkin has long been an outspoken oppo-
nent of biotechnology and genetic engineering in particular. He
holds a BA in Economics from the University of Pennsylvania and
an MA in international relations from the Fletcher School of Law
and Diplomacy at Tufts University. He helped organize the first
protest against the Vietnam War in 1967 and worked as a volunteer in New York City. Among his books are* How to Commit Revolution American Style *(1973),* Common Sense II: The Case Against
Corporate Tyranny *(1975) and* Own Your Own Job: Economic
Democracy for Working Americans *(1977).* "A Heretic's View on the
New Bioethics" is from his controversial book, *Algeny* (1983). The
title is a play upon the word "alchemy" suggesting that the modern quest to manipulate genes is analogous to the medieval quest
for gold.

. . . even though we profess to be a democratic republic, we give over
much of our individual responsibility for decision making to elites, especially scientific and corporate elites. . . . I'm afraid we're going to lose the
sense of a democratic republic if we don't start to assert our rightful role
and participate in the political process. I don't think you have to be a
physicist to speak up and speak out on the issues of nuclear power and nuclear bombs and nuclear war. I don't think you have to be a chemist to be
informed and to speak out on the questions of petrochemical pollution in

"A Heretic's View of Bioethics," by Jeremy Rifkin, reprinted from *Algeny,* edited by Writers
and Artists Agency, 1983, Foundation on Economic Trends.

the environment. And I certainly don't think you have to be a molecular biologist to be informed about the issues on genetic engineering and to speak out forcefully and passionately and intelligently on those issues.

Darwin's world was populated by machine-like automata. Nature was conceived as an aggregate of standardized, interchangeable parts assembled into various functional combinations. If one were to ascribe any overall purpose to the entire operation, it would probably be that of increased production and greater efficiency with no particular end in mind.

The new temporal theory of evolution replaces the idea of life as mere machinery with the idea of life as mere information. By resolving structure into function and reducing function to information flows, the new cosmology all but eliminates any remaining sense of species identification. Living things are no longer perceived as carrots and peas, as foxes and hens, but as bundles of information. All living things are drained of their aliveness and turned into abstract messages. Life becomes a code to be deciphered. There is no longer any question of sacredness and inviolability. How could there be when there are no longer any recognizable boundaries to respect? Under the new temporal theory, structure is abandoned. Nothing exists at the moment. Everything is pure activity, pure process. How can any living thing be deemed sacred when it is just a pattern of information?

By eliminating structural boundaries and reducing all living things to information exchanges and flows, the new cosmology provides the proper degree of desacralization for the bioengineering of life. After all, in order to justify the engineering of living material across biological boundaries, it is first necessary to desacralize the whole idea of an organism as an identifiable, discrete structure with a permanent set of attributes. In the age of biotechnology, separate species with separate names gradually give way to systems of information that can be reprogrammed into an infinite number of biological combinations. It is much easier for the human mind to accept the idea of engineering a system of information than it is for it to accept the idea of engineering a dog. It is easier still, once one has fully internalized the notion that there is really no such thing as a dog in the traditional sense. In the coming age it will be much more accurate to describe a dog as a very specific pattern of information unfolding over a specific period of time.

Life as information flow represents the final desacralization of nature. Conveniently, humanity has eliminated the idea of fixed biological borders and reduced matter to energy and energy to information in its cosmological thinking right at the very time that bioengineers are preparing to cut across species boundaries in the living world.

THE NEW ETHICS

Civilization is experiencing the euphoric first moments of the next age of history. The media are already treating us to glimpses of a future where the engineering of life by design will be standard operating procedure. Even as the corporate laboratories begin to dribble out the first products of bioengineering, a subtle shift in the ethical impulse of society is becoming perceptible to the naked eye. As we begin to reprogram life, our moral code is being similarly reprogrammed to reflect this profound change in the way humanity goes about organizing the world. A new ethics is being engineered, and its operating assumptions comport nicely with the activity taking place in the biology laboratories.

Eugenics is the inseparable ethical wing of the age of biotechnology. First coined by Charles Darwin's cousin Sir Francis Galton, eugenics is generally categorized in two ways, negative and positive. Negative eugenics involves the systematic elimination of so-called biologically undesirable characteristics. Positive eugenics is concerned with the use of genetic manipulation to "improve" the characteristics of an organism or species.

Eugenics is not a new phenomenon. At the turn of the century the United States sported a massive eugenics movement. Politicians, celebrities, academicians, and prominent business leaders joined together in support of a eugenics program for the country. The frenzy over eugenics reached a fever pitch, with many states passing sterilization statues and the U.S. Congress passing a new immigration law in the 1920s based on eugenics considerations. As a consequence of the new legislation, thousands of American citizens were sterilized so they could not pass on their "inferior" traits, and the federal government locked its doors to certain immigrant groups deemed biologically unfit by then-existing eugenics standards.

While the Americans flirted with eugenics for the first thirty years of the twentieth century, their escapades were of minor historical account when compared with the eugenics program orchestrated by the Nazis in the 1930s and '40s. Millions of Jews and other religious and ethnic groups were gassed in the German crematoriums to advance the Third Reich's dream of eliminating all but the "Aryan" race from the globe. The Nazis also embarked on a "positive" eugenics program in which thousands of S.S. officers and German women were carefully selected for their "superior" genes and mated under the auspices of the state. Impregnated women were cared for in state facilities, and their offspring were donated to the Third Reich as the vanguard of the new super race that would rule the world for the next millennium.

Eugenics lay dormant for nearly quarter of a century after World War II. Then the spectacular breakthroughs in molecular biology in the 1960s raised the specter of a eugenics revival once again. By the mid-1970s, many scientists were beginning to worry out loud that the potential for genetic engineering might lead to a return to the kind of eugenics hysteria that had swept over America and Europe earlier in the century. Speaking at a National Academy of Science forum on recombinant DNA, Ethan Signer, a biologist at M.I.T., warned his colleagues that

> this research is going to bring us one more step closer to genetic engineering of people. That's where they figure out how to have us produce children with ideal characteristics. . . . The last time around, the ideal children had blond hair, blue eyes and Aryan genes.

The concern over a re-emergence of eugenics is well founded but misplaced. While professional ethicists watch out the front door for telltale signs of a resurrection of the Nazi nightmare, eugenics doctrine has quietly slipped in the back door and is already stealthily at work reorganizing the ethical priorities of the human household. Virtually overnight, eugenics doctrine has gained an impressive if not an impregnable foothold in the popular culture.

Its successful implantation into the psychic life of civilization is attributable to its going largely unrecognized in its new guise. The new eugenics is commercial, not social. In place of the shrill eugenic cries for racial purity, the new commercial eugenics talks in pragmatic terms of increased economic efficiency, better performance standards, and improvement in the quality of life. The old eugenics was steeped in political ideology and motivated by fear and hate. The new eugenics is grounded in economic considerations and stimulated by utilitarianism and financial gain.

Like the ethics of the Darwinian era, the new commercial eugenics associates the idea of "doing good" with the idea of "increasing efficiency." The difference is that increasing efficiency in the age of biotechnology is achieved by way of engineering living organisms. Therefore, "good" is defined as the engineering of life to improve its performance. In contrast, not to improve the performance of a living organism whenever technically possible is considered tantamount to committing a sin.

For example, consider the hypothetical case of a prospective mother faced with the choice of programming the genetic characteristics of her child at conception. Let's assume the mother chooses not to have the fertilized egg programmed. The fetus develops naturally, the baby is born, the child grows up, and in her early teenage years discovers that she has a rare genetic disease that will lead to a premature and painful death. The mother could have avoided the calamity by having that defective genetic trait eliminated from the fertilized egg, but she chose not to. In the age of biotechnology, her choice not to intervene might well constitute a crime for which she might be punished. At the least, her refusal to allow the fetus to be programmed would be considered a morally reprehensible and irresponsible decision unbefitting a mother, whose duty it is always to provide as best she can for her child's future well-being.

Proponents of human genetic engineering contend that it would be irresponsible not to use this powerful new technology to eliminate serious "genetic disorders." The problem with this argument, says the *New York Times* in an editorial entitled "Whether to Make Perfect Humans," is that "there is no discernible line to be drawn between making inheritable repairs to genetic defects, and improving the species." The *Times* rightly points out that once scientists are able to repair genetic defects, "it will become much harder to argue against adding genes that confer desired qualities, like better health, looks or brains."

Once we decide to begin the process of human genetic engineering, there is really no logical place to stop. If diabetes, sickle cell anemia, and cancer are to be cured by altering the genetic makeup of an individual, why not proceed to other "disorders"; myopia, color blindness, left-handedness? Indeed, what is to preclude a society from deciding that a certain skin color is a disorder?

As knowledge about genes increases, the bioengineers will inevitably gain new insights into the functioning of more complex characteristics, such as those associated with behavior and thoughts. Many scientists are already contending that schizophrenia and other "abnormal" psychological states result from genetic disorders or defects. Others now argue that "antisocial" behavior, such as criminality and social protest, are also examples of malfunctioning genetic information. One prominent neurophysiologist has gone so far as to say, "There can be no twisted thought without a twisted molecule." Many sociobiologists contend virtually all human activity is in some way determined by our genetic makeup, and that if we wish to change this situation, we must change our genes.

Whenever we begin to discuss the idea of genetic defects, there is no way to limit the discussion to one or two or even a dozen so-called disorders, because of a hidden assumption that lies behind the very notion of "defective." Ethicist Daniel Callahan penetrates to the core of the problem when he observes that "behind the human horror at genetic defectiveness lurks . . . an image of the perfect human being. The very language of 'defect,' 'abnormality,' 'disease,' and 'risk,' presupposes such an image, a kind of proto-type of perfection."

The idea of engineering the human species is very similar to the idea of engineering a piece of machinery. An engineer is constantly in search of new ways to improve the performance of a machine. As soon as one set of imperfections is eliminated, the engineer immediately turns his attention to the next set of imperfections, always with the idea in mind of creating a perfect piece of machinery. Engineering is a process of continual improvement in the performance of a piece of machinery, and the idea of setting arbitrary limits to how much "improvement" is acceptable is alien to the entire engineering conception.

The question, then, is whether or not humanity should "begin" the process of engineering future generations of human beings by technological design in the laboratory. What is the price we pay for embarking on a course whose final goal is the "perfection" of the human species? How important is it that we eliminate all the imperfections, all the defects? What price are we willing to pay to extend our lives, to ensure our own health, to do away with all the inconveniences, the irritations, the nuisances, the infirmities, the suffering, that are so much a part of the human experience? Are we so enamored with the idea of physical perpetuation at all costs that we are even willing to subject the human species to rigid architectural design?

With human genetic engineering, we get something and we give up something. In return for securing our own physical well-being we are forced to accept the idea of reducing the human species to a technologically designed product. Genetic engineering poses the most fundamental of questions. Is guaranteeing our health worth trading away our humanity?

People are forever devising new ways of organizing the environment in order to secure their future. Ethics, in turn, serves to legitimize the drive for self-perpetuation. Any organizing activity that a society deems to be helpful in securing its future is automatically blessed, and any activity that undermines the mode of organization a society uses to secure its future is automatically damned. The age of bioengineering brooks no exception. In the years to come a multitude of new bioengineering products will be forthcoming. Every one of the breakthroughs in bioengineering will be of benefit to someone, under some circumstances, somewhere in society. Each will in some way appear to advance the future security of an individual, a group, or society as a whole. Eliminating a defective gene trait so that a child won't die prematurely; engineering a new cereal crop that can feed an expanding population; developing a new biological source of energy that can fill the vacuum as the oil spigot runs dry. Every one of these advances provides a modicum of security against the vagaries of the future. To forbid their development and reject their application will be considered ethically irresponsible and inexcusable.

Bioengineering is coming to us not as a threat but as a promise; not as a punishment but as a gift. We have already come to the conclusion that bioengineering is a boon for humanity. The thought of engineering living organisms no longer conjures up sinister images. What we see before our eyes are not monstrosities but useful products. We no longer feel dread but only elated expectation at the great possibilities that lie in store for each of us.

How could engineering life be considered bad when it produces such great benefits? Engineering living tissue is no longer a question of great ethical import. The human psyche has been won over to eugenics with little need of discussion or debate. We have already been convinced of the good that can come from engineering life by learning of the helpful products it is likely to spawn.

As in the past, humanity's incessant need to control the future in order to secure its own well-being is already dictating the ethics of the age of biotechnology. Engineering life to improve humanity's own prospects for survival will be ennobled as the highest expression of ethical behavior. Any resistance to the new technology will be castigated as inhuman, irresponsible, morally reprehensible, and criminally culpable.

Prologue

Philip Roth

Philip Roth was born (in 1933) and raised in Newark, New Jersey. He began writing for literary magazines while studying for a Ph.D. in English at the University of Chicago. His first published work was a collection of short stories entitled Goodbye Columbus *(1959). Since then, Roth has written and published numerous novels among which* Portnoy's Complaint *(1969),* The Great American Novel *(1973), the trilogy* Zuckerman Bound *(1985), and* I Married a Communist *(1998). The following is the Prologue to his autobiographical book* Patrimony *(1994).*

One day in late October 1944, I was astonished to find my father, whose workday ordinarily began at seven and many nights didn't end until ten, sitting alone at the kitchen table in the middle of the afternoon. He was going into the hospital unexpectedly to have his appendix removed. Though he had already packed a bag to take with him, he had waited for my brother, Sandy, and me to get home from school to tell us not to be alarmed. "Nothing to it," he assured us, though we all knew that two of his brothers had died back in the 1920s from complications following difficult appendectomies. My mother, the president that year of our school's parent-teacher association, happened, quite unusually, to be away overnight in Atlantic City at a statewide PTA convention. My father had phoned her hotel, however, to tell her the news, and she had immediately begun preparations to return home. That would do it, I was sure: my mother's domestic ingenuity was on a par with Robinson Crusoe's, and as for nursing us all through our illnesses, we couldn't have received much better care from Florence Nightingale. As was usual in our household, everything was now under control.

"Prologue," by Phillip Roth, reprinted from *The Facts: A Novelist's Autobiography*, 1988, Farrar, Strauss & Giroux.

By the time her train pulled into Newark that evening, the surgeon had opened him up, seen the mess, and despaired for my father's chances. At the age of forty-three, he was put on the critical list and given less than a fifty-fifty chance to survive.

Only the adults knew how bad things were. Sandy and I were allowed to go on believing that a father was indestructible—and ours turned out to be just that. Despite a raw emotional nature that makes him prey to intractable worry, his life has been distinguished by the power of resurgence. I've never intimately known anyone else— aside from my brother and me—to swing as swiftly through so wide a range of moods, anyone else to take things so hard, to be so openly racked by a serious setback, and yet, after the blow has reverberated down to the quick, to clamber back so aggressively, to recover lost ground and get going again.

He was saved by the new sulfa powder, developed during the early years of the war to treat battlefront wounds. Surviving was an awful ordeal nonetheless, his weakness from the near-fatal peritonitis exacerbated by a ten-day siege of hiccups during which he was unable to sleep or to keep down food. After he'd lost nearly thirty pounds, his shrunken face disclosed itself to us as a replica of my elderly grandmother's, the face of the mother whom he and all his brothers adored (toward the father—laconic, authoritarian, remote, an immigrant who'd trained in Galicia to be a rabbi but worked in America in a hat factory—their feelings were more confused). Bertha Zahnstecker Roth was a simple old-country woman, good-hearted, given to neither melancholy nor complaint, yet her everyday facial expression made it plain that she nursed no illusions about life's being easy. My father's resemblance to his mother would not appear so eerily again until he himself reached his eighties, and then only when he was in the grip of a struggle that stripped an otherwise physically youthful old man of his seeming impregnability, leaving him bewildered not so much because of the eye problem or the difficulty with his gait that had made serious inroads on his self-sufficiency but because he felt all at once abandoned by that masterful accomplice and overturner of obstacles, his determination.

When he was driven home from Newark's Beth Israel Hospital after six weeks in bed there, he barely had the strength, even with our assistance, to make it up the short back staircase to our second-story apartment. It was December 1944 by then, a cold winter day, but through the windows the sunlight illuminated my parents' bedroom. Sandy and I came in to talk to him, both of us shy and grateful and, of course, stunned by how helpless he appeared seated weakly in a lone chair in the corner of the room. Seeing his sons together like that, my father could no longer control himself and began to sob. He was alive, the sun was shining, his wife was not widowed nor his boys fatherless—family life would now resume. It was not so complicated that an eleven-year-old couldn't understand his father's tears. I just didn't see, as he so clearly could, why or how it should have turned out differently.

I knew only two boys in our neighborhood whose families were fatherless, and thought of them as no less blighted than the blind girl who attended our school for a while and had to be read to and shepherded everywhere. The fatherless boys seemed almost equally marked and set apart; in the aftermath of their fathers' deaths, they too struck me as scary and a little taboo. Though one was a model of obedience and the other a troublemaker, everything either of them did or said seemed determined by his being a boy with a dead father and, however innocently I arrived at this notion, I was probably right.

I knew no child whose family was divided by divorce. Outside of the movie magazines and the tabloid headlines, it didn't exist, certainly not among Jews like us. Jews didn't get divorced—not because divorce was forbidden by Jewish law but because that was the way they were. If Jewish fathers didn't come home drunk and beat their wives—and in our neighborhood, which was Jewry to me, I'd never heard of any who did—that too was because of the way they were. In our lore, the Jewish family was an inviolate haven against every form of menace, from personal isolation to gentile hostility. Regardless of internal friction and strife, it was assumed to be an indissoluble consolidation. *Hear, O Israel, the family is God, the family is One.*

Family indivisibility, the first commandment.

In the late 1940s, when my father's younger brother, Bernie, proclaimed his intention of divorcing the wife of nearly twenty years who was the mother of his two daughters, my mother and father were as stunned as if they'd heard that he'd killed somebody. Had Bernie committed murder and gone to jail for life, they would probably have rallied behind him despite the abominable, inexplicable deed. But when he made up his mind not merely to divorce but to do so to marry a younger woman, their support went instantly to the "victims," the sister-in-law and the nieces. For his transgression, a breach of faith with his wife, his children, his entire clan—a dereliction of his duty as a Jew *and* as a Roth—Bernie encountered virtually universal condemnation.

That family rupture only began to mend when time revealed that no one had been destroyed by the divorce; in fact, anguished as they were by the breakup of their household, Bernie's ex-wife and his two girls were never remotely as indignant as the rest of the relatives. The healing owed a lot to Bernie himself, a more diplomatic man than most of his judges, but also to the fact that for my father the demands of family solidarity and the bond of family history exceeded even *his* admonishing instincts. It was to be another forty-odd years, however, before the two brothers threw their arms around each other and hungrily embraced in an unmistakable act of unqualified reconciliation. This occurred a few weeks before Bernie's death, in his late seventies, when his heart was failing rapidly and nobody, beginning with himself, expected him to last much longer.

I had driven my father over to see Bernie and his wife, Ruth, in their condominium in a retirement village in northwestern Connecticut, twenty miles from my own home. It was Bernie's turn now to wear the little face of his unillusioned, stoical old mother; when he came to the door to let us in, there in his features was that stark resemblance that seemed to emerge in all the Roth brothers when they were up against it.

Ordinarily the two men would have met with a handshake, but when my father stepped into the hallway, so much was clear both about the time that was left to Bernie and about all those decades, seemingly stretching back to the beginning of time, during which they had been alive as their parents' offspring, that the handshake was swallowed up in a forceful hug that lasted minutes and left them in tears. They seemed to be saying goodbye to everyone already gone as well as to each other, the last two surviving children of the dour hatblocker Sender and the imperturbable *balabusta* Bertha. Safely in his brother's arms, Bernie seemed also to be saying goodbye to himself. There was nothing to guard against or defend against or resent anymore, nothing even to remember. In these brothers, men so deeply swayed, despite their dissimilarity, by identical strains of family emotion, everything remembered had been distilled into pure, barely bearable feeling.

In the car afterward my father said, "We haven't held each other like that since we were small boys. My brother's dying, Philip. I used to push him around in his carriage. There were nine of us, with my mother and father. I'll be the last one left."

While we drove back to my house (where he was staying in the upstairs back bedroom, a room in which he says he never fails to sleep like a baby) he recounted the struggles of each of his five brothers—with bankruptcies, illnesses, and in-laws, with marital dissension and bad loans, and with children, with their Gonerils, their Regans, and their Cordelias. He recalled for me the martyrdom of his only sister, what she and all the family had gone through when her husband the bookkeeper who liked the horses had served a little time for embezzlement.

It wasn't exactly the first time I was hearing these stories. Narrative is the form that his knowledge takes, and his repertoire has never been large: family, family, family, Newark, Newark, Newark, Jew, Jew, Jew. Somewhat like mine.

I naïvely believed as a child that I would always have a father present, and the truth seems to be that I always will. However awkward the union may sometimes have been, vulnerable to differences of opinion, to false expectations, to radically divergent experiences of America, strained by the colliding of two impatient, equally willful temperaments and marred by masculine clumsiness, the link to him has been omnipresent. What's more, now, when he no longer commands my attention by his bulging biceps and his moral strictures, now, when he is no longer the biggest man I have to contend with—and when I am not all that far from being an old man myself—I am able to laugh at his jokes and hold his hand and concern myself with his well-being, I'm able to love him the way I wanted to when I was sixteen, seventeen, and eighteen but when, what with dealing with him and feeling at odds with him, it was simply an impossibility. *The* impossibility, for all that I always respected him for his particular burden and his struggle within a system that he didn't choose. The mythological role of a Jewish boy growing up in a family like mine—to become the hero one's father failed to be—I may even have achieved by now, but not at all in the way that was preordained. After nearly forty years of living far from home, I'm equipped at last to be the most loving of sons—just, however, when he has another agenda. He is trying to die. He doesn't say that, nor, probably, does he think of it in those words, but that's his job now and, fight as he will to survive, he understands, as he always has, what the real work is.

Trying to die isn't like trying to commit suicide—it may actually be harder, because what you are trying to do is what you least want to have happen; you dread it but there it is and it must be done, and by no one but you. Twice in the last few years

251

he has taken a shot at it, on two different occasions suddenly became so ill that I, who was then living abroad half the year, flew back to America to find him with barely enough strength to walk from the sofa to the TV set without clutching at every chair in between. And though each time the doctor, after a painstaking examination, was unable to find anything wrong with him, he nonetheless went to bed every night expecting not to awaken in the morning and, when he did awaken in the morning, he was fifteen minutes just getting himself into a sitting position on the edge of the bed and another hour shaving and dressing. Then, for God knows how long, he slouched unmoving over a bowl of cereal for which he had absolutely no appetite.

I was as certain as he was that this was it, yet neither time could he pull it off and, over a period of weeks, he recovered his strength and became himself again, loathing Reagan, defending Israel, phoning relatives, attending funerals, writing to newspapers, castigating William Buckley, watching MacNeil-Lehrer, exhorting his grown grandchildren, remembering in detail our own dead, and relentlessly, exactingly—and without having been asked—monitoring the caloric intake of the nice woman he lives with. It would seem that to prevail here, to try dying and to *do* it, he will have to work even harder than he did in the insurance business where he achieved a remarkable success for a man with his social and educational handicaps. Of course, here too he'll eventually succeed—though clearly, despite his record of assiduous application to every job he has ever been assigned, things won't be easy. But then they never have been.

Needless to say, the link to my father was never so voluptuously tangible as the colossal bond to my mother's flesh, whose metamorphosed incarnation was a sleek black sealskin coat into which I, the younger, the privileged, the pampered papoose, blissfully wormed myself whenever my father chauffeured us home to New Jersey on a winter Sunday from our semiannual excursion to Radio City Music Hall and Manhattan's Chinatown: the unnameable animal-me bearing her dead father's name, the protoplasm-me, boy-baby, and body-burrower-in-training, joined by every nerve ending to her smile and her sealskin coat, while his resolute dutifulness, his relentless industriousness, his unreasoning obstinacy and harsh resentments, his illusions, his innocence, his allegiances, his fears were to constitute the original mold for the American, Jew, citizen, man, even for the writer, I would become. To be at all is to be her Philip, but in the embroilment with the buffeting world, my history still takes its spin from beginning as his Roth.

252

Simplicity

Scott Russell Sanders

Scott Russell Sanders teaches at Indiana University and lives in Bloomington, Indiana with his wife and two children. He has written many books of both fiction and nonfiction. The Paradise of Bombs, *a book of personal essays, won the Associated Writing Programs Award for Creative Nonfiction. He also won a Lannan Literary Award in 1995 and the Great Lakes Book Award in 1996.*

Too many things, too little time,
too many obligations? Sometimes
The best solution is just to let go.

On our last night in Rocky Mountain National Park, after a week of backpacking near the continental divide, my son, Jesse, and I sat on a granite ledge overlooking a creek just below our campsite. The water crashed through a jumble of boulders, churning up an icy mist and turning the current whiter than the surrounding snow.

Though it was June, glacial air poured down the creek from snowfields higher up. I pulled up the hood of my jacket, stuffed hands into pockets and hunkered down to soak in the spray. Still I trembled. I couldn't tell whether my shivering was from the cold or from the spell of moving water.

After a while, Jesse murmured, "This is a good place."

"It is."

In the waning light, the trees along the banks merged into a velvety blackness, and the froth of the creek shone like the Milky Way. Waves rose from the current, fleeting shapes that would eventually dissolve—like my own body, like the mountains, like the earth and the stars. I blinked at my son, who rode the same current. Our time in the mountains had left me feeling cleansed and clarified.

The spell of the high country began to evaporate as soon as we climbed into our rental car at the trailhead the next day. The ignition key, the steering wheel, and the sun-fried upholstery chafed my skin; the thrum of pavement under the wheels and the press of traffic hustling into Denver chafed my brain. Everything moved too fast. The car felt like a cage on wheels, hurtling along against a backdrop of dry plains and snowcapped peaks.

Never one to stare at scenery through windows, my son dived into his book, and he said scarcely a word until we reached the motel. At 17 and 49, both of us moody, Jesse and I had learned that keeping quiet was less wearisome than shouting at each other. We'd quarreled at the start of our trip, but the mountains had soon calmed us, and we had made peace. In the morning we would fly home to Indiana, streaking along at 500 miles an hour.

The truce between Jesse and me also began to evaporate as soon as we returned to the land of electricity, money, and clocks. His first act on entering our motel room was to switch on the television, and the sound of it was like a file scraping my nerves. "Does that have to be so loud?" I snapped.

"If you want it off, why don't you say so?" He jabbed the remote control, and the picture blinked out. "It's all trash anyhow."

I didn't argue, because I could feel tension rising between us like the onset of fever. Now that we'd left the trail, I was in charge once more of budget and schedule, and that alone would have irked him. Back in the city, where much of what I saw struck me as wasteful, ugly, or mad, I was also prone to the ranting and lamentation that so disturbed Jesse. In our quarrels he had accused me of casting a shadow over his life, because my grief over the fate of the earth filled him with despair. For his sake, I would have to find a way back through this confusion to the sanity I had felt in the mountains.

From our window I could see, beyond a thicket of billboards, the Rockies glowing serenely in the last light. While I stood watching, Jesse came to join me.

He gazed quietly, then let out a deep breath. "It's hard to believe we were up there only this morning."

"It does seem a long way," I agreed. I wanted to embrace him, the mountains, the light. But he soon backed away, and we both set about sorting our gear. To still the panic I was feeling from the crush of the city, I summoned up an image from the mountains: my green poncho spread on the ground, with everything I needed to live in the wild—food, fuel, water, clothes, tent, sleeping bag, tools—covering no more than a quarter of the fabric. I carried that image with me into sleep.

Whenever I return from a sojourn in the woods or waters or mountains, I'm dismayed by the noise and jumble of the workaday world. One moment I can lay everything I need on the corner of a poncho, tally my responsibilities on the fingers of one hand. The next moment, it seems, I couldn't fit all my furniture and tasks into a warehouse. Time in the wild, like time in meditation, reminds me how much of what I ordinarily do is mere dithering, how much of what I own is mere encumbrance. Coming home, I can see there are too many appliances in my cupboards, too many clothes in my closet, too many files in my drawers, too many strings of duty jerking me in too many directions. The opposite of simplicity, as I understand it, is not complexity but clutter.

Returning from a back-country trip, I yearn to pare my life down to essentials. I vow to live more simply, by purchasing nothing that I don't really need, giving away everything that is excess, refusing all chores that don't arise from my central concerns. I make room for silence. I avoid television, with its blaring novelties, and advertising, with its phony bait. I go about town on bicycle or foot. I resolve to slow down and savor each moment, instead of always rushing on into the future.

The simplicity I seek is not the enforced austerity of the poor. I seek instead the richness of a gathered and deliberate life, the richness that comes from letting one's belongings and commitments be few in number and high in quality. I aim to preserve, in my ordinary days, the lightness and purpose I've discovered on my clarifying journeys.

As our plane banked after takeoff, we caught one last glimpse of the Front Range shining to the west.

I pressed my cheek against the window. Viewed from the air, Denver seemed to be blundering outward in every direction, flinging subdivisions and strip malls and roads into the foothills and plains. No doubt many who lived there felt the city was already large enough. But more people were eagerly joining the sprawl or making fortunes from it, and who was going to stop them? Like other American cities, Denver swells on a blind faith in abundance, a faith that there will always be enough water and land and metal and wood, and that oil will always be cheap. While I reflected on the folly of this addiction to growth, cheap oil carried Jesse and me home toward Indiana.

Except for the patchwork of irrigated fields and the green tendrils of waterways, the shortgrass steppes of Colorado were the color of pancakes. In these arid lands, the drainage patterns branching down from the hills were as clear as the seams on an outdoor face. In western Nebraska and Kansas we began seeing vast circular fields defined by pivoting irrigation equipment. Set within the grid of section lines, they looked like solar arrays, turning sunlight into beans or wheat. But they were clumsy by comparison to the grass that once flourished there, without fertilizers or pesticides or pumps.

From the air, Missouri and Illinois and Indiana appeared more densely patterned, the rectangles of farms and the patches of woods carved up by housing developments and highways. Buildings clung to the roads, huddled into clumps to form towns, piled into great drifts to make cities. Roads and rails and powerlines bound settlement to settlement, a net flung over the land.

Gazing down on all of this from six miles in the air, I realized that nothing will prevent us from expanding our human numbers and extending our sway over every last inch of earth—nothing except outward disaster or inward conversion. Since I couldn't root for disaster, I would have to work for a change of heart and mind. The word that came to me was *restraint.* If we hope to survive on this planet, if we wish to leave breathing room for other creatures, we must learn restraint. We need not merely to will it but to desire it, to say "Enough!" with relish and conviction.

But how are we to achieve restraint when we seem mindlessly devoted to growth? Like birds and bees and bacteria, we yearn to propagate our kind. Nothing could be more natural. We're unusual among species only in being able to escape, for the short run, the natural constraints on our population or appetites, and in being able to magnify our hungers through the lens of technology.

It seems that our evolutionary history has shaped us to equate well-being with increase, to yearn not merely for more offspring but more of everything, more shoes and meat and horsepower and loot. In a hunting and gathering society, the fruits of an individual's search for more food, better tools, and richer land were shared with the tribe. The more relentless the search, the more likely the tribe would flourish. As a result of that history, observes anthropologist Lionel Tiger, "We are calculating organisms exquisitely equipped to desire more and truculent and grim about enduring less."

How much any group can accumulate or use is limited, of course, by its level of technology. Hunters on foot armed with stone-tipped weapons can wipe out woolly mammoths and giant beavers; they can open up grasslands by burning; they can alter the mix of plants in their home territory; but they can't turn a mountain inside out in search of glittering metal or erase a forest or poison the sea. The harnessing of mechanical power dramatically increased our ability to make the world over to suit ourselves; the rise of towns enabled us to pile up wealth, since we no longer had to haul it from campsite to campsite. I suspect that we're no more greedy than our ancestors, no more eager for comfort, only far more potent in pursuing our desires.

The constant hankering for more, which served hunting and gathering peoples well, has become a menace in this age of clever machines and burgeoning populations. Our devotion to growth endangers the planet, by exhausting resources and accelerating pollution and driving other species to extinction; it upsets community, by swelling the scale of institutions and settlements beyond reach of our understanding; and it harms the individual, by encouraging a scramble for possessions and a nagging discontent even in the midst of plenty.

What are we poor ravenous creatures to do? We may keep riding the exponential curves higher and higher on every graph—widgets produced, oil burned, hamburgers sold, acres paved, trees felled, babies born—until nature jerks us back toward the zero point. Or we may choose to live more simply and conservingly, and therefore more sustainably. I doubt that there's anything in our biology to lead us onto the saner, milder path. Biology, I'm afraid, is on the side of gluttony and compulsive growth. If we are to achieve restraint, it will have to come from culture, that shared conversation by which we govern our appetites. Just as our short-term ability to ignore the constraints of nature distinguishes us from other species, so we're also distinguished by the ability to impose limits on ourselves through reason and ritual and mindfulness.

As I write, National Public Radio carries a report about the culling of elephants in a South African park. Animal rights activists protest the killing, but rangers insist that the elephants have multiplied beyond the land's carrying capacity. They are devastating the park: uprooting trees, trampling vegetation, exposing soil to erosion. In the absence of predators, beavers also can devastate a woods, and deer can graze fragile plants beyond the point of recovery. These animals possess no inborn curb to prevent them from destroying their own habitat. The growth of their population is checked only by the supply of water or food, by predators, or by disease.

Many anthropologists now believe that early humans behaved much like elephants and beavers and deer, degrading one habitat after another, then moving on. As our ancestors spread over the globe, they left deserts and the bones of extinct species in their wake. North America is dotted with sites of ancient social experiments that failed, from the Maya to the mound builders. Even now some indigenous peoples in the rainforests of Asia and South America pursue slash-and-burn agriculture at a pace that the forests cannot sustain. Such evidence suggests that the ecological wisdom surviving today in traditional cultures had to be learned over long periods of time, through trial and error. Only gradually did humans, here and there, develop cultural practices—stories and taboos, methods of birth control, rituals for hunting, rules about the use of common land—that curbed our instinct to follow hunger wherever it leads.

The capacity for restraint based on knowledge and compassion is a genuine source of hope, though an embattled one. Whenever the Environmental Protection Agency proposes higher standards for emissions from smokestacks and cars, for example, critics attack the standards as too expensive, claiming that the richest country in the world can't afford to pay the real price of energy, nor to cut back on the use of electricity and gasoline in exchange for breathable air. You can see the pattern repeated in debates over offshore drilling, the cutting of old-growth timber, the draining of wetlands, the release of greenhouse gases, and the building of new highways. For every voice that echoes Thoreau's famous plea, "Simplify, simplify," a dozen cry, "Amplify, amplify!"

The present scale of human destructiveness is unprecedented, but the impulse to eat whatever's within reach is entirely natural. Although it may be channeled, it can't be eradicated. What is unnatural, what comes only from culture, is reflection and a regard for other forms of life. We're the only species capable of acting, through love and reason, to preserve our fellow creatures.

If our addiction to growth is rooted in evolutionary history, we can't just decide to feel good about living with less. We can, however, shift the focus of our expansive desires. We can change the standard by which we measure prosperity. We can choose to lead a materially simpler life not as a sacrifice but as a path toward fulfillment. In ancient terms, we can learn to seek spiritual rather than material growth.

Meditation, contemplation, pilgrimage, and other forms of religious inquiry are only part of what I mean by *spiritual.* I also mean the nourishment that comes to us through art, literature, and science, through conversation, through skillful and useful work, through the sharing of bread and stories, through encounters with beauty and wildness. I mean a slowing down and focusing on the present moment, with its inexhaustible depths, rather than a dashing through life toward some ever-retreating goal.

If we imagine that the fullness we yearn for can be reckoned in dollars or yen, if we imagine it can be purchased in stores, then there will be no end to our craving. Every time we jump in the car merely for the sake of motion, every time we browse the aisles of stores without needing a thing, or switch on the television to banish silence, or surf the Net for distraction, or pump ourselves full of chemicals in search of a jolt, we are hunting for a freshness that we're far more likely to find in the place from which we set out, had we but eyes to see.

We could cut back dramatically on our consumption of food and fuel, our use of wood and metal, and the size of our houses and wardrobes without suffering any deprivation. We could free this surplus for others to use, now and in the future, and free ourselves from the burden of lugging it around. Just as we run ourselves ragged by chasing after too many thrills and tasks, so we may become centered and calm by remaining faithful to a few deep concerns. As we increase the likelihood of strife by scrambling for more wealth, so we may increase the likelihood of peace by living modestly and sharing what we have. Thus our needs and the needs of the planet coincide.

Less burdened by possessions, less frenzied by activities, we might play more with our children, look after our elders, plant flowers, read books, make music, come to know the local birds and rocks and trees. We might take better care of the land. We might lie down at night and rise up in the morning without feeling the cramp of anxiety. Instead of leaping around like grasshoppers from notion to notion, we might sit still and think in a connected way about our families, our communities, and the meaning of life.

For days after reaching home from the Rockies, I felt oppressed by the glut of things. My desk was mounded with mail. My floor was littered with unopened parcels. Lights blinked on the answering machine, and messages lurked in the computer. Family and friends, students and colleagues, neighbors and strangers marked my return by calling for help. Meanwhile, the kitchen faucet had sprung a leak, the car's engine was tapping ominously, our wildflower patch had all but disappeared under a surf of weeds, and grass too high for our tired mower waved in the June sunshine. Despite my yearning for simplicity, the life to which I had returned was crowded with duties and demands.

"You don't have to do everything your first day home," my wife, Ruth, pointed out to me as I set to work with my usual fury. Even though I knew better, I kept imagining that if I could first answer every request, fix every broken thing, *then* I would simplify my life. But trying to catch up once and for all is like digging a hole in sand: No matter how fast you shovel, new sand keeps pouring in. Unable to make any headway, missing the mountains, missing the company of my son, who'd been caught up once more in his whirl of teenage friendships, I began to slide down the slope toward gloom.

Familiar with my moods from 30 years of marriage, Ruth kept an eye on me to make sure I didn't slide too far—and also to make sure I didn't throw out any crucial mail or junk the car or put up a FOR SALE sign in the front yard.

One evening that first week home, friends called to invite us out to their farm for a look at the stars. Ruth covered the mouthpiece on the phone and told me she thought it would be a shame to squander this clear night.

"I've got too much work to do," I told her, pausing on my way upstairs with an armload of papers. Ruth looked at me hard, then said into the phone, "We'll be there in half an hour."

On our drive into the country, whenever I began to speak about fixing the car or balancing the checkbook, Ruth asked me about my time in the Rockies. So I told her of snowshoeing with Jesse up into avalanche country, of laying out all my gear on a corner of the poncho, of meeting hummingbird and coyote and elk, of watching sunlight pour through lodgepole pines, of listening all night to a creek. By the time we rolled down the gravel drive to John and Beth's place, the mountain memories had steadied me. We could see our friends walking to meet us, their silhouettes tall and thin against a background of stars.

I climbed out of the car with a greeting on my lips, but the sky hushed me. From the black bowl of space countless fiery lights shone down, each one a sun or a swirl of suns, the whole brilliant host of them enough to strike me dumb. The Milky Way arced overhead, reminding me of froth glimmering on the dark surface of a mountain creek. I know the names of a dozen constellations and half a dozen of the brightest stars, but I wasn't thinking in words right then. I was too busy feeling brimful of joy, without need of any props except the universe. The deep night drew my scattered pieces back to the center, stripped away all clutter and weight, and set me free.

On Reading a Videotext

Robert Scholes

Robert Scholes is Andrew W. Melon Professor of Humanities at Brown University, based in the Department of Modern Cultures and Media. He teaches courses in modernism, modern literature, art, opera, and thought. Scholes has a Ph.D. from Cornell University and has written numerous academic books and articles on literature, theory, and the media. His most recent books are Protocols of Reading *(1989),* Hemingway's Genders *(1994) and* The Rise and Fall of English *(1998). Recently, Scholes has started experimenting with publishing on line, taking advantage of the possibility of including color pictures within his essays about painters. For the past several years, he has been working with the College Board, the ETS, the NCTE and a group of energetic and creative teachers to develop a new version of a final course in English for all high school students. This course is now being taught in programs all over the country. It is called Pacesetter English. "On Reading a Videotext" is an excerpt from* Protocols of Reading.

We must consider the rhetoric of video, because it is so powerful, so ubiquitous in our culture, and because it brings into play the temporal or narrative dimension of evaluative discourse in a very vivid manner. Appealing, as it does, to a wide audience, it will also provide an appropriate occasion to consider the relation of specific texts to the cultural codes against which they must be read.

The moments of surrender proposed to us by video texts come in many forms, but all involve a complex dynamic of power and pleasure. We are, for instance, offered a kind of power through the enhancement of our vision. Close-ups position us where we could never stand. Slow motion allows us an extraordinary penetration into the mechanics of movement, and, combined with music, lends a balletic grace to ordinary forms of locomotion. Filters and other devices cause us to see the world through jaundiced or rose-colored optics, coloring events with emotion more effectively than verbal pathetic fallacy and less obtrusively. These derangements of normal visual processing can be seen as either constraints or extensions of visual power—that is, as power over the viewer or as extensions of the viewer's own optical power, or both. Either way they offer us what is perhaps the greatest single virtue of art: change from the normal, a defense against the ever-present threat of boredom. Video texts, like all except the most utilitarian forms of textuality, are constructed upon a base of boredom, from which they promise us relief.

Visual fascination—and I have mentioned only a few of its obvious forms—is just one of the matrices of power and pleasure that are organized by video texts. Others include narrativity and what I should like to call, at least tentatively, cultural reinforcement. By narrativity, of course, I mean the pleasures and powers associated with the reception of stories presented in video texts. By cultural reinforcement, I mean the process through which video texts confirm viewers in their ideological positions and reassure them as to their membership in a collective cultural body. This function, which operates in the ethical-political realm, is an extremely important element of video textuality and, indeed, an extremely important dimension of all the mass media. This is a function performed throughout much of human history by literature and the other arts, but now, as the arts have become more estranged from their own culture and even opposed to it, the mass media have come to perform this role. What the epic poem did for ancient cultures, the romance for feudalism, and the novel for bourgeois society, the media—and especially television—now do for the commodified, bureaucratized world that is our present environment.

It is time, now, to look at these processes as they operate in some specific texts. Let us begin with a well-known Budweiser commercial, which tells—most frequently in a format of twenty-eight seconds, though a longer version also exists—the life story of a black man pursuing a career as a baseball umpire. In this brief period of time, we are given enough information to construct an entire life story—provided we have the cultural knowledge upon which this construction depends. The story we construct is that of a young man from the provinces, who gets his "big break," his chance to make it in the big city, to rise to the top of his profession. We see him working hard in the small-time, small-town atmosphere of the minor leagues, where the pace of events is slower and more relaxed that it is "at the top." He gets his chance for success—the voice-over narrator says, "In the minors you got to make all the calls, and then one day you *get* the call"—after which we see him face his first real test. He must call an important and "close" play correctly and then withstand the pressure of dispute, neither giving ground by changing his mind (which would be fatal) nor reacting too vigorously to the challenge of his call by an offended manager. His passing of this test and being accepted is presented through a later scene in a bar, in which the manager who had staged the protest "toasts" the umpire with a bottle of Budweiser beer, with a chorus in the background singing, "You keep America working. This Bud's for you." From this scene we conclude that the ump has now "made it" and will live happily ever after. From a few scenes, then, aided by the voice-over narration and a music track, we construct an entire life. How do we do this? We draw upon a storehouse of cultural information that extends from fairy tales and other basic narrative structures to knowledge about the game and business of baseball.

In processing a narrative text we actually construct the story, bringing a vast repertory of cultural knowledge to bear upon the text that we are contemplating. Our pleasure in the narrative is to some extent a constructive pleasure, based upon the sense of accomplishment we achieve by successfully completing this task. By "getting" the story, we prove our competence and demonstrate our membership in a cultural community. And what is the story that we "get"? It is the myth of America itself, of the racial melting pot, of upward mobility, of justice done without fear or favor. The corporate structure of baseball, with minor leagues offering a path for the talented to the celebrity and financial rewards of the majors, embodies values that we all possess, we Americans, as one of the deepest parts of our cultural heritage or ideology. It is, of course, on the playing field that talent triumphs most easily over racial or social barriers. Every year in baseball new faces arrive. Young men, having proved themselves in the minors, get their chance to perform at the highest level. Yale graduates and high-school dropouts who speak little or no English are judged equally by how well they hit, run, throw, and react to game situations. If baseball is still the national pastime, it is because in it our cherished myths materialize—or appear to materialize.

The commercial we are considering is especially interesting because it shows us a black man competing not with his body but with his mind, his judgment and his emotions, in a cruelly testing public arena. Americans who attend to sports are aware that black athletes are just beginning to find acceptance at certain "leadership" positions, such as quarterback in professional football, and that there is still an active scandal over the slender representation of blacks at baseball's managerial and corporate levels. The case of the black umpire reminds viewers of these problems, even as it suggests that here, too, talent will finally prevail. The system works, America works. We can take pride in this. The narrative reduces its story to the absolutely bare essentials, making a career turn, or seem to turn, on a single decision. The ump must make a close call, which will be fiercely contested by a manager who is deliberately testing him. This is a story of initiation, in that respect, an ordeal that the ump must meet successfully. The text ensures that we know this is a test, by showing us the manager plotting in his dugout, and it gives us a manager with one of those baseball faces (Irish? German?) that have the history of the game written on them. This is not just partisan versus impartial judge, it is old man against youth, and white against black. We root for the umpire because we want the system to work—not just baseball but the whole thing: America. For the story to work, of course, the ump must make the right call, and we must know it to be right. Here, the close-up and slow motion come into play—just as they would in a real instant replay—to let us see both how close the call is and that the umpire has indeed made the right call. The runner is out. The manager's charge from dugout is classic baseball protest, and the ump's self-control and slow walk away from the angry manager are gestures in a ritual we all know. That's right, we think, that's the way it's done. We know these moves the way the contemporaries of Aeschylus and Sophocles knew the myths upon which the Greek tragedies were based. Baseball is already a ritual, and a ritual we partake of mostly through the medium of television. The commercial has only to organize these images in a certain way to create a powerful narrative.

At the bar after the game, we are off stage, outside that ritual of baseball, but we are still in the world of myth. The manager salutes the ump with his tilted bottle of beer; the old man acknowledges that youth has passed its test. The sword on the shoulder of knighthood, the laying on of hands, the tilted Bud—all these are ritual gestures in the same narrative structure of initiation. To the extent that we have wanted this to happen we are gratified by this closing scene of the narrative text, and many things, as I have suggested, conspire to make us want this ending. We are dealing with an archetypal narrative that has been adjusted for maximum effect within a particular political and social context, and all this has been deployed with a technical skill in casting, directing, acting, photographing, and editing that is of a high order. It is very hard to resist the pleasure of this text, and we cannot accept the pleasure without, for the bewildering minute at least, also accepting the ideology that is so richly and closely entangled with the story that we construct from the video text. To accept the pleasure of this text is to believe that America works; and this is a comforting belief, itself a pleasure of an even higher order—for as long as we can maintain it. Does the text also sell Budweiser? This is something only market research (if you believe it) can tell. But it surely sells the American way first and then seeks to sell its brand of beer by establishing a metonymic connection between the product and the nation: a national beer for the national pastime.

An audience that can understand this commercial, successfully constructing the ump's story from the scenes represented in the text and the comments of the narrative voice, is an audience that understands narrative structure and has a significant amount of cultural knowledge as well, including both data (how baseball leagues are organized, for instance, and how the game is played) and myth (what constitutes success, for example, and what initiation is). At a time when critics such as William Bennett and E. D. Hirsch are bewailing our ignorance of culture, it is important to realize that many Americans are not without culture; they simply have a different culture from that of Bennett and Hirsch. What they really lack, for the most part, is any way of analyzing and criticizing the power of a text like the Budweiser commercial—not its power to sell beer, which is easily resisted, especially once you have tasted better beer—but its power to sell America. For the sort of analysis that I am suggesting, it is necessary to recover (as Eliot says) from the surrender to this text, and it is also necessary to have the tools of ideological criticism. Recovery, in fact, may depend upon critical analysis, which is why the analysis of video texts needs to be taught in all our schools.

Before moving on to the consideration of a more complex textual economy; we would do well to pause and consider the necessity of ideological criticism. One dimension of the conservative agenda for this country has been conspicuously anticritical. The proposals of William Bennett and E. D. Hirsch, for instance, different as they are in certain respects, are both recipes for the indoctrination of young people in certain cultural myths. The great books of past ages, in the eyes of Bennett, Hirsch, and Allan Bloom, are to be mythologized, turned into frozen monuments of Greatness in which our "cultural heritage" is embodied. This is precisely what Bloom does to Plato, for instance, turning the dialectical search for truth into a fixed recipe for "greatness of soul." The irony of this is that Plato can only die in this process. Plato's work can better be kept alive in our time by such irreverent critiques as that of Jacques Derrida, who takes Plato seriously as an opponent, which is to say, takes him dialectically. In this age of massive manipulation and disinformation, criticism is the only way we have of taking something seriously. The greatest patriots in our time will be those who explore our ideology critically, with particular attention to the gaps between mythology and practice. Above all, we must start with our most beloved icons, not the ones we profess allegiance to, but those that really have the power to move and shake us.

Regeneration Through Violence: The Language of the Myth

Richard Slotkin

Richard Slotkin, a Ph. D. from Brown University, teaches interdisciplinary courses on American culture, literature, film, and history. He recently completed the last volume of a trilogy on the American myth of the frontier: Gunfighter Nation: The Myth of the Frontier in Twentieth Century America *(1992). Both the first volume,* Regeneration through Violence: The Mythology of the American Frontier *(1973), and the second,* The Fatal Environment: The Myth of the Frontier in the Age of Industrialization *(1985) received academic prizes. He also wrote and published two historical novels:* The Crater *(1980), a novel of the civil war; and* The Return of Henry Starr *(1988), about the end of the Old West and the beginning of the Western. The essay below is an excerpt from* Gunfighter Nation.

The Myth of the Frontier is our oldest and most characteristic myth, expressed in a body of literature, folklore, ritual, historiography, and polemics produced over a period of three centuries. According to this myth-historiography, the conquest of the wilderness and the subjugation or displacement of the Native Americans who originally inhabited it have been the means to our achievement of a national identity, a democratic polity, an ever-expanding economy, and a phenomenally dynamic and "progressive" civilization. The original ideological task of the Myth was to explain and justify the establishment of the American colonies; but as the colonies expanded and developed, the Myth was called on to account for our rapid economic growth,

"Regeneration Through Violence: The Language of the Myth," by Richard Slotkin, reprinted from *Gunfighter Nation: The Myth of the Frontier in Twentieth Century America*, 1992, Atheneum Press.

our emergence as a powerful nation-state, and our distinctively American approach to the socially and culturally disruptive processes of modernization.

The peculiarities of the American version of this myth/ideology derived from our original condition as a settler-state, a colonial outpost of the European "metropolis." In America, all the political, social, and economic transformations attendant on modernization began with outward movement, physical separation from the originating "metropolis." The achievement of "progress" was therefore inevitably associated with territorial expansion and colored by the experience, the politics, and the peculiar psychology of emigration.

Euro-American history begins with the self-selection and abstraction of particular European communities from their metropolitan culture, and their transplantation to a wilderness on the other side of the ocean where conditions were generally more primitive than those at home. These colonies in turn would expand by reproducing themselves in subcolonial settlements, projected at some distance from the colonial metropolis into a further and more primitive wilderness. Thus the processes of American development in the colonies were linked from the beginning to a historical narrative in which repeated cycles of *separation* and *regression* were necessary preludes to an improvement in life and fortune.

Conflict was also a central and peculiar feature of the process. To establish a colony or settlement, the Europeans had to struggle against an unfamiliar natural environment and against the non-European, non-White natives for whom the wilderness was home. Violence is central to both the historical development of the Frontier and its mythic representation. The Anglo-American colonies grew by displacing Amerindian societies and enslaving Africans to advance the fortunes of White colonists. As a result, the "savage war" became a characteristic episode of each phase of westward expansion.

Conflict with the Indians defined one boundary of American identity: though we were a people of "the wilderness" we were *not* savages. The other boundary was defined by the emergence of conflicts between the colonies and the "mother country," and (later) between the regional concerns of the "borderers" and those of American metropolitan regimes. The compleat "American" of the Myth was one who had defeated and freed himself from both the "savage" of the western wilderness and the metropolitan regime of authoritarian politics and class privilege.

In each stage of its development, the Myth of the Frontier relates the achievement of "progress" to a particular form or scenario of violent action. "Progress" itself was defined in different ways: the Puritan colonists emphasized the achievement of spiritual regeneration through frontier adventure; Jeffersonians (and later, the disciples of Turner's "Frontier Thesis") saw the frontier settlement as a re-enactment and democratic renewal of the original "social contract"; while Jacksonian Americans saw the conquest of the Frontier as a means to the regeneration of personal fortunes and/or of patriotic vigor and virtue. But in each case, the Myth represented the redemption of American spirit or fortune as something to be achieved by playing through a scenario of separation, temporary regression to a more primitive or "natural" state, and *regeneration through violence.*

At the core of that scenario is the symbol of "savage war," which was both a mythic trope and an operative category of military doctrine. The premise of "savage war" is that ineluctable political and social differences—rooted in some combination of "blood" and culture—make coexistence between primitive natives and civilized Europeans impossible on any basis other than that of subjugation. Native resistance to European settlement therefore takes the form of a fight for survival; and because of the "savage" and bloodthirsty propensity of the natives, such struggles inevitably become "wars of extermination" in which one side or the other attempts to destroy its enemy root and branch. The seventeenth-century Puritans envisioned this struggle in biblical terms—"Two Nations [are in] the Womb and will be striving"—and urged their soldiers to exterminate the Wampanoags as God commanded Israel to wipe out the Amalekites. But similar ideas informed the military thinking of soldiers in the Age of Reason, like Colonel Henry Bouquet, who described an "American war" as "a rigid contest where all is at stake and mutual destruction the object . . . [where] everything is terrible; the face of the country, the climate, the enemy . . . [where] victories are not decisive but defeats are ruinous; and simple death is the least misfortune that can happen." Military folklore from King Philip's War to Braddock's Defeat to Custer's Last Stand held that in battle against a savage enemy you always saved the last bullet for yourself; for in savage war one side or the other must perish, whether by limitless murder or by the degrading experience of subjugation and torture.

In its most typical formulations, the myth of "savage war" blames Native Americans as instigators of a war of extermination. Indians were certainly aggressors in particular cases, and they often asserted the right to exclude settlers from particular regions. But with the possible exception of Tecumseh's abortive attempt at a confederacy of western tribes, after 1700 no tribe or group of tribes pursued (or was capable of pursuing) a general "policy" of exterminating or removing White settlements on a large-scale basis. The accusation is better understood as an act of psychological projection that made the Indians scapegoats for the morally troubling side of American expansion: the myth of "savage war" became a basic ideological convention of a culture that was itself increasingly devoted to the extermination or expropriation of the Indians and the kidnaping and enslavement of black Africans.

In American mythology, the Indian war also provides a symbolic surrogate for a range of domestic social and political conflicts. By projecting the "fury" of class resentment outward against the Indian, the American expands his nation's resources and thereby renders class struggle unnecessary. All the antipathies that make for Revolutionary Terror and/or dictatorial oppression in Europe are projected onto the American savage, who becomes the only obstacle to the creation of a perfect republic. But this historical myth and its hopeful political scenario can only be realized so long as a frontier exists: a reservoir of natural resources sufficient to requite the ambitions of all classes without prejudice to the interests of any.

In analyzing the structure and meaning of this mythology of violence, it is vital that we not confuse mythic representation with political reality. The mythic tales and polemics we will be examining are rife with visions of border wars that turn overnight into preludes to Armageddon and with proposals for genocide and wars of extermination. And there has been enough actual violence along these lines—the Indian wars, the slave trade, "lynch law" and race riots, the labor/management violence of 1880—1920, and our currently high levels of domestic and criminal violence—to support the belief that America has been a peculiarly violent nation. However, most of these apparently distinctive forms of political and social violence have also figured with comparable prominence in the histories of other settler-states, and of Europe. Neither the slave trade nor the subjugation/extermination of natives by colonists was an exclusively Anglo-American enterprise. The mass genocides of modern times belong not to the history of the Americas, but to Europe, Asia, and Africa. What is distinctively "American" is not necessarily the amount or kind of violence that characterizes our history but the mythic significance we have assigned to the kinds of violence we have actually experienced, the forms of symbolic violence we imagine or invent, and the political uses to which we put that symbolism.

When history is translated into myth, the complexities of social and historical experiences are simplified and compressed into the action of representative individuals or "heroes." The narrative of the hero's action exemplifies and tests the political and/or moral validity of a particular approach to the use of human powers in the material world. The hero's inner life—his or her code of values, moral or psychic ambivalence, mixtures of motive—reduces to personal motive the complex and contradictory mixture of ideological imperatives that shape a society's response to a crucial event. But complexity and contradiction are focused rather than merely elided in the symbolizing process. The heroes of myth embody something like the full range of ideological contradictions around which the life of the culture revolves, and their adventures suggest the range of possible resolutions that the culture's lore provides.

The moral landscape of the Frontier Myth is divided by significant borders, of which the wilderness/civilization, Indian/White border is the most basic. The American must cross the border into "Indian country" and experience a "regression" to a more primitive and natural condition of life so that the false values of the "metropolis" can be purged and a new, purified social contract enacted. Although the Indian and the Wilderness are the settler's enemy, they also provide him with the new consciousness through which he will transform the world. The heroes of this myth-historical quest must therefore be "men (or women) who know Indians"—characters whose experiences, sympathies, and even allegiances fall on both sides of the Frontier. Because the border between savagery and civilization runs through their moral center, the Indian wars are, for these heroes, a spiritual or psychological struggle which they win by learning to discipline or suppress the savage or "dark" side of their own human nature. Thus they are mediators of a double kind who can teach civilized men how to defeat savagery on its native grounds—the natural wilderness, and the wilderness of the human soul.

Born in the U.S.A.

Bruce Springsteen

*New Jersey is proud to claim Bruce Springsteen as its native. Spring-
steen joined his first band at the age of fourteen. For many years he
was known only locally and his first albums, both released in 1973,
were commercial failures. In 1975, Springsteen finally achieved
national recognition with his best-selling album* Born to Run. *In
1994, Springsteen received the Academy Award for his original
song "Streets of Philadelphia," about the victims of AIDS. "Born in
the U.S.A." is the title song of the 1984 album, which enjoyed an extreme popularity.*

Born down in a dead man's town
The first kick I took was when I hit the ground
You end up like a dog that's been beat too much
Till you spend half your life just covering up
    Born in the U.S.A.
    I was born in the U.S.A.
    I was born in the U.S.A.
    Born in the U.S.A.
Got in a little hometown jam so they put a rifle in my hand
Sent me off to a foreign land to go and kill the yellow man
    Born in the U.S.A.
    I was born in the U.S.A.
    I was born in the U.S.A.
    I was born in the U.S.A.
    Born in the U.S.A.
Come back home to the refinery
Hiring man says "son if it was up to me"

Went down to see my V.A. man
He said "son don't you understand now"

Had a brother at Khe Sanh fighting off the Viet Cong
They're still here, he's all gone
He had a woman he loved in Saigon
I got a picture of him in her arms now

Down in the shadow of the penitentiary
Out by the gas fires of the refinery
I'm ten years burning down the road
Nowhere to run ain't got nowhere to go
   Born in the U.S.A.
   I was born in the U.S.A.
   Born in the U.S.A.
   I'm a long gone Daddy in the U.S.A.
   Born in the U.S.A.
   Born in the U.S.A.
   Born in the U.S.A.
   I'm a cool rocking Daddy in the U.S.A.

(1984)

In Novel Conditions:
The Cross-Dressing Psychiatrist

Allucquère Rosanne Stone

Allucquère Rosanne (Sandy) Stone is Associate Professor and Director of the Advanced Communication technologies Laboratory (ACTLab) in the department of Radio-TV-Film at the University of Texas at Austin, where she studies issues related to interface, interaction, and desire. She was program chair and organizer for the 1991 Second International Conference on Cyberspace, member of the program committee for the Third International Conference on Cyberspace in 1993, and director of the subsequent Conferences on Cyberspace up to and including the present ones. Her academic publications include numerous articles on psychoanalysis and cyberspace. Her book The War of Desire and Technology at the Close of the Mechanical Age *was published by MIT Press in September 1995 (hardcover) and September 1996 (paperback), and it is currently available in English, Italian, Japanese, Swedish, and Chinese. The following essay is a chapter from this book.*

One of our Western industrialized cultural assumptions is that subjectivity is invariably constituted in relation to a physical substance—that social beings, people, exist by virtue of possessing biological bodies through which their existence is warranted in the body politic. Another is that we know unproblematically what "body" is. Let me tell you a boundary story, a tale of the nets, as a means of anchoring one corner of the system of discourse within which this discussion operates. It is also a fable of loss of innocence—which, I have begun to notice, is the tenor of more than one story

"In Novel Conditions: The Cross-Dressing Psychiatrist," by Allucquère Rosanne Stone, reprinted from *The War of Desire and Technology at the Close of the Mechanical Age*, 1996, MIT Press.

here. In the course of this essay a number of chapters partake of the loss-of-innocence motif . . . in retrospect, a surprising number. People who still believe that I have some sort of rosy vision of the future of virtual systems are advised to reread a few of the origin myths I present in these pages. Herewith, another.

This one begins in 1982, on the CompuServe conference system. CompuServe is owned by Reader's Digest and Ziff-Davis. CompuServe began in 1980 as a generalized information service, offering such things as plane reservations, weather reports, and the "Electronic Shopping Mall," which is simply lists of retail items that can be purchased through CompuServe and ordered on-line. It was one of perhaps three major formation services that started up within a year or so of each other. The others were The Source, Prodigy, and America Online. All of these were early attempts by business to capture some of the potential market formed by consumers with computers and modems, an attempt to generate business of a kind that had not previously existed. None of the on-line services knew what this market was or where it lay, but their thinking, as evidenced by reports in the *Wall Street Journal,* was along the lines of television. That is, computers would be media in which goods could be sold visually, like a shopping service. Prodigy implemented this theory by having banners advertising products running along the bottom of the screen, while permitting conferencing to go on in the main screen area. The companies who financed The Source seem to have believed that unrestricted conversation was against the American Way, because it was never permitted to occur within the system. Both Prodigy and The Source saw their primary mission as selling goods. They attracted audiences in the same way that broadcasters did, as a product to be delivered to manufacturers in the form of demographic groups meant to watch commercials. The Source went quietly bankrupt in 1986. Prodigy, by virtue of having permitted on-line conferencing, weathered the storms of the shakeout days in which it became clear that whatever on-line services were good for, it was *not* to deliver audiences to manufacturers. CompuServe, however, found out quite early that the thing users found most interesting was on-line conferencing and chat—that is, connectivity. Or, as an industry observer put it, "People are willing to pay money just to connect. Just for the opportunity to communicate." America Online never saw itself as a medium for selling goods and concentrated on connectivity in various forms from the beginning.

Most on-line conferences now offer what are called chat lines, which are virtual places where many people can interact simultaneously in real time. In the Internet world there are many such places with quite elaborately worked out geographies; these are known as multiple-user thisses-and-thats. The first of these were direct descendants of real-life things called role-playing games, or RPGs.

Role-playing games were developed within a rather small community whose members shared certain social traits. First, most were members of the Society for Creative Anachronism, or SCA, one of the driving forces behind the Renaissance Faires. The SCA sponsors medieval tournaments with full regalia as well as medieval banquets in medieval style, which is to say, 16-course meals of staggering richness. Once one has attended such a banquet, the shorter life span of people in the Middle Ages becomes much more understandable.

Participants are extremely dedicated to the principles of the SCA, one of which is that tournaments go on as scheduled, rain or shine. In California, where many SCA members live, this can be risky. There is something not exactly bracing about watching two grown men in full armor trying to whack each other with wooden swords while thrashing and wallowing through ankle-deep mud and pouring rain. During this phase of my research I got a glimpse of what it must be like to be trained as a traditional anthropologist, and finally to be sent to some godforsaken island where one thrashes out one's fieldwork in a soggy sleeping bag while being wracked by disabling parasites and continuous dysentery.

Second, many of the people who belong to the SCA also consider themselves part of what is sometimes called the neopagan movement. And third, particularly in California, many of the people who participate in SCA events and who belong to the neopagan movement are also computer programmers.

Originally RPGs seemed to be a way for SCA members to continue their fantasy roles between tournaments. Role-playing games are also a good deal less expensive and more energy efficient than tournaments. They have tremendous grab for their participants, are open-ended, and improve with the players' imaginations. Some RPG participants have kept a good game going for years, meeting monthly for several days at a time to play the game, eating, sleeping, and defecating in role. For some, the game has considerably more appeal than reality. They express an unalloyed nostalgia for a time when roles were clearly defined, folks lived closer to nature, life was simpler, magic was afoot, and adventure was still possible. They are aware, to a certain extent, that their Arthurian vision of the Middle Ages is thoroughly bogus, but they have no intention of allowing reality to temper their enthusiasm.

The first RPG was published as a set of rules and character descriptions in 1972 and was called, appropriately enough, Dungeons and Dragons. It was an extension, really, of SCA into a textual world. D&D, as it quickly became known, used a set of rules invented by the Austin game designer Steve Jackson called the Generic Universal Role Playing System, or GURPS, for constructing characters, and voluminous books containing lists of character attributes, weapons, and powers. A designated Dungeon Master acted as arbiter of disputes and prognosticator of events and had considerable effect on the progress of the game; creative Dungeon Masters, like good tops, were hard to find and, once discovered, were highly prized.

The first 120- and 300-baud modems became available in the mid-1970s, and virtually the instant that they became available, the programmers among the D&D community began to develop versions of the game that could be played on-line. The first on-line systems ran on small personal computers (the very first were developed for Apple II's). Because of the problems of writing multitasking operating systems, which allow several people to log in on-line at once, the first systems were time-aliased; that is, only one person could be on-line at a time, so simultaneous real-time interaction was impossible. The first of these to achieve a kind of success was an on-line game called *Mines of Moria*. The program contained most of the elements that are still ubiquitous in on-line RPG systems: Quests, Fearsome Monsters, Treasure, Wizards, Twisty Mazes, Vast Castles, and, because the systems were written by young heterosexual males, the occasional Damsel in Distress.

As the Internet came into being from its earlier and more cloistered incarnation as ARPANET, more people had access to multitasking systems. The ARPANET had been built around multitasking systems such as Bell Laboratories' UNIX and had packet-switching protocols built in; these enabled multiple users to log in from widely separated locations. The first on-line multiple-user social environments were written in the early 1980s and were named, after their origins, Multiple-User Dungeons or MUDs. When the staid academics and military career persons who actually oversaw the operation of the large systems began to notice the MUDs in the mid-1980s, they took offense at such cavalier misuse of their equipment. The writers of the MUDs then tried the bald public-relations move of renaming their systems Multiple-User *Domains* in an effort to distance themselves from the offensive odor of play that accompanied the word *dungeon*. The system administrators were unimpressed by this move. Later multiple-user social environments came to be called MUSEs (for Multiple-User Social Environment), MUSHes (for Multiple-User Social Host), MUCKs, and MOOs (MUD Object-Oriented). Of these, all are somewhat similar except for the MOO, which uses a different and much more flexible method of creating objects within the simulation. Unlike MUDs, objects and attributes in a MOO are persistent; when the MOO crashes, everything is still in place when it comes back up. This property has importance for large systems such as Fujitsu's *Habitat* and smaller ones that contain many complex objects, such as the MIT Media Lab's MediaMOO and the U. Texas ACTLab's PointMOOt.

The multiple-user social environments written for the large, corporate-owned, for-pay systems betray none of their origins in low culture. They do not contain objects, nor can objects be constructed within them. They are thoroughly sanitized, consisting merely of bare spaces within which interactions can take place. They are the Motel 6 of virtual systems. Such an environment is the CB chat line on the CompuServe. It was on CompuServe, some time early in 1982, that a New York psychiatrist named Sanford Lewin opened an account.

In the conversation channels, particularly the real-time chat conferences such as CB, it is customary to choose an on-line name, or "handle," that may have no relationship to one's "real" name, which CompuServe does not reveal. Frequently, however, participants in virtual conversations choose handles that express some part of their personalities, real or imagined. Lewin, with his profession in mind, chose the handle "Doctor."

It does not appear to have dawned on him that the term was gender-neutral until a day not long after he first signed on. He had been involved in a general chat in public virtual space, had started an interesting conversation with a woman, and they had decided to drop into private mode for a few minutes. In private mode two people who have chosen to converse can only "hear" each other, and the rest of the people in the vicinity cannot "hear" them. The private conversation was actually under way for a few minutes before Lewin realized it was profoundly different from any conversation he'd been in before. Somehow the woman to whom he was talking had mistaken him for a *woman* psychiatrist. He had always felt that even in his most personal conversations with women there was always something missing, some essential connection. Suddenly he understood why, because the conversation he was now having was deeper and more open than anything he'd experienced. "I was stunned," he said later, "at the conversational mode. I hadn't known that women talked among themselves that way. There was so much more vulnerability, so much more depth and complexity. And then I thought to myself, Here's a terrific opportunity to help people, by catching them when their normal defenses are down and they're more able to hear what they need to hear."

Lewin reasoned, or claimed to have reasoned, that if women were willing to let down their conversational barriers with other women in the chat system, then as a psychiatrist he could use the chat system to do good. The obvious strategy of continuing to use the gender-neutral "Doctor" handle didn't seem like the right approach. It appears that he became deeply intrigued with the idea of interacting with women *as a woman,* rather than using a female persona as a masquerade. He wanted to become a female persona to such an extent that he could feel what it was like to be a woman in some deep and essential way. And at this point his idea of helping women by becoming an on-line woman psychiatrist took a different turn.

He opened a second account with CompuServe under the name Julie Graham. He spent considerable time working out Julie's persona. He needed someone who would be fully functioning on-line, but largely unavailable off-line in order to keep her real identity secret. For the most part, he developed an elaborate and complex history for Julie, but creating imaginary personae was not something with which he had extensive experience. So there were a few minor inconsistencies in Julie's history from time to time; and it was these that provided the initial clues that eventually tipped off a few people on the net that something was wrong. As it turned out, though, Julie's major problems didn't arise from the inconsistencies in her history, but rather from the consistencies—from the picture-book life Lewin had developed for her.

Julie first signed on in 1982. She described herself as a New York neuropsychologist who, within the last few years, had been involved in a serious automobile accident caused by a drunken driver. Her boyfriend had been killed, and she had suffered severe neurological damage to her head and spine, in particular to Broca's area, which controls speech. She was now mute and paraplegic. In addition, her face had been severely disfigured, to the extent that plastic surgery was unable to restore her appearance. Consequently she never saw anyone in person. She had become a recluse, embittered, slowly withdrawing from life, and seriously planning suicide, when a friend gave her a small computer and modem and she discovered CompuServe.

After being tentatively on-line for a while, her personality began to flourish. She began to talk about how her life was changing, and how interacting with other women in the net was helping her reconsider her situation. She stopped thinking of suicide and began planning her life. Although she lived alone and currently held no job, she had a small income from an inheritance; her family had made a fortune in a mercantile business, so at least she was assured of a certain level of physical comfort. She was an atheist, who enjoyed attacking organized religion; smoked dope, and was occasionally quite stoned on-line late at night; and was bisexual, from time to time coming on to the men and women with whom she talked. In fact, as time went on, she became flamboyantly sexual. Eventually she was encouraging many of her friends to engage in net sex with her.

Some time during this period Julie changed her handle, or sign-on pseudonym, as a celebration of her return to an active social life, at least on the net. She still maintained her personal privacy, insisting that she was too ashamed of her disfigurements and her inability to vocalize, preferring to be known only by her on-line persona. People on the chat system held occasional parties at which those who lived in reasonable geographic proximity would gather to exchange a few socialities in biological mode, and Julie assiduously avoided these. Instead she ramped up her social profile on the net even further. Her standard greeting was a huge, expansive "HI!!!!!!!!!!!!"

Julie started a women's discussion group on CompuServe. She also had long talks with women outside the group, and her advice was extremely helpful to many of them. Over the course of time several women confided to her that they were depressed and thinking about suicide, and she shared her own thoughts about her brush with suicide and helped them to move on to more life-affirming attitudes. She also helped several women with drug and chemical dependencies. An older woman confided her desire to return to college and her fear of being rejected; Julie encouraged her to go through with the application process. Once the woman was accepted, Julie advised her on the writing of several papers (including one on MPD) and in general acted as wise counsel and supportive sister.

She also took it upon herself to ferret out pretenders in the chat system, in particular men who masqueraded as women. As Van Gelder pointed out in her study of the incident, Julie was not shy about warning women about the dangers of letting one's guard down on the net. "Remember to be careful," Van Gelder quotes her as saying, "Things may not be as they seem."

There is a subtext here, which has to do with what I have been calling the on-line persona. Of course we all change personae all the time, to suit the social occasion, although with on-line personae the act is more purposeful. Nevertheless, the societal imperative with which we have been raised is that there is one primary persona, or "true identity," and that in the off-line world—the "real world"—this persona is firmly attached to a single physical body, by which our existence as a social being is authorized and in which it is grounded. The origin of this "correct" relationship between body and persona seems to have been contemporaneous with the Enlightenment, the same cultural moment that gave birth to what we like to call the sovereign subject. True, there is no shortage of examples extending far back in time of a sense of something in the body other than just meat. Usually this has to do with an impalpable soul or a similar manifestation—some agency that carries with it the seat of consciousness, and that normally may be decoupled from the body only after death. For many people, though, the soul or some impalpable avatar routinely journeys free of the body, and a certain amount of energy is routinely expended in managing the results of its travels. Partly the Western idea that the body and the subject are inseparable is a worthy exercise in wish fulfillment—an attempt to explain why ego-centered subjectivity terminates with the substrate *and* to enforce the termination. Recently we find in science fiction quite a number of attempts to refigure this relationship, notably in the work of authors like John Varley, who has made serious tries at constructing phenomenologies of the self (e.g., Varley 1986).

Julie worked off her fury at drunk drivers by volunteering to ride along in police patrol cars. Because of her experience at neuropsychology, she was able to spot erratic driving very quickly, and by her paralysis she could offer herself as a horrible example of the consequences. During one of these forays she met a young cop named John. Her disability and disfigured face bothered him not a whit, and they had a whirlwind romance. Shortly he proposed to her. After Julie won his mother over (she had told him "he was throwing his life away by marrying a cripple"), they were married in a joyous ceremony. Rather than having a live reception, they held the reception online, toasting and being toasted by friends from remote sites around the country. They announced that they intended to honeymoon in the Greek Islands, and soon real postcards from Greece began showing up in their friends' mailboxes.

Julie's professional life began to bloom. She began attending conferences and giving papers around the States, and shortly in Europe as well. Of course there were problems, but John was the quintessential caring husband, watching out for her, nurturing her. Her new popularity on the conference circuit allowed them to take frequent trips to exotic places. While they were on safari, if there was a place her wheelchair couldn't reach, he simply carried her. When they were home he was frequently out on stakeouts in the evenings, which gave her lots of time to engage with her on-line friends. Occasionally he would talk to her friends on the chat system.

Julie began talking about becoming a college teacher. She felt that she could overcome her handicap by using a computer in the classroom. This would be hooked to a large screen to "talk" with her students. Throughout the planning of her new career, John was thoroughly supportive and caring.

It was some time during this period that Julie's friends first began to become suspicious. She was always off at conferences, where presumably she met face to face with colleagues. And she and John spent a lot of time on exotic vacations, where she must also be seeing people face to face. It seemed that the only people who never got to see her were her on-line friends. With them she maintained a firm and unyielding invisibility. There were beginning to be too many contradictions. But it was the other disabled women on-line who pegged her first. They knew the real difficulties—personal and interpersonal—of being disabled. Not "differently abled," that wonderful term, but rather the brutal reality of the way most people—including some friends—related to them. In particular they knew the exquisite problems of negotiating friendships, not to mention love relationships, in close quarters with the "normally" abled. In that context, Julie's relationship with the unfailingly caring John was simply impossible. John was a Stepford husband.

Still, nobody had yet pegged Julie as other than a disabled woman. The other disabled women on-line thought that she was probably a disabled woman, but also felt that she was probably lying about her romantic life and about her frequent trips. But against that line of argument they had to deal with the reality that they had hard evidence of some of those trips—real postcards from Greece—and in fact Julie and John had gone back to Greece next year, accompanied by another flurry of postcards.

Julie, John, Joan—they are all wonderful examples of the war of desire and technology. Their complex virtual identities are real and productive interventions into our cultural belief that the unmarked social unit, besides being white and male, is a single self in a single body. Multiple personality "disorder" is another such intervention. As I tried to make clear in "Identity in Oshkosh," MPD is generally considered to be pathological, the result of trauma. But we can look to the construction and management of pathology for the circumstances that constitute and authorize the unmarked, so that we may take the pathologization of MPD and in general the management and control of any manifestations of body-self, other than the one body—one self norm, to be useful tools to take apart discourses of the political subject so we can see what makes them work. There are other interventions to be made, and here we interrogate a few Harawayan elsewheres—in this case, virtual space, the phantasmic "structure" within which real social interactions take place—for information. Of course, the virtual environment of the chat lines is just beginning, a look at a single event when such events were still singular.

Julie's friends weren't the only ones who were nervous over the turns her life was taking and the tremendous personal growth she was experiencing. In fact, Lewin was getting nervous too. Apparently he'd never expected the impersonation to succeed so dramatically. He thought he'd make a few contacts on-line, and maybe offer helpful advice to some women. What had happened instead was that he'd found himself deeply engaged in developing a whole new part of himself that he'd never known existed. His responses had long since ceased to be a masquerade; with the help of the on-line mode and a certain amount of textual prosthetics, he was in the process of *becoming* Julie. She no longer simply carried out his wishes at the keyboard; she had her own emergent personality, her own ideas, her own directions. Not that he was losing his own identity, but he was certainly developing a parallel one, one of considerable puissance. Jekyll and Julie. As her friendships deepened and simultaneously the imposture began to unravel, Lewin began to realize the enormity of his deception.

And the simplicity of the solution.

Julie had to die.

And so events ground inexorably onward. One day Julie became seriously ill. With John's help, she was rushed to the hospital. John signed on to her account to tell her on-line friends and to explain what was happening: Julie had been struck by an exotic bug to which she had little resistance, and in her weakened state it was killing her. For a few days she hovered between life and death, while Lewin hovered, setting up her demise in a plausible fashion.

The result was horrific. Lewin, as John, was deluged with expressions of shock, sorrow, and caring. People offered medical advice, offered financial assistance, sent cards, sent flowers. Some people went into out-and-out panic. The chat lines became jammed. So many people got seriously upset, in fact, that Lewin backed down. He couldn't stand to go through with it. He couldn't stand to engineer her death. Julie recovered and came home.

The relief on the net was enormous. Joyous messages were exchanged. Julie and John were overwhelmed with caring from their friends. In fact, sometime during the great outpouring of sympathy and concern, while Julie was at death's door, one of her friends managed to find out the name of the hospital where she was supposed to be staying. He called, to see if he could help out, and was told there was no one registered by that name. Another thread unraveled.

Lewin was still stuck with the problem that he hadn't had the guts to solve. He decided to try another tack, one that might work even better from his point of view. Shortly, Julie began to introduce people to her new friend, Sanford Lewin, a New York psychiatrist. She was enormously gracious about it, if not downright pushy. To hear her tell it, Lewin was absolutely wonderful, charming, graceful, intelligent, and eminently worthy of their most affectionate attention. Thus introduced, Lewin then began trying to make friends with Julie's friends himself.

He couldn't do it.

Sanford simply didn't have the personality to make friends easily on-line. Where Julie was freewheeling and jazzy, Sanford was subdued and shy. Julie was a confirmed atheist, an articulate firebrand of rationality, while Sanford was a devout conservative Jew. Julie smoked dope and occasionally got a bit drunk on-line; Sanford was, how shall we say, drug-free—in fact, he was frightened of drugs—and he restricted his drinking to a little Manischewitz on high holy days. And to complete the insult, Julie had fantastic luck with sex on-line, while when it came to erotics Sanford was a hopeless klutz who didn't know a vagina from a virginal. In short, Sanford's Sanford persona was being defeated by his Julie persona.

What do you do when your imaginary playmate makes friends better than you do?

With Herculean efforts Lewin had succeeded in striking up at least a beginning friendship with a few of Julie's friends when the Julie persona began to come seriously unraveled. First the disabled women began to wonder aloud, then Lewin took the risk of revealing himself to a few more women with whom he felt he had built a friendship. Once he started the process, word of what was happening spread rapidly through the net. But just as building Julie's original personal had taken some time, the actual dismantling of it took several months, as more clearly voiced suspicion gradually turned to factual information and the information was passed around the conferences, repeated, discussed, and picked over. Shortly the process reached a critical level where it became self-supporting. In spite of the inescapable reality of the deception, though, or rather in spite of the inescapable unreality of Julie Graham, there was a kind of temporal and emotional mass in motion that, Newton-like, tended to remain in motion. Even as it slowly disintegrated like one of the walking dead, the myth of Julie still tended to roll ponderously ahead on its own, shedding shocked clots of ex-Julie fans as it ran down. The effect, though spread out over time, was like a series of bombing raids interspersed throughout a ground war.

Perhaps to everyone's surprise, the emotion that many of those in the chat system felt most deeply was mourning. Because of the circumstances in which it occurred, Julie's unmasking as a construct, a cross-dressing man, had been worse than a death. There was no focused instant of pain and loss. There was no funeral, no socially supported way to lay the Julie persona to rest, to release one's emotions and to move on. The help Julie had given people in that very regard seemed inappropriate in the circumstance. Whatever else Julie was or wasn't, she had been a good friend and a staunch supporter to many people in need, giving unstintingly of her time and virtual energy wherever it was required. Her fine sense of humor and ability to see the bright side of difficulties had helped many people, mostly women, over very difficult places in their lives. At least some of her charm and charisma should have rubbed off on Lewin. But it didn't. And, quite understandably, some of the women did not bounce back with forgiveness. At least one said that she felt a deep emotional violation which, in her opinion, was tantamount to sexual assault. "I felt raped," she said, "I felt as if my deepest secrets were violated. The good things Julie did . . . were all done by deception." Some of the women formed a support group to talk about their sense of betrayal and violation, which they referred to wryly as "Julie-anon."

The Julie incident produced a large amount of Monday morning quarterbacking among the habitués of CompuServe's chat system. In retrospect, several women felt that Julie's helpfulness had exceeded the bounds of good sense—that what she had actually fostered was dependency. Others focused on her maneuvers for net sex, which sometimes amounted to heavy come-ons even with old friends. Perhaps most telling was the rethinking, among Julie's closest friends, of their attitudes toward Julie's disability. One said, "In retrospect, we went out of our way to believe her. We wanted to give her all the support we could, because of what she was trying to do. So everybody was bending over backward to extend praise and support and caring to this disabled person. We were all so supportive when she got married and when she was making all the speaking engagements . . . in fact there was a lot of patronizing going on that we didn't recognize at the time."

Sanford Lewin retained his CompuServe account. He has a fairly low profile on the net, not least because the Sanford person is inherently low-key. Many of Julie's friends made at least a token attempt to become friends with him. Not too many succeeded, because, according to them, there simply wasn't that much in common between them. Several of the women who were friends of Julie have become acquaintances of Lewin, and a few have become friends. One said, "I've been trying to forget about the Julie thing. We didn't think it through properly in the first place, and many of the women took risks that they shouldn't have. But whether he's Julie or Sanford, man or woman, there's an inner person that must have been there all along. That's the person I really like."

The hackers in my study population, the people who wrote the programs by means of which the nets exist, just smiled tiredly. A few sympathized with the women whom Julie had taken in, and understood that it takes time to realize, through experience, that social rules do not necessarily map across the interface between the physical and virtual worlds. But all of them had understood from the beginning that the nets presaged radical changes in social conventions, some of which would go unnoticed. That is, until an event like a disabled woman who is revealed to be "only" a persona— not a true name at all—along with the violated confidences that resulted from the different senses in which various actors understood the term *person,* all acted together to push these changes to the foreground. Some of these engineers, in fact, wrote software for the utopian possibilities it offered. Young enough in the first days of the net to react and adjust quickly, they had long ago taken for granted that many of the pre-net assumptions about the nature of identity had quietly vanished. Even though they easily understood and assimilated conflictual situations such as virtual persona as mask for an underlying identity, few had yet thought very deeply about what underlay the underlying identity. There is an old joke about a woman at a lecture on cosmology who said that she understood quite clearly what kept the earth hanging in space; it actually rested on the back of a giant turtle. When asked what the turtle was standing on, she replied that the turtle was standing on the back of yet another turtle, and added tartly, "You can't confuse me, young man; it's turtles all the way down."

Is it personae all the way down?

Say amen, somebody.

Mother Tongue

Amy Tan

Amy Tan is an only daughter of Chinese immigrants. Her Chinese name "An-mei" means "blessing from America." Her family moved constantly when she was a child and eventually settled in Santa Clara, California. She won an essay contest at the age of eight, and from that day on, she dreamed only of becoming a fiction writer. After becoming a free-lance business writer, a job she found unfulfilling, she began writing fiction as a hobby. She soon quit the free-lance business and in four months, her most famous book, The Joy Luck Club, *was written. Other books by Tan include* The Kitchen God's Wife *(1991) and* The Hundred Secret Senses *(1995). "Mother Tongue" originally appeared in* The Three Penny Review *(1990) and was selected by Joyce Carol Oates for* The Best American Essays.

I am not a scholar of English or literature. I cannot give you much more than personal opinions on the English language and its variations in this country or others.

I am a writer. And by that definition, I am someone who has always loved language. I am fascinated by language in daily life. I spend a great deal of my time thinking about the power of language—the way it can evoke an emotion, a visual image, a complex idea, or a simple truth. Language is the tool of my trade. And I use them all—all the Englishes I grew up with.

Recently, I was made keenly aware of the different Englishes I do use. I was giving a talk to a large group of people, the same talk I had already given to half a dozen other groups. The nature of the talk was about my writing, my life, and my book, *The Joy Luck Club.* The talk was going along well enough, until I remembered one major difference that made the whole talk sound wrong. My mother was in the room. And it was perhaps the first time she had heard me give a lengthy speech, using the kind

"Mother Tongue," by Amy Tan, reprinted from *The Best American Essays*, edited by Robert Atwan, 1988, Sandra Dijkstra Literary Agency.

of English I have never used with her. I was saying things like, "The intersection of memory upon imagination" and "There is an aspect of my fiction that relates to thus-and-thus"—a speech filled with carefully wrought grammatical phrases, burdened, it suddenly seemed to me, with nominalized forms, past perfect tenses, conditional phrases, all the forms of standard English that I had learned in school and through books, the forms of English I did not use at home with my mother.

Just last week, I was walking down the street with my mother, and I again found myself conscious of the English I was using, the English I do use with her. We were talking about the price of new and used furniture and I heard myself saying this: "Not waste money that way." My husband was with us as well, and he didn't notice any switch in my English. And then I realized why. It's because over the twenty years we've been together I've often used that same kind of English with him, and sometimes he even uses it with me. It has become our language of intimacy, a different sort of English that relates to family talk, the language I grew up with.

So you'll have some idea of what this family talk I heard sounds like, I'll quote what my mother said during a recent conversation which I videotaped and then transcribed. During this conversation, my mother was talking about a political gangster in Shanghai who had the same last name as her family's, Du, and how the gangster in his early years wanted to be adopted by her family, which was rich by comparison. Later, the gangster became more powerful, far richer than my mother's family, and one day showed up at my mother's wedding to pay his respects. Here's what she said in part:

> "Du Yusong having business like fruit stand. Like off the street kind. He is Du like Du Zong—but not Tsung-ming Island people. The local people call putong, the river east side, he belong to that side local people. That man want to ask Du Zong father take him in like become own family. Du Zong father wasn't look down on him, but didn't take seriously, until that man big like become a mafia. Now important person, very hard to inviting him. Chinese way, came only to show respect, don't stay for dinner. Respect for making big celebration, he shows up. Mean gives lots of respect. Chinese custom. Chinese social life that way. If too important won't have to stay too long. He come to my wedding. I didn't see, I heard it. I gone to boy's side, they have YMCA dinner. Chinese age I was nineteen."

You should know that my mother's expressive command of English belies how much she actually understands. She reads the *Forbes* report, listens to *Wall Street Week*, converses daily with her stockbroker, reads all of Shirley MacLaine's books with ease—all kinds of things I can't begin to understand. Yet some of my friends tell me they understand 50 percent of what my mother says. Some say they understand 80 to 90 percent. Some say they understand none of it, as if she were speaking pure Chinese. But to me, my mother's English is perfectly clear, perfectly natural. It's my mother tongue. Her language, as I hear it, is vivid, direct, full of observation and imagery. That was the language that helped shape the way I saw things, expressed things, made sense of the world.

Lately, I've been giving more thought to the kind of English my mother speaks. Like others, I have described it to people as "broken" or "fractured" English. But I wince when I say that. It has always bothered me that I can think of no way to describe it other than "broken," as if it were damaged and needed to be fixed, as if it lacked a certain wholeness and soundness. I've heard other terms used, "limited English," for example. But they seem just as bad, as if everything is limited, including people's perceptions of the limited English speaker.

I know this for a fact, because when I was growing up, my mother's "limited" English limited *my* perception of her. I was ashamed of her English. I believed that her English reflected the quality of what she had to say. That is, because she expressed them imperfectly her thoughts were imperfect. And I had plenty of empirical evidence to support me: the fact that people in department stores, at banks, and at restaurants did not take her seriously, did not give her good service, pretended not to understand her, or even acted as if they did not hear her.

My mother has long realized the limitations of her English as well. When I was fifteen, she used to have me call people on the phone to pretend I was she. In this guise, I was forced to ask for information or even to complain and yell at people who had been rude to her. One time it was a call to her stockbroker in New York. She had cashed out her small portfolio and it just so happened we were going to go to New York the next week, our very first trip outside California. I had to get on the phone and say in an adolescent voice that was not very convincing, "This is Mrs. Tan."

And my mother was standing in the back whispering loudly, "Why he don't send me check, already two weeks late. So mad he lie to me, losing me money."

And then I said in perfect English, "Yes, I'm getting rather concerned. You had agreed to send the check two weeks ago, but it hasn't arrived."

Then she began to talk more loudly. "What he want, I come to New York tell him front of his boss, you cheating me?" And I was trying to calm her down, make her be quiet, while telling the stockbroker, "I can't tolerate any more excuses. If I don't receive the check immediately, I am going to have to speak to your manager when I'm in New York next week." And sure enough, the following week there we were in front of this astonished stockbroker, and I was sitting there red-faced and quiet, and my mother, the real Mrs. Tan, was shouting at his boss in her impeccable broken English.

We used a similar routine just five days ago, for a situation that was far less humorous. My mother had gone to the hospital for an appointment, to find out about a benign brain tumor a CAT scan had revealed a month ago. She said she had spoken very good English, her best English, no mistakes. Still, she said, the hospital did not apologize when they said they had lost the CAT scan and she had come for nothing. She said they did not seem to have any sympathy when she told them she was anxious to know the exact diagnosis, since her husband and son had both died of brain tumors. She said they would not give her any more information until the next time and she would have to make another appointment for that. So she said she would not leave until the doctor called her daughter. She wouldn't budge. And when the doctor finally called her daughter, me, who spoke in perfect English—lo and behold—we had assurances the CAT scan would be found, promises that a conference call on Monday would be held, and apologies for any suffering my mother had gone through for a most regrettable mistake.

I think my mother's English almost had an effect on limiting my possibilities in life as well. Sociologists and linguists probably will tell you that a person's developing language skills are more influenced by peers. But I do think that the language spoken in the family, especially in immigrant families which are more insular, plays a large role in shaping the language of the child. And I believe that it affected my results on achievement tests, IQ tests, and the SAT. While my English skills were never judged as poor, compared to math, English could not be considered my strong suit. In grade school I did moderately well, getting perhaps B's, sometimes B-pluses, in English and scoring perhaps in the sixtieth or seventieth percentile on achievement tests. But those scores were not good enough to override the opinion that my true abilities lay in math and science, because in those areas I achieved A's and scored in the ninetieth percentile or higher.

This was understandable. Math is precise; there is only one correct answer. Whereas, for me at least, the answers on English tests were always a judgment call, a matter of opinion and personal experience. Those tests were constructed around items like fill-in-the-blank sentence completion, such as, "Even though Tom was _____, Mary thought he was_____." And the correct answer always seemed to be the most bland combinations of thoughts, for example, "Even though Tom was shy, Mary thought he was charming," with the grammatical structure "even though" limiting the correct answer to some sort of semantic opposites, so you wouldn't get answers like, "Even though Tom was foolish, Mary thought he was ridiculous." Well, according to my mother, there were very few limitations as to what Tom could have been and what Mary might have thought of him. So I never did well on tests like that.

The same was true with word analogies, pairs of words in which you were supposed to find some sort of logical, semantic relationship, or for example, *"Sunset* is to *nightfall* as _____ is to _____." And here you would be presented with a list of four possible pairs, one of which showed the same kind of relationship: *red* is to *stoplight, bus* is to *arrival, chills* is to *fever, yawn* is to *boring.* Well, I could never think that way. I knew what the tests were asking, but I could not block out of my mind the images already created by the first pair, *"sunset* is to *nightfall"*—and I would see a burst of colors against a darkening sky, the moon rising, the lowering of a curtain of stars. And all the other pairs of words—red, bus, stoplight, boring—just threw up a mass of confusing images, making it impossible for me to sort out something as logical as saying: "A sunset precedes nightfall" is the same as "a chill precedes a fever." The only way I would have gotten that answer right would have been to imagine an associative situation, for example, my being disobedient and staying out past sunset, catching a chill at night, which turns into feverish pneumonia as punishment, which indeed did happen to me.

I have been thinking about all this lately, about my mother's English, about achievement tests. Because lately I've been asked, as a writer, why there are not more Asian Americans represented in American literature. Why are there few Asian Americans enrolled in creative writing programs? Why do so many Chinese students go into engineering? Well, these are broad sociological questions I can't begin to answer. But I have noticed in surveys—in fact, just last week—that Asian students, as a whole, always do significantly better on math achievement tests than in English. And this makes me think that there are other Asian-American students whose English spoken in the home might also be described as "broken" or "limited." And perhaps they also have teachers who are steering them away from writing and into math and science, which is what happened to me.

Fortunately, I happen to be rebellious in nature and enjoy the challenge of disproving assumptions made about me. I became an English major my first year in college, after being enrolled as pre-med. I started writing nonfiction as a freelancer the week after I was told by my former boss that writing was my worst skill and I should hone my talents toward account management.

But it wasn't until 1985 that I finally began to write fiction. And at first I wrote using what I thought to be wittily crafted sentences, sentences that would finally prove I had mastery over the English language. Here's an example from the first draft of a story that later made its way into *The Joy Luck Club,* but without this line: "That was my mental quandary in its nascent state." A terrible line, which I can barely pronounce.

Fortunately, for reasons I won't get into today, I later decided I should envision a reader for the stories I would write. And the reader I decided upon was my mother, because these were stories about mothers. So with this reader in mind—and in fact she did read my early drafts—I began to write stories using all the Englishes I grew up with: the English I spoke to my mother, which for lack of a better term might be described as "simple"; the English she used with me, which for lack of a better term might be described as "broken"; my translation of her Chinese, which could certainly be described as "watered down"; and what I imagined to be her translation of her Chinese if she could speak in perfect English, her internal language, and for that I sought to preserve the essence, but neither an English nor a Chinese structure. I wanted to capture what language ability tests can never reveal: her intent, her passion, her imagery, the rhythms of her speech and the nature of her thoughts.

Apart from what any critic had to say about my writing, I knew I had succeeded where it counted when my mother finished reading my book and gave me her verdict: "So easy to read."

Wouldn't You Rather Be at Home?

The Internet and the Myth of the Powerful Self

Ellen Ullman

Ellen Ullman is a software engineering consultant and writer based in San Francisco, who has been involved in the computer industry since 1978. She is the author of Close to the Machine: Technophilia and Its Discontents *(City Lights, 1997). Her writings have also appeared in* Harper's *magazine and in several anthologies among which* Resisting the Virtual Life, *and* Wired Women: Gender and New Realities in Cyberspace *(ed. Lynn Cherny and Elizabeth Reba Wise, Seal Press, 1996), as well as at* <u>salon.com</u>. *She is a commentator on National Public Radio's "All Things Considered."*

———————————

Years ago, before the Internet as we know it had come into existence—I think it was around Christmas, in 1990—I was at a friend's house, where her nine-year-old son and his friend were playing the video game that was the state of the art at the time, Sonic the Hedgehog. They jumped around in front of the TV and gave off the sort of rude noises boys tend to make when they're shooting at things in a video game, and after about half an hour they stopped and tried to talk about what they'd just been doing. The dialogue went something like this:

"I wiped out at that part with the ladders."

"Ladders? What ladders?"

"You know, after the rooms."

"Oh, you mean the stairs?"

"No, I think they were ladders. I remember, because I died there twice."

"I never killed you around any ladders. I killed you where you jump down off this wall."

Excerpt from "Wouldn't You Rather Be At Home? The Internet and the Myth of the Powerful Self," by Ellen Ullman, reprinted from *Harper's Magazine*, 1999.

"Wall? You mean by the gates of the city?"

"Are there gates around the city? I always called it the castle."

The boys muddled along for several more minutes, making themselves more confused as they went. Finally they gave up trying to talk about their time with Sonic the Hedgehog. They just looked at each other and shrugged.

I didn't think about the two boys and Sonic again until I watched my clients try out the World Wide Web. By then it was 1995, the Internet as we know it was beginning to exist, but the two women who worked for my client, whom I'd just helped get online, had never before connected to the Internet or surfed the Web. They took to it instantly, each disappearing into nearly an hour of obsessive clicking, after which they tried to talk about it:

"It was great! I clicked that thing and went to this place. I don't remember its name."

"Yeah. It was a link. I clicked here and went there."

"Oh, I'm not sure it was a link. The thing I clicked was a picture of the library."

"Was it the library? I thought it was a picture of City Hall."

"Oh, no. I'm sure it was the library."

"No, City Hall. I'm sure because of the dome."

"Dome? Was there a dome?"

Right then I remembered Sonic and the two boys; my clients, like the two boys, had experienced something pleasurable and engaging, and they very much wanted to talk about it—talking being one of the primary ways human beings augment their pleasure. But what had happened to them, each in her own electronic world, resisted description. Like the boys, the two women fell into verbal confusion. How could they speak coherently about a world full of little wordless pictograms, about trails that led off in all directions, of idle visits to virtual places chosen on a whim-click?

Following hyperlinks on the Web is like the synaptic drift of dreams, a loosening of intention, the mind associating freely, an experience that can be compelling or baffling or unsettling, or all of those things at once. And like dreams, the experience of the Web is intensely private, charged with immanent meaning for the person inside the experience, but often confusing or irrelevant to someone else.

At the time, I had my reservations about the Web, but not so much about the private, dreamlike state it offered. Web surfing seemed to me not so much antisocial as asocial, an adventure like a video game or pinball, entertaining, sometimes interesting, sometimes a trivial waste of time; but in a social sense it seemed harmless, since only the person engaged in the activity was affected.

Something changed, however, not in me but in the Internet and the Web and in the world, and the change was written out in person-high letters on a billboard on the corner of Howard and New Montgomery Streets in San Francisco. It was the fall of 1998. I was walking toward Market Street one afternoon when I saw it, a background of brilliant sky blue, with writing on it in airy white letters, which said: *now the world really does revolve around you.* The letters were lower-case, soft-edged, spaced irregularly, as if they'd been skywritten over a hot August beach and were already drifting off into the air. The message they left behind was a child's secret wish, the ultimate baby-world narcissism we are all supposed to abandon when we grow up: the world really does revolve around me.

What was this billboard advertising? Perfume? A resort? There was nothing else on it but the airy, white letters, and I had to walk right up to it to see a URL written at the bottom; it was the name of a company that makes semiconductor equipment, machinery used by companies like Intel and AMD to manufacture integrated circuits. Oh, chips, I thought. Computers. Of course. What other subject produces such hyperbole? Who else but someone in the computer industry could make such a shameless appeal to individualism?

The billboard loomed over the corner for the next couple of weeks. Every time I passed it, its message irritated me more. It bothered me the way the "My Computer" icon bothers me on the Windows desktop, baby names like "My Yahoo" and "My Snap"; my, my, my; two-year-old talk; infantilizing and condescending.

But there was something more disturbing about this billboard, and I tried to figure out why, since it simply was doing what every other piece of advertising does: whispering in your ear that there is no one like you in the entire world, and what we are offering is for you, special you, and you alone. What came to me was this: Toyota, for example, sells the idea of a special, individual buyer ("It's not for everyone, just for you"), but chip makers, through the medium of the Internet and the World Wide Web, are creating the actual infrastructure of an individualized marketplace.

What had happened between 1995, when I could still think of the Internet as a private dream, and the appearance of that billboard in 1998 was the near-complete commercialization of the Web. And that commercialization had proceeded in a very particular and single-minded way: by attempting to isolate the individual within a sea of economic activity. Through a process known as "disintermediation," producers have worked to remove the expert intermediaries, agents, brokers, middlemen, who until now have influenced our interactions with the commercial world. What bothered me about the billboard, then, was that its message was not merely hype but the reflection of a process that was already under way: an attempt to convince the individual that a change currently being visited upon him or her is a good thing, the purest form of self, the equivalent of freedom. The world really does revolve around you.

In Silicon Valley, in Redmond, Washington, the home of Microsoft, and in the smaller silicon alleys of San Francisco and New York, "disintermediation" is a word so common that people shrug when you try to talk to them about it. Oh, disintermediation, that old thing. Everyone already knows about that. It has become accepted wisdom, a process considered inevitable, irrefutable, good.

I've long believed that the ideas embedded in technology have a way of percolating up and outward into the nontechnical world at large, and that technology is made by people with intentions and, as such, is not neutral. In the case of disintermediation, an explicit and purposeful change is being visited upon the structure of the global marketplace. And in a world so dominated by markets, I don't think I go too far in saying that this will affect the very structure of reality, for the Net is no longer simply a zone of personal freedoms, a pleasant diversion from what we used to call "real life"; it has become an actual marketplace that is changing the nature of real life itself.

Removal of the intermediary. All those who stand in the middle of a transaction, whether financial or intellectual: out! Brokers and agents and middlemen of every description: good-bye! Travel agents, real-estate agents, insurance agents, stockbrokers, mortgage brokers, consolidators, and jobbers, all the scrappy percentniks who troll the bywaters of capitalist exchange—who needs you? All those hard-striving immigrants climbing their way into the lower middle class through the penny-ante deals of capitalism, the transfer points too small for the big guys to worry about—find yourself some other way to make a living. Small retailers and store clerks, salespeople of every kind—a hindrance, idiots, not to be trusted. Even the professional handlers of intellectual goods, anyone who sifts through information, books, paintings, knowledge, selecting and summing up: librarians, book reviewers, curators, disc jockeys, teachers, editors, analysts—why trust anyone but yourself to make judgments about what is more or less interesting, valuable, authentic, or worthy of your attention? No one, no professional interloper, is supposed to come between you and your desires, which, according to this idea, are nuanced, difficult to communicate, irreducible, unique.

The Web did not cause disintermediation, but it is what we call an "enabling technology": a technical breakthrough that takes a difficult task and makes it suddenly doable, easy; it opens the door to change, which then comes in an unconsidered, breathless rush.

We are living through an amazing experiment: an attempt to construct a capitalism without salespeople, to take a system founded upon the need to sell ever greater numbers of goods to ever growing numbers of people, and to do this without the aid of professional distribution channels—without buildings, sidewalks, shops, luncheonettes, street vendors, buses, trams, taxis, other women in the fitting room to tell you how you look in something and to help you make up your mind, without street people panhandling, Santas ringing bells at Christmas, shop women with their perfect makeup and elegant clothes, fashionable men and women strolling by to show you the latest look—in short, an attempt to do away with the city in all its messy stimulation, to abandon the agora for home and hearth, where it is safe and everything can be controlled.

The first task in this newly structured capitalism is to convince consumers that the services formerly performed by myriad intermediaries are useless or worse, that those commissioned brokers and agents are incompetent, out for themselves, dishonest. And the next task is to glorify the notion of self-service. Where companies once vied for your business by telling you about their courteous people and how well they would serve you—"Avis, We Try Harder"—their job now is to make you believe that only you can take care of yourself. The lure of personal service that was dangled before the middle classes, momentarily making us all feel almost as lucky as the rich, is being withdrawn. In the Internet age, under the pressure of globalized capitalism and its slimmed-down profit margins, only the very wealthy will be served by actual human beings. The rest of us must make do with Web pages, and feel happy about it.

One evening while I was watching television, I looked up to see a commercial that seemed to me to be the most explicit statement of the ideas implicit in the disiater-mediated universe. I gaped at it, because usually such ideas are kept implicit, hidden behind symbols. But this commercial was like the sky-blue billboard: a shameless and naked expression of the Web world, a glorification of the self, at home, alone.

It begins with a drone, a footstep in a puddle, then a ragged band pulling a dead car through the mud—road warriors with bandanas around their foreheads carrying braziers. Now we see rafts of survivors floating before the ruins of a city, the sky dark, red-tinged, as if fires were burning all around us, just over the horizon. Next we are outside the dead city's library, where stone lions, now coated in gold and come to life, rear up in despair. Inside the library, red-coated Fascist guards encircle the readers at the table. A young girl turns a page, loudly, and the guards say, "Shush!" in time to their march-step. We see the title of the book the girl is reading: *Paradise Lost.* The bank, too, is a scene of ruin. A long line snakes outside it in a dreary rain. Inside, the teller is a man with a white, spectral face, who gazes upon the black spider that is slowly crawling up his window. A young woman's face ages right before us, and in response, in ridicule, the bank guard laughs. The camera now takes us up over the roofs of this post-apocalyptic city. Lightning crashes in the dark, red-tinged sky. On a telephone pole, where the in-sulators should be, are skulls.

Cut to a cartoon of emerald-green grass, hills, a Victorian house with a white pick-et fence and no neighbors. A butterfly flaps above it. What a relief this house is after the dreary, dangerous, ruined city. The door to this charming house opens, and we go in to see a chair before a computer screen. Yes, we want to go sit in that chair, in that room with candy-orange walls. On the computer screen, running by in teasing suc-cession, are pleasant virtual reflections of the world outside: written text, a bank check, a telephone pole, which now signifies our connection to the world. The cam-era pans back to show a window, a curtain swinging in the breeze, and our sense of calm is complete. We hear the Intel-Inside jingle, which sounds almost like chimes. Cut to the legend: Packard Bell. Wouldn't you rather be at home?

In sixty seconds, this commercial communicates a worldview that reflects the ultimate suburbanization of existence: a retreat from the friction of the social space to the supposed idyll of private ease. It is a view that depends on the idea that desire is not social, not stimulated by what others want, but generated internally, and that the satisfaction of desires is not dependent upon other persons, organizations, struc-tures, or governments. It is a profoundly libertarian vision, and it is the message that underlies all the mythologizing about the Web: the idea that the civic space is dead, useless, dangerous. The only place of pleasure and satisfaction is your home. You, home, family; and beyond that, the world. From the intensely private to the global, with little in between but an Intel processor and a search engine.

In this sense, the ideal of the Internet represents the very opposite of democracy, which is a method for resolving differences in a relatively orderly manner through the mediation of unavoidable civil associations. Yet there can be no notion of resolving differences in a world where each person is entitled to get exactly what he or she wants. Here all needs and desires are equally valid and equally powerful. I'll get mine and you'll get yours; there is no need for compromise and discussion. I don't have to tolerate you, and you don't have to tolerate me. No need for messy debate and the whole rigmarole of government with all its creaky, bothersome structures. There's no need for any of this, because now that we have the World Wide Web the problem of the pursuit of happiness has been solved! We'll each click for our individual joys, and our only dispute may come if something doesn't get delivered on time. Wouldn't you really rather be at home?

But who can afford to stay at home? Only the very wealthy or a certain class of knowledge worker can stay home and click. On the other side of this ideal of work-anywhere freedom (if indeed it is freedom never to be away from work) is the reality that somebody had to make the thing you ordered with a click. Somebody had to put it in a box, do the paperwork, carry it to you. The reality is a world divided not only between the haves and have-nots but between the ones who get to stay home and everyone else, the ones who deliver the goods to them.

The Net ideal represents a retreat not only from political life but also from culture—from that tumultuous conversation in which we try to talk to one another about our shared experiences. As members of a culture, we see the same movie, read the same book, hear the same string quartet. Although it is difficult for us to agree on what we might have seen, read, or heard, it is out of that difficult conversation that real culture arises. Whether or not we come to an agreement or understanding, even if some decide that understanding and meaning are impossible, we are still sitting around the same campfire.

But the Web as it has evolved is based on the idea that we do not even want a shared experience. The director of San Francisco's Museum of Modern Art once told an audience that we no longer need a building to house works of art; we don't need to get dressed, go downtown, walk from room to room among crowds of other people. Now that we have the Web, we can look at anything we want whenever we want, and we no longer need him or his curators. "You don't have to walk through *my* idea of what's interesting to look at," he said to a questioner in the audience named Bill. "On the Web," said the director, "you can create the museum of Bill."

And so, by implication, there can be the museums of George and Mary and Helene. What then will this group have to say to one another about art? Let's say the museum of Bill is featuring early Dutch masters, the museum of Mary is playing video art, and the museum of Helene is displaying French tapestries. In this privatized world, what sort of "cultural" conversation can there be? What can one of us possibly say to another about our experience except, "Today I visited the museum of me, and I liked it."

Reassurance

Alice Walker

Alice Walker was born on February 9, 1944, in Eatontown, Georgia, the eighth and last child of Willie Lee and Minnie Lou Grant Walker, who were sharecroppers. She received her BA from Sarah Lawrence College in 1965. After finishing college, Walker lived for a short time in New York, then from the mid-1960s to the mid-1970s, she lived in Tougaloo, Mississippi. Alice Walker was active in the Civil Rights Movement of the 1960's, and in the 1990's she is still an involved activist. She currently resides in Northern California.

Alice Walker received the Pulitzer Prize in 1983 for The Color Purple. *Among her numerous books are* The Third Life of Granger Copeland *(1970),* In Love and Trouble *(1973),* You Can't Keep a Good Woman Down *(1981),* The Temple of My Familiar *(1989) and* Possessing the Secret of Joy *(1992). The Following poem is part of an essay interspersed with poems, "What Can I Give My Daughters Who Are Brave," published in the volume* Anything We Love Can Be Saved *(1997).*

I must love the questions
themselves
as Rilke said
like locked rooms
full of treasure
to which my blind
and groping key
does not yet fit.

"Reassurance," by Alice Walker, reprinted from *Revolutionary Petunias & Other Poems*, 1997, Harcourt Brace & Company.

and await the answers
as unsealed
letters
mailed with dubious intent
and written in a very foreign
tongue.

and in the hourly making
of myself
no thought of Time
to force, to squeeze
the space
I grow into.

The Distribution of Distress

Patricia Williams

Patricia Williams is a professor of Law. She received a B.A. (1972) from Wellesley College and a J.D. (1975) from Harvard University. She has worked both as a lawyer and a professor of law. She is the author of The Alchemy of Race and Rights: A Diary of a Law Professor *(1991),* The Rooster's Egg: On the Persistence of Prejudice *(1995), and* Seeing a Color-Blind Future: The Paradox of Race *(1997). Influential not only in legal circles but in the public domain as well, she is a columnist for* The Nation. *Her essays and columns have challenged what many take for granted in our society, particularly with regard to race and gender.*

Many years ago, I was standing in a so-called juice bar in Berkeley, California. A young man came in whom I had often seen begging in the neighborhood. A more bruised-looking human one could not imagine: he was missing several teeth, his clothes were in rags, his blond hair was matted, his eyes red-rimmed, his nails long and black and broken. On this particular morning he came into the juice bar and ordered some sort of protein drink from the well-scrubbed, patchouli-scented young woman behind the counter. It was obvious that his presence disturbed her, and when he took his drink and mumbled, "Thanks, little lady," she exploded.

"Don't you dare call me 'little lady'!" she snarled with a ferocity that turned heads. "I'm a *woman* and you'd better learn the difference!"

"Sorry," he whispered with his head bowed, like a dog that had been kicked, and he quite literally limped out of the store.

"Good riddance," the woman called after him.

This took place some fifteen years ago, but I have always remembered the interchange because it taught me a lot about the not so subliminal messages that can

"The Distribution of Distress," by Patricia Williams, reprinted from *Seeing a Color-Blind Future*, Noonday Press (Farrar, Straus & Giroux).

be wrapped in the expression of Virtue Aggrieved, in which antibias of one sort is used to further the agenda of bias of another kind.

In an abstract sense, I understood the resentment for girlish diminutives. Too often as a lawyer I have been in courtroom situations where coy terms of endearment were employed in such a way that "the little lady, God-bless-her" became a marginalizing condescension, a precise condensation of "She thinks she's a lawyer, poor thing." Yet in this instance, gender power was clearly not the issue, but rather the emotional venting of a revulsion at this man's dirty and bedraggled presence. It wasn't just that he had called her a little lady; she seemed angry that he had dared address her at all.

If, upon occasion, the ploughshare of feminism can be beaten into a sword of class prejudice, no less can there be other examples of what I call battling biases, in which the impulse to antidiscrimination is defeated by the intrusion or substitution of a different object of enmity. This revolving door of revulsions is one of the trickiest mechanisms contributing to the enduring nature of prejudice; it is at heart, I suppose, a kind of traumatic reiteration of injurious encounters, preserving even as it transforms the overall history of rage.

I was in England several years ago when a young Asian man was severely beaten in East London by a young white man. I was gratified to see the immediate renunciation of racism that ensued in the media. It was a somewhat more sophisticated and heartfelt collective self-examination than sometimes occurs in the United States in the wake of such incidents, where, I fear, we are much more jaded about all forms of violence. Nevertheless, what intrigued me most about the media coverage of this assault was the unfortunate way in which class bias became a tool for the denunciation of racism.

"Racial, Ethnic, or Religious Prejudice Is Repugnant," screamed the headlines.

Hooray, I thought.

And then the full text: "It is repugnant, *particularly*"—and I'm embellishing here—"when committed by a miserable low-class cockney whose bestial nature knows no plummeted depth, etc. etc."

Oh dear, I thought.

In other words, the media not only defined anti-Asian and anti-immigrant animus as ignorance, as surely it is, but went on to define that ignorance as the property of a class, of "the" lower classes, implying even that a good Oxbridge education inevitably lifts one above that sort of thing. As surely it does not.

And therein lies a problem, I think. If race or ethnicity is not a synonym for either ignorance or foreignness, then neither should class be an explanatory trashbin for racial prejudice, domestic incivility, and a host of other social ills. If the last fifty years have taught us nothing else, it is that our "isms" are no less insidious when beautifully polished and terribly refined.

None of us is beyond some such pitfalls, and in certain contexts typecasting can even be a necessary and helpful way of explaining the social world. The hard task is to untangle the instances where the categoric helps us predict and prepare for the world from those instances where it verges on scapegoating, projection, and prejudice.

To restate the problem, I think that the persistence of racism, ethnic and religious intolerance, as well as gender and class bias, is dependent upon recirculating images in which the general and the particular duel each other endlessly.

"*En garde,* you heathenish son of an inferior category!"

"Brute!" comes the response. "I am inalienably endowed with the unique luminosity of my rational individualism; it is you who are the guttural eruption of an unspeakable subclassification . . ."

Thrust and parry, on and on, the play of race versus ethnicity versus class versus blood feud. One sword may be sharper or quicker, but neither's wound is ever healed.

Too often these tensions are resolved simply by concluding that stereotyping is just our lot as humans so let the consequences fall where they may. But stereotyping operates as habit not immutable trait, a fluid project that rather too easily flows across the shifting ecology of human relations. And racism is a very old, very bad habit.

This malleability of prejudice is underscored by a little cultural comparison. If class bias has skewed discussions of racism in the British examples I have just described, it is rather more common in the United States for race to consume discussions of class altogether. While I don't want to overstate the cultural differences between the United States and the United Kingdom—there is enough similarity to conclude that race and class present a generally interlocking set of problems in both nations—the United States does deem itself classless with almost the same degree of self-congratulation that the United Kingdom prides itself on being largely free of a history of racial bias. Certainly these are good impulses and desirable civic sentiments, but I am always one to look closely at what is deemed beyond the pale. *It will never happen here* . . . The noblest denials are at least as interesting study as the highest ideals.

Consider: for a supposedly classless society, the United States nevertheless suffers the greatest gap of any industrialized nation between its richest and poorest citizens. And there can be no more dramatic and ironic class consciousness than the Dickensian characteristics ascribed to those in the so-called underclass, as opposed to the rest—what are we to call them, the *over*class? Those who are deemed to have class versus those who are so far beneath the usual indicia of even lower class that they are deemed to have no class at all.

If this is not viewed by most Americans as a problem of class stasis, it is perhaps because class denominations are so uniformly understood to be stand-ins for race. The very term *underclass* is a *euphemism* for blackness, class operating as euphemism in that we Americans are an upbeat kind of people and class is usually thought to be an easier problem than race.

Middle-classness, on the other hand, is so persistently a euphemism for whiteness, that middle-class black people are sometimes described as "honorary whites" or as those who have been deracinated in some vaguely political sense. More often than I like to remember, I have been told that my opinion about this or that couldn't possibly be relevant to "real," "authentic" black people. Why? Simply because I don't sound like a Hollywood stereotype of the way black people are "supposed" to talk. "Speaking white" or "Talking black." No in-between. Speaking as a black person while

297

sounding like a white person has, I have found, engendered some complicated sense of betrayal. "*You're* not black! You're not *white!*" No one seems particularly interested in the substantive ideas being expressed; but everyone is caught up with the question of whether anyone should have to listen to a white-voiced black person.

It is in this way that we often talk about class and race such that we sometimes end up talking about neither, because we insist on talking about race as though it were class and class as though it were race, and it's hard to see very clearly when the waters are so muddied with all that simile and metaphor.

By the same token, America is usually deemed a society in which the accent with which one speaks Does Not Matter. That is largely true, but it is not so where black accents are concerned. While there is much made of regional variations—New Yorkers, Minnesotans, and Southerners are the butts of a certain level of cheap satire— an accent deemed "black" is the one with some substantial risk of evoking outright discrimination. In fact, the speech of real black people ranges from true dialects to myriad patois, to regional accents, to specific syntactical twists or usages of vocabulary. Yet language identified as black is habitually flattened into some singularized entity that in turn becomes synonymous with ignorance, slang, big lips and sloppy tongues, incoherent ideas, and very bad—terribly unruly!—linguistic acts. Black speech becomes a cipher for all the other stereotypes associated with racial discrimination; the refusal to understand becomes rationalized by the assumption of incomprehensibility.

My colleague Professor Mari Matsuda has studied cases involving accent discrimination. She writes of lawsuits whose transcripts revealed an interesting paradox. One case featured a speaker whose accent had been declared incomprehensible by his employer. Nevertheless, his recorded testimony, copied down with no difficulty by the court reporter, revealed a parlance more grammatically accurate, substantively coherent, and syntactically graceful than any other speaker in the courtroom, including the judge. This paradox has always been the subject of some interest among linguists and sociolinguists, the degree to which language is understood in a way that is intimately linked to relations among speakers.

"Good day," I say to you. Do you see me as a genial neighbor, as part of your day? If so, you may be generously disposed to return the geniality with a hearty "Hale fellow, well met."

"Good day," I say. Do you see me as an impudent upstart the very sound of whose voice is an unwelcome intrusion upon your good day? If so, the greeting becomes an act of aggression; woe betide the cheerful, innocent upstart.

"Shall we consider race?" I say to you. If you are disposed to like me, you might hear this as an invitation to a kind of conversation we have not shared before, a leap of faith into knowing more about each other.

"Shall we consider race?" I say. *Not* "Shall I batter you with guilt before we riot in the streets?" But only: "Shall we *consider* race?" Yet if I am that same upstart, the blood will have boiled up in your ears by now, and very shortly you will start to have tremors from the unreasonable audacity of my meddlesome presumption. Nothing I actually say will matter, for what matters is that I am out of place . . .

This dynamic, this vital ingredient of the willingness to hear, is apparent in the contradiction of lower-status speech being simultaneously understood yet not understood. Why is the sound of black voices, the shape of black bodies so overwhelmingly agreeable, so colorfully comprehensible in some contexts, particularly in the sports and entertainment industries, yet deemed so utterly incapable of effective communication or acceptable presence when it comes to finding a job as a construction worker?

This is an odd conundrum, to find the sight and the sound of oneself a red flag. And it is a kind of banner, one's face and one's tongue, a banner of family and affiliation—that rhythm and stress, the buoyance of one's mother's tongue; that plane of jaw, that prominence of brow, the property of one's father's face. What to make of those social pressures that would push the region of the body underground in order to allow the purity of one's inner soul to be more fully seen? When Martin Luther King, Jr., urged that we be judged by the content of our character, surely he meant that what we looked like should not matter. Yet just as surely that enterprise did not involve having to deny the entirely complicated symbolic character of one's physical manifestation. This is a hard point, I confess, and one fraught with risk of misunderstanding. The color of one's skin is a part of ourselves. It does not matter. It is precious, and yet it should not matter; it is important and yet it must not matter. It is simultaneously our greatest vanity and anxiety, and I am of the opinion, like Martin Luther King, that none of this should matter.

Yet let me consider the question of self-erasure. I've written elsewhere about my concern that various forms of biotechnological engineering have been turned to such purposes—from skin lighteners to cosmetic surgery to the market for sperm with blond hair and eggs with high IQs. Consider the boy I read about who had started some sort of computer magazine for children. A young man of eleven, celebrated as a computer whiz, whose family had emigrated from Puerto Rico, now living in New York. The article recounted how much he loved computers because, he said, nobody judged him for what he looked like, and he could speak without an accent. What to make of this freedom as disembodiment, this technologically purified mental communion as escape from the society of others, as neutralized social space. What a delicate project, this looking at each other, seeing yet not staring. Would we look so hard, judge so hard, be so hard—what would we look like?—if we existed unself-consciously in our bodies—sagging, grayhaired, young, old, black, white, balding and content?

Let me offer a more layered illustration of the way in which these issues of race and class interact, the markers of class distinction and bias in the United Kingdom emerging also in the United States as overlapping substantially with the category of race. A few years ago, I purchased a house. Because the house was in a different state than where I was located at the time, I obtained my mortgage by telephone. I am a prudent little squirrel when it comes to things financial, always tucking away sufficient stores of nuts for the winter, and so I meet all the criteria of a quite good credit risk. My loan was approved almost immediately.

A short time after, the contract came in the mail. Among the papers the bank forwarded were forms documenting compliance with what is called the Fair Housing Act. It is against the law to discriminate against black people in the housing market, and one of the pieces of legislation to that effect is the Fair Housing Act, a law that monitors lending practices to prevent banks from doing what is called "red-lining." Redlining is a phenomenon whereby banks circle certain neighborhoods on the map and refuse to lend in those areas for reasons based on race. There are a number of variations on the theme. Black people cannot get loans to purchase homes in white areas; or black people cannot get start-up money for small businesses in black areas. The Fair Housing Act thus tracks the race of all banking customers to prevent such discrimination. Unfortunately, some banks also use the racial information disclosed on the Fair Housing forms to engage in precisely the discrimination the law seeks to prevent.

I should repeat that to this point my entire mortgage transaction had been conducted by telephone. I should also say that I speak what is considered in the States a very Received-Standard-English, regionally northeastern perhaps, but not marked as black. With my credit history, with my job as a law professor, and no doubt with my accent, I am not only middle-class but match the cultural stereotype of a good white person. It is thus perhaps that the loan officer of this bank, whom I had never met in person, had checked off a box on the Fair Housing form indicating that I *was* "white."

Race shouldn't matter, I suppose, but it seemed to in this case, and so I took a deep breath, crossed out "white," checked the box marked "black," and sent the contract back to the bank. That will teach them to presume too much, I thought. A done deal, I assumed.

Suddenly said deal came to a screeching halt. The bank wanted more money as a down payment, they wanted me to pay more points, they wanted to raise the rate of interest. Suddenly I found myself facing great resistance and much more debt.

What was most interesting about all this was that the reason the bank gave for its newfound recalcitrance was not race, heaven forbid—racism doesn't exist anymore, hadn't I heard? No, the reason they gave was that property values in that neighborhood were suddenly falling. They wanted more money to cover the increased risk.

Initially, I was surprised, confused. The house was in a neighborhood that was extremely stable; prices in the area had not gone down since World War II, only slowly, steadily up. I am an extremely careful shopper and I had uncovered absolutely no indication that prices were falling at all.

It took my real estate agent to make me see the fight. "Don't you get it," he sighed. "This is what they always do."

And even though I work with this sort of thing all the time, I really hadn't gotten it: for of course, *I* was the reason the prices were in peril.

The bank was proceeding according to demographic data that show any time black people move into a neighborhood in the States, whites are overwhelmingly likely to move out. In droves. In panic. In concert. Pulling every imaginable resource with them, from school funding to garbage collection to social workers who don't want to work in black neighborhoods to police whose too frequent relation to black communities is a corrupted one of containment rather than protection.

It's called a tipping point, this thing that happens when black people move into white neighborhoods. The imagery is awfully catchy you must admit: the neighborhood just tipping right on over like a terrible accident, whoops! Like a pitcher I suppose. All that nice fresh wholesome milk spilling out, running away . . . leaving the dark, echoing, upended urn of the inner city.

This immense fear of "the black" next door is one reason the United States is so densely segregated. Only two percent of white people have a black neighbor, even though black people constitute approximately thirteen percent of the population. White people fear black people in big ways, in small ways, in financial ways, in utterly incomprehensible ways.

As for my mortgage, I threatened to sue and eventually procured the loan on the original terms. But what was fascinating to me about this whole incident was the way in which it so exemplified the new problems of the new rhetoric of racism. For starters, the new rhetoric of racism never mentions race. It wasn't race but risk with which the bank was concerned. Second, since financial risk is all about economics, my exclusion got reclassified as just a consideration of class, and there's no law against class discrimination, after all, for that would present a restraint on one of our most precious liberties, the freedom to contract or not. If public schools, trains, buses, swimming pools, and neighborhoods remain segregated, it's no longer a racial problem if someone who just happens to be white keeps hiking the price for someone who just accidentally and purely by the way happens to be black. White people set higher prices for the "right," the "choice" of self-segregation. If black people don't move in, it's just that they can't *afford* to. Black people pay higher prices for the attempt to integrate, even as the integration of oneself is a threat to one's investment by lowering its value.

By this measure of mortgage worthiness, the ingredient of blackness is cast not just as a social toll but as an actual tax. A fee, an extra contribution at the door, an admission charge for the higher costs of handling my dangerous propensities, my inherently unsavory properties. I was not judged based on my independent attributes or individual financial worth as a client; nor even was I judged by statistical profiles of what my group actually do. (For, in fact, anxiety-stricken, middle-class black people make grovelingly good cake-baking neighbors when not made to feel defensive by the unfortunate, historical welcome strategies of bombs, burnings, or abandon.)

Rather, I was being evaluated based on what an abstraction of White Society writ large thinks we—or I—do, and that imagined "doing" was treated and thus established as a self-fulfilling prophecy.

However rationalized, this form of discrimination is a burden: one's very existence becomes a lonely vacuum when so many in society not only devalue *me*, but devalue *themselves* and their homes for having me as part of the landscaped view from the quiet of their breakfast nook.

I know, I know, I exist in the world on my own terms surely. I am an individual and all that. But if I carry the bank's logic out with my individuality rather than my collectively imagined effect on property values as the subject of this type of irrational economic computation, then I, the charming and delightful Patricia J. Williams, become a bit like a car wash in your backyard. Only much worse in real price terms. I am more than a mere violation of the nice residential comfort zone in question; my blackness can rezone altogether by the mere fortuity of my relocation.

"Dumping district," cringes the nice, clean actuarial family next door; "there goes the neighborhood . . ." as whole geographic tracts slide into the chasm of impecuniousness and disgust. I am the economic equivalent of a medical waste disposal site, a toxic heap-o'-home.

In my brand-new house, I hover behind my brand-new kitchen curtains, wondering whether the very appearance of my self will endanger my collateral yet further. When Benetton ran an advertisement that darkened Queen Elizabeth II's skin to a nice rich brown, the *Sun* newspaper ran an article observing that this "obviously cheapens the monarchy." Will the presentation of my self so disperse the value of my own, my ownership, my property?

This is madness, I am sure, as I draw the curtain like a veil across my nose. In what order of things is it *rational* to thus hide and skulk?

It is an intolerable logic. An investment in my property compels a selling of myself.

I grew up in a white neighborhood where my mother's family had been the only black people for about fifty years. In the 1960s, Boston began to feel the effects of the great migration of Southern blacks to the north that came about as a result of the Civil Rights Movement. Two more black families moved into the neighborhood. There was a sudden churning, a chemical response, a collective roiling with streams of froth and jets of steam. We children heard all about it on the playground. The neighborhood was under siege. The blacks were coming. My schoolmates' parents were moving out *en masse.*

It was remarkable. The neighborhood was entirely black within about a year.

I am a risk pool. I am a car wash.

I was affected, I suppose, growing up with those children who frightened themselves by imagining what it would be like to touch black bodies, to kiss those wide unkissable lips, to draw the pure breath of life through that crude and forbidden expanse of nose; is it really possible that a gentle God—their God, dear God—would let a *human* heart reside within the wet charred thickness of black skin?

I am, they told me, a jumble of discarded parts: low-browed monkey bones and infected, softly pungent flesh.

In fact, my price on the market is a variable affair. If I were crushed and sorted into common elements, my salt and juice and calcinated bits are worth approximately five English pounds. Fresh from the kill, in contrast, my body parts, my lungs and liver, heart and healthy arteries, would fetch some forty thousand. There is no demand for the fruit of my womb, however; eggs fresh from their warm dark sanctuary are worthless on the open market. "Irish Egg Donor Sought," reads an ad in the little weekly newspaper that serves New York City's parent population. And in the weird economy of bloodlines, and with the insidious variability of prejudice, "Irish eggs" command a price of upwards of five thousand pounds.

This silent market in black worth is pervasive. When a certain brand of hiking boots became popular among young people in Harlem, the manufacturer pulled the product from inner-city stores, fearing that such a trend would "ruin" the image of their boot among the larger market of whites.

It's funny . . . even shoes.

Last year I had a funny experience in a shoe store. The salesman would bring me only one shoe, not two.

"I can't try on a pair?" I asked in disbelief.

"When you pay for a pair," he retorted. "What if there were a hundred of you," he continued. "How would we keep track?"

I was the only customer in the store, but there were a hundred of me in his head.

In our Anglo-American jurisprudence there is a general constraint limiting the right to sue to cases and controversies affecting the individual. As an individual, I could go to the great and ridiculous effort of suing for the minuscule amount at stake in waiting for the other shoe to drop from his hand; but as for the real claim, the group claim, the larger defamation to all those other hundreds of me . . . well, that will be a considerably tougher row to hoe.

I am one, I am many.

I am amiable, orderly, extremely honest, and a very good neighbor indeed. I am suspect profile, market cluster, actuarial monster, statistical being.

My particulars battle the generals.

"Typecasting!" I protest.

"Predictive indicator," assert the keepers of the gate.

"Prejudice!" I say.

"Precaution," they reply.

Hundreds, even thousands, of me hover in the breach.

Virtual Worlds

Benjamin Woolley

British author Benjamin Woolley, a correspondent for The Late Show, *was the first to introduce the idea of virtual reality in Britain. He has contributed numerous articles to national newspapers and magazines on technology. He also writes 'Signs of Life,' an edition of* Horizon *on the use of computers in the study and simulation of life forms. In 1992, Benjamin Woolley won the BP Arts Journalism television award.* Virtual Worlds. A Journey in Hyperreality *examines the dramatic intellectual and cultural changes brought about by the development of technology.*

In our days everything seems pregnant with its contrary.

Karl Marx, 1856.

On 7 May, 1987, the US multinational Proctor & Gamble submitted Olestra, a new food substitute, to the American Food and Drug Administration (FDA) for approval. Olestra was, in the judgement of the world's media as well as Proctor & Gamble's publicity, potentially one of the most significant nutritional breakthroughs of its time. It promised what every dieter desired, the realization of an impossible dream: fat-free fat.

For a dietary aid, Olestra is made out of unpromising ingredients, sugar and fat. However, when they are chemically bonded together in the correct way, they form a new and very strange substance: sucrose polyester. It may sound better suited to manufacturing shirts than food, but sucrose polyester has interesting nutritional qualities. It retains the culinary and textural qualities of the fat, but in a form that the body is unable to digest. Result: a fat that passes straight through the body. In tests, obese subjects who ate a diet that used Olestra lost weight even if they were allowed to supplement the diet with conventional fatty snacks.

"Introduction to Virtual Worlds: A Journey in Hype and Hyperreality," by Benjamin Woolley, reprinted from *Virtual Worlds: A Journey in Hype and Hyperreality*, 1992, Blackwell Publishers, Ltd.

Fat-free fat. It is a concept pregnant with its own contrary. When Marx used the phrase in 1856, he was commenting on an era that was having to come to terms with the violent impact of industrialization on the order of nature. This book is about the impact of an even more disorientating era: artificialization, of making dreams come true, of 'imagineering' as the Disney Corporation calls it. What are the extent and limits of the artificial? Is there, can there be, any contact with reality when it is possible to make fat that is not fat, when the fake becomes indistinguishable from—even more authentic than—the original, when computers can create synthetic worlds that are more realistic than the real world, when technology scorns nature?

Evidence of artificialization seemed to be abundant at the time of writing this book. Wherever one looked, artificiality was triumphing over reality. In the closing months of 1991, as the Soviet Union broke apart, the fate of the embalmed body of Lenin, which had been lying in state since 1924, was in doubt. Some had questioned whether, indeed, it was his 'real' body at all, Lenin's unblemished facial complexion suggesting that it might be a waxwork. But who cares? Most British politicians would happily become a waxwork if it meant a position at Madame Tussaud's, the most popular tourist site in London. In an artificial world, there is no need for Lenin's material substance any more than there is a need for the great materialist state he founded. It is, perhaps, a fitting symbol of the triumph of the land of dreams over the empire of iron, the 'end of history', that Lenin should be left to decay while the cryogenically preserved Walt Disney waits in suspended animation (an appropriate state for a cartoonist) to return to the world that is now his.

As the worms awaited Lenin, a book entitled *Fly Fishing* by J. R. Hartley entered the British bestseller list. Unremarkable though it may have seemed, this was no ordinary book. British Telecom had run a series of television commercials featuring an elderly man locating a copy of the out-of-print *Fly Fishing* by J. R. Hartley using the Yellow Pages. The man turns out at the end of the commercial to be J. R. Hartley. So moved was the audience by this story that bookshops and even the British Library were reportedly overwhelmed with requests for it—even though, of course, no such book and no such author had ever existed. So the publisher Random Century decided to create one. It commissioned the writer Michael Russell to ghost write the book, and hired the actor Norman Lumsden, who had played Hartley in the original advertisement, to pose as the author. The result was a fiction turned into fact—artificial reality.

Few of us think about 'reality' much—those of us who intend to write books about it have to keep reminding ourselves that we are rare exceptions. It is, perhaps, the conceptual equivalent of unconscious motor functions such as breathing. It is vital to life—without it, we would be unable to distinguish the real from the imaginary, the true from the false, the natural from the artificial. But we do not have to think about it to use it—indeed, as soon as we do start thinking about it, it becomes extremely difficult to continue using it. For this reason, perhaps, some may regard it as a peculiar subject for any sort of analysis: it is a given, a fact of life, and best left hidden behind the curtain of unconsciousness.

To extend (but I hope not exhaust) the breathing metaphor, the problem is that just as a polluted environment can make us short of breath, so an increasingly complex, artificial environment can diminish our sense of reality. And, as that sense diminishes, so innumerable troubling side-effects start to creep in. Soon after Olestra's announcement, an American pressure group, the Center for Science in the Public Interest, quoted the results of tests using rats which showed that nearly a half of the rats fed on Olestra died during the period of the experiment, compared with under a third of the rats fed a normal diet. 'Aha!' said the critics, 'There you have it: you think you can have fat for free, but there is really a price, the price that nature usually exacts, cancer.'

The prejudice that favours the products of nature over our own is, perhaps, understandable. Nature's approvals process is slower even that the FDA's, working at the pace of evolutionary time to separate dangerous substances from those to whom they are a danger. We are part of a natural order poised in a state of delicate equilibrium, safe as long as we keep to our position within it. This 'natural order' is a very basic, important structure. It is independent of us, uncontaminated by us. The problem with synthetic substances like Olestra is that they are not a part of it—worse, that they seem to ignore it, even violate it. Fat-free fat, like alcohol-free alcoholic drinks, sugar-free sweets and caffeine-free coffee, flouts the reality principle, the principle that you cannot have something for nothing, that everything has its price, that nothing in life is free, that there is no such thing as a free lunch, that there can be no gain without pain. Science and technology have arrogantly ignored this principle, and the result is a world filled with disease and pollution.

But must it be thus? Surely there *could* be gain without pain or, more appropriately given that Olestra is a dietary aid, less without distress, crapulence without corpulence? As the *US News & World Report* put it in a rather breathless report about food substitutes entitled 'Have your cake and eat it, too', 'the foodstuffs of which dieters dream are fast becoming realities'. And why not? A few cancerous rats prove nothing: there is no law of science (though perhaps one of logic) that says a fat-free fat is impossible.

It is this sort of debate, and what for most of us is a genuine feeling of uncertainty as to exactly what we can believe that makes any secure, unexamined notion of reality increasingly troublesome. How is it possible to hold a clear view of the distinction between reality and fantasy when the unreal is continually being realized?

There has never been a totally secure view of reality, certainly not in the industrial era of history. People say that the world is not as real than it used to be. Well, to adapt what an editor of *Punch* said in response to a tiresome criticism of his magazine: the world was *never* as real as it used to be. Indeed, it is industry, the power to manufacture what previously had to be taken from nature, that has made the world progressively more artificial and less real, that provided the wealth and energy to change the natural landscape, even to replace it with one of our own making. But equally the industrial era has been about the discovery of reality. The ability to manipulate nature, to turn its operation to our own ends, shows how successful science has been in discovering how it works, and technology in exploiting that discovery.

The industrial experience, in other words, seems to have both destroyed reality and reinforced it.

As we enter the so-called post-industrial era, the crisis continues. It is a favourite theme of nearly all commentaries about the times we live in. There is a 'legitimation crisis', a 'crisis of representation', and one great big 'crisis of modernity'. As Umberto Eco observed: 'Crisis sells well. During the last few decades we have witnessed the sale (on newsstands, in bookshops, by subscription, door-to-door) of the crisis of religion, of Marxism, of representation, the sign, philosophy, ethics, Freudianism, presence, the subject . . . Whence the well-known quip: "God is dead, Marxism is undergoing crisis, and I don't feel so hot myself." The question such crises pose is whether this means that attitudes to reality have been undermined by the experience of modernity, or whether reality itself, something firm and objective, something underpinning the uncertain world of appearance, has been shown to be an illusion. Is the lesson we should have learnt from the last century that *there is no reality?* When the newspapers and the food manufacturers tell us that dreams are fast becoming realities, does that really mean that reality is fast becoming a dream?

For centuries the issue of what does and does not count as real has been a matter of philosophy. There have been two main questions, what could be called the ontological and epistemological questions. The ontological question is about being: what is real? Is there a reality behind appearance? The epistemological question is about knowing: what is truth? Is knowledge the product of reason or of experience? For most people, and certainly for most scientists, neither question is particularly relevant, because there are working systems that are used to tell reality from appearance, truth from falsity. When a court assesses the truth of a witness's evidence, epistemology does not come into it. The judge does not ask the members of the jury whether or not they are rationalists or empiricists. Similarly, the result of an experiment does not rest on whether the scientist performing the experiment is an idealist or materialist.

At Britain's first virtual reality conference, held in the summer of 1991, the chairman, Tony Feldman, tried to emphasize that the agenda he had drawn up was concerned with hard-headed, pragmatic business issues, but conceded that 'the metaphysics are inescapable'. Technology, he and the subsequent speakers observed, could manipulate reality to the point of being able to create it. Artificialization is no longer just a matter of cultural observation or intellectual angst, it had become, well, real. It is for this reason that reality is no longer secure, no longer something we can simply assume to be there.

Most people probably now have some idea of what virtual reality is. It is the technology used to provide a more intimate 'interface' between humans and computer imagery. It is about simulating the full ensemble of sense data that make up 'real' experience. Ideally, the user wears a device that substitutes the sense data coming from the natural world with that produced by a computer. Computer screens are placed before the eyes, 'effectors' cover the body, providing the sights of this artificial world, and the feelings that result from touching it. Furthermore, tracking devices attached to the body monitor its movements, so, as the user moves, so what he or she sees and feels is altered accordingly. This book does not provide a technical description or assessment of this technology. I am more concerned with the two issues that underlie its emergence as one of the 'Big Ideas' of the 1990s, issues that remain neglected by the computer industry, but which I hope to show are essential to making sense of the developments that have lead to this rude instrusion of metaphysics into ordinary life.

The first issue is simulation. Computers are unique in that they are all, in a sense, simulations of some ideal computer, a 'universal machine'. Everything a computer does can be seen as a simulation, except that many of the things it simulates do not exist beyond the simulation. What, then, is simulation? Is it just another form of imitation or representation, fiction for the computer age? Can anything be simulated—even reality and human intelligence? These questions raise important mathematical and scientific questions, and in attempting to answer them I hope to show what is 'special' about the computer, why it is not just a glorified calculator, and why those who have developed it have attributed to it such extraordinary creative powers.

The second issue concerns artificial reality. It is a strange, provocative notion. It is hard to tell on first acquaintance whether it is meaningful or meaningless. It could be a new paradigm, it could be pretentious. It could be an oxymoron, a figure of speech that uses what sounds like a contradiction to suggest a much deeper truth. It could just be a contradiction. It has become a general-purpose metaphor for both the present and the future, one that is easy to pick up but impossible to put down. Its attractions are obvious. It is a term full of novelty and puzzle, provocatively coined to intensify a deep-seated insecurity as well as capture a sense of technological adventure.

The term's origin is generally attributed to Myron Krueger, an American 'computer artist and educator' (his own description), who used it as the title of a book written in the 1970s but not published until 1983. The book's subject was what he called 'responsive environments', art installations in which lighting and sound would change according to the movement of people walking around them. He did not, however, use the term 'artificial reality' as a technological label. He had a more ambitious use for it: 'The world described in Genesis, created by mysterious cosmic forces, was a volatile and dangerous place. It moulded human life through incomprehensible caprice. Natural beneficence tempered by natural disaster defined reality. For centuries, the goal of human effort was to tap Nature's terrible power. Our success has been so complete, that a new world has emerged. Created by human ingenuity, it is an artificial reality.'

The champions of virtual reality and computer simulation—who are not just pioneering visionaries but powerful commercial interests—are wanting to make artificial reality real. To them, it promises not just a world where you can eat fat without getting fat, not just a metaphor, but the actual creation of any world you could ever want or imagine—fantastical, fabulous, terrifying, infinite, enclosed, utopian, Stygian. I want to look at the validity of such promises, and to discover their influence over the whole notion of reality. Artificial reality has acquired the role of a sort of Barium meal ingested by the body of society and culture, its spreading glow revealing, under the X-ray of critical examination, the growths and malfunctions of the internal organs.

Just like a Barium meal, some people find any discussion about artificial or virtual reality hard to swallow. Upon introducing the idea to innocent members of the lay public, I discovered that, far from showing mild interest or no interest, they would look at me as though I had announced myself to be the risen Messiah. Life, they seemed to say, is complicated enough without making it more complicated with such outlandish ideas. Such an attitude has a proud and long tradition in Anglo-Saxon culture. You could say it was formulated as long ago as the fourteenth century, when it came to be known as 'Occam's razor', after the English philosopher William of Occam. Occam was a ferociously ascetic Franciscan, so ascetic he actually led a revolt in favour of poverty, when Pope John XXII threatened to end it as a monastical principle. He was an equally ferocious intellectual ascetic, demanding that in philosophical theory, 'entities are not to be multiplied beyond necessity', a principle more economically expressed in the phrase 'cut the crap'. Judged in such terms, most contemporary theory, especially that coming from the fields of information technology and cultural criticism, seems in need of a good shave.

Some contemporary theorists positively encourage the multiplication of entities. One of the most enthusiastic is the influential French sociologist Roland Barthes, who died in 1980. His most important work was *Mythologies,* a book that unblushingly used the most sophisticated analytical techniques to examine the most commonplace objects and activities: wrestling, margarine, photos of Greta Garbo, polystyrene. It was Barthes's explicit aim to break the illusion of 'naturalness' that is used by mass media to dress up reality. He wanted to show that our notion of the natural and the real is really a highly political construction, a product of history. 'In short, in the account given of our contemporary circumstances . . . I wanted to track down, in the decorative display of *what-goes-without-saying,* the ideological abuse which, in my view, is hidden there.' He set out to be reality's party pooper, to show that, in his language, it is the product of myth.

Neologisms are, Barthes claims, essential precisely because of this myth. What we take to be fixed and certain is, in fact, constantly changing, and so the language used to analyse it must change too. The words that appear in dictionaries, words that are presented as having meaning independent of history, are no use. We need new ones: 'neologism is therefore inevitable. China is one thing, the idea which a French petit-bourgeois could have of it not so long ago is another: for this peculiar mixture of bells, rickshaws and opium-dens, no other word is possibly but *Sininess.* Unlovely? One should at least get some consolation from the fact that conceptual neologisms are never arbitrary: they are built according to a highly sensible proportional rule'. Artificial reality. Unlovely, or built according to a highly sensible proportional rule? Just another example of intellectual stubble and a candidate for Occam's cutthroat, or a perfectly legitimate example of a new term for something that has not been previously recognized or expressed?

My belief is that artificial reality does reveal a great deal about the 'myth' of reality—about the way that the idea of reality is used and understood, at least within the Western culture that gave birth to it. If nothing else, it reveals that much of what we take to be reality *is* myth, just as Olestra reveals that the idea of fat is a myth. It reveals that the things we assume to be independent of us are actually constructed by us. It reveals that being 'real', like being 'natural', is not simply a value-free, un-problematic, apolitical, objective state—though part of its mythology is to make itself appear to be so. It reveals that, like 'new' and, indeed, 'natural', 'real' has been ab-ducted by business as a marketing term.

Artificial reality, then, expresses the ambiguity of current attitudes to reality. But that ambiguity is not, as most commentators on the subject have taken it to be, evi-dence that there is no reality. Just because there is a reality myth does not mean that reality is a myth. The absurdity of such a position is revealed in attempts by some an-tirealists to argue that they cannot assert reality to be a myth because that would be to assert that what is real is that reality is a myth, which cannot be asserted as there is no reality (because it is a myth).

I want to show that such denials of reality are mistaken, that there is a reality, and that the virtual form of it, far from releasing us from it, can help us recover it. I also believe we need it. Take away reality, and all that is left is relativism, a belief that truth can be established simply by asserting it, that the self is all that exists—no, that *myself* is all that exists. The computing industry was built on the liberal belief in the individual as the only legitimate political entity, and virtual reality has, in some hands, been promoted as the ultimate embodiment of that principle. What better way of ex-pressing your individualism than by creating your own, individual reality? Empowered by the personal computer, liberated by virtual reality, the individual becomes the God of his or her own universe. The sight of someone wearing a virtual reality headset is the ultimate image of solipsistic self-absorption, their movements and gestures mean-ingless to those left outside.

We have to look, then, at how virtual reality and artificial reality, the technolo-gy and culture, are changing public reality. Because the formidable might of com-merce and in particular the computing industry have been deployed in defining reality, we need to look at what they mean to do with it.

CONCATENATIONS

The following writing assignments have been conceived as successive links between individual texts leading to a concatenation of essays. Every concatenation has five links, and each link can include from one to four texts. The links give you the opportunity to consider the texts included from different angles and to discover new layers of meaning with each new essay you write. The number of possible links between texts in this book is virtually unlimited. You are invited both to test some of the following links and to create your own by generating other combinations.

Each link has a theme that can be the topic of your paper. The first paragraph of the link reveals the premise on which the assignment is built. You need not take the premise for granted. On the contrary, you should check its assumptions against the texts. The second paragraph in the link is asking a number of questions that you may use to start brainstorming and discovering ideas for your paper. Finally, the last paragraph is asking the central question of the assignment that has to be answered in an essay form. This format gives you the freedom to take the premise of the assignment in whichever direction you want.

You can establish relations between texts by looking closely at details. The closer you read, the more connections you will be able to make and the more ideas you will generate. Before starting to write, reread the texts with the assignment in mind and mark the passages relevant to the topic. At this stage you will also start noticing the connections that can be made between details from various texts. Later, you may use some of these passages as quotations in your paper. By analyzing the quotations, you can support the claims that you will be making.

Although rooted in the texts, the assignments ask you to construct an original argument that will show your own interpretation of the readings, and that will make claims from your point of view. It is very important that your voice should be heard in the paper above the voices of the authors included. It is a good idea to regard the texts as sources of evidence for your case rather than as static objects for analysis. Analysis, comparison, and description are discrete operations that contribute to the building of an argument, not purposes in themselves. By argument, we mean a claim supported by evidence. In order to be able to make a claim, you must examine the evidence first.

CONCATENATION I

Link 1

Text: Louise Erdrich, "The Red Convertible"

Louise Erdrich's story, "The Red Convertible," functions on many levels. We can say it is a story about two brothers and their relationship. It may also be seen as a story about a Vietnam vet who cannot cope with the memory of the war. But the main purpose of Louise Erdrich's prose in general is to speak about the life of contemporary American Indians. She does so without ostentation, and the many aspects of reservation life are mainly seen in details.

Reread the story and single out the details that let us know the characters are American Indians and reflect their way of life. Look back on these details and try to figure out the bigger picture that they compose.

In a short essay, show the main characteristics of Native American life in our time as portrayed by Erdrich in her story.

Link 2

Texts: Michael Dorris, "Indians on the Shelf"
Louise Erdrich, "The Red Convertible"

Michael Dorris speaks about the ways American Indians have been transformed into mythical figures by literature, folklore, and the media. Their mythical images are inevitably contradictory: "As folklore, Indians seem infinitely flexible; they can be tough and savage, as in the Washington Redskins football team, or, starring in environmental commercial, turn maudlin and weepy at the sight of litter" (97). Therefore, it is hard for American Indians to live up to the images others have of them. In Louise Erdrich's story "The Red Convertible" the characters are American Indians living in the contemporary United States. How do they compare with the Indians of the myth?

Reconsider both the essay and the story. Look for evidence from the story that either supports or invalidates Dorris' argument. Think of questions like: What are the consequences of the media images for the lives of these real people? What strategies have they developed to interact with mainstream Americans who romanticize them? And how does this romantic image contribute to the tragedy that takes place in the story?

Write an essay in which you relate Michael Dorris' argument about the transformation of American Indians into myth to Louise Erdrich's portrayal of contemporary American Indians in "The Red Convertible."

Link 3

Texts: Gary Engle, "What Makes Superman So Darned American?"
Dika Lam, "The Ramble"

      Gary Engle argues that the myth of Superman gives expression to the aspirations of immigrants who feel at once alienated and empowered by American culture. The girl portrayed by Dika Lam in her story is such an immigrant. Had she been a boy, she would probably have identified with Superman. But as she is a young woman, so she has to construct her own mythology. In what ways does the girl resemble the immigrants described by Engle?

      Reread Engle's argument and locate the passages that best apply to the girl's problems in the story. Think of questions like: How does she find an outlet for her dreams and creativity? How does her conflict with her mother mirror the contradictory feelings of immigrants toward the country they have left? In what way is her fantasy similar to the Superman myth?

      Write an essay in which you relate the myth of Superman as analyzed by Engle to the circumstances of the young woman in Lam's story. Make sure that you find a meaningful relation whether you argue that the story confirms or denies his argument.

Link 4

Texts: Louise Erdrich, "The Red Convertible"
Michael Dorris, "Indians on the Shelf"
Gary Engle, "What Makes Superman So Darned American?"

      Both Dorris and Engle speak about the process by which reality is transformed into myth. But mythmaking is not without purpose. Who makes the myth and whom the myth is about may make a difference. Because of the myths about them, the American Indians portrayed by Erdrich feel discouraged and lost when facing the world outside the reservation. On the contrary, the immigrants who find their own image in Superman are empowered by the myth.

      These contrary functions of the myth raise a number of questions: Is the process of mythmaking itself good or bad? What purposes does it serve? How does the myth relate to identity? How can a myth be appropriated? Reread the texts and consider such questions.

      Write an essay about the importance and functions of myth for a particular group of people. Look at the ways myths are generated, perpetuated, and used for political purposes. Establish how myth making is an activity related to power and social order.

Link 5

Texts: Michael Dorris, "Indians on the Shelf"
Gary Engle, "What Makes Superman So Darned American?"
Benjamin Woolley, "Virtual Worlds"

In "Virtual Worlds" Benjamin Woolley shows how, due to scientific developments, more and more human fantasies have become reality. This phenomenon raises an interesting question: How do we determine what is real? Looking back on the other two essays, we can see that fantasies and myths have always existed, and in many ways, have determined political and social realities.

The question then arises: How do we distinguish these fantasies from the new fantasy called virtual reality? What is the difference between fiction, fantasy, and virtuality? What is real after all? Reconsider the mythology concept in this new light and think of these questions.

Write an essay in which you debate the issue of reality and its relation to fantasy, fiction, and virtuality. Establish whether such notions should be distinguished from each other or the distinction has no practical use.

(With this concatenation, you can also include movies: *Smoke Signals* and *The Matrix*).

CONCATENATION II

Link 1

Text: Hilton Als, "My Pin-Up"

In his memoir, Als seems to have unresolved issues regarding his heritage and his identity. In many ways, the essay is an homage to his mother, a hard-working woman who raised her children with dignity. At times, however, Als seems to be insulting her and all black women, by reiterating descriptions of the "negress" as a category of people without dignity.

Isolate the most difficult to understand passages in the essay and determine the target of Als' criticism. When is Als speaking on his own behalf and when is he covertly quoting public opinion about race and racial issues? What do his anecdotal examples prove? What is his position on racial issues? Consider questions like these and look closely at the rhetorical movements of the essay.

Write an essay of your own in which you explain what Als's attitude toward black women is and what determines this attitude.

Link 2

Texts: Hilton Als, "My Pin-Up"
Toni Morrison, "Hagar"

In his discussion of the "negress," Hilton Als mentions Toni Morrison's character, Pilate. In "Hagar," which is a chapter of the novel *Song of Solomon* by Toni Morrison, we get a glimpse of Pilate, the grandmother who vainly tries to rescue Hagar from her madness.

Think of questions like: Why does Als use a derogatory term to characterize, among others, his mother? To what extent is he speaking of a real person and to what extent is he speaking of a myth? How does Pilate, as a fictional character, help to make his point? How "real" is Pilate? How does the character of the "negress" relate to American culture in general? What does it actually say about this culture?

Write an essay in which you explain what Hilton Als means by "negress," and how the description applies to Pilate.

Link 3

Texts: Francine Du Plessix Gray, "On Friendship"
Toni Morrison, "Hagar"

In her essay "On Friendship," Francine Du Plessix Gray speaks about "the sexual industrial complex" as a way to exploit and demean women in our society. She relates this "complex" with the notion of romantic love. In Morrison's story, Hagar is a victim of romantic love as well as of the "sexual industrial complex."

Reread Toni Morrison's "Hagar" and consider the behavior of the heroine. What acts show her passion? What would be her idea about love? Why is she worried about her appearance? To what extent does she behave like any woman would in her situation? Think about such questions before you start writing.

Write an essay in which you explain the concept of romantic love and its relation to the cosmetic industry and illustrate it with Hagar's case. Compare the "romantic love" as defined by Gray with your own notion of love and show what Hagar has done wrong from that perspective.

Link 4

Texts: Francine Du Plessix Gray, "On Friendship"
Hilton Als, "My Pin-Up"
Ariel Dorfman, "September, 1973"

Both Hilton Als and Francine Du Plessix Gray talk about how women are seen. These ways of seeing women are determined by cultural and social conditions that are beyond the control of individual men or women. However, the reason that the images function socially is that individuals tailor their perceptions according to the prevailing social view. Als catches himself in the process of doing so on more than one occasion. The memoir written by Dorfman also shows that the author both understands the process, by which women are transformed into images, and is participating in it at the same time.

Have another look at the texts. Where do the authors detach themselves from their former opinions? Where do they render traditional views or public opinions? Where do they establish their own opinions? Consider such questions and examine the writing carefully before starting your paper.

Write an essay in which you explore the roles we each play in the formation and perpetuation of images and decide whether a change of perspective at the individual level could produce a change in society at large.

Link 5

Texts: Hilton Als, "My Pin-Up"
Ariel Dorfman, "September, 1973"
Alluquere Rosanne Stone, "In Novel Conditions: The Cross Dressing Psychiatrist"

You have been reading and writing about women and images of women. All these discussions have been based on the assumption that women are different from men. The differences may be either biological or cultural, but they are assumed to exist. "The Cross Dressing Psychiatrist," however, makes us wonder about these differences.

Think about questions like: Are there any differences between men and women, and if so, what are they? How much does biology have to do with our codes of behavior and our perceptions? What would happen if the differences disappeared? In what ways do the texts support ideas about either biologically or culturally determined differences? Can such differences be erased? Should the differences be erased?

Write an essay in which you explore the differences between genders, their roots in biology, their social construction, and their usefulness.

(With this concatenation, you can also include movies: *Boys Don't Cry* or *Working Girl*)

CONCATENATION III

Link 1

Text: Daniel Orozco, "Orientation"

In "Orientation," Daniel Orozco gives us an image of office life through the "orientation" of a new employee. We find out a lot of things about the office, in this way. Some of them are typical of any office, but others are a bit peculiar. Orozco may exaggerate in order to make a point.

To what extent is Orozco's image of office life believable? How does it compare with your experience (or knowledge of) office work? Why do you think the author exaggerates the characteristics of an office environment? What does he want to say with this story?

After you have thought about the above questions, write an essay in which you discuss Orozco's implied argument about office environments.

Link 2

Texts: Daniel Orozco, "Orientation"
Tim O'Brien, "The Man I Killed"

The difference between office work and war is obvious to everyone, but few people think of the similarities between these two situations. However, soldiers marching in rows and employees in cubicles look pretty much the same. As if to prove this point, the stories written by Daniel Orozco and Tim O'Brien share the same direct and simplified style. It looks like the narrators are pointing at things for us to see.

Think of questions like: What do wars and offices have in common? What happens to people in such environments? What makes people conform to the rules? What do the person who receives the orientation and O'Brien's soldier have in common?

Starting from the stylistic similarities of the two stories, write a paper in which you develop an argument about the elements that office work and war have in common.

Link 3

Texts: Tim O'Brien, "The Man I Killed"
Steve Hasset, "And What Would You Do, Ma?"
Steve Hasset, "Christmas"
Bruce Springsteen, "Born in the USA"

In O'Brien's story "The Man I Killed," we get only a snapshot of the Vietnam War, but one that is powerful enough to remember for a long time. This image includes a condemnation of the Vietnam War and other wars as well. Hasset's poems invent little war scenarios that also include his protest against the war. Springsteen speaks, also obliquely, about what happened to the Vietnam vets when they returned.

How do we know that O'Brien, Hasset, and Springsteen are talking about the same war? And what makes this war so special? In what ways do the story, the poems and the lyrics of the song protest the war?

After thinking about such questions, write a paper about the way the Vietnam War is represented by Tim O'Brien, Hasset, and Springsteen and decide what they consider most abominable about the war. You may want to think of this paper as an evaluation of the job the authors do reflecting on the war and the historical perspective we get from their work. You may also consider your experience as readers knowing the war second hand, as it were.

Link 4

Texts: Jean Baudrillard, "Xerox and Infinity"
Daniel Orozco, "Orientation"

Jean Baudrillard thinks that the presence of intelligent machines in our society dehumanizes us. But what does he mean by humanity? The people, in Orozco's story, though undoubtedly human, are acting as if they were machines.

What characteristics that are human do the machines lack? Do we need machines in order to be dehumanized? How human is the environment of the office in Orozco's story? In what ways do they resemble the machines? In what ways do they resist the dehumanizing environment in which they work?

After thinking about such questions, write a paper in which you establish what it means to be human by Baudrillard's standards and compare his implicit definitions to your own and to the sample of humanity that Orozco portrays in his story.

Link 5

Texts: Daniel Orozco, "Orientation"
Tim O'Brien, "The Man I Killed"
Jean Baudrillard, "Xerox and Infinity"

Various aspects of humanity emerge from the three texts above. In "Orientation," people are expected to act like machines. In "The Man I Killed," a soldier asserts his humanity against the machine of the war. In "Xerox and Infinity," the danger of technology is clearly dehumanization.

Under what conditions do we lose our humanity? What elements of the environment contribute to such a loss? What traits of human nature cooperate with the environment to make us less human? Think about such questions before starting to write your paper.

Write a paper in which you investigate the various ways that lead to dehumanization and decide what we can do to preserve our humanity.

(With this concatenation you can also include movies: *Office Space* and *Platoon*, or *Full Metal Jacket*, or *Apocalypse Now*)

CONCATENATION IV

Link 1

Text: Debra Dickerson, "Who Shot Johnny?"

Dickerson describes a family crisis in great detail, but is Johnny's shooting a unique, isolated incident? We hear about shootings like this every day on the news.

Have another look at the story and select those passages that indicate the author is talking about more than just her family or Johnny's shooting. To what extent is this incident representative of a variety of situations? Why is Dickerson disclosing her family's misfortune? What does she want to prove with this story after all? Consider such questions before starting to write.

After you have established the more general validity of Dickerson's statements, write an essay in which you show what Dickerson argues through her story. Make your points carefully and use quotations to support them.

Link 2

Texts: Debra Dickerson, "Who Shot Johnny?"
Philip Roth, "Prologue"

Both Dickerson and Roth talk about minority communities with specific ideas about the roles that men and women have to play in the family and in society.

How does Dickerson describe herself? What are the other women like in her story? To what extent do they resemble Roth's mother? How does Roth's father compare to the man who shot Johnny? What kind of standards do the two communities have for men and women? Ponder these questions before you start writing.

After you have established the common points of the two stories, write a paper in which you discuss both similarities and differences between the two communities with regard to the roles of men and women.

Link 3

Texts: Debra Dickerson, "Who Shot Johnny?"
Philip Roth, "Prologue"
Jonathan Franzen, "Imperial Bedroom"

Jonathan Franzen makes a case for the need of public space and public behavior. In the process, he implies that the difference between the private and the public is, or should be, clear. But is it always easy to decide what is a private and what is a public matter?

What is the difference between private and public according to Franzen? To what extent is Johnny's shooting a private issue for his family and to what extent is it a public issue? Why does Dickerson choose to discuss a private matter in a public forum (her story)? How does her disclosure of private matters compare to Roth's account of his family? In what ways is the notion of family related to privacy? Only after you have thought about these questions and others like them can you start writing.

After you have finished examining the difference between private and public in the texts above, write a paper in which you establish whether the difference between private and public is clear or not, and whether it is necessary for the good functioning of society.

Link 4

Texts: Jonathan Franzen, "Imperial Bedroom"
Ellen Ullman, "Wouldn't You Rather Be At Home?"

Jonathan Franzen speaks of privacy in social and political terms. However, as Ullman's essay demonstrates, technology may have an important role to play in the relation between the private and public domains.

How does technology relate to our private lives? How does technology make possible a more engaged public life? To what extent does technology contribute to the invasion of privacy?

Create an argument around the reasons why the private and public domains may overlap and establish whether the cause of this is social or technological.

Link 5

Texts: Ellen Ullman, "Wouldn't You Rather Be At Home?"
Andrei Codrescu, "Intelligent Electronics"

The invention of the intelligent machine has brought about many changes in society as well as in the way we think and learn. Both Ullman and Codrescu seem to look at the negative side of these developments. They do, however, suggest or at least imply ways to use the machines to our advantage.

How does the amount of information available on the Internet influence the way we think? How do machines encourage changes in behavior? What kind of human tendencies do the ads for computers exploit?

Keeping your findings in mind, write an essay about the social and cultural changes brought about by the use of intelligent machines. Establish whether machines are dangerous and should be abandoned or we can harness their power to our advantage.

(With this concatenation you can include movies: *Demon Seed* or *Enemy of the State*)

CONCATENATION V

Link 1

Text: ZZ Packer, "Brownies"

The girls portrayed by ZZ Packer in her story "Brownies" are involved in complicated social situations. Some of their problems arise from the lack of knowledge about their situation as well as knowledge about the world in general. Because they are young, and because they are being instructed, we can see how their knowledge is formed. What do the Brownies learn from their environment?

Before starting to write, consider a few questions like: what do the girls know about interracial relations? What do they know about the words they learn out of the dictionary? How does their troop leader convey knowledge to them? What do the girls learn from their own experience? How does this knowledge they gain compare to education in school?

Write an essay in which you consider the learning experiences of the girls portrayed in the story as well as your own experiences and draw some conclusions about the learning process. You might want to differentiate between this process and the more familiar notion of education.

Link 2

Texts: ZZ Packer, "Brownies"
Walter Mosley, "Pet Fly"

In "Pet Fly," Walter Mosley portrays a young man who has trouble relating to his environment because he approaches others without prejudice. He is part of a power structure whose mechanism he does not understand. His innocence regarding power is unusual since, as we can see in Packer's story, power relations, pecking orders, and means of domination are established early in childhood. What keeps Mosley's hero from understanding what is going on in his office?

Reread both stories and locate the passages where relations of domination are established. What gives Arnetta the upper hand over the other brownies? Why do the black brownies decide to raid the camp of the white brownies? In what ways do the leaders exercise power over either brownies or employees? How are race and gender used to establish domination? How do victims turn their situation into a dominant position?

After pondering such questions, write an essay in which you examine the idea of power, the way it is obtained and exercised, and the kind of relationships it gives rise to.

Link 3

Texts: ZZ Packer, "Brownies"
Walter Mosley, "Pet Fly"
Patricia Williams, "The Distribution of Distress"

Patricia Williams uses personal experience and anecdotes to show the complexities of interracial relations in this country in recent years. In many ways, you have discovered some of these complexities by analyzing the power issues in the two stories. How do interracial relations relate to power?

Look closely at Patricia Williams' argument and compare her examples with the examples you have discussed in your previous paper. To what extent is power intertwined with race? Why is it so difficult to ignore race altogether? How is victimization used by some in order to gain the upper hand?

Write an essay in which you discuss Patricia Williams' argument about the distribution of distress in relation to examples from the two stories. You may decide to enlarge or refute her argument based on the analysis of your examples.

Link 4

Texts: Walter Mosley, "Pet Fly"
Patricia Williams, "The Distribution of Distress"
Alluquère Rosanne Stone, "In Novel Conditions: The Cross-Dressing Psychiatrist"

In her essay "The Distribution of Distress," Patricia Williams talks about the Puerto Rican computer wiz who enjoys not being seen by the people with whom he carries on conversations on the Internet. This is the ideal situation where indeed the color of the skin does not matter. In a less fortunate circumstance, the psychiatrist portrayed by Stone also enjoys the neutrality afforded by the computer. Does this mean that the end of racism can happen only virtually, that is, in cyberspace?

Consider all the three texts and look at ways in which the physical presence of people matters or does not matter. What prevents people from forgetting what others look like? What would happen if Mosley's character interacted with the girl on the Internet? Why did the psychiatrist lose the relationships he forged in the chat room?

Write an essay in which you make a case for the importance or lack of importance of physical appearance, including racial markers.

Link 5

Texts: ZZ Packer, "Brownies"
Patricia Williams, "The Distribution of Distress"
Breyten Breytenbach, "Write and Wrong"

In his essay "Write and Wrong," Breyten Breytenbach reflects on history and the role it plays in our lives. Visiting a German town, he is astonished by the care with which the locals have preserved and reconstructed all the possessions of their great poet Wolfgang Goethe. But when visiting the museums preserving the remains of the fascist camps, Breytenbach wonders at the use of preserving or remembering the past. In what ways is history useful, and in what ways does it prevent us from forming productive relationships in the present?

Read Breytenbach's essay with special care as it contains many metaphors that stand in need of interpretation. Consider also the other texts and the role that the past plays in establishing relationships or getting to know other people. What can Breytenbach mean when he advises his Russian friend to look in the faces of ants? How would the girls from "Brownies" be helped by knowing more or less about the past of racial relationships in America? What is Patricia Williams' sense of history?

Write an essay in which you decide whether history is useful, or not or how it should be taught in order to be useful.

(With this concatenation you may also include movies: *The Crying Game*)

Pam
"Crystal